THE CAMBRIDGE COMPANION TO
BRITISH LITERATURE AND EMPIRE

The volume outlines modern British literature's relation to global empire from the sixteenth century to the present. Spanning the interactions between Britain, Europe, and the world outside, in Asia, Africa, Australasia, North America, and the Caribbean, it suggests the centrality of colonial-capitalist empire and global exchanges in the development of major genres of literary fiction, poetry, drama, and nonfiction. Illuminating the vital role of categories such as race, class, gender, religion, commerce, war, slavery, resistance, and decolonization, the twenty-one chapters of the book chart major aspects of British literature and empire. In rigorous yet accessible prose, an international team of experts provides an updated account of earlier and latest scholarship. Suitable for a general readership and academics in the field, the Companion will aid readers in familiarizing themselves with Britain's imperial past and its continuing relevance for the present.

Auritro Majumder is Associate Professor of English at the University of Houston. His research includes modern and comparative world literature, theory, and intellectual history. He is the author of *Insurgent Imaginations: World Literature and the Periphery* (2021) and past chair of the Modern Language Association's South Asia forum.

*A complete list of books in the series is at the back of this book*

# THE CAMBRIDGE COMPANION TO
# BRITISH LITERATURE AND EMPIRE

EDITED BY
AURITRO MAJUMDER
*University of Houston*

Shaftesbury Road, Cambridge CB2 8EA, United Kingdom

One Liberty Plaza, 20th Floor, New York, NY 10006, USA

477 Williamstown Road, Port Melbourne, VIC 3207, Australia

314–321, 3rd Floor, Plot 3, Splendor Forum, Jasola District Centre, New Delhi – 110025, India

103 Penang Road, #05–06/07, Visioncrest Commercial, Singapore 238467

Cambridge University Press is part of Cambridge University Press & Assessment, a department of the University of Cambridge.

We share the University's mission to contribute to society through the pursuit of education, learning and research at the highest international levels of excellence.

www.cambridge.org
Information on this title: www.cambridge.org/9781009554404
DOI: 10.1017/9781009554435

© Cambridge University Press & Assessment 2025

This publication is in copyright. Subject to statutory exception and to the provisions of relevant collective licensing agreements, no reproduction of any part may take place without the written permission of Cambridge University Press & Assessment.

When citing this work, please include a reference to the DOI 10.1017/9781009554435

First published 2025

*A catalogue record for this publication is available from the British Library*

*A Cataloging-in-Publication data record for this book is available from the Library of Congress*

ISBN 978-1-009-55438-1 Hardback
ISBN 978-1-009-55440-4 Paperback

Cambridge University Press & Assessment has no responsibility for the persistence or accuracy of URLs for external or third-party internet websites referred to in this publication and does not guarantee that any content on such websites is, or will remain, accurate or appropriate.

For EU product safety concerns, contact us at Calle de José Abascal, 56, 1°, 28003 Madrid, Spain, or email eugpsr@cambridge.org

# CONTENTS

| | |
|---|---|
| *List of Figures* | *page* viii |
| *List of Contributors* | ix |
| *Acknowledgments* | xv |
| *Chronology* | xvi |

Introduction: Situating British Literature and Empire  1
AURITRO MAJUMDER

### PART I  EARLY INTIMATIONS AND LITERARY GENRES: 1500–1800

1  Early Modern Utopia: Capitalism, Colonialism, and Private Property  19
CRYSTAL BARTOLOVICH

2  Trade, Race, and Class in Early Modern England  36
ANIA LOOMBA

3  Peripheral Heroics on the Renaissance Stage  50
SU FANG NG

4  Travel Narratives and the Early Novel  64
JASON PEARL

5  Anglophone Epics and Ruin Poetry in Eighteenth-Century India  77
JAMES MULHOLLAND

6  The Black Atlantic, Slave Narratives, and Empire  93
NICOLE N. ALJOE

## CONTENTS

### PART II ENTANGLEMENTS OF PROSE, POETRY, AND EMPIRE: 1800–1900

7  Romantic Orientalist Poetry and the Spectacle of Revolution  109
   ARIF CAMOGLU

8  The Historical Novel and Nineteenth-Century Empire  122
   IAN DUNCAN

9  Gothic Plots and the Nineteenth-Century Irish Novel  136
   CHRISTINA MORIN

10 The Victorian Industrial Novel and the Working Classes  149
   AVIVA BRIEFEL

11 Victorian Liberalism, Settler Character, and Literary Form  161
   PHILIP STEER

12 The Imperial Romance: Colonialism in Ritual Form  174
   SANDEEP BANERJEE

### PART III FIGURES, MOVEMENTS, AND HISTORIES: 1900–1945

13 Unraveling Adventure Fictions: Modernist Compressions and Anti-imperial Connections  189
   DOMINIC DAVIES

14 Poetic Accumulation, Modernist Verse, and Imperial Capital  202
   PAUL STASI

15 Modernist Women, Technologies of Whiteness, and Undoing Empire  216
   SONITA SARKER

16 Joyce and His Contemporaries: Revivalism, Modernism, and Irish Anti-imperialism  230
   JOE CLEARY

17 Popular Front Aesthetics, Imperialism, and the People  244
   ELINOR TAYLOR

CONTENTS

PART IV PATHWAYS AND LEGACIES: 1945–2020

18  British Fiction, Decolonization, and the Cold War  259
    ANDREW HAMMOND

19  Beyond the Empire: Black Caribbean British Writing  279
    LISA TOMLINSON

20  Reimagining the First World War in Contemporary
    British-Arab Writing  293
    NADIA ATIA

21  Multiculturalism and Muslim Writing after Brexit  307
    AMINA YAQIN

    *Further Reading*  321
    *Index*  326

# FIGURES

5.1 George Willison, *Eyles Irwin*, oil on canvas, c. 1776. This portrait was composed when Irwin was about twenty-five years old and employed in Madras (Archer 106). Private collection © Christie's Images/Bridgeman Images. *page* 82

5.2 Thomas Daniell, "Ruins of the Palace, Madura," c. 1790s, hand-colored aquatint on paper. This image was engraved by William Daniell and included in *Oriental Scenery* (1797–98). Courtesy of the President and Fellows of Trinity College, Oxford. 85

5.3 "Tremal Naig's Choultry, Madura." Etching and aquatint, drawn by Thomas Daniell and engraved by Thomas and William Daniell, 1798, showing the long hall and succession of Madurai Nayaka rulers. Included in *Oriental Scenery* (1797–98). Courtesy of the President and Fellows of Trinity College, Oxford. 86

5.4 "Architectural drawing of Tirumala Nayak at Madura," pen and ink on paper, c. 1780s. This drawing, thought to be commissioned by Adam Blackader and drawn by an Indian artist, shows Tirumala Nayaka and his wives on a pillar of the new hall. The writing at the top is in Tamil and includes marks reading "68 N," "68 W," "68 S," and "68 E." © Victoria and Albert Museum, London (AL 7766:87) (Guy 209–10). 87

CONTRIBUTORS

NICOLE N. ALJOE is Professor of English and Africana Studies at Northeastern University in Boston. She is Codirector of the Early Caribbean Digital Archive and Mapping Black London and Director of the Early Black Boston Digital Almanac. Her research and teaching focuses on eighteenth and early nineteenth-century Black Atlantic and Caribbean literatures with specializations in slave narrative, early novels about race, and digital humanities. The author of *Creole Testimonies: Slave Narratives from the British West Indies, 1709–1836* (2012) and coeditor of *Journeys of the Slave Narrative in the Early Americas* (2014) as well as *A Literary History of the Early Anglophone Caribbean: Islands in the Stream* (2018), her essays have appeared in *African American Review*, *American Literary History*, *Anthurium*, *Eighteenth-Century Fiction*, *Early American Literature*, and *Women's Studies*.

NADIA ATIA is Reader in Postcolonial and Global Literature at Queen Mary University of London. Her research examines Britain's ever-evolving relationship with Iraq and the ways in which Iraq and its people are represented in contemporary Iraqi literature. She is currently working on a Leverhulme-funded project that examines representations of home in diasporic Iraqi writing. She is the author of *World War I in Mesopotamia: The British and the Ottomans in Iraq* (2016) and coeditor of *Popular Postcolonialisms: Discourses of Empire and Popular Culture* (2018).

SANDEEP BANERJEE is Associate Professor in the Department of English at McGill University, Canada. His scholarship lies at the intersection of the environmental humanities, empire and decolonization, aesthetics in the global periphery, and the cultures of global communism. He is the author of *Space, Utopia and Indian Decolonization: Literary Pre-figurations of the Postcolony* (2019) and is currently completing his second monograph on the environmental imagination of the colonial Himalaya. His articles have appeared in venues such as *Victorian Literature and Culture*, *Comparative Literature Studies*, *Modern Fiction Studies*, *Modern Asian Studies*, and *Cambridge Critical Concepts: Space and Literary Studies*. He is one of the series editors of the Routledge Series in the Cultures of the Global Cold War and serves on the editorial boards of the journals *positions: asia critique* and *Mediations*.

CRYSTAL BARTOLOVICH is Associate Professor of English at Syracuse University where she teaches courses in early modern studies, cultural studies, and Marxism. With Neil Lazarus, she edited *Marxism, Modernity and Postcolonial Studies* and, with Jean Howard and David Hillman, she is the author of *Marx and Freud: The Great Shakespeareans*. Her many essays have appeared in venues such as *PMLA*, *Angelaki*, and *Cultural Critique*. Her current book project is entitled *Hating Utopia Properly*.

AVIVA BRIEFEL is Edward Little Professor of English and Cinema Studies at Bowdoin College. She is the author of *The Deceivers: Art Forgery and Identity in the Nineteenth Century* (2005) and *The Racial Hand in the Victorian Imagination* (2015), and coeditor of *Horror after 9/11: World of Fear, Cinema of Terror* (2011) and *Labors of Fear: The Modern Horror Film Goes to Work* (2023). Her most recent book is titled *Ghosts and Things: The Material Culture of Victorian Spiritualism* (2025).

ARIF CAMOGLU is Assistant Professor of English at University of California, Davis. His research focuses on the British and Ottoman Turkish literatures of the eighteenth and nineteenth centuries. His most recent writing appeared in *Eighteenth-Century Studies*, *Global Nineteenth Century Studies*, *Essays in Romanticism*, and *European Romantic Review*. Currently he is at work on a book manuscript that reconceptualizes empire by foregrounding affect in its analysis of imagined and actual Anglo-Ottoman encounters in the long nineteenth century.

JOE CLEARY is Professor of English at Yale University and author of *Modernism, Empire, World Literature* (2021), *The Irish Expatriate Novel and Late Capitalist Globalization* (2021), *Outrageous Fortune: Capital and Culture in Modern Ireland* (2007), and *Literature, Partition and the Nation-State: Culture and Conflict in Ireland, Israel and Palestine* (2002). He has edited *The Cambridge Companion to Modern Irish Culture* (2005) and *The Cambridge Companion to Irish Modernism* (2014) and edited or coedited special issues of *Éire-Ireland*, *Modern Language Quarterly*, and *Boundary 2*.

DOMINIC DAVIES is in English at City, University of London, where he has directed both BA and MA English programs. He holds a DPhil and British Academy Postdoctoral Fellowship from the University of Oxford. He has written extensively on the relationship between infrastructure, literature, and visual culture, particularly in contexts of empire and colonialism and their aftermath. His books include *Imperial Infrastructure (2017)* and *The Broken Promise of Infrastructure* (2023).

LIST OF CONTRIBUTORS

IAN DUNCAN is Distinguished Professor and Florence Green Bixby Chair in English at the University of California, Berkeley. He is the author of *Human Forms: The Novel in the Age of Evolution* (2019), *Scott's Shadow: The Novel in Romantic Edinburgh* (2007), and *Modern Romance and Transformations of the Novel: The Gothic, Scott, Dickens* (1992). He has coedited essay collections on Scottish Romantic period writing and edited works of fiction by Walter Scott, James Hogg, Robert Louis Stevenson, and Arthur Conan Doyle. A general editor of the *Collected Works of James Hogg* and *Edinburgh Critical Studies in Romanticism*, he is currently editing *The Cambridge History of Scottish Literature* and *The Cambridge Companion to Walter Scott*.

ANDREW HAMMOND has taught at the University of Nizwa, the University of Brighton and the Swansea Metropolitan University and has specialized in Cold War literature, postcolonial writing, and post-1945 British fiction. He is the author and editor of ten book-length studies, including *The Palgrave Handbook of Cold War Literature* (2020), *The Novel and Europe* (2016), *British Fiction and the Cold War* (2013), and *British Literature and the Balkans* (2010).

ANIA LOOMBA is Catherine Bryson Professor Emerita at the University of Pennsylvania. Her monographs include *Gender, Race, Renaissance Drama* (1989), *Colonialism/Postcolonialism* (1998; 2005; 2015), *Shakespeare, Race, and Colonialism* (2002), and *Revolutionary Desires: Women, Communism, and Feminism in India* (2018). Edited books include *Cultural History of Western Empires in the Renaissance* (2018), *Rethinking Feminism: Gender, Race and Sexuality in the Early Modern World* (2016), *South Asian Feminisms* (2012), a critical edition of Shakespeare's *Antony and Cleopatra* (2011), *Race in Early Modern England: A Documentary Companion* (2007), *Postcolonial Studies and Beyond* (2005), and *Post-Colonial Shakespeares* (1998).

AURITRO MAJUMDER is Associate Professor of English and India Studies at the University of Houston. His research covers modern and comparative world literature, literary theory, film studies, and intellectual history. His recent book is *Insurgent Imaginations: World Literature and the Periphery* (2021). Some of his essays appear in *The Oxford Handbook of Modern Indian Literatures*, *Cambridge Journal of Postcolonial Literary Inquiry*, *Critical Asian Studies*, *Comparative Literature Studies*, *Interventions*, *Journal of Multicultural Discourses*, *Journal of Postcolonial Writing*, *Mediations*, *Research in African Literatures*, and *South Asian Review*. He is past chair of the Modern Language Association's South Asia forum.

CHRISTINA MORIN lectures in English literature at the University of Limerick, where she also currently serves as Assistant Dean of Research for the Faculty of Arts, Humanities and Social Sciences. She is the author of *The Gothic Novel in Ireland, c. 1760–1829* (2018) and *Charles Robert Maturin and the Haunting* of *Irish Romantic Fiction* (2011), and has coedited a special issue of the *Irish University Review* on "Irish Gothic Studies Today" (2023; with Ellen Scheible) as well as the collections *Traveling Irishness in the Long Nineteenth Century* (with Marguérite Corporaal, 2017) and *Irish Gothics: Genres, Forms, Modes and Traditions* (with Niall Gillespie, 2014).

JAMES MULHOLLAND is Professor of English at North Carolina State University. He is the author of *Before the Raj: Writing Early Anglophone India* (2021) and *Sounding Imperial: Poetic Voice and the Politics of Empire, 1730–1820* (2013). His work has been supported by the American Council of Learned Societies Frederick Burkhardt Fellowship, the Marion Jasper Whiting Foundation, and the Fox Center for Humanistic Inquiry. He is the winner of the Srinivas Aravamudan Prize from the American Society for Eighteenth-Century Studies and has been honorably mentioned for the Modern Language Association's William Riley Parker Prize and American Society for Eighteenth-Century Studies' Louis Gottschalk Prize and James L. Clifford Prize.

SU FANG NG is Cutchins Professor of English at Virginia Tech. She has published numerous articles and is the author of *Literature and the Politics of Family in Seventeenth-Century England* (2007) and *Alexander the Great from Britain to Southeast Asia: Peripheral Empires in the Global Renaissance* (2019); the latter won the Renaissance Society of America's 2020 Gordan Prize for best book. Her recent publications include a Cambridge Element on *Writing "Discovery" in the Early Modern East Indies* (2022) and a coedited collection of essays, *England's Asian Renaissance* (2021). Her work has been generously supported by fellowships at the Radcliffe Institute at Harvard, the National Humanities Center, the University of Texas at Austin, Heidelberg University, All Souls College, Oxford, the University of Wisconsin at Madison, and the Folger Shakespeare Library.

JASON PEARL is Associate Professor of English at Florida International University, where he teaches courses on British literature of the eighteenth century. He is author of *Utopian Geographies and the Early English Novel* (2014), as well as essays and reviews in *Eighteenth-Century Studies*, *Studies in English Literature*, *Review of English Studies*, *Studies in the Novel*, *Eighteenth-Century Life*, *Eighteenth-Century Fiction*, *The Eighteenth Century: Theory and Interpretation*, *Studies in Eighteenth-Century Culture*, *The Scriblerian*, and *Digital Defoe*. His public-facing work has appeared in *The Atlantic*, *Los Angeles Review of Books*, *Public Books*, *Times Literary Supplement*, *Literary Review*, *Public Domain Review*, *The Millions*, *LensCulture*, *Gastronomica*, *The Chronicle of Higher Education*, *Inside Higher Ed*, *The Rambling*, *Age of Revolutions*, and *London School of Economics Review of Books*. His current project is entitled "Aerial Vistas: The Advent of Flight and the View from Above."

LIST OF CONTRIBUTORS

SONITA SARKER is Professor of Women's, Gender, and Sexuality Studies, and English at Macalester College, located on the lands of the Sisseton and Wahpeton peoples, in St. Paul, Minnesota. She is the author of *Women Writing Race, Nation, and History: N/native* (2022), the editor of *Sustainable Feminisms* (2007), and coeditor of *Trans-Status Subjects: Gender in the Globalization of South and Southeast Asia* (2002). Her monograph-in-progress is tentatively titled "Breathing: Whiteness in Post/Modernist Literature." She has written numerous articles on modernist women writers, on transnational feminist literature of the Cold War, on post/modern and post/colonial cultural theories of mass production, knowledge-making, history, and subalternity (Benjamin, Gramsci, Foucault), and on comparative Indigenous modernisms. She teaches feminist theories and literary production in the context of neo/liberal and neo/colonial histories and economies on the basis of decolonial pedagogy.

PAUL STASI teaches twentieth-century Anglophone literature at SUNY Albany. He is the author of *The Persistence of Realism in Modernist Fiction* (2022) which was shortlisted for the Modern Studies Association 2022 Book Prize, and *Modernism, Imperialism and the Historical Sense* (2012), as well as the editor of several volumes, including *Raymond Williams at 100* (2021) and *Realism and the Novel: A Global History* (2025). His work has appeared in, among other places, *ELH*, *Novel*, *James Joyce Quarterly*, *Mediations*, *Twentieth-Century Literature*, *Comparative Literature*, and *Historical Materialism*.

PHILIP STEER is Associate Professor of English in the School of Humanities, Media and Creative Communication at Massey University, New Zealand. His research explores the cultural, economic, and environmental aspects of settler colonialism from the nineteenth century to the present day, with a focus on Australia and New Zealand. He is author of *Settler Colonialism in Victorian Literature: Economics and Political Identity in the Networks of Empire* (2020), and coeditor with Nathan K. Hensley of *Ecological Form: System and Aesthetics in the Age of Empire* (2019). His chapter was supported by the Marsden Fund Council (grant no. MFP-19-MAU-022), managed by Royal Society Te Apārangi.

ELINOR TAYLOR is Senior Lecturer in English Literature at the University of Westminster, London. She is the author of *The Popular Front Novel in Britain* (2018) and coeditor, with Nick Hubble and Luke Seaber, of *The 1930s: A Decade of Modern British Fiction* (2021). She is a member of the executive committee of the Raymond Williams Society and an editor of its journal, *Key Words: A Journal of Cultural Materialism*.

LISA TOMLINSON is Senior Lecturer at the University of the West Indies, Mona, in the Department of Literatures in English. She is the author of the books *The African Jamaican Aesthetic: Cultural Retention and Transformation across Borders* (2017) and *Una Marson* (2019) from the Caribbean Biography Series.

Her research interests include film and visual culture, literary theory and criticism, diaspora studies, and Black popular culture.

AMINA YAQIN is Professor of World and Postcolonial Literatures at the University of Exeter. Her publications include *Gender, Sexuality and Feminism in Pakistani Urdu Writing* (2022), *Framing Muslims: Stereotyping and Representation after 9/11* (coauthored with Peter Morey, 2011), and the coedited volumes *Contesting Islamophobia: Media, Politics and Culture* (2019), *Muslims, Trust and Multiculturalism: New Directions* (2018), and *Culture, Diaspora and Modernity in Muslim Writing* (2012). She has coedited several journal special issues and her articles have appeared in peer-reviewed journals. Currently, she is cofounding coeditor of the interdisciplinary journal *Critical Pakistan Studies*. She is coinvestigator on a new Arts and Humanities Research Grant, "Empathy, Narrative and Cultural Values." The BBC, Sky News, Euronews, TRT World, Indus News, and Pakistan Television Network have aired her commentary and interviews. She has written for *The National UAE*, *Times Higher Education UK*, the British Film Institute, *The Friday Times*, and *The Conversation*.

ACKNOWLEDGMENTS

Like all edited volumes, this one is a collective effort. The editor thanks all the contributors – the credit for this book belongs to them. At various stages, the generous suggestions provided by Margot Backus, Timothy Brennan, Sreya Chatterjee, Suvir Kaul, Laura Murphy, and Ato Quayson strengthened various aspects of the work. The anonymous referees' comments proved helpful in clarifying the scope of the volume. Ray Ryan, publisher at Cambridge University Press, provided invaluable guidance. Thanks to Edgar Mendez, Biju Singh, Nicola Maclean, and Emma Goff-Leggett at the Press, the copyeditor Jane Hamilton, and Santhamurthy Ramamoorthy at Lumina Datamatics.

# CHRONOLOGY

| | |
|---|---|
| 1397 | Richard Whittington becomes Lord Mayor of London |
| 1452 | Papal Bull authorizing Christian enslavement of "Pagans" |
| 1492 | Onset of European colonization projects in the Americas |
| 1516 | Thomas More's *Utopia* published in Latin |
| c. 1530–1754 | The reign of the Madurai Nayaka, one of the successor states to the Vijayanagara Empire in southern India, especially Tirumala Nayaka (also known as Tirumalai Nayaka), who reigned c. 1623–1659 |
| 1547 | City of London sets up five charities for poor relief |
| 1553 | Bridewell Prison and Hospital set up to punish vagrants and house poor children |
| 1562–63 | John Hawkins undertakes first slave-trading voyage |
| 1577–80 | Francis Drake's circumnavigation of the world |
| 1581 | Founding of the Levant Company, following Queen Elizabeth I's ambassador William Harborne securing of commercial rights in the form of Capitulations on an embassy from 1579–80 from the Ottoman Sultan Murad III (r. 1574–1595) |
| 1585 | The Marocco or Barbary Company established by patent from Queen Elizabeth I |
| 1600 | Visit of the Moroccan ambassador 'Abd al-Wāḥid ben Mas'ūd sent by Sultan Aḥmad al-Manṣūr (r. 1578–1603) to the court of Queen Elizabeth I to negotiate an Anglo-Moroccan alliance against Spain |

# CHRONOLOGY

| | |
|---|---|
| 1600 | Founding of the East India Company (EIC), with its first voyage, 1601–03, led by James Lancaster |
| 1639 | Founding of the Ft. St. George Presidency in Madras, the locus of the EIC's power in southern India |
| 1652 | First Dutch settlement in modern-day South Africa |
| 1657 | Publication of Richard Ligon's *A True and Exact History of the Island of Barbados* |
| 1675–76 | Great Narragansett War (Indigenous uprising against New England colonization) |
| 1680 | Pueblo Revolt (Indigenous uprising against Spanish colonization in New Mexico) |
| 1688 | Publication of Aphra Behn's *Oroonoko* |
| 1697 | Publication of William Dampier's *New Voyage Round the World* |
| 1707 | Act of Union of Scotland and England |
| 1709 | Publication of the pamphlet *A Letter from a Merchant at Jamaica to a Member of Parliament in London, Touching the African Trade; to which is added, A Speech Made by a Black of Gardaloupe [sic], at the Funeral of a Fellow-Negro* |
| 1711 | Richard Steele's "The History of Inkle and Yarico" published in *The Spectator* |
| 1719 | Publication of Daniel Defoe's *Robinson Crusoe* |
| 1726 | Publication of Jonathan Swift's *Gulliver's Travels* |
| 1734 | Publication of Thomas Bluett, *Some Memoirs of the Life of Job, the Son of Solomon, the High Priest of Boonda in Africa; Who Was a Slave about Two Years in Maryland; and Afterwards Being Brought to England, Was Set Free, and Sent to His Native Land in the Year 1734* |
| 1749 | Publication of *The Royal African: or, Memoirs of the Young Prince of Annamaboe [William Ansah Sessarakoo]* |
| 1756–63 | Seven Years' War between Great Britain and France and British imperial gains in Canada and India |

CHRONOLOGY

| | |
|---|---|
| 1757 | EIC forces led by Robert Clive defeat the army of Siraj-ud-Daulah, the last independent Nawab of Bengal. The nominal beginning of British colonialism in Bengal and South Asia |
| 1764 | The Battle of Buxar. EIC troops defeat the combined forces of the Nawabs of Bengal (Mir Qasim), Awadh (Shuja-ud-Daula), and the Mughal Emperor (Shah Alam II) |
| 1765 | Treaty of Allahabad. EIC awarded *diwani*, serving as a tax collecting agent for the Mughal Empire in Bengal and Orissa |
| 1767–99 | Four successive and short Anglo-Mysore wars between the state of Mysore and the EIC and its allies, culminating in the defeat and death of Mysore ruler Tipu Sultan at Seringapatam in 1799, marking the dominance of the EIC in southern India |
| 1769–73 | The Great Famine in Bengal. The first of almost 200 years of deadly famines in South Asia under British rule, the famine killed 10 million people or about one-third of the population of the province |
| 1770 | Publication of J. A. U. Gronniosaw's (1712–1775), *A Narrative of the Most Remarkable Particulars in the Life of James Albert Ukawsaw Gronniosaw, an African Prince* |
| 1772 | The Mansfield Decision, stopping the forced removal of James Somerset, an enslaved African, from England to Jamaica |
| 1779 | Death of James Cook in Hawaii at the hands of natives |
| 1782 | Establishment of Grattan's Parliament (free independent parliament in Ireland, subsequently dissolved with the passing of Anglo-Irish Union) |
| 1787 | Publication of Ottobah Cugoano's (b. 1757?), *Narrative of the Enslavement of Ottobah Cugoano, a Native of Africa; Published by Himself on the Year 1787* |
| 1787 | Founding of the Committee for the Abolition of the Slave Trade (first formal abolitionist society) |

| | |
|---|---|
| 1788 | Arrival of First Fleet at Sydney Cove, Australia |
| 1789 | Publication of Olaudah Equiano's (1745?–1797), *The Interesting Narrative of the Life of Olaudah Equiano, or Gustavus Vassa, the African. Written by Himself* |
| 1791–1804 | The Haitian Revolution |
| 1793–1815 | Napoleonic Wars |
| 1798 | Rebellion in Ireland |
| 1803 | Rebellion in Ireland (Robert Emmet) |
| 1800–1801 | The Act of Anglo-Irish Union (1800) and Anglo-Irish Union (1801) |
| 1801 | Anglo-Persian Treaty |
| 1806 | Vellore Revolution undertaken by the Indian infantry against the EIC |
| 1807 | Anglo-Turkish War |
| 1814 | Publication of Walter Scott's *Waverley* |
| 1821–29 | The Greek War of Independence |
| 1824–31 | Black War, Van Diemen's Land/Tasmania, Australia |
| 1829 | Publication of Edward Gibbon Wakefield's *A Letter from Sydney, the Principal Town of Australasia* |
| 1835 | The English Education Act. Legislative act of the Council of India making English the language of colonial administration and higher law courts, replacing Persian |
| 1840 | Signing of Te Tiriti o Waitangi/Treaty of Waitangi, Aotearoa New Zealand |
| 1840 | Publication of Frances Trollope's *The Life and Adventures of Michael Armstrong, The Factory Boy*, often considered to be the first British industrial novel |
| 1845 | Publication of Friedrich Engels's *The Condition of the Working Class in England* |
| 1851 | Discovery of gold in New South Wales, Australia |
| 1854 | Publication of Charles Dickens's *Hard Times* |

CHRONOLOGY

| | |
|---|---|
| 1855 | Publication of Elizabeth Gaskell's *North and South* |
| 1857–58 | Rebellion of 1857, called "Sepoy Mutiny" by the British and first war of independence by Indians. EIC rule ends and British India comes under the Crown's direct rule |
| 1860–72 | Colonial wars throughout the central North Island, Aotearoa New Zealand |
| 1863 | Publication of F. E. Maning's *Old New Zealand, a Tale of the Good Old Times* |
| 1868 | Arrival of final convict transport, Australia |
| 1867 | Dominion of Canada created |
| 1870–72 | Marcus Clarke, serialization of *His Natural Life* |
| 1877 | Victoria, Queen of Great Britain and Ireland, crowned Empress of India |
| 1879 | Irish National Land League founded in County Mayo, Ireland, to abolish landlordism and advance tenant rights. Concerted agitation in the following decades forced successive Westminster Acts that undermined the Landlord Ascendancy and led to land redistribution and the creation of a small-farmer class. (In 1870 just 3 percent of those farming the land owned their own farms; by 1920, thanks to the Land League, 97 percent of farmers owned their own properties.) The farming class becomes a decisive force in Irish politics across the twentieth century |
| 1882 | British invasion of Egypt |
| 1883 | Publication of J. R. Seeley's *The Expansion of England* |
| 1884–85 | Berlin Conference divides Africa into European colonies |
| 1885 | The first meeting of the Indian National Congress in Bombay |
| 1893 | All adult women granted suffrage in parliamentary elections, Aotearoa New Zealand, through the Electoral Act of the same year |
| 1895–96 | The Jameson Raid launched in the South African Republic |

| | |
|---|---|
| 1899 | Second Boer War |
| 1899 | Rudyard Kipling pens "The White Man's Burden," a paean to US imperialism in the Philippines |
| 1901 | The South African War comes to an end and Milner's Kindergarten is founded |
| 1901 | Formation of the Commonwealth of Australia |
| 1902 | Publication of Barbara Baynton's *Bush Studies* |
| 1904 | The Abbey Theatre opens in Dublin and over the following decades produces landmark Revivalist works by William Butler Yeats, John M. Synge, Lady Augusta Gregory, Seán O'Casey, George Moore, George Bernard Shaw, and others |
| 1905 | Sinn Féin party founded in Dublin by Arthur Griffith |
| 1907 | Kipling awarded Nobel Prize in Literature, becoming the first English-language Nobel laureate |
| 1910 | The Union of South Africa is established |
| 1912 | Ulster Solemn League and Covenant signed by some 471,414 unionists to resist Irish Home Rule Bill passed in Westminster by the British government. The Ulster Volunteers, a loyalist paramilitary organization, formed to resist the imposition of Home Rule. The Irish Volunteers, formed to ensure the granting of Home Rule, is set up in 1913 |
| 1913 | Rabindranath Tagore wins the Nobel Prize in Literature, becoming the first Asian laureate |
| 1914–18 | First World War |
| 1914 | The Ottoman Empire enters the war in alliance with the Central Powers (October) |
| 1914 | Indian Expeditionary Force D captures the port of Basra, Mesopotamia, under the Command of General Sir Arthur Barrett (November) |
| 1915 | Publication of the first of John Buchan's trilogy of the Hannay adventure stories, *The Thirty-Nine Steps* |

| | |
|---|---|
| 1916 | Patrick Pearse and James Connolly lead an armed republican insurrection, with breakaway groups of the Irish Volunteers and the Irish Citizen Army in Dublin, and declare an independent Irish Republic from the steps of Dublin's General Post Office on Easter Monday (April 24). Dublin city center shelled by British forces, about 1,800 people taken prisoner, and 16 rebel leaders tried by secret court martial and executed, turning popular opinion against Britain and in support of the rebels |
| 1916 | Sykes–Picot Agreement (May) between Britain and France for the control and partition of Ottoman Empire territories |
| 1916–18 | Great Arab Revolt against the Ottoman Empire, led by the Sharif of Mecca and his sons |
| 1917 | Vladimir Lenin's *Imperialism: The Highest Stage of Capitalism* is published; October Revolution in Russia led by the Bolsheviks |
| 1917 | Indian and British forces capture Baghdad under the command of General Sir Frederick Stanley Maude (March) |
| 1917 | Balfour Declaration, supporting national homeland for Jews in Palestine (November) |
| 1917 | British forces capture Jerusalem under the command of General Edmund Allenby (December) |
| 1918–19 | Sweeping Sinn Féin victory in the General Election and the demise of the Irish Home Rule Party represents a shift in nationalist opinion toward full sovereignty. Dáil Éireann (Irish Parliament) declared and Irish War of Independence commences |
| 1919 | Gandhi becomes leader of Indian National Congress |
| 1919 | Jallianwala Bagh massacre in Amritsar, India |
| 1919 | Formation of the Third International (Comintern) in Moscow |
| 1919–21 | Irish War of Independence |
| 1920 | Paris Peace Conference (January) of the victorious Allied and defeated Central Powers, leading to the Treaty of Versailles |

| | |
|---|---|
| 1920 | British Mandates for Mesopotamia and Palestine, and French Mandate over Greater Syria (Syria and Lebanon), confirmed by the League of Nations at the San Remo Conference (April) |
| 1920 | Nebi Musa riots in Jerusalem (April) |
| 1921–23 | Northern Irish Parliament opened in Belfast by George V on June 22, 1921 to govern six Northern Irish counties; Anglo-Irish Treaty signed in London on December 6, 1921 to establish Ireland as a self-governing dominion of the British Empire; Irish Free State established December 1922 to govern twenty-six counties. Irish Civil War between pro- and anti-Treaty forces in Ireland begins in June 1922 and ends in May 1923 with victory for the pro-Treaty forces |
| 1922 | James Joyce's *Ulysses* is published in Paris (February) |
| 1923 | W. B. Yeats awarded the Nobel Prize for Literature on November 14, 1923. "The Shadow of a Gunman," the first part of Seán O'Casey's "Dublin Trilogy" opens in the Abbey Theatre. "Juno and the Paycock" follows in 1924 and "The Plough and the Stars," a satirical take on the Easter Rising, opens to theatre protest and riots in 1926 for the Easter Rising's tenth anniversary. |
| 1924 | Publication of E. M. Foster's *A Passage to India* |
| 1925 | George Bernard Shaw awarded the Nobel Prize for Literature, though the prize is not conferred until 1926 |
| 1927 | Publication of Edward Thompson's *An Indian Day* |
| 1930 | Gandhi begins the Salt March, initiating a campaign of civil disobedience |
| 1931 | Statute of Westminster gives Dominions constitutional autonomy and equality of status with respect to Britain; at this point these included Canada, Australia, New Zealand, South Africa, the Irish Free State, and Newfoundland |
| 1932 | End of the British Mandate in Iraq (October) |
| 1935 | Progressive Writers' Association founded in London |
| 1935 | Government of India Act ratified, giving some autonomy to provinces |

CHRONOLOGY

| | |
|---|---|
| 1935 | Publication of Mulk Raj Anand's *Untouchable* |
| 1935 | Italian invasion of Abyssinia (Ethiopia) |
| 1936 | All India Progressive Writers' Association founded in Lucknow |
| 1937 | Irish Constitution ratified |
| 1939–45 | The Second World War: The struggle against fascism brings the major European colonial powers, Britain and France, in alliance with the United States and the Soviet Union; the Allied military forces included significant numbers of colonial personnel such as 2 million recruits from British India alone; colonial contribution to the war efforts as well as the rising international status of communism, bolstered by the fall of Berlin and the liberation of the Auschwitz camp by Soviet forces, accelerated decolonization and independence in the British Empire |
| 1943–58 | Influential BBC radio broadcast series, *Caribbean Voices* |
| 1945 | The Colonial Development and Welfare Act, signaling British commitment to continued colonialism |
| 1947–48 | Dissolution of the British Raj in South Asia and Partition of India; creation of the independent Dominion of India and the Dominion of Pakistan in August 1947; independent Dominion of Sri Lanka (Ceylon) in February 1948; later, East Pakistan secedes from West Pakistan to become independent Bangladesh in 1971 |
| 1948 | *Nakba* (catastrophe), the forced dispossession and displacement of the Palestinians during the Arab–Israeli War; establishment of the state of Israel |
| 1948 | The HMT *Empire Windrush* arrives at Tilbury Docks on June 22, bringing the first large group of Caribbean emigrants to Britain after the Second World War |
| 1948 | The passing of the British Nationality Act |
| 1949 | North Atlantic Treaty signed (April) between United States, Canada, and Western European countries including Britain and France, leading to the establishment of the North Atlantic Treaty Organization (NATO) |

| | |
|---|---|
| 1951–76 | British decolonization in sub-Saharan Africa (including territories in present-day Libya, Sudan, South Sudan, Ghana, Cameroon, Somalia, Nigeria, Sierra Leone, Uganda, Kenya, Zanzibar, Malawi, Zambia, Gambia, Zimbabwe, Botswana, Lesotho, Mauritius, and Seychelles, among others). Previously in the African continent, Egypt had become independent in 1922 and South Africa in 1910 |
| 1956 | Egyptian President Gamal Abdel Nasser declares the nationalization of the British and French-owned Suez Canal Company (the Suez Crisis) |
| 1956 | Publication of Sam Selvon's *The Lonely Londoners* |
| 1958 | Notting Hill race riots (August–September) |
| 1960 | British Prime Minister Harold Macmillan delivers the "Wind of Change" speech to the South African Parliament (February, previously given in Accra, in January), signaling British willingness to decolonize in Africa |
| 1962 | The passing of the Commonwealth Immigrants Act |
| 1968 | Race Relations Act against discrimination in housing and employment |
| 1981 | "Sus" (Suspect Person) Law repealed by the Criminal Attempts Act |
| 1981 | The passing of the British Nationality Act |
| 1982 | Falklands/Malvinas conflict between Britain and Argentina |
| 1998 | Belfast (Good Friday) Agreement between Northern Ireland political parties, the British and Irish governments |
| 2016 | Brexit referendum in the UK to leave the European Union (EU). Fifty-two percent vote Leave, 48 percent vote Remain. David Cameron resigns as Prime Minister. Theresa May wins the Conservative Party leadership contest |
| 2017 | The Conservative Party lose their majority in the General Election and Theresa May strikes a deal with Northern Irish unionists from the Democratic Unionist Party to stay in power (June) |

CHRONOLOGY

| | |
|---|---|
| 2017 | Article 50 triggered by Theresa May, setting the date for UK departure (March) |
| 2018–19 | Brexit delays and extensions over exit terms. Theresa May faces vote of no confidence from the Conservative Party. Eighteen ministers quit over Brexit, including Brexit Minister David Davis and Foreign Secretary Boris Johnson |
| 2019 | Boris Johnson wins the Conservative Party internal leadership contest and becomes Prime Minister (July), and wins the General Election (December) |
| 2020 | European Parliament approves Brexit Deal and the UK leaves the EU on January 31 |

AURITRO MAJUMDER

# Introduction
## *Situating British Literature and Empire*

### Rethinking British Literature

The subject of the British Empire exerts an uncanny influence in contemporary Britain and elsewhere. Opinion polls, unreliable except perhaps as a vague measure of the times, suggest that many Britons continue to hold a positive view of the empire. Per surveys carried out in 2014 and 2020 by the data analytics company YouGov, 59 percent (2014) and 32 percent (2020) of respondents were "proud" of the empire, compared to 37 percent who felt neither pride nor shame (2020) and 19 percent who were "ashamed" (both 2014 and 2020). Of course, "empire" here evokes the image of a fictional past rather than a historical one, having to do more with feelings than facts. The longing for a vanished age and space of supposedly heroic values is hardly unique to Britain, after all, and common to nearly every modern nation. Which explains the stubborn persistence of these opinions despite the painstaking corrections done by scholars and activists, and the vocal condemnations from a significant minority within Britain and the vast majority in her former colonies. The nostalgia for the glories of empire is impossible to dislodge by highlighting the depredations committed in the name of the latter, or demonstrating how these may parallel the imperium of our own times. The key issue is how the bygone empire serves our decidedly pedestrian here and now.

Arguably, literature provides an indispensable site to explore the relation between the past and the present of empire. It illuminates the ordinary everyday within the epochal, the intimate realm of feelings amidst the rigid structures of social life. To argue for the special value of literary matters might appear paradoxical today. Surely, the study of literature faces a dire situation evidenced by the devaluation of humanistic knowledge in public discourse and in schools and universities, where learning outcomes are increasingly shaped by a gray vision of neoliberal, technocratic education and governance. However, as one of its objectives, *The Cambridge*

*Companion to British Literature and Empire* demonstrates the value of literature when it comes to understanding Britain's place in the modern world and situating the global present in relation to the past. Not in any straightforward sense, let us add; texts are not mere reflections of history or geography even if they are often erroneously treated as such. Nor is the field of literary studies devoid of aesthetic value, a pursuit reserved for the privileged yet increasingly precarious few. But then, to tweak the famous lines by Kipling, what do they know of English literature that only English literature know?

The term, "literature," adapted from Latin, has at least a dual meaning: It refers to a range of texts providing discursive *knowledge* on a broad or narrow subject, for example, medical literature or literature on the feeding habits of ducks. Alternatively, in a more specific sense, a set of creative, subjective works that exist in *writing* in distinction to oral, plastic, visual, and other forms of cultural and aesthetic expression. Likewise, the title of the present volume, "British literature and empire" indicates another ambiguity: Does the proper adjective British qualify both nouns that follow it (literature and empire), so that one is describing literature and its relation to the British Empire specifically? Or does the phrase refer to British literature and empire separately, in which case the latter includes the entire system of modern empire including other European, American, and Asian competitors? Furthermore, how to understand the evolving relation between Britain and the various commonwealths, Crown- and trading company-administered territories, dominions, protectorates, semi-colonies, and informal dependencies that defined empire once, and that constitute diverse independent nation-states today?

Even these preliminary issues of description foreground the problem of literary language: the polyvalent connotations of words, their many possible relations among themselves and what they reference in the world outside the text, and the subtle connections between knowledge, writing, and power. The collection of essays presented here grapples with these issues and more, providing a synoptic overview of the literatures produced or otherwise circulated in Britain and the racialized, classed, and gendered imaginaries of empire over the last five hundred years. Together, the chapters survey a wide range of works from the sixteenth century to the present and how these articulate the consciousness of an imperialized world through creative language, literary perspective, and narrative form. Alongside, they revaluate literary genres such as typologies of fiction, poetry, and drama, and reconsider periodization emphasizing overlaps and recurrences rather than linear episodic development. In doing so, this collection traces transnational literary histories connecting the British Isles to Australasia, the Caribbean, the United States and Canada, South, Southeast, and West Asia, and North and sub-Saharan Africa.

The objective truth made available by any literary archive is complex. This is because literary works are produced at the intersection of many forces, personal and subjective factors for one but also ideological, economic, and political flows that extend beyond a single individual, group, or nation. Alongside, the reading of literature seldom reproduces an unchanging meaning, which itself changes over time as well as space, albeit unevenly, and is shaped by varying concerns. To take but one instance, students of Shakespeare would recall that for nearly three centuries *The Tempest* (first performed in 1611) held a minor place in the Shakespearean oeuvre limited to discussions of esoteric Renaissance knowledge represented by Prospero, the play's aristocratic protagonist. But at the start of the last century, the text's reputation and significance altered. From an outpost far from Britain, the Uruguayan intellectual José Enrique Rodó published his influential essay, "Ariel" in 1900, which claimed the play's ethereal servant, Ariel, to be embodying a Latin American spiritual and artistic ethic, one that was distinct to, and superior from, his fellow serf Caliban's vulgar materialism. Over the century's course, successive intellectuals in the hemispheric Americas would turn to the defiant Caliban previously dismissed by Rodó and situate him as the classic victim of European colonial violence. Prominent figures in this latter tradition included Aimé Césaire, the Martiniquan bard of Négritude; Roberto Fernández Retamar, the Cuban communist poet; and Sylvia Wynter, the Jamaican author and critic. Writing in European languages, French, Spanish, and English, respectively, but guided by the anticolonial spirit, their works reilluminated *The Tempest*'s relationship to diasporic blackness and Indigenous Americanness, and the intersections of literary culture and global empire in Shakespeare's times as much as in their own.

In other words, what is minor for or overlooked by one generation may be quite crucial for the next; a creed favoring empire may reveal a subversive manifesto, conversely, once-progressive texts can lose their auratic sheen. Crystal Bartolovich's opening piece for this volume tracks the case of Thomas More's *Utopia* (originally published in Latin in 1516), viewed by many recent scholars as a blueprint for European settler colonialism but whose radical call for abolishing private property and especially land ownership drew dismay through the sixteenth and seventeenth centuries. Bartolovich highlights the emerging link between the loss of the commons, the subsequent consolidation of capitalist property relations in England, and the rise of settler colonialism in the New World. This intimate relation between early capitalism and empire is illuminated from another perspective by Ania Loomba, whose chapter on a popular English tale or legend of the London mayor, Dick Whittington, and his lucky cat charts evolving categories of race and racial capitalism through global trade networks in the early modern world. Mercantilism in the texts of Renaissance drama is the focus of Su Fang Ng, whose essay unveils a "peripheral heroics" that articulated the aspirational but marginal English bourgeoisie's anxieties about intra-European rivalry especially against the Spanish and Dutch, as well as sexual and religious contamination and pollution, issues that continue to resonate today albeit in changed form and content. These critics maintain that English literature was informed by imperial concerns and anti-capitalist/colonial critique alike since the sixteenth and seventeenth centuries, even as England was a minor player among European imperial powers. However, what is termed the "first British Empire," manifested by English expansion over the rest of the British Isles (Wales, Scotland, Ireland), goes back to the eleventh and twelfth centuries.

To turn to the ascendant rather than merely aspirational British Empire, consider Percy Bysshe Shelley's well-known poem, "Ozymandias," first published in 1818, which traces the question of imperial decline in the embodied figure of the king. "I met a traveller from an antique land, / Who said – 'Two vast and trunkless legs of stone / Stand in the desert.... Near them, on the sand, / Half sunk a shattered visage lies.'" The opening riffs on the overused symbolism of monuments ravaged by the passage of time. The enigmatic "traveller" marks an aporia in the poem; likewise, the "two vast and trunkless legs of stone" that once might have marched to faraway lands, contrast with the hapless "half sunk ... shattered visage"; what had been the "frown[ing], "sneer[ing]" face of conquest lies buried in "the sand." It is the second part of the poem beginning with "on the pedestal these words appear: 'My name is Ozymandias, king of kings; / Look on my works, ye Mighty, and despair!'" that Shelley advances the strikingly poetic idea central to this volume – namely, that writing captures invisible contradictions and prophesies futures before those are realized in fact. Appearing to proclaim the glory of the "king of kings," the epitaph articulates defeat instead of triumph and, moreover, threatens a similar fate like Ozymandias' to all with imperial ambition. The epitaph persists while the statue crumbled, yet the former produces meaning by reference to the vanished latter.

Needless to add, for Shelley the symbol of imperial hubris and decline is a non-European other, an ancient Egyptian king, at the precise moment when the British Empire was beginning to overtake its competitors both in Europe and Asia. The inscription's source is the *Bibliotheca historica*, a compendious history of the classical world by Diodorus Siculus in the first century BCE, which describes the Egyptian Pharaoh, Ramses II, in these

Introduction

terms. Rather than overt citation, Shelley's poem subsumes the reference in the form of intertextuality. The poem both observes and contravenes the Italianate sonnet meter of Petrarch (1304–74): In terms of its theme and form, "Ozymandias" reflects what might be called a general principle of literary reflections on empire, it is indebted to and freely borrows from works of the past but with an altered significance. Late eighteenth- and early nineteenth-century English musings on the rise and fall of other empires were shaped as much by the ancient and the premodern as the contemporary world, by events near home as well as distant shores that were often foreign as the past itself. James Mulholland's chapter excavates the late eighteenth-century Anglophone epic poetry of ruins crafted by colonial administrator-authors that reconciled the East India Company's (EIC's) growing presence in South and Southeast Asia with the decline of Asian power. In another case, Arif Camoglu's essay takes stock of Romantic attitudes toward the "Muslim" and "Hindu" regions of West and South Asia, where the cycles of failed political revolutions supposedly attested to their chronic instability and justified Western interventions. The English Orientalists' and Romantics' fascination with ruins and insurrections in the non-European and especially the Islamic world were symptomatic of deeper culturalist assumptions which carry to the present day – in 2003, a CNN reporter, moved no doubt by literary inspiration, would invoke Ozymandias to describe the fall of Saddam Hussein to invading US forces.

The corpus of what has been called British literature may be works written by, and even arguably primarily for, Britons, but it was not disconnected from global others – we'll return to this point shortly. Another related issue is the changing foundations of studying British literature: Today, students are no longer restricted to the canonical figures of a Shakespeare or a Shelley, or even the protocols and assumptions of a once formidable Western humanist tradition. They can, if they choose to, turn their attention to previously marginalized authors: for instance, women, immigrants, minorities, and working-class, providing a broader range of perspectives and better reflecting the composite histories of Britain and an interconnected modern world. The connections between English-language literature and the world beyond Europe have also been made more explicit; scholars have persuasively demonstrated that diverse branches of literature, prose especially but also drama and verse genres, were shaped by expanding trade, global markets, territorial and resource appropriations, military conquests, human emigration/immigration, and the resulting cultural contact from all these forces. Jason Pearl's contribution to this volume outlines a fresh understanding of the rise of the English novel, juxtaposing early fiction with seafaring and land voyage accounts and natural scientific explorations in the Atlantic New

World as well as Pacific Australasia. On the other hand, Nicole N. Aljoe's essay reframes the vital corpus of Black Atlantic slave narratives in terms of literary modes of voice, narrative form, and style, marking the vital agency and aesthetic-political impact of African-descended persons in eighteenth- and nineteenth-century Britain.

## Orientalism and Ideology

Pioneering scholarship on the forms of knowledge and writing engendered by empire include works (in both cases, focused on British India) such as David Kopf's *British Orientalism and the Bengal Renaissance: The Dynamics of Indian Modernization 1773–1835* (published in 1969) and Benita Parry's *Delusions and Discoveries: India in the British Imagination, 1880–1930* (appearing in 1972). The landmark text was Edward Said's *Orientalism: Western Conceptions of the Orient* (1978), which offered a sweeping survey of British and French self-perpetuating representations of the "Middle East." Said's text not only marked the end of the hopeful, tumultuous decades of the 1960s and 1970s, but also popularized the term "Orientalism" and its neglected imperial dimensions to broad readerships outside the academy. Few later scholars followed the epic scale of Said's work, instead focusing on more narrowly defined periods and revising some of his formulations in view of their more specific findings. Since the 1980s, literary research has engaged in a range of conversations with other disciplines such as history, economics, sociology, geography, and anthropology, among others, and incorporated the theories and insights of world-system analysis, critical race, colonial discourse analysis, post-structuralism, Marxism, psychoanalysis, feminism, and new historicism, to name a few. The overtly "political" focus of much of this scholarship derived from the events of the 1960s and 1970s: the rise and fall of liberation struggles in the Third World (and anti-imperialist trends within the New Left in the West) and, relatedly, the interventions of diasporic intellectuals and professors arrived in Britain and North America from the former colonies. This body of work eventually led to the institutionalization of "postcolonial studies" in various avatars in the 1990s and 2000s, with scholars continuing to excavate the histories of European empires but also the implications of the United States–led unipolar world order after the fall of the Soviet Union and the end of the Cold War.

Since the early 2000s, however, the postcolonial perspectives have been contested in academic circles. Michael Hardt and Antonio Negri's succinctly titled *Empire* (2000) argued for the obsolescence of imperialism in the twenty-first century from an avowedly "communist" perspective. Much more significant was the conservative backlash. The historian Niall

# Introduction

Ferguson's *Empire: How Britain Made the Modern World* (2003) rehearsed wearisome tropes of the British Empire's modernizing influence, spawning a range of revisionist works that downplayed or simply denied the human (and environmental) costs of imperial modernization. Not only politicians and the mainstream media, but sections of Western academia too would be affected by colonial nostalgia, a case in point being the political scientist Bruce Gilley's essay "The Case for Colonialism," which advocated for twenty-first-century recolonization. To unravel such loathsome sentiments, which, contrary to appearances, are not unique to the present moment but often draw from older narratives, it would be useful to underline those texts and genres of literature that registered as well as articulated empire to varying degrees: Also, conversely, it would be useful to consider how literature played a crucial role in the consolidation – and eventual unraveling – of British imperial hegemony.

Over the long nineteenth century, a mix of ideologies spawned to rationalize British overseas presence as not only inevitable (such sentiments had been expressed even earlier) but indeed beneficial for the colonized, extending the eighteenth-century concept of *bienfaisance* (literally, good act) in new directions. These included Indo-Europeanism and Orientalism noted earlier in this chapter; the notion of "Greater Britain" from Charles Dilke's 1868 book of the same name linking the English metropole to the rest of the British Isles and the Atlantic and Pacific settler colonies, all the way to the infamous "White Man's burden," in Rudyard Kipling's phrasing (1899), passing the torch of colonial "improvement" from British to US hands. Such notions of empire normalized Anglo-British dominance, sidelining the murkier aspects of rapine and genocide, famine and war. Moreover, they would be endlessly reproduced and broadcast through cultural media – oratory, books, films, newspapers, TV shows – consolidating one of the foundational myths of the modern West.

In the present volume, Ian Duncan's chapter illustrates how nineteenth-century historical novels articulated the discourse of "progress" and scientific rationality while also registering the keen contestations arising from different colonial contexts: from British "internal colonialism" or the unions of Scotland and Ireland with England, through the settler colonies in Canada and the United States, to the administered colony in India. Christina Morin's contribution discusses Irish Romantic gothic fiction and its fraught negotiation of Ireland's subordinate position and colonial history on the one hand and Irish cultural nationalist participation in anti-blackness and racial hierarchies of the British Empire on the other hand. In other words, English but also Irish literature and the empire complemented and reinforced one another, albeit in different ways.

Alongside, the British literary canon took shape through the networks of empire, the latter enabling the dissemination of texts and the formation of global reading publics stratified by race, gender, class, and location. Often, this process involved a motley range of personnel, media, and institutions: administrators, adventurers, missionaries, and philanthropists; technologies of print, radio, and other media; reviews, periodicals, and publishing houses; training colleges, universities, and libraries; white-only clubs in the colonies; amateur and professional playhouses, and so on. Charting such networks might be one way of understanding the enduring reach, and appeal, of classic or "timeless" British authors in the hearts and minds of readers. Aided by the lingua franca of English, readers around the world read not merely about England but her "leading" role in widely disparate regions. In this collection, Aviva Briefel's chapter highlights the genre of the industrial novel, where the localized tropes and motifs of worker resistance in the factories of Victorian Britain and the distant imagery of dehumanized and enslaved peoples of the colonial empire informed each other. Comparably, Sandeep Banerjee's piece explores the influential body of Victorian imperial romance and their juxtaposition of British anxieties over anticolonial revolt (such as the Indian Uprising of 1857) and sexual miscegenation in India and Africa.

It is noteworthy that nineteenth-century English fiction incorporated a variety of imaginative landscapes as well as representational modes ranging from realism to fantasy. More than clear distinctions of highbrow and popular genres, what mattered was the distance traveled by fictional texts whether in the depths of the reader's imagination or the actual geographical spread of the novels. Further, the extroversion through literature of British identity effected a reciprocal nationalist consolidation at home: With print culture and rising literacy, the lower social orders, that is, the working classes and not only the elite could be trained in the rudiments of imperial thinking, which proved to be useful given the omnipresent strands of dissent in Britain and threats to the status quo.

However, rather than suggest a homogeneous context of British literature, we should emphasize literature's specific iterations in the different colonies. Providing a useful counterpoint to metropolitan Victorian texts, Philip Steer's essay explores the corpus of nonfiction, novels, and short stories from Australia and New Zealand and *their* elaboration of "Greater Britain" liberalism, newfangled settler identity, and contact with the Indigenous populations; many of these texts traveled back to Britain through the same networks already described. Threading unevenly through varied geographies and cultures, and marked by distinct trajectories of negotiation and refraction, such exchanges between metropole and periphery accumulated more layers than any brief outline can suggest. Moreover, despite its top-down imposition as an aspect of the dominating culture, colonial receptions of British literature were neither passive nor uniform but highly divergent, attesting to the complex relation between texts and their interpretive communities. One noteworthy aspect in this context was the expansion of English both as literature and language to encompass the domain of the Anglophone. Here, an analogy from political economy would be useful to illuminate the issue.

At the most basic level, European colonialism, as it did with local systems of commodity production and property relations, baldly annihilated or modified native languages. In tandem with trade, the English language's export to the Atlantic Empire and competition with Spanish, Dutch, Portuguese, and French marked England's ascent from a marginal European power. The spread of the English language fostered new forms of pidgin and creole, some of them developing into vital oral and literary traditions as in the Caribbean. By the middle third of the nineteenth century, English, along with French, another imperial language, had attained extraordinary circulation and eminence. English's global status – or what is termed the Anglophone today – was made possible by a disparate range of British imperial activities in far-flung regions, persuasive and coercive in equal measure: in the 1830s in South Asia, the replacement of Persian by English as the official language; in Ireland around the same time, the erasure of indigenous language and place names; in the independent nations of United States and Canada starting in the 1870s, the forced assimilation of Native American children through the residential school system; the movement of masses of indentured and precarious labor from one corner of the world to another seeking recourse to a common idiom, and so on. However, it is important to emphasize that not despite but precisely because of its roots in imperial domination, English as a language of contact also enabled the formation of contrarian currents to empire, as discussed in the section "Lineages of the Present."

The literary critic Aamir Mufti has argued that Orientalist and Anglicist philology, seeking to analyze non-Western literary traditions and fine-tune administrative policy in colonial India, was instrumental in developing the methods of a global comparative literature. It was English's function as a "vanishing mediator," Mufti suggests, more than the German theories of *Weltliteratur* espoused by Goethe, Marx, et al., that provided the conceptual basis for the modern and Eurocentric discipline of world literature as a hierarchical space of literary exchange among unequal nations. For Western-educated colonized intellectuals, on the other hand, literature and culture more broadly became the preferred vehicles (in the absence of real economic and political power) for asserting and elaborating alternative visions of national pasts that selectively borrowed and departed from the confines of colonial discourse. Unsurprisingly, Britain itself did not remain inured to the rising chorus of anti-imperial voices from the colonies and upheavals within Europe for long.

## Lineages of the Present

Like our contemporary moment when the idea of literature is undergoing profound transformation, at the beginning of the twentieth century too the most profound changes of British literary style were wrought through (and in turn mediated) demotic challenges within and outside Britain. Dominic Davies' chapter examines what he usefully terms the "modernist compressions" in post–First World War British adventure fiction, which unlike their flamboyant Victorian predecessors anxiously articulated intra-European conflict, especially rival German nationalism and the decline of British influence in South Africa and India, through formal techniques of fragmentation and nonlinearity as well as textual silences and aporias. In even more tangible ways, interimperial warfare and anti-imperial dissent were foregrounded in modernism thanks to the presence of diverse intellectuals in London.

As the principal city of the British Empire, London attracted immigrants and visitors from all over the world but especially the colonies. Between the 1900s and the 1940s, a nonexhaustive list of writers and activists from the latter might include illustrious names such as Mulk Raj Anand, Roy Campbell, T. S. Eliot, Miles Franklin, C. L. R James, James Joyce, Dorothy Livesay, Katherine Mansfield, Una Marson, Ezra Pound, F. R. Scott, A. J. M Smith, Christina Stead, and W. B. Yeats. Paul Stasi's contribution reads influential male and female modernist poets arrived in Britain from the Caribbean, India, and the United States, and how their ebullient conceptions of poetic autonomy stood at odds with dehistoricized approaches of "art-for-art's-sake" canonized in metropolitan modernism. Considering the same milieu, Sonita Sarker complicates modernist fiction's much-discussed estrangement of narrative form and artistic persona by drawing attention to the subtexts of empire and whiteness, unpacking the combination of race, gender, and nationalism in "New Women" authors from Canada, Ireland, New Zealand, and South Africa relocating to the "mother country" of England.

Colonial writers also fraternized with England-born members of the avant-garde in London (such as the famed Bloomsbury Group): Like the Romantics' circles a century earlier, modernism came to be defined by the cosmopolitan exchange of ideas as well as loosely anchored artistic groups and factions. The reception of foreign intellectuals was of course filtered through identity categories alongside their overt or assumed political sympathies: Predictably, Asians, Africans, women, and the indigent found themselves at the margins of both the avant-garde and the mainstream cultural world far more frequently than their Euro-American male counterparts. Nonetheless, these itinerant figures profoundly shaped the course of modernism and more generally intellectual and political life in Britain. As Joe Cleary's chapter on Irish revivalism and Irish modernism demonstrates through a discussion of James Joyce, not only Joyce but many writers in and from the peripheries of the British Empire surpassed their English counterparts as the major innovators of modernist prose, poetry, and drama. In parallel, English-language literature's center of gravity started to shift from a once-dominant, now-shrinking England to an increasingly globally influential United States in the first half of the twentieth century. Admittedly, these large-scale transformations were protracted in scope and neither immediate nor restricted to literature but also covered other arts such as painting, theater, and cinema.

Elinor Taylor's contribution in the volume focalizes another type of transnational collective: the gathering of antifascist writers in Britain under the Popular Front banner of the 1930s. Considering a wide range of left-wing journals, nonfiction, poetry, and novels, Taylor illuminates the complex role of English, Australian, Caribbean, Indian, and Welsh activists negotiating the relationship between British working-class radicalism, resistance to capitalist imposition, and anticolonial movements in the British Empire. Collectives such as the Popular Front and similar organizations of the 1930s and 40s afforded opportunities for socialist, feminist, and anticolonial activists to cross-fertilize their ideas. Consequently, in contrast to dominant assumptions, these activist circles would eloquently articulate the parallels between empire and fascism. Undermining the British elite self-image of enlightenment and democracy, the ideologies and practices of not only British but Euro-American imperialism as a whole marked uncanny continuities with those of the contemporary fascist regimes in Germany, Italy, and Spain: To mention a few, the idea of "Aryan race"-based right to rule; nationalist-masculinist mobilizations of the lower classes; labor camps, mass internment, dispossession, and resettlement of "suspect" colonized populations; racialized science and eugenics; endless war; collective punishment of entire populations including women, children, and the infirm; the coordination between transnational corporations, financial institutions, and the state. These represented interlinked aspects of imperial expansion and systemic responses to recurrent capitalist crisis, whether by the English EIC or Nazi Germany, rather than aberrant, exceptional moments in the development of the modern West.

Particularly, interwar and postwar Marxists in Britain, both "natives" and "outsiders," such as C. L. R James, Eric Williams, Claudia Jones, Agnes Smedley, Sylvia Pankhurst, George Thompson, Nancy Cunard, Rajani Palme Dutt, Eric Hobsbawm, Joseph Needham, Victor Kiernan, Ruth First, Raymond Williams, Ambalavaner Sivanandan, and Stuart Hall among others provided outstanding insights on the relation between capitalism, empire, and mass resistance. Aimed at broad audiences, their ideas circulated through innovative channels: speeches, pamphlets, adult education, and community-based organizations in addition to books and articles. These developments need to be juxtaposed with the global ferment of decolonization especially the national liberation movements after 1945. Thus, the ideas of "Black self-determination" that C. L. R James had traced in the Haitian Revolution (1790–1804) found renewed expression in the contemporary struggles of the peasantry in Africa and urban underclasses in North America. Northern Irish nationalists made common cause with anti-Zionist and anti-Apartheid movements in Palestine and South Africa respectively. English models of "history from below" traveled to India, where Subaltern historians would refashion it to undermine the then-dominant "Cambridge School" historiography. Finally, the theory and field of cultural materialism and cultural studies, respectively, initiated new methodologies for exploring social contestations in Thatcherite Britain and beyond.

At the same time, as Andrew Hammond demonstrates in his chapter, the long shadow of the Cold War, associated with the Soviet Union and United States–led blocs' contest for hegemony, especially in the Third World, had a decisive impact on British literary production. Hammond's wide-ranging study of Anglo-British "mainstream" and diasporic "postcolonial" writing reveals antithetical attitudes to England's loss of its former colonies. The former group manifested a retrograde nostalgia for English prestige and benevolence, while demonizing both anticolonial insurgents abroad and communities of color in Britain in crudely racist, stereotypical terms. On the other hand, for diasporic postcolonial authors, literature and especially fiction became one of the key means of negotiating marginalization and asserting citizenship. This latter group included the famed "Windrush Generation" of early Caribbean writers and successive cohorts of Caribbean-, South Asian-, and African-origin authors in Britain in the 1960s, 70s, and 80s.

Postcolonial writers introduced readers to the vocabulary and grammar as well as the rhythm and memory of colonized lands, foregrounding the perspectives of the formerly colonized peoples and adding yet another layer to the historical contestations around standard written English. The Guyanese-origin British author, John Agard, pithily described the latter process in his poem, "Listen Mr. Oxford Don" (1967), as "mugging de Queen's

English," which parodied the racialized and gendered discourse of Black male criminality ("mugging") and elite nationalist anxieties about linguistic and cultural purity ("Queen's English"). Lisa Tomlinson's contribution in this volume foregrounds a vital corpus of formally and linguistically subversive writing: namely, the dub poetry and fiction of Black British writers in the 1980s and 1990s. Tomlinson signals both the continuities and the departures in post–Windrush generations of Afro-Caribbean diasporic writers, as they staked claim to a multicultural Britishness in aesthetic as well as political terms.

The volume's final two pieces consider twenty-first-century British fiction's engagement with the contradictions of liberal multiculturalism and revanchist nationalism, as fiction writers and poets articulate oppressed Arab and Muslim identities – in the face of institutional and cultural censure – while refashioning the tropes and techniques of mainstream narrative. Nadia Atia's chapter explores contemporary Arab British historical novels that focus on the Great War (First World War) in the Middle East and the war's less-discussed aftermath in the 1920s, namely, Arab nationalist independence movements in Mesopotamia and the European–Zionist colonial project in Palestine. Similarly, the negotiations between Britishness and Islam (the latter doubly mediated by post-9/11 US discourse on the "War on Terror" and aggressive English nationalism after Brexit) inform Amina Yaqin's essay, which situates new directions in British Muslim writing and how these deploy ideas of English landscape and modes of the pastoral to present imaginative alternatives to dominant notions of Britain and her relationship to the world beyond.

To conclude, the *Companion* provides an accessible yet nuanced introduction to the vast colonial interactions that shaped Britain, propelling the rise of English-language literature as a global phenomenon. Taken together, the essays carefully map the developing genres of literary texts – fiction and nonfiction prose, poetry, and their different typologies – over multiple periods and several locations, connecting these texts to transnational contexts. Not every key area of British literature could be engaged with, for reasons of space and practicality. Altogether, the volume covers a period of over five hundred years, with more focus on the last century given its proximity and greater relevance to the present (the earliest work considered, Thomas More's *Utopia*, was published in 1516; the latest, Ayisha Malik's *This Green and Pleasant Land*, appeared in 2019 – both, not incidentally, focus on lived and imagined relationships to an island). The capacious geographical coverage of the anthology will benefit the reader, especially nonspecialists, in discovering often-unexpected patterns and continuities in literary and imperial space and networks of circulation. The *Companion* underscores that many themes of contemporary cultural politics (racial hierarchies, for one, or settler colonialism, for another) are neither unique to the present nor limited to the regions of Britain or even the West, but iterations and variations of contests spread across far-flung corners of the world. In terms of methodology, the compendium charts both the classical concerns of literary studies, that is, aesthetic and humanistic considerations, and critical trends of the past decades that insist on literature's imbrication in, and inseparability from, material and ideological practices of world making. Accordingly, the survey and the close readings of the selected literary texts – both canonical and little-discussed – are grounded in, and in turn illuminate, the cultural implications of domination, resistance, and negotiation in a world shaped unevenly by Western capitalism and colonialism. Put another way, literature, in its ability to articulate important shifts in perception, sensibilities, and social relations before such changes are actualized, provides an indispensable index to comprehending "the human condition."

Meanwhile, the violence of empire continues: The grim double standards of the Western ruling classes when it comes to their contrasting attitude to the victims in Gaza and Ukraine, respectively, are on plain display for the world to watch. Unfortunately, across the West, media houses, universities, arts and culture organizations have been complicit in this regard, censoring protesting voices and opinions. Surely, there is no greater proof of the dehumanizing impact of empire? The selective indifference to lives and suffering and the resulting shrinking of open, democratic culture? The study of literature or history cannot change this present situation. But certainly, it can equip students with the resources, narratives, and capacities to strive for a shared vision, a world to come after empire.

## Works Cited

Césaire, Aimé. *A Tempest*. 1969. Translated by Richard Miller, Theater Communications Group, 1992.
Dilke, Charles W. *Greater Britain*. 1868. Cambridge UP, 2009, 2 vols.
Ferguson, Niall. *Empire: How Britain Made the Modern World*. Allen Lane, 2003.
Gilley, Bruce. "The Case for Colonialism." *Academic Questions*, vol. 31, no. 2, 2018, pp. 167–85.
Hardt, Michael, and Antonio Negri. *Empire*. Harvard UP, 2000.
Kipling, Rudyard. "The White Man's Burden: The United States and the Philippine Islands," 1899, www.kiplingsociety.co.uk/poem/poems_burden.htm. Accessed Feb. 5, 2024.
Kopf, David. *British Orientalism and the Bengal Renaissance: The Dynamics of Indian Modernization 1773–1835*. U of California P, 1969.
Mufti, Aamir R. *Forget English! Orientalisms and World Literatures*. Harvard UP, 2016.

Parry, Benita. *Delusions and Discoveries: India in the British Imagination 1880–1930*. 1972. Verso, 1998.

Retamar, Roberto F. "Caliban: Notes toward a Discussion of Culture in Our America [1971]." *Caliban and Other Essays*. Translated by Edward Baker, U of Minnesota P, 2002, pp. 3–45.

Rodó, José E. *Ariel*. 1900. Translated by Margaret S. Peden, U of Texas P, 1988.

Said, Edward W. *Orientalism*. 1978. Vintage Books, 2014.

Shakespeare, William. *The Tempest*. 1611. Edited by Peter Hulme and William H. Sherman, W.W. Norton, 2019.

Shelley, Percy B. "Ozymandias," 1818, www.poetryfoundation.org/poems/46565/ozymandias. Accessed Feb. 5, 2024.

Wynter, Sylvia. "Beyond Miranda's Meanings: Un/Silencing the 'Demonic Ground' of Caliban's 'Woman.'" *Out of the Kumbla: Caribbean Women and Literature*, edited by Carole Boyce Davies and Elaine Savory Fido, Africa World P, 1990, pp. 355–70.

PART I
# Early Intimations and Literary Genres: 1500–1800

# I

CRYSTAL BARTOLOVICH

# Early Modern Utopia
## Capitalism, Colonialism, and Private Property

Thomas More's *Utopia* (1516) emerged into a world with no British Empire, at least not in the sense that this collection of essays probably conjures up for most readers. As James Knapp put it, England had an "empire nowhere" in the early modern period. Nevertheless, when James I combined the kingdoms of Scotland and England in 1603, he, like monarchs before him, claimed to rule an "empire." His cartographer, John Speed, faithfully records this assertion in his atlas, *Theatre of the Empire of Great Britain* (1612). But England – unlike Portugal and Spain – had no successful New World colonies at the time, much less in Asia or Africa; its holdings in France were long lost, Ireland was doubtful, and even its trade network was modest compared to that of the Dutch. Speed's volume included maps of England, Scotland, Wales, Ireland, and "the iles adjoining" only. The "British Empire," in the modern sense of an expansive network of distant settler and extractive colonies, did not yet exist, though nineteenth-century colonial propagandists tendentiously backdated their own assumptions to the Renaissance (see Armitage).

What did exist, though, was what James Harrington's *Oceana* (1656) later described as "domestic" empire. "Empire," for Harrington, resulted from relations of dependency, predicated on uneven control over land, wherever it occurs. Speed's volume, with its detailed maps and accounts of each British shire, "with her cities and earls described," illustrates this state of affairs emphatically. When land is held overwhelmingly by the Crown, aristocracy, and urban corporations, dependency ensues. "He who wanteth bread, is his servant that will feed him," Harrington observed, a relationship that he attributed to lack of access to land (4).[1] Writing during the Interregnum, his main concern is casting doubt on domestic empire, which, he argues, makes the freeholders' commonwealth he longed for impossible; he thus proposes distributing private property in land among a large enough number of citizen-owners to obviate monarchy and aristocracy. Intriguingly, "foreign" empire, too, was undesirable in his view, not least because he (presciently) worried it would lead in time to rebellion.

The key immediate point, though, is that his understanding of "empire," whether domestic or foreign, is materialist: based on control over land. Marx later decries unequal landholding as well when he lays out the long process of dispossession of land, specifically, as necessary to producing the "capital relation" in both Europe and the colonies in the Primitive Accumulation chapters of *Capital*; unlike Harington, however, Marx proposes abolition of private property altogether as the antidote – as do More's Utopians. Though their assessments are different, More, Harington, and Marx all recognize that the dependency required by colonialism and capitalism alike was well underway domestically in England by the sixteenth century because of unequal control of land.

But what do *Utopia* – and utopia – have to do with what Harrington calls "foreign" empire? A great deal according to many critics (including Knapp) who have dedicated themselves to "decolonizing" utopia, sometimes by exploring the "utopian" production of non-Western peoples, but more often by denouncing the damage that "utopia" has purportedly done in supporting European colonization.[2] Karl Hardy, for example, asserts that "without a doubt, More's *Utopia*, much of the ensuing modern utopian literary tradition, and the utopianism of settler societies are substantial contributors to the naturalization of settler societies" (133). Earlier, John Mohawk, himself a Seneca, traced a "history of conquest and oppression in the Western World," which he describes as a "utopian legacy." Defining utopia as a vision of a "perfect society," he claims that though such visions can be found in all cultures, the insidiousness of "Western" utopia is its collapsing with what he, following Isaiah Berlin, calls "pursuit of the ideal," a tendency to package up brutal self-interest *as* "utopia." Similarly, Sylvia Wynter devastatingly observes that "White Utopia was the Black inferno" (210). All this sounds damning indeed for utopia, and yet I want to pose some dialectical "doubt" where Hardy sees none, because his claim is only part of the story. At the same time as Wynter excoriates "White" utopia, she also uses "utopian" affirmatively to describe resistance to dehumanizing treatment of the enslaved in, for example, song and dance. And, while Mohawk denounces a "utopian legacy," he does not include *Utopia* itself as part of that project, instead describing it as a "reaction to the wretched conditions of poverty and injustice being produced in England" by enclosure (144). It would be more accurate, then, to view "utopia" as a site of struggle from the sixteenth century onward rather than dismissing it *tout court* as a thoroughly contaminated colonialist project.[3]

One problem for Hardy's contention about *Utopia*, at least, is that early English references to *Utopia* in print – including in colonial propaganda – are ambivalent, skeptical, or forthrightly hostile, far more likely to distance themselves from utopia than to embrace it.[4] Particularly disturbing to early English commentators is *Utopia*'s refusal of private property, which they saw as threatening to social stability at home and retrograde to advancing trade and empire abroad. Such responses raise the question of whether a social order that eschews private property can be "colonialist" at all, given that not only Marxists, but Indigenous studies, as I will discuss shortly, view the imposition of private property in land as an irreducible aspect of capitalist colonization.

Many early English readers, in any case, viewed *Utopia* as worrisomely hostile to private property from the start. In his influential *The Governor* (1531), Thomas Elyot, one of More's closest associates, explicitly denies that "Commonwealth" means that "every thing should be to all men in common without discrepance of any estate or condition," declaring not only that this is a misuse of the word, but also – reversing Hythloday's charge in *Utopia* that private property is an insidious conspiracy of the rich – that persons who advocate for such a commonwealth are "moved more by sensuality than by any good reason or inclination to humanity" (A[1]r). David Weil Baker observes that with this move Elyot is attempting to "dispel the notion that *The Governor* will be an English *Utopia*" (92). A century later, Robert Burton's "poetical commonwealth," in the *Anatomy of Melancholy* (1621), still finds it necessary to assert the sanctity of inequality and private property against what he calls "Utopian parity." "That which is common, and every mans," he complains, "is no man's"; it "takes away all splendor and magnificence" (57–8). Gerard Malynes (1622), likewise rejects *Utopia*'s "all things ... common" because "the same was never used in any age, nor by the Word of God commanded, when from the beginning he willed man to subdue the earth and rule over the fish" (*Lex Mercatoria* 186). Earlier (1603), Malynes had protested that all countries that are "decent and of estimation" value gold and gems, while the "Indian and Blackamoor" do not, before launching into an extended paraphrase of *Utopia*, whose invented citizens he associates with actual "Indian[s] and Blackamoor[s]" in their (perverse, to him) devaluation of gold (*View* 98–103). He then attempts to refute *Utopia*'s "strange" account further, adding: "with great reason therefore hath gold his due estimation above other things," at least in places where people live "in the most civil manner above other nations which live barbarously" (105–6). So far is he from seeing *Utopia* as a how-to manual for colonization, Malynes associates it with the lifeways and attitudes of peoples ripe for it. Apparently, utopia had to be made useful to colonialism if *Utopia* is to be associated positively with actual colonial projects.

And it was. Early English colonies were retrospectively described as "utopia" after they were well established, as when Cotton Mather observes in his 1693 *Wonders of the Invisible World* that readers "who mistook Sir *Thomas More's Utopia*, for a Country really existent ... might now have certainly found a Truth in their Mistake; *New-England* was a true Utopia" (10). Much later, ignoring the withering judgment on the present of Cotton's past tense, Ronald Reagan deployed John Winthrop's New England "City on a Hill" as if it described not only an actually-existing utopia (it did not) but also the twentieth-century United States.[5] English colonization demonstrably becomes entangled with "utopian" tropes. But questions remain: Does this entanglement completely suppress other work that "utopia" might perform? And: What is the significance of the struggle over utopia that ensues in the gap between the time of More and Mather, given that English writers in the first century following *Utopia*'s publication generated a fervent "rhetoric of reaction" in response to it, rejecting not only objectionable (to them) aspects of More's book, but often utopianism *tout court*, associating utopia with the false, the suspect, and the seditious.[6]

In the face of this rhetoric, ideological effort was required by organic intellectuals of colonization for it to cohabit cozily with utopia. Of particular interest in making utopia safe for colonization is *A Letter Sent by I. B.* (1572) that unfolds in a fictional dialogue a plan for "peopling and replenishing [Ireland] with the English nation," despite "doubts and exceptions" circulating in England against such projects. This pamphlet has recently been described as deploying "eutopia" in a positive sense in relation to colonization (Hogan, 97–104), which it does do, but only, I would underscore, by positioning itself against *Utopia*. Although this dialogue was published anonymously, it depicts the plan it unfolds as originating with Thomas Smith, the yeoman's son who, weathering a series of preferments and setbacks, had managed to rise from "beggarly scholar" to Secretary of State in 1572 (*ODNB*). Smith had been granted land in Ireland by Elizabeth in 1571, so had a personal stake in its colonization. By the 1570s, he also had a lot of practical political experience and was well known as a political theorist, having first written *Discourse of the Commonweal* in the 1540s and *De Republica Anglorum* in the 1560s, both of which explicitly reject *Utopia* as a prominent example of "feigned commonwealths such as never was nor never shall be, vain imaginations, phantasies of Philosophers to occupy the time" (118). The *Letter* is canny about entering a rhetorical milieu in which such views are the norm. Smith is confident that his project is no "vain imagining," not only because it is overtly speculative but also because he takes it to be based on human nature: "man is more moved by particular gain than of respect they have to common profit," he avers, an understanding of human motivation pointedly contrary to that embraced by More's Utopians (Smith D1r). Like a later (Adam) Smith, Thomas insists that the economy should direct the (putatively) inherent selfishness of individuals to serve its ends, a view that would become a conservative commonplace. He advocates rewarding soldiers sent to Ireland with private property in land, which will give them an enduring material incentive to suppress rebellions by dispossessed Irish peoples. Having laid out this plan, the narrator gleefully declares: "have I not set forth to you *another* Eutopia?" (Smith E1r, emphasis mine). The meaning of "eutopia" here, it should be emphasized, is purposefully distant from that of More's Utopians, whose views had already been rejected by Smith. "Another" and the shift in spelling signal as much. The latter implies – as Smith had already observed in his dismissal of it – *Utopia* is merely nowhere (*ou*-topos), a "vain imagining," while Smith's own proposal is "good" (*eu*-topos), not only as theory but because it is practical and amendable to empire, while *Utopia* was not.[7]

Why, then, do so many critics since the 1970s declare *Utopia* to be "colonialist"? The claim seems to have originated with D. B. Quinn, who observed that *Utopia* puts an "emphasis on the legitimacy of colonization" and "hint[s] … [that] to colonize can … even [be] good" (75). This now widespread view – often inflating "hint" to full-blown advocacy – took hold at a time when Ronald Reagan and other conservative politicians, as I noted earlier, were tendentiously touting American exceptionalism by way of "City on a Hill," which they erroneously took to be a "utopian" assessment, rather than the warning that it was. Rightly rejecting such rhetoric, decolonizers conflate *Utopia* (and utopia) with a specifically conservative use of it. Still, given the weight and implications of the charge, it is important to look closely at the passage from *Utopia* that is inevitably cited as proof of the book's colonialist inclinations.

When the population of Utopian towns exceed the "due number," they "build up a town [coloniam] under their own laws in the next land where the inhabitants have much waste and unoccupied ground, receiving also of the same country people to them, if they will join and dwell with them." Hythloday adds:

> if the inhabitants of that land will not dwell with them to be ordered by their laws, then they drive them out of those bounds which they have limited and appointed out for themselves. And if they resist and rebel, then they make war against them. For they count this the most just cause of war, when any people holdeth a piece of ground void and vacant to no good nor profitable use, keeping others from the use and possession of it which notwithstanding by the law of nature ought thereof to be nourished and relieved. (Bruce 63)

Indicting this passage, decolonizing critics typically note that "excess" population is a frequent preoccupation of early European colonial propaganda, as is the deployment of "improvement" and just war ideologies they see in it. Slavery and Utopus's "conquest" also have an odor of imperialism about them, and More's Latin text even uses "coloniam," they underscore.[8] One might counter, as David Armitage does, that modern colonialism is not implied by "coloniam," and, in any case, Ralph Robinson's sixteenth-century translation, cited earlier, does not use the word at all (Armitage 109). Furthermore, *Utopia* describes migration as motivated by balancing humans and habitat – a not incidental consideration in our times of impending eco-disaster – rather than manifest destiny, a civilizing mission, or profit. But even assuming the worst, the more important issue is: What is lost when we focus on these "colonial" parts of the text in isolation, if we agree that *Utopia* demands to be read dialectically, as Louis Maran and Fredric Jameson insist?

To assess *Utopia*'s relation to empire properly, then, I think we need to add at least two things to the discussion: *Utopia*'s form and Stephen Greenblatt's still salient observation that More addressed questions that many others ignore, not just in utopias but in politics more generally: "who slaughters the meat? Who disposes of the filth?" (39). Greenblatt's immediate point is that (entirely justified) consternation with Utopian slavery cannot stop at denunciation, but also must address the problems it raises: How should societies deal with behavior they deem unacceptable? How are undesirable jobs to be filled? We do not have to advocate either slavery or the prison industrial complex to recognize that some mechanism for allocating unattractive tasks would need to be devised in any social order and that individuals might engage in infelicitous behavior, even during the struggle for a good society, especially in the period before it is fully realized when it is surrounded by enemies keen to see it fail.

In short: The pressures imposed by a "wrong" totality cannot be ignored without feeding into well-established conservative anti-utopian tropes. Elsewhere I have discussed the dilemma of "communism in one country,"[9] and pointed out that failure of revolutions to achieve full liberation is very poorly understood when attributed – as conservatives would have it – solely to internal corruption and the impossibility (indeed catastrophic danger) of attempting to enact utopian aspirations at all. The daunting difficulty of enacting liberatory hopes in what Adorno called a "wrong" world demands attention to constraints at every scale. Such a view by no means excuses the problems and excesses of actually existing communisms and other liberatory projects, but it does cast them in a rather different light than the manifestly ideological localizing determinism of Karl Popper and colleagues, who insist that even attempting to create an equal and just world is *inherently* bound to end in disaster, a view that Raymond Williams took to task long ago, for its role in justifying the sufferings imposed by capitalism, which are at least as "tragic" as any imposed by the usual conservative targets (66). How might actually existing communism have fared without Cold War pressures? Or, for that matter, what might Haiti have become if crippling reparations had not been imposed on it after the revolution? We can't know. But such questions should give us pause when considering both past and current world historical dynamics and make it possible to distinguish at least some current land seizures by peasants, or border breaches by migrants, in order to live, from corporate and state annexations to enhance the profit and power of elites.

Minimally, critics who argue that *Utopia* is "colonialist" need to indicate appreciation of the pressures of "wrong" totality *and* propose a better approach to human ecological pressure on localities, the book's rationale for human migration. In any case, *Utopia* should be judged by the questions it raises rather than its "solutions," since the latter are undermined at every turn. As Marin shows, More encodes the text with contradiction – not only via the "More" character's direct refutation of some of Hythloday's views (including of private property), but also in its formal ambiguity and tension: place and character names that undermine themselves, litotes, irony, and humor. According to Marin and Jameson, this self-questioning form indicates that utopia is a provocation not a blueprint. It is worth underscoring, then, that virtually none of the other early English texts identified as "utopias" today resemble it in this respect: They are emphatically anti-*Utopian* in form as they aspire to recode what "utopia" will be and mean in a direction more favorable to primitive accumulation and empire, domestic and foreign.[10]

Marin emphatically draws attention to the peculiarities of *Utopia*'s form. Not only does it bear the traces of contradictions inherent to the society in which it emerged (all texts do), but it refuses to "resolve" them, presenting detailed plans for cities that, as described, are unmappable (and therefore unbuildable), social orders that couldn't function, systems of exchange that don't add up. Unlike critics of utopianism (whether conservative, liberal, or "radical") that leap on such anomalies as evidence that utopian texts give readers dangerously false hope in unrealizable dreams – an argument that relies on treating utopian content as "positive" – Marin argues that such assertions misread *Utopia*'s "negative" form. The dissonance of More's text renders it a "utopic practice" or "ideological critique of the dominant ideology" – a negative gesture in relation to history (Marin xiv). That is, because of the way its content undermines itself, *Utopia* bears a critical relation to the historical situation from which it emerges, along the lines of its oxymoronic titular pun (u/topia: ou = no; eu = good), or, Anyder, its river "without water." For Marin, utopia (as a form) provokes: It is a dynamic opening to "limitless contradiction" rather than being prescriptive (7). As Jameson elaborates, utopias figure social contradictions as troubling antinomies rather than attempting to settle them in the reassuring imaginary resolution of myth (5). Myth (and ideology) attempt to close down and contain questioning of the status quo, and are thus formally anti-utopian. Against myth, including its own (irreducible) ideological aspects, *Utopia*'s form negates itself as a blueprint to redirect pursuit of the "common ... to all" in questioning, flexible, collective praxis.

This need not have been fully intentional. More himself – along with other elites at the time – seems to have been horrified by the power of utopian form, especially after *Utopian* communism became linked to Anabaptist sedition. He claims he would rather see his own books burned than for them to be so used and tries to deflect the association with sedition from *Utopia* to Protestantism.[11] This effort did not succeed. When Joseph Hall parodies *Utopia*, his land of "Moronia" – a jab at More less playful than Erasmus's *Moriae Encomium* – is populated with Anabaptists among other sectaries and trouble-makers. Widespread association of *Utopia* with domestic sedition as well as distant "savagery" demonstrates how thoroughly it was viewed as infelicitous to the emergence of capitalism, including colonial projects. Thus, other early English "utopias" are typically earnest *un*-writings of More (such as Lupton's *Siuqila*), or pointed mockery, as Hall's *Alter Mundus*: anti-*Utopias* that reject *Utopia*'s content and form. "*Another* utopia," as I. B. put it, that attempts to divert utopia onto paths favorable to private property and empire.

Examples of this struggle at work in early English colonial propaganda abound. *True Declaration* (1610) explicitly distinguishes itself from "utopian and legendary fables" (Anon. 33) with one hand, while cherry-picking tropes from *Utopia* with the other, thereby transforming them. It claims, for example, that Virginian colonists work only six hours a day – like More's Utopians, though the tract doesn't admit this – a preposterous assertion, inserted to allay fears of potential colonists that "the sap of their bodies should be spent for other men's profit" (Anon. 49). Another colonial pamphlet from that year makes the even more *Utopian* suggestion that colonists in times of crisis should practice "natural and primary community" (Anon. (2) 11). That is, they should embrace common ("community") property instead of seeking individual private gain under catastrophic conditions.

And yet an actual practice of common property by shipwrecked Virginia-bound English colonists in Bermuda is pointedly omitted from much early English colonial propaganda. William Strachey's "True Reportory" didn't appear in print until 1625 in Samuel Purchas *Pilgrims*, but circulated in manuscript from 1610. It details "diverse mutinies" that ensued among the shipwrecked in Bermuda when, in the absence of private property and repressive apparatuses, dissidents claim that "all ... were freed from the government of any man" and resist going on to Virginia, where they anticipated not only privation but servitude, "their whole life to serve the turns of the adventurers with their travails and labors" – an accusation that the *True Declaration*, as we have seen, takes care to address (1744). Though it, too, describes the shipwreck in Bermuda, it omits mentioning dissent there because one of its main arguments about the failure of early plantations in Virginia is lack of proper leadership, given that the bulk of the spiritual and secular authorities ended up in Bermuda, with the upshot that in Virginia "every man overvaluing his own worth would be a commander. Every man underprizing others value denied to be commanded," a state of affairs that led to a "tempest of dissension" (Anon. 34). A "tempest," however, also arose on Bermuda, despite the presence of numerous traditional authority figures, who, in the absence of repressive apparatuses and unequal property, had no local means of enforcing hierarchy, except by rhetoric and threats of company and state retaliation down the line. These threats ultimately prevailed, given *global* conditions in which the imperialist state and corporation could send reinforcements at any moment, but not without a struggle. Shakespeare's *Tempest* and other early modern texts identified as "utopian" are inflected by – and participate in – this struggle.

## What Are the Stakes?

When capitalism was emergent in England, property relations necessary to it were produced through dispossession (foreign *and* domestic), in the first instance of land, the fundamental means of production, a process that becomes bound up with an ideological imperative for humans to "master" nonhuman "nature," encouraged by the success of Baconian "new knowledge" and the rationalizations to which it gave rise in "improvement" campaigns. Thus, when Bermuda was officially colonized by England, it was immediately surveyed – and garrisoned – to avoid a repeat of the earlier "tempest." Theodor Adorno and Max Horkheimer argued that Enlightenment develops such practices of "mastery" over most humans as well as "Nature" because it unfolds in a "bourgeois" form in which unequal control over private property enabled elite interests to prevail – a view that is hard to see as celebrating "Eurocentric" norms.[12] The "Dialectic of Enlightenment," Enlightenment's promise of freedom, while – in its capitalist form – delivering the opposite for most people and the nonhuman world, was an effect of particular material struggles in which private property and colonialism triumph.

Failing to link Baconian "mastery" to these struggles has made it possible for some critics to read *New Atlantis* as anticolonial despite its explicit advocacy of "enlarging the bounds of human Empire" – an "empire" in which all peoples are by no means considered equal participants or beneficiaries (see Welburn for an overview). Not only does Bensalem have private property and commerce, but Bacon envisions a society in which knowledge is controlled by "Fellows" who take an "oath of secrecy" that instantiates inequality both domestically and in relation to other nations, from whom Fellows collect knowledge while hiding their own, thereby defining the vast majority of Earth's inhabitants (human and nonhuman) as *objects of* knowledge rather than direct participants in its "empire" (Bruce 184). Horkheimer and Adorno underscore that this hierarchy and objectification would be impossible to maintain without disproportionate control over planetary "resources" by elites. That *Utopia* was widely viewed as antagonistic to such mastery in early modern England is precisely what gave rise to a (negative) "rhetoric of reaction" in relation to it and a positive (anti-*Utopian*) utopianism (including Bacon's) – "another" utopia, more readily reconciled to elite interests. To fail to take this struggle over utopia into account not only gives a false picture of how primitive accumulation, ideology, and utopia work (and therefore how to undo them) but also of how best to approach cultural forms, resulting in readings that can all too readily dovetail with right-wing anti-Marxist anti-utopianism, even when they come from the left (see Jacoby).

Thus, while James Holstun's linking of *Utopia* to the "mastery" side of the *Dialectic of Enlightenment* was a provocative intervention in the context of "utopian" American exceptionalism promulgated by Reagan and other elites, reading Horkheimer and Adorno via Foucault has the unfortunate consequence of limiting his view of utopian form problematically. Defining early modern utopia *as* a disciplinary apparatus – "a literary form, political rhetoric, and social practice that envisions the displaced populations of early modern Europe and North America as the raw materials for an act of millennial poieis" comes at the cost of obviating the struggle *over* utopia I am foregrounding (Holstun 3). Not only *Utopia*, but the communist Diggers, the (proto-liberal) New Model Army, and Harrington, as well as John Eliot's colonial "praying towns," are flattened in their repressive "utopianism" for him. In his later work, Holstun corrects his view of the Diggers, who he sees – rightly – as offering an alternative to capitalist "improvement" rather than an instantiation of it, given that their communes are both egalitarian and revolutionary in their refusal of private property. He never, however, revises his view of *Utopia*; thus, the significance of *its* "colonialism" *without private property* never appears to him as a contradiction, like its river without water, and therefore as potentially revolutionary.

This contradiction should give us pause, however, because "bourgeois" colonial practices – whether domestic or foreign – all share a predication on mastery and dispossession to install private property regimes. Indigenous ways of life – as Malynes and many others recognized early on – resisted this. Aileen Moreton-Robinson argues that "indigenous ontological relations to land are incommensurate with those developed through capitalism, and they continue to unsettle ... white possession and power configured through the logic of capitalism and profound individual attachment" (xxi). One does not have to assume that all native peoples are alike, or that native peoples were a model for *Utopia* (à la Morgan) to see that the Utopian way of life shares more in common with many native practices than emergent English propertarian ones. All Utopians consider their relation to the land to be – as Robinson's English translation puts it – "good husbands rather than owners," which, Hythloday comments, is what keeps them from "enlarging the bounds" of their settlements, and propels them to establish "colonies" on "unused" land beyond Utopia if its human population disrupts local ecological balance – not elite property hierarchies. Denouncers of Utopian "colonialism" must, then, confront the questions that *Utopia* is asking by raising migration concerns: What *are* the right relations of humans to the nonhuman world and to each other as part of that world, not its masters? Leanne Simpson has underscored Indigenous rejection of ownership in pursuit of right relations: "The opposite of dispossession," she explains "is not possession, it is deep, reciprocal, consensual attachment. Indigenous bodies don't relate to the land by possessing or owning it or having control over it. We relate to the land through connection – generative, affirmative, complex, overlapping and nonlinear relationship" (43). Malynes was perhaps right to compare Utopians with Indigenous peoples, then, despite his repellently racist agenda.

Holstun's insightful but underdeveloped observation in the conclusion of *Ehud's Dagger* of a family resemblance between Digger struggle and Indigenous resistance to capitalism thus demands elaboration. From the point of view of either "traditional" community or emergent absolute property, the Diggers were suspect "strangers" making claims on already settled localities. "As a society gathered together from all parts of the nation," the agrarian handbook writer Walter Blith observed in 1653, the Diggers could not "claim a right to any particular common," since common "rights" were determined by local tenancy and custom (C3r). In this way, Blith was hoping to divert local prejudices against outsiders among commoners into support for his capitalist improvement agenda, just as landowners did in their campaigns of terror against the Digger communes, and as elites still do today in anti-migrant campaigns and in promoting private property and state sovereignty as absolute.

Alternatively, Gerrard Winstanley, the Digger leader and pamphleteer, not only emphatically rejected primogeniture, which made an accident of birth into a rationale for rendering the rest of the "sons" dependent on a landowning firstborn, but also rejected land ownership and, effectively, state borders, period, declaring the Earth to be a site of collective responsibility and cohabitation. Neither natality nor conquest nor purchase can confer any absolute privilege of possession; right relations have to continuously be worked out for the good of all inhabitants, human and nonhuman, and not only locally. Indeed, it is crucial to recognize that, although the Diggers have been appropriated in some representations solely to the causes of narrowly English and male liberalism, both their pamphlets and program explicitly promote human – and even creaturely – mutuality far beyond England, addressed as they are not only to the "Powers of England," but to "all the Powers of the World" (*Complete Works* II: 1) and directed as they are to "restoring the whole Creation" (*Complete Works* I: 472). The Diggers might have been starting from a tiny network of communes in one nation, but they appeared to understand that communism in one locale – whatever the scale – was doomed from the get-go if hostile, propertarian forces surround them – something that I argued earlier that *Utopia* recognizes also. Only right relations – relations that nurture and protect the Earth rather than attempt to "master" it and fellow humans – can lead to thriving for *all*: another overlap of Diggers with Indigenous anti-propertarian perspectives.

But how can "right relations" be enacted in a world of inequalities, oppressions, and depredations established and maintained through a global capitalism that gathers all localities – unevenly – into an insidious totality? Jodi Byrd notes that, in such a world, a "cacophony" of conflicting claims necessarily emerge. In North America these include Indigenous demands for "sovereignty" and the struggles of the formerly enslaved (unwilling "settlers"); we might add migrants from the Global South, fleeing localities undermined by globalization and disproportionate effects of ecological crises, which they have not caused, as well as the claims of nonhumans to habitat. None of these claims (nor that of queers, crips, or other groups seeking redress) can be peremptorily dismissed in the struggle for right relations to land today. It is worth underscoring, then, that although "cacophonous" claims are not fully reconcilable with each other, they do meet in one respect: Transformation of land into capitalist property underwrites all oppression in the final instance; as Byrd laments, expropriation of "our lands became the grounds for others' oppressions" ("Weather" 213). For this very reason, we might also note that "our land" – though one understands the strategic importance of such claims in a world dominated by private property and ongoing suppression of native sovereignty – seems to contradict Simpson's insistence on native rejection of "ownership or possession," a predicament that Robert Nichols has thoughtfully engaged, pointing out that Indigenous originary *owner* arguments rely on the very property claims that they also deny. This dilemma is not the fault of native peoples, he underscores, but, to the contrary, of the systemic triumph of capitalist colonial relations, which is what must be undone.

This point enjoins us to grapple with the very real problems of all "occupation" in settler colonies that Eve Tuck and K. Wayne Yang have influentially brought to the fore. Even struggles for social justice, like the "Occupy" movement, take place on *already* "stolen" land, such that "occupation" can repeat, rather than undo, oppression. While attending to their devastating critique of the numerous techniques that settlers deploy to render themselves innocent, however, it is also crucial not to homogenize native peoples in a universally virtuous abstraction, which, like the abstraction of "decolonization" itself, can obviate the hard work of forging solidarities. As Tuck and Yang point out, unequivocally insisting on the "incommensurability" of "native sovereignty" with other struggles for social justice "won't get anyone off the hook of the hard, unsettling work of decolonization" (4). Given that, as Nick Estes observes, "many Indigenous nations actively participate in resource extraction and capitalist economies," the "repatriation" that Tuck and Wang call for cannot succeed in a decolonization that would undermine property and capitalism unless all native peoples, too, were decapitalized – that is, if the world is no longer organized in a capitalist way (Estes 22). De-*propertization* is not an automatic effect of repatriation of "native" land, which also, as Robin Kelley has argued in response to Patrick Wolfe, can participate in a fantasy of "life before and beyond invasion," a process so complicated by intersectional differences – especially, but not only, race – that it cannot be sustained without creating political problems of its own (274). The complexities of how to describe the relation of revolutionary slaves in Haiti, for example, to land that had been inhabited by the Taino – themselves migrants – for centuries, simply does not accede to any easy answers.

Sensitive to this dilemma, Kim TallBear has taken a different approach to exclusive sovereignty arguments, provocatively wondering recently "how things might have been different had more newcomers respected long-established ways of relating [to land] already in place" (38) in the encounter of Europeans and native peoples – ways of relating that eschewed private property and emphasized reciprocity and mutual care for the Earth. Perhaps "the two parties [might have] gradually and easily merge[d] together and absorb[ed] the same way of life and the same customs, much to the great advantage of both peoples" (More 137); this quotation is not from TallBear – though it is, arguably, her sentiment. It's drawn from the ostensibly "colonialist" paragraph of *Utopia*. With her counterfactual experiment, TallBear recognizes, as many theorists do today, that "migration" and "sovereignty" demand reassessment in ever-changing conditions that global capital has deformed, not least ecologically, and that the totality of existing relations must be taken into account (see Sharma).

How can those of us committed to global social justice at every scale support peoples disproportionately deprivileged by "dispossession," as well as the always fragile communities established by attempting to live alternatively to oppressive norms and borders (whether Diggers, or Black Panther Oakland, or insurgencies by Indigenous and other dispossessed peoples and migrants today), while also refusing propertarian and exclusionary logics wherever they manifest? If Palestinians got back "their" land and proceeded to simply turn the tables on all non-Palestinians, or tribal nations use their "sovereignty" to allocate mining concessions to global conglomerates, has planetary justice been served? And who decides? One essay – one person – cannot *solve* this dilemma. I am simply suggesting that given the complex politics of human (and nonhuman) settlement and migration, and its deformation by the propertization of land, *Utopia's questions* deserve more nuanced consideration than they have been getting from critics who would "decolonize" it. I'm not calling, then, for a "positive" (in any sense) reading of Utopian "colonization," but rather insisting that answers to its questions have to be worked out, as Marin and Jameson suggest, in collective *praxis*, while recognizing, relentlessly, what Byrd calls "cacophony." Via Campesina's solidarities of peasants and Indigenous peoples against agribusiness offer an example of the hard and fraught work of forging such solidarities in struggles for land (see Wiebe). This is what utopia as a site of struggle *means*, I would suggest. Rather than rejecting *Utopia* as "colonialist" then, a more productive response would be what Jameson calls anti-anti-utopianism (*Archaeologies*, 14). The latter requires us not only to read utopia dialectically and negatively, but also to struggle collectively for liberatory alternatives to the empire of private property, a struggle that utopia and Marxism both provoke, but whose ends toward a thriving planet for all neither can fully prescribe.

## Notes

1. All references to pre-modern texts are from Early English Books Online (EEBO). Spelling in quotations from pre-modern texts has been modernized.
2. https://utopia.ac/resources/decolonisation/ (accessed April 27, 2025).

3. Visions of good societies are ancient and widespread, but More's was the first to be *called* "utopia," inaugurating a historically specific tradition that emerged with capitalism.
4. My book project, "Hating Utopia Properly," examines every accessible mention of "utopia" and its variants in English print between 1530 and 1639, tracing the overwhelming suspicion of *Utopia* from the start, a tendency that has been partially, or in passing, observed by scholars such as Baker, Kendrick, Sarkar, and Sacks (4–5).
5. The reactionary appropriation of "City on a Hill" has been discussed by Gamble, Rogers, and Van Engen.
6. "Rhetoric of Reaction," Albert Hirschman's term for hegemonizing projects that seek to undermine radically liberatory possibilities as soon as they emerge, begins with the French Revolution, in his view. I extend this concept to the response to the publication of *Utopia*, which was met in England with reactionary suspicion that parallels Hirschman's account of later developments.
7. English orthography was not regularized, but eu/u spellings of *Utopia were* recognized as significant from the earliest Latin editions – and Robinson's English translation (1556, second edition) – via the celebratory poem of "Anemolius" that depends on the spelling shift: "Wherefore not Utopie, but rather rightly / My name is Eutopie: a place of felicity," as Robinson renders it.
8. See More's Latin in the Yale edition, 136.
9. For elaboration, see my "Utopia and Its New Enemies".
10. For a listing of early modern utopias in English, see https://openpublishing.psu.edu/utopia/ (accessed May 3, 2025). On an exception to early modern English utopias eschewing *Utopia*'s form, see my "Optimism of the Wyll".
11. See Baker on the early association of *Utopia* with Anabaptism.
12. While a dismissal of the Frankfurt School as irreducibly Eurocentric and therefore irredeemably suspect, not least in the wake of Edward Said's damning characterization in *Culture and Imperialism* (278), has proved both influential and enduring, negative dialectics has also had strong defenders, including Keya Ganguly, Neil Lazarus, and Asha Varadharajan, all of who deploy it toward specifically Marxist postcolonial critique. See Spencer.

## Works Cited

Anon. *True and Sincere Declaration*. 1610.
Anon. (2). *True and Sincere Declaration*. London, 1610.
Armitage, David. "Literature and Empire." *Origins of Empire*, edited by Nicholas Canny, Oxford UP, 1998, pp. 99–123.
Baker, David Weil. *Divulging Utopia*. U of Massachusetts P, 1999.
Bartolovich, Crystal. "Utopia and Its New Enemies." *Journal for Early Modern Cultural Studies*, vol. 13, no. 3, 2013, pp. 33–65.
———. "'Optimism of the Wyll': Isabella Whitney and Utopia." *Journal of Medieval and Early Modern Studies*, vol. 39, no. 2, 2009, pp. 407–32.
Blith, Walter. *English Improver Improved*. 1653.
Burton, Robert. *Anatomy of Melancholy*. 1621.
Byrd, Jodi. *Transit of Empire*. U of Minnesota P, 2011.

"Weather with You." *Critical Ethnic Studies*, vol. 5, nos. 1–2, 2019, pp. 207–14.
Bruce, Susan (ed). *Three Early Modern Utopias*. Oxford University Press, 1999.
Elyot, Thomas. *The boke Named the Governor*. London, 1531.
Estes, Nick. *Our History Is the Future*. Verso, 2019.
Gamble, Richard. *In Search of a City on a Hill*. Continuum, 2012.
Greenblatt, Stephen. *Renaissance Self-Fashioning*. U of Chicago P, 1980
Hardy, Karl. "Unsettling Hope." *Spaces of Utopia*, 2nd series, vol. 1, 2012, pp. 123–6.
Harington, John. *Oceana*. 1656.
Hirschman, Albert. *Rhetoric of Reaction*. Harvard UP, 1991.
Hogan, Sarah. *Other Englands*. Stanford UP, 2018.
Holstun, James. *A Rational Millennium*. Oxford UP, 1987.
  *Ehud's Dagger*. Verso, 2000.
Horkheimer, Max, and Theodor Adorno. *Dialectic of Enlightenment*. Translated by Edmund Jephcott, Stanford UP, 2002.
Jacoby, Russell. *Picture Imperfect*. Columbia UP, 2007.
Jameson, Fredric. "Of Islands and Trenches." *Diacritics*, vol. 7, no. 2, 1977, pp. 2–21.
  *Archaeologies of the Future*. Verso, 2005.
Kendrick, Christopher. *Utopia, Carnival and Commonwealth*. U of Toronto P, 2004.
Kelley, Robin D. G. "The Rest of Us: Rethinking Settler and Native." *American Quarterly*, vol. 69, no. 2, 2017, pp. 267–76.
Knapp, James. *An Empire Nowhere*. U of California P, 1992.
Malynes, Gerard. *England's View*. 1603.
Malynes, Gerard. *Lex Mercatoria*. 1622.
Marin, Louis. *Utopics*. Translated by Robort Vollrath, Humanity Books, 1984.
Marx, Karl. *Capital*, vol. 1. Translated by Ben Fowkes, Penguin, 1990.
Mather, Cotton. *Wonders of the Invisible World*. 1693.
Mohawk, John. *Utopian Legacies*. Clear Light Publishers, 2000.
More, Thomas. *Utopia* in *The Complete Works of Thomas More*, vol. 4. Yale UP, 1965.
Moreton-Robinson, Aileen. *The White Possessive*. U of Minnesota P, 2015.
Morgan, Arthur. *Nowhere Was Somewhere*. U of North Carolina P, 1946.
Nichols, Robert. *Theft is Property*. Duke UP, 2020.
Popper, Karl. *The Open Society and Its Enemies*. Princeton UP, 1966, 2 vols.
Quinn, D. B. "Renaissance Influences in English Colonization." *Transactions of the Royal Historical Society*, 5th series, vol. 26, 1976, pp. 73–92.
Rogers, Daniel. *As a City on a Hill*. Princeton UP, 2018.
Sacks, David Harris. "Introduction." *Utopia*. Bedford, 1999.
Said, Edward. *Culture and Imperialism*. Vintage Books, 1994.
Sarkar, Debapriya. "Utopian," https://shc.stanford.edu/arcade/interventions/utopian (accessed April 28, 2025).
Sharma, Nandita. *Home Rule*. Duke UP, 2020.
Simpson, Audra. *Mohawk Interruptus*. Duke UP, 2014.
Simpson, Leanne. *As We Have Always Done*. U of Minnesota P, 2017.
Smith, Thomas. *Letter sent by I.B.* 1572.
Smith, Thomas. *De Republica Anglorum*. 1583.
Spencer, Robert. "Thoughts from Abroad: Theodor Adorno as Postcolonial Theorist." *Culture, Theory and Critique*, vol. 51, no. 3, 2010, pp. 207–21.

Tallbear, Kim. "Caretaking Relations, Not American Dreaming." *Kalfou*, vol. 6, no. 1, 2019, pp. 24–41.
Tuck, Eve, and K. Wayne Yang. "Decolonization Is Not a Metaphor." *Decolonization: Indigeneity, Education and Society*, vol. 1, no. 1, 2012, pp. 1–40.
Van Engen, Abram. *City on a Hill*. Yale UP, 2020.
Welburn, Jude. "Empire and Utopia." *English Literary Renaissance*, vol. 48, no. 2, 2018, pp. 160–90.
Wiebe, Nettie. "Shaping Our Collective Futures: Activism, Analysis, Solidarity." *Journal of Peasant Studies*, vol. 50, no. 2, 2023, pp. 627–39.
Williams, Raymond. *Modern Tragedy*. Stanford UP, 1996.
Winstanley, Gerrard. *Complete Works*, 2 vols. Edited by Thomas Corns, Ann Hughes, and David Loewenstein, Oxford UP, 2009.
Wynter, Sylvia. "Black Metamorphosis." unpublished manuscript. Schomburg Center for Research in Black Culture.

## 2

ANIA LOOMBA

# Trade, Race, and Class in Early Modern England

Of all the countries in the continent we now call Europe, England was a latecomer to international ventures, colonial and mercantile. But by the eighteenth century, it had overtaken its rivals, Spain, Portugal, Holland, and France, and was poised to become the dominant imperial and mercantile power. There are two persistently difficult issues in scholarly analyses of the fifteenth to the eighteenth centuries. The *first* is this: Despite a vast scholarship on the growth of trade on the one hand, and the growth of colonization and slavery on the other, the two phenomena are often addressed in isolation from one another. But to bifurcate these histories is to obfuscate the dynamic of both and to ignore the violence and force, both material and ideological, that accompanied "free" trade.

Slavery *and* colonialism developed precisely within the ideological crucible of trade, as Karl Marx pointed out in a classic passage from *Capital*:

> The discovery of gold and silver in America, the extirpation, enslavement and entombment in mines of the aboriginal population, the beginning of the conquest and looting of the East Indies, the turning of Africa into a warren for the commercial hunting of black-skins, signaled the rosy dawn of the era of capitalist production. These idyllic proceedings are the chief moments of primitive accumulation. Hard on their heels follows the commercial war of the European nations, which has the globe as its battlefield ... (915–16).

Despite his global awareness, Marx emphasized English developments such as the enclosures of the commons and accelerated urbanization in his account of capital accumulation, rather than the international developments of the time. Later, other Marxists, including Rosa Luxemburg and V. I. Lenin, amplified the way in which capitalism was dependent upon international markets as well as imperial domination. However, they had little vocabulary for analyzing how cultural and ideological factors, including racial ideologies and practices, were also central to the making, spread, and justifications of capitalism. This braiding of racial ideologies with capitalist ones is the *second* issue that has not been sufficiently addressed in early modern studies. In this essay, I shall suggest some ways in which literature and cultural texts of the period help us illuminate both questions – that is, the organic links between domestic and global capitalism on the one hand, and racial and capitalist ideologies on the other.

The term "racial capitalism" indicates this nexus, but it is often invoked without any attention to its history. In the US it was first used by Robert Blauner in *Racial Oppression in America* (1972), arguing that "colonial theory" and "Marxist models of capitalism" needed to be brought together because the United States was "clearly a mixed society that might be termed colonial capitalist or racial capitalist" (13). In 1976, Martin Legassick and David Hemson used it in a pamphlet entitled "Foreign Investment and the Reproduction of Racial Capitalism in South Africa," published by the anti-Apartheid movement in London, which argued that racism in South Africa was strengthened, not weakened by capitalism. Today, the term is most often attributed to Cedric Robinson, who, in his now classic book *Black Marxism* (1983), sought to connect the genesis of capitalism with racism, arguing that:

> The historical development of world capitalism was influenced in a most fundamental way by the particularistic forces of racism and nationalism. This could only be true if the social, psychological, and cultural origins of racism and nationalism both anticipated capitalism in time and found a piece with those events that contributed directly to its organization of production and exchange ... European civilization is not the product of capitalism. On the contrary, the character of capitalism can only be understood in the social and historical context of its appearance ... (9, 24)

Robinson was drawing upon the ideas of South African and British Marxists but making a different point – whereas they suggest that racism fertilizes and emerges from capitalism, Robinson suggests that capitalism emerged from social structures that *were already* racist, although the forms of racism changed. Robinson also argued that class differences provided the ideological and material structures for ethnic and racial categories.

Premodern scholarship has corroborated both insights. Robert Bartlett has discussed the ways in which "the mental habits and institutions of European racism and colonialism were born out of the medieval world; the conquerors of Mexico knew the problem of the Mudejars; the planters of Virginia had already been planters in Ireland" (313). These mental habits and institutions were deeply rooted in the expansion of European feudalism from the tenth to the thirteenth centuries. Robin Blackburn shows how Atlantic slavery was shaped by the long histories of enslavement in medieval

Europe, even as he also emphasizes the crucial changes that took place: "The persecution of every type of deviant [in the twelfth and thirteenth centuries] perfected a will to ideological subordination that had ominous implications for those who came into the path of European expansion. It helped to forge the identity of Europe" (74). A host of scholars have discussed how the Irish, Jews, Roma, and Slavs were victims of dispossession, colonialism, and slavery within Europe; all these peoples were racialized in different ways. Class differences in feudal Europe also shaped ethnic and racial categories and vice versa. From the medieval period on, Muslims and Jews were widely described in terms of both blackness and servitude by white Christians. Peasants were often described as the children of Ham, condemned by Noah to slavery. The idea morphed over time – the peasant was replaced by "man of Inde" and then "the blackamoor." In other words, class conflicts at home were renegotiated in tandem with an expanding world, one result of which was that, to use Robinson's words, "the effects of racialism were bound to appear in the social expression of every strata of every European society no matter the structures upon which they were formed. None was immune ... this proved to be true for the rebellious proletariat as well as the radical intelligentsias" (28). Hence, Robinson urged scholars to attend to the underpinnings of race in the very construction of class and nation.

The study of late medieval and early modern period can do much to thicken Robinson's argument that capitalism did not inaugurate racism but was itself shaped by its changing forms. However, his work also reminds us about the *obverse* implications of this dynamic, that the history of racial ideologies is impossible to extract from the histories and structures of capitalism. Today, there is a tendency to neglect the economic underpinnings of racial structures, and thus simply invert the earlier neglect of race in studies of capitalism. Within the US, there is also the tendency to define race in narrow and exclusionary terms and to privilege skin color to the point where class hierarchies and economics, as well as the different forms taken by racial ideologies, are explicitly downplayed. Given the power of the US academy today, this is a particularly dangerous trend, for it bypasses the *global* history of racial capitalism.

As early modernists, we can attend to a crucial historical juncture in the formation of racial capitalism, one whose *multiple* legacies resonate today. In the rest of this essay, I want to trace the simultaneous formation of class and race ideologies in early modern England and show how they were grounded in the logic of both nationalism and overseas trade and colonialism. I will do so by tracing the evolution of a story about a poor boy that acquired the status of a fairy tale in English culture. This evolution also reminds us how powerful literature is in *creating* ideologies of class, nation, and race by creating powerful images that penetrate deep within the social fabric. As will become clear, this process was shaped by the histories of contact in different parts of the world, histories that were diverse but intersected in the formation of colonial and capitalist ideologies.

\* \* \*

Some years ago, I was taking a group of students around London's famous Guildhall, built in 1440. We came upon a stained-glass window depicting a medieval mayor – the legend informed us that this was Richard Whittington, who was thrice mayor of London.

As a child in India, I had grown up on English books that narrated the story of a poor boy called Dick Whittington who ended up becoming the mayor of London. This is how the story goes: Dick comes from the countryside to London because he has heard that the city's streets are paved with gold. Disappointed to find the rumor untrue, Dick starts working at the kitchens of a rich merchant and is lodged in a rat-infested garret; unable to sleep, he spends his only penny on a cat. When the merchant organizes a trade expedition, he asks everyone in his household to contribute something to the venture. Having nothing else, Dick ventures his cat.

Now he is plagued both by the rats and by a mean-spirited cook in the kitchens. He decides to run away from London, back to where he came from. But on his way out, Dick hears the famous Bow Bells of London ringing; they seem to be saying:

> Turn again, Whittington,
> Once Lord Mayor of London!
> Turn again, Whittington,
> Twice Lord Mayor of London!
> Turn again, Whittington,
> Thrice Lord Mayor of London!

Struck by this prophecy, Dick returns to the merchant's house.

Meanwhile, the ship carrying his cat sails to the Barbary Coast, where the Moorish king purchases the entire cargo for a load of gold and insists on feasting the English traders. But the banquet is disrupted by legions of rats and mice. The English factor tells the king and queen that they have a creature which could exterminate these vermin, and produces Dick's cat, which proceeds to decimate them, to the astonishment and delight of the Moors. Upon hearing that the cat is pregnant, they offer to buy the creature for ten times the price of the rest of the ship's cargo. The ship returns to London, the merchant informs Dick that he is now a rich man and offers him his daughter's hand in marriage. Dick joins the merchant in his business and ends up becoming the mayor of London, three times, just as the bells had predicted.

Over time, the story morphed into a rags-to-riches fable, accumulating the cat, the overseas trade, and the prediction by the London bells. Children everywhere absorbed its message about race and wealth. It circulated in chap books and ballads and has been adapted to virtually every medium. Samuel Pepys noted that he watched a "puppet-show of Whittington" at Southwark Fair; the clown Joseph Grimaldi acted as the female cook in Dick's scullery; by the nineteenth century it was a pantomime that is still performed at Christmas.

While the fable circulated around the world, the history did not. The way the story changed over time, and the way in which its crucial features became absorbed in English literature, illustrates how dreams of class mobility at home were shaped by the promises of international wealth; how these promises in turn molded the ideology of nationalism whereby the nobility and the mercantile classes came together despite the tensions between them; how existing geographic differences were rewritten to present European superiority; and finally, how peoples from different parts of the world were represented as both necessary and dangerous to the advancement of the European self.

The historical Richard Whittington was not poor, but the third son of a Gloucestershire family who was sent to London to learn the textile trade. Born in 1354, he became a successful merchant, importing velvet and silk, and exporting English broadcloth to Europe. He supplied luxury items to King Richard II and began moneylending, including to the king. When Richard was deposed, Whittington transitioned smoothly to the new regime, supplying goods and money to Henry IV and then to *his* son, Henry V. Legend has it that, in a banquet for the latter, Whittington burnt the bonds for 60,000 pounds that the king owed him. Henry repaid him by asking him to supervise the completion of Westminster Abbey and, even though Whittington was a moneylender himself, to sit on usury trials in 1421. This is consistent with the racial history of usury in medieval England – Jews in England had been typecast as usurers and demonized for the practice, partly because Christian moneylending was not openly acknowledged. Whittington was also allowed to export broadcloth without paying duties. He benefitted a range of London institutions, renovating not just Westminster Abbey, but the Guildhall, St. Bartholomew's Hospital, and Newgate Prison, founding Whittington College, a library at Greyfriars, and multiple almshouses. At these almshouses, the poor had to pray daily for Whittington and his family. His transformation into an English icon is, as Patrick Parrinder puts it, "one of the founding myths of British mercantile capitalism" (413).

Parrinder contrasts Whittington's story with another rags-to-riches tale, that of Simon Eyre, a shoemaker who rose to become Lord Mayor of London, told by Thomas Deloney in 1597 and by the playwright Thomas Dekker two years later in *The Shoemaker's Holiday*. In Deloney's story, Eyre hears of a merchant from Candy, who comes in on a ship called the Black Swan "laden with all minds of lawns and cambricks, and other linen cloth, which commodities at that time in London were very scant and exceedingly dear" (62). Eyre plots to trick the Greek and acquire these goods because he wants to become "a gentleman forever" (64). He seeks a rank backed up by property, guaranteed by wealth, a status that has real material basis. Historically, no shoemaker rose to mayoral rank; indeed, the historical Simon Eyre was not a shoemaker but belonged to the more prestigious Drapers' Company.[1] In stories about him, the accumulation of wealth and class mobility turns on an interaction with a foreigner, and on acquiring the foreign goods that were then transforming all of Europe. In Deloney's version, the outsiders are Catholics from other parts of Europe; in Dekker's play, they are the Dutch, the greatest trading rivals of the English. In both cases, the wealth comes *to* English shores. In the Whittington story, the foreigners are North Africans and it is the English who must journey in search for their riches.

Scholars have neglected the question of foreign trade in the Whittington saga, but a racialized nationalism is evident from its earliest invocation in an anonymous jingoistic poem written fifteen years after the historical Whittington's death in 1423. *The Libell of English Policy*, the earliest known treatise in English on economic and political geography, bemoans the restrictions on English merchants abroad, contrasting them to the liberties allowed foreign merchants in England. It recommends that England tighten her control of the surrounding seas and keep a firm colonial hold on Ireland and Wales. It expounds on the fertility of Irish soil and on the large quantities of Irish gold, offering an argument that was later used in English colonies in the Americas – that colonial rule was necessary because the natives were not disciplined enough to make proper use of natural resources. It warned that if "a wyld Yrishe wyrlynge" (a deformed creature or monster) became its king, Ireland would ally with Scotland, Spain, and other enemies of England (37). To strengthen England, the *Libell* advocates an alliance of the nobility and merchants – if English merchants thrive, so will the country's nobility. The merchant upholds English honor, not just internally, but globally. It is to bolster this argument that the poem offers the example of Whittington as this "son of marchaundy," a "loodes sterre and chief-chosen floure," who contributed so much to English honor that "penne and papere may not me suffice / Him to describe" (25). As Roger A. Ladd astutely notes, in Whittington, the two classes are organically aligned because he "also remains the son of a knight" (16).[2]

It is important to note that *The Libell* was written on the brink of what is called "the Great Slump" of the fifteenth century. English wool exports were jeopardized because of English hostilities with Burgundy and France. Internally there were food shortages and rebellions, including the Lollard Rising of 1431. In this climate, the figure of the merchant who sustains and is sustained by the nobility, and who, in turn, gives to the poor, works as an accommodative ideal smoothening over social tensions by bolstering a nationalistic vision of trade and empire.

This alignment is especially evident in the earliest and most detailed prose version of the Whittington story – *The Famous and Remarkable History of Sir Richard Whittington*, written by none other than Thomas Heywood. Heywood details how Whittington, during a feast for King Henry V, brings out the "security for tenne thousand Markes, lent you for the maintenance of your Royall Warrs in France, by the Right Worshipfull Company of the Mercer" and burns it, along with loans to the king by other livery companies such as Grocers, the Merchant Tailors, the Drapers, the Skinners, the Ironmongers, the Goldsmiths, the Haberdashers and other companies.[3] He then also forgives other members of the nobility several of their debts to merchants and the city.

Whittington's lowly birth entered the tale at the end of the sixteenth century, when the story suffused popular culture.[4] Thomas Heywood's 1606 play, *If You Know Not Me You Know Nobody* (Part 2) suggests that it is a rumor. But a 1612 ballad claimed *both* knighthood for Dick *and* his poor birth in Lancashire.[5] By 1608 Whittington featured in an epigram for class transformation:

> 'Tis said that *Whittington* was rais'd of nought,
> And by a Cat hath many wonders wrought:
> But *Fortune* (not his Cat) makes it appeare,
> Hee may dispend a thousand markes a yeare. (Parrot, no. 4)

By mid-century, an anonymous ballad called "London's Glory, and Whittingtons Renown" offered Dick's story as a "Looking-Glass for Citizens of London," reminding "brave London prentices" that in Dick's fortunes, "you poor Country Lads, / though born of low degree / See by gods providence, / what you in time may be" (n.p.).

Heywood's rewriting of the Whittington story embellishes each stage of poor Dick's journey; here, the merchant's sympathetic daughter is "of a good and gentle persuasion," and she persuades her rich father to take

Dick in and offers her own money for him to venture. Dick is the ideal servant with ample "willingnesse, to runne, or goe, or to doe any service, how meane soever." His master is benevolent and eager to expand the profits of overseas trade to his minions – he insists that even the poorest member of his household must venture something abroad. When the wealth from Barbary comes in, the merchant calls Dick, saying:

> Indeed Mr. Whittington, ... you are at this time a better man than myself in estate; and then showed him all those Cabinets and Caskets, and how richly they were lined.... [T]urning to his Master, [Dick] presented all his Riches before him, and told him, that all he had was at his disposing and service: who answered him again, that for his own part, God had lent him sufficient of his own; neither would he take from him the value of one *Barbary* Ducket.

Dick is appropriately grateful and humble, offering his master all his wealth; the master appropriately honest and generous, refusing it and overseeing Dick's "strange and suddain Metamorphosis; for out of a smoaky and dirty Kitchin-drudge, there appeared a proper and well-proportioned man, and a gentile Merchant."

In Heywood's hands, Dick's story actively rewrites the enormous tensions between masters and servants and between the authorities and rebellious working classes prevalent in England during the late sixteenth and early seventeenth centuries, when the country was "troubled by economic crisis, political crisis, social tension and popular disorder" resulting from "a sequence of harvest failures, dearth, and food riots, as well as unemployment in the clothing trades ..." Manning (157). Dick's migration to London, because he was "almost starved in the Countrey," indexes the historical influx into the city, which doubled its population between 1580 and 1600. The enclosures and privatization of land had violently dislocated agrarian workers, turning them into proletarians in search of employment. But laws prohibited laborers from leaving their shires without written passes or without hiring themselves out for at least a year: "Unless a person owed property worth 40 shillings per annum, was an heir to property of that value, or possessed goods worth 10 pounds, or belonged to certain specified callings ... he was not free to dispose of his own labour" (160). In *The Famous History*, Dick spends two days "gaping among the shops, and gazing upon the buildings." In fact, a boy roaming about the city would have been labeled a vagrant, for which the punishment was severe – according to the Vagrancy and Poor Relief Act of 1572, "first offenders were to be imprisoned ... and upon conviction were to be whipped and burnt in the ear unless some worthy householder accepted them in service for one year. Second offenders were to be judged felons unless a householder took them into service for two years; a second offender who ran away was to be hanged" (165). Earlier, a short-lived parliamentary legislation threatened to impose slavery on individuals who refused to work. As Michael Guasco observes, "the willingness to address vagabondage with actual bondage suggests the nature of the crisis Tudor elites perceived" (121).

In Heywood's story, Dick's future master first threatens him "with the Stocks, and Whipping-post," and offers him employment only when his daughter pleads Dick's case. Dick's miserable life in the scullery, and his running away, obliquely acknowledge the conditions of servitude at the time. Runaway servants accounted for two-thirds of the vagrants punished by Bridewell Court between 1597 and 1608 (Manning 193). This was hardly surprising, because many domestic servants were treated like slaves in English households, as the Swiss ambassador Thomas Platter noted. Apprentices' lives were barely better – there was what Roger Manning has called an "epidemic of apprentice' riots, lasting nearly two decades" (157). Roger A. Ladd points out too that Dick must be established as a worthy recipient of his master's benevolence, and he connects this to the contemporary distinction between deserving and undeserving poor, the former worthy of charity and the latter deserving of severe punishment. The story of Dick's assimilation into a benign household thus smoothens over some of the sharpest class divides of the time, just as his rise among the mercantile and civic structures of London glosses over their increasingly oligarchic nature.

By the late sixteenth century, when the Whittington story acquired its stable features, England had its eyes on a much larger world market. After 1570, it tried with new vigor to emulate and disrupt Spanish and Portuguese domination in both East and West, to trade with "Moorish" lands (including Turkey, Persia, India, the Moluccas, Morocco, Tunis, Malta, and Algiers), and to establish colonies in the New World. Over the same time, the English slave trade had been firmly established – between 1551 and 1600, 1,900 slaves were carried from Africa to the new world on *English* ships. By 1642, this number was to rise to 3,400 (Eltis and Richardson 25). Fables like Dick Whittington's express several features of racial capitalism – they juxtapose changing landscapes at home and abroad and they fuse together a variety of foreign locales to offer a romance of class transformations that hinge upon acquisitions from outsiders, who are both the fulcrum of the story and marginal to it. The wide circulation and popularity of such fables thus shapes and expresses the fantasies of upward mobility and of racial superiority.

Let me elaborate. In Heywood's tale, the ship carrying Dick's cat comes to the utmost coast of *Barbary*, where never any English man, (or scarse any Christian) had ever traded before: Where they shewed some of their commodities, and offered them to be bended. The Moores came down in multitudes, much taken with the beauty of their ship for they had never seen any of that building, or burden before: But when they had taken a serious view of their commodities, as Hatchets, Knives, Looking-glasses, Fish-hooke, &c. but especially their Cloth and Kersies of severall sizes and colours, they brought them Gold in abundance; for it was more plentifull with them then Leade, or Copper is with us ...

Heywood's story suggests a first, primal, encounter between Christians and Moors, between the English and Barbary Coast inhabitants. The Moors are dazzled by English ships and are desperate for English objects. Historically, there had been centuries of previous contact and, well before Heywood was writing, Queen Elizabeth had established an arms trade with the Moroccan Sultan Ahmad al-Mansur, whose secretary spent six months in London to negotiate an alliance against Spain.

At the same time, the English were at the mercy of Barbary pirates in the region, who captured 466 English ships between 1609 and 1616. Ironically, many of these pirates were English – one famous one being John Ward, who converted to Islam, was known as Yusuf Reis, and was represented in plays such as *A Christian Turn'd Turk* by Robert Daborne and *The Renegado* by Philip Massinger.

The idea of Moors who gape at English ships and are willing to give all their gold for rudimentary armaments also neatly inverts the actual geopolitics in North Africa, and indeed in Ottoman Turkey and Mughal India. Far from desiring English commodities, in most "Moorish" territories the English were desperate to gain trading facilities, bringing rich gifts for the monarchs, which, however, regularly failed to impress. The persistent European dream of unequal gift exchange turned into an endless nightmare in these regions. This dream was partly honed by New World travelogues, which had for long spun scenarios of natives innocent of the value of their own goods. These narratives are careful to emphasize that the Americans did not have to work for the gold even though other reports, such as those of Bartolomé de Las Casas, detailed how gold was extracted by violently forced labor. The Dick Whittington story transposes such scenarios to Barbary, where too, we are told, gold was more abundant than lead in England.

Edward Bonahue makes the astute observation that Heywood's text anticipates Daniel Defoe's 1719 novel *Robinson Crusoe* (38). Recall that the English Crusoe weans his servant Friday off human flesh by teaching him how to eat barbequed goat; he also teaches him how to make a canoe

European style. These two key episodes in Friday's education, as Peter Hulme points out, center

> on precisely the two aspects of Carib technology, the barbecue and the canoe, that Europe learned from the Caribbean, both "barbecue" and "canoe" being Carib (or strictly speaking Island Arawak) words. The "ignorance" of the savage Caribs is *produced by* the text of *Robinson Crusoe*, which enacts a denial of those very aspects of Carib culture from which Europe had learned. (210–11)

To this list we can add corn, which was first cultivated in Mexico and imported to Europe by Columbus, and yet it is Crusoe who teaches Friday how to cultivate it. Analogously, the Whittington tale produces the cultural and natural backwardness of the Moorish world by precisely appropriating those aspects in which England lagged. Discussing the moment that Crusoe is stunned to find that he is a wealthy man, Hulme also makes the important point that "it marks the discovery of the secret of capital itself, that it accumulates in magical independence from the labour of its owner" (219–20). In Whittington's case, even more than in Crusoe's, the reality behind this "magical independence" remains unseen – whereas we know that Crusoe has invested in slaves, Dick's fortunes depend upon a cat, which we can read as a mythos of English goods, which historically, amounted to, well, not much.

It is also noteworthy that Dick's cat neatly reverses the historical trajectory of the feline. All domesticated cats have a North African lineage and likely came to England from there via Cyprus. Dick was unlikely to possess a cat in the first place – cats were generally not kept as pets in medieval or early modern Europe, being associated with female sexuality and witchcraft and thus reviled. Indeed, the spread of bubonic plague through the proliferation of rats has been attributed to their widespread persecution. It is significant, then, that the explosion of rats occurs in Barbary, rather than in England in the Whittington story. But sections of the clergy members of the upper classes had started to keep feline pets. These elites could flout the association of cats with evil because of their privileged status. In *The Great Cat Massacre*, Robert Darnton argues that when, in the 1790s, a group of apprentices tortured and ritually killed all the cats they could find, they were enacting a kind of class revolt against their masters who fed the cats better than they did the workers. Ladd is correct to note that Heywood's "depiction of a scullion being fond of a cat might ... serve a similar ideological function to its story of a scullion (not even officially an apprentice) achieving mastery effortlessly" (25). But it is important to emphasize that if the cat allows Dick to climb the social ladder, it is only because it acquires its real value overseas.

The Whittington story, as it changes over time, sediments and mythologizes the idea that overseas travel, colonial mastery, and trade would enable class and cultural mobility. This theme proliferates in the literature of the period. So does the flip side of this idea – that the lands and people whom the Europeans encounter will recognize their own inferiority, or else will be made to do so by force.

Take for example Shakespeare's *The Tempest* (1611). Here, two lowly servants – Stephano, a drunken butler, and Trinculo, a court jester – aspire to become rulers of the island where they have been shipwrecked by harnessing the labors of Caliban, whom they view as their subject and as a subhuman "monster" whom they can display for profit if they take him back to England. In this play, there is no mention of trade, but Caliban, the "abhorrèd slave" (as Miranda calls him), is the means through which power and profit will be made. And indeed, by the time Shakespeare was writing the play, the slave trade was poised to become the most lucrative source of European wealth.

But Caliban has several features attributed to the European poor – he is ungrateful, incapable of learning, rude, rebellious, and physically repellent, a manual laborer, a "slave" who aspires to unite with the princess. Miranda tells him that "thy vile race / Though thou didst learn / had that in't which good natures / Could not abide to be with" (1.2.354–62); at the time, the word "race" indicated lineage, or class; exactly during this time it began to accrue the other connotations with which we are more familiar.

It is Heywood's play *Fair Maid of the West* (1597–1601) that most fully elaborates the dynamic of the Whittington story. Bess Bridges, an English barmaid, becomes rich through her adventures in Barbary where she goes to find her gentleman lover in a ship that she names *The Negro*. Here, there is no cat; in fact, the English have nothing to trade with the Moors. Except Bess's sexuality. Just a kiss from Bess is enough to make Mullisheg, King of Fez, lavish her and other Europeans with favors, including trading privileges. But because, unlike Dick, Bess comes into direct contact with the Moors, the dangers of such encounters need to be emphasized. Even Bess's servants, who themselves dream of being miraculously transformed into wealthy men in Moorish lands, recoil from the spectacle of a Moor kissing this "girl worth gold." While early modern critics have attended to the racial nationalism of this play, they have not noticed the connections between it and Heywood's other text, *The History of Whittington*. Juxtaposing the two and bringing into simultaneous focus other texts of the period, we see how the romance of class transformation and the romance of racial mastery become inextricably and obviously fused.

Let me take, as a last example, Philip Massinger's play *The Renegado* (1624). Here Gazet, a servant of the Italian nobleman Vitelli, imagines himself becoming enriched and powerful in the court of Tunis. In *The Fair Maid* Bess's servant Clem mistakenly understands "gelded" to mean "gilded" and is castrated – he then mourns that his "current commodity" has been "tickled," making manifest the play's connections between sexuality and wealth. In *The Renegado*, Gazet nearly suffers the same fate, because he too imagines becoming rich at the Ottoman court. In all three plays, these servants are the butt of class-inflected humor – their dreams are seen as ridiculous, even as they mirror those of their class superiors in each play. In *The Tempest*, it is Prospero's control over the colonial space of the island that repositions him to gain power over his European rivals. In *The Fair Maid*, Mullisheg's adoration of Bess translates directly into English victories over the Spanish as well as her own advancement. And in *The Renegado*, Gazet's master wins over the Ottoman princess Donusa, who, at the end of the play, escapes with him. All these plays simultaneously evoke the possibilities afforded by foreign spaces for European subjects, poor and rich, and warn against the dangers for these subjects abroad.

I have shown how the story of Dick Whittington, as it develops from the later medieval to the early modern period, indicates the organic connections between domestic class transformations and overseas expansion, connections that are visible in wide array of other literary texts as well. The process illustrates that, as Cedric Robinson puts it, "[t]he tendency of European civilization through capitalism was thus not to homogenize but to differentiate – to exaggerate regional, subcultural, and dialectical differences into 'racial' ones" (26). These texts not only allow us to glimpse this process, but they testify to the power of the stories in which it was embedded, stories that simultaneously testified to the place of empire in the making of national, racial, and class identities, and erased it.

## Notes

1. One of the 111 livery or guild companies of the City of London. Established in 1361, it was a trade association of wool and cloth merchants.
2. I am deeply indebted to this essay.
3. There are no page numbers in this edition.
4. See Ladd.
5. See Johnson.

## Works Cited

Anon. "London's Glory, and Whittington's Renown Or, a Looking-Glass for Citizens of London." G. Eld for Iohn Wright, 1612.

Anon. *The Libelle of Englyshe Polycye, a Poem on the Use of Sea-power 1436.* Edited by George Warner, Clarendon P, 1926.

Bartlett, Robert. *The Making of Europe: Conquest, Colonization, and Cultural Change, 950–1350.* Princeton UP, 1993.

Blackburn, Robin. "The Old World Background to European Colonial Slavery." *William and Mary Quarterly*, vol. 54, no. 1, Jan. 1997, pp. 65–102.

Blauner, Robert. *Racial Oppression in America.* Harper & Row, 1972.

Bonahue, Edward T. "Heywood, the Citizen Hero, and the History of Dick Whittington." *English Language Notes*, vol. 36, Mar. 1999, pp. 33–41.

Deloney, Thomas. *The Gentle Craft.* Edited by Alexis F. Lange, Mayer and Müller, 1903.

Eltis, David, and David Richardson. *Atlas of the Transatlantic Slave Trade.* Yale UP, 2010.

Guasco, Michael. "Labor." *A Cultural History of the Western Empires in the Renaissance.* Edited by Ania Loomba, Bloomsbury Academic, 2019, pp. 101–26.

Heywood, Thomas. *The Famous and Remarkable History of Sir Richard Whittington.* W. Wilson, 1656.

Hulme, Peter. *Colonial Encounters, Europe and the Native Caribbean, 1492–1797.* Methuen, 1986.

Johnson, Richard. "A Crowne Garland of Roses Gathered Out of Englands Royall Garden." G. Eld for Iohn Wright, 1612.

Ladd, Roger A. "From 'Sonne of Marchaundy' to 'Obsurely Bred': The Nine Lives of Richard Whittington." *English Language Notes*, vol. 43, no. 1, Jan. 2005, pp. 12–33.

Manning, Roger B. *Village Revolts, Social Protests and Popular Disturbances in England, 1509–1640.* Oxford UP, 1988.

Marx, Karl. *Capital*, vol. 1. Vintage Books, 1977.

Parrinder, Patrick. "'Turn Again, Dick Whittington!': Dickens, Wordsworth, and the Boundaries of the City." *Victorian Literature and Culture*, vol. 32, no. 2, 2004, pp. 407–19.

Parrot, Henry. *Epigrams.* Imprinted at London by R. B., 1608.

Robinson, Cedric J. *Black Marxism: The Making of a Black Radical Tradition.* U of North Carolina P, 1983.

# 3

SU FANG NG

# Peripheral Heroics on the Renaissance Stage

*Non illi imperium pelagi saevumque tridentem,*
*sed tibi sorte datum.*

"Not to him, but to you, were given by fate the empire of the sea and the ferocious trident": Modifying Virgil's *Aeneid* 1.139–40 by substituting *tibi* for *mihi*, Richard Hakluyt's epistle dedicatory to *Principal Navigations* praises the Lord High Admiral Charles Howard's victory against the Spanish Armada (sig.*2v). Hakluyt underlines England's oceanic imperial destiny by linking naval defense to the "high courage" of pursuing voyages to "unknowen quarters of the world" (sig.*2). Later, John Dryden translated *imperium pelagi* with the evocative phrase, "liquid empire" (*Aeneis* 1.198). This empire of trade is celebrated and discursively produced by travel literature promoting exploration and overseas ventures. The explosion of travel narratives, fueled by trade expansion, in turn engendered new literary forms. This included tragicomedy but also, preeminently, the voyage or adventure drama, whose rise arguably parallels the popularity of English theatre itself (Forman; Jowitt and McInnis 12).

Like travel narratives, adventure dramas present trade and nationalist expansion as linked projects. Voyage drama's capitalist imperatives even reshaped history plays like Thomas Heywood's *If You Know Not Me, You Know No Bodie, Part Two* (1606), in which seafaring heroes – Sir Francis Drake, and in the 1633 printing, jointly with Martin Frobisher – deliver news of the Armada victory to Queen Elizabeth (sig. K; sig. K3ᵛ). In stitching a city comedy to a history play, Heywood's bifurcated structure highlights the link between national pride and capitalist ventures: While the second half stages Queen Elizabeth's life, the first features the apprentices of Thomas Gresham, building the Royal Exchange as a commercial center. Voyage dramas call attention to London theatre's fascination with the foreign. Over sixty plays featuring Islamic themes, characters, and settings appeared between 1579 and 1624 (Burton, *Traffic* 11). But even London

## 3 Peripheral Heroics on the Renaissance Stage

city comedies frequently allude to the Indies, linking urban and oceanic navigation (Howard 2–4). In the Restoration, adventure plays continued to capture audience interest (Orr).

Yet early modern England was hardly an imperial power. Supplicants to Islamic empires of the East – the Ottomans, Safavids, and Mughals – the English envied and emulated the Hapsburg Spanish. The internal consolidation and colonization of the British Isles, from Ireland to Scotland, proceeded in an uneven fashion; termed the First British Empire, it was an enlargement of the composite monarchy, acquired by "conquest, annexation, inheritance and secession" (Armitage 23). American settlements had slow and difficult beginnings. The Virginia colony in Jamestown, established 1607, remained troubled and unprofitable for much of the seventeenth century, encountering considerable Native resistance, finally ceasing to be a town in 1699. In Asia, the British established not colonial plantations but trading factories, exerting influence through joint-stock companies like the East India Company (EIC). Challenging previous views of European dominance, Holden Furber named this the "Age of Partnership," in which Europeans cooperated with Asian merchants in trade (Kling and Pearson). Although this assessment has been revised to account for rivalry as well as cooperation, scholars acknowledge the "severe competition from Asian merchants" to call it the "Age of Competition" (Chaudhury and Morineau 9). It was only in the late eighteenth century that an ascendant Europe came to world domination.

English drama both celebrated and criticized trading ventures. Renaissance drama's mercantile poetics lionized middle-class traders, but foreign exotica also provoked unease, for commerce was thought to deplete national wealth. However, an "absence of America" on the London stage, with only three plays focusing on the Americas from 1576 to the theatres' closing in 1642, marks the precariousness of New World settler colonies (Hollis). Adventure plays are primarily set in the Mediterranean and Indian Ocean. In them, ambivalence defines English heroism. For Hakluyt, Howard's bravery – and by synecdoche the English's – lie in their meagre numbers: He was "accompanied with ten ships onely of her Majesties Navie Royall, environed their Fleet in most strange and warrelike sort, enforced them to stoope gallant, and to vaile their bonnets for the Queene of England" (Hakluyt sig.*2–*2v). The monarch's gender symbolized a vulnerability displaced onto the Spanish. Flexibly adopting a counter-imperial stance, the English both emulated and distanced themselves from rivals like the Spanish or Dutch. This emergent imperial consciousness is at once ambitious – in imagining the overturning of great empires – and anxious in the awareness of its own lack.

The nascent British Empire's dynamic of emulation and disavowal produces what I term "peripheral heroics." The decidedly middle-class status of English protagonists is defensively justified by nobility of character. A strong Christian strain frames that valor in terms of humility and even martyrdom. Defined by English marginality, this heroism is marked by ambivalences, with shifting and flexible modes of gendering and racializations. Hakluyt's capsule Armada account broadly sketches the constituent myths of English heroism: A small scrappy band defeats a great imperial power through sheer audacity. This essay traces in representative plays – Marlowe's *Tamburlaine*; Day, Wilkins, and Rowley's *Travels of the Three English Brothers*; Heywood's *Fair Maid of the West;* and Dryden's *Amboyna* – the strand of ambivalent imperialism, or "peripheral heroics," running through early modern adventure drama, defined by figures that emerge from the margins.

\*\*\*

I begin with Christopher Marlowe's widely imitated *Tamburlaine* plays. Bajazeth provided the model for ranting Turks (Burton, *Traffic*; Vitkus). Tamburlaine – a humble nomadic shepherd bursting seemingly out of nowhere to world conquest – engendered boundary-crossing, upstart protagonists, including pirates, ambassadors, and merchants. Inaugurating an audacious type of bombastic ranter, the *Tamburlaine* plays present a new literary model for articulating English imperial aspiration. Emily Bartels views *Tamburlaine* as "[i]mperialist self-construction" (54), while Stephen Greenblatt relates "Tamburlaine's restlessness, aesthetic sensitivity, appetite, and violence" to nascent capitalism, "the acquisitive energies of English merchants, entrepreneurs, and adventurers" (194). Scholars detect a resemblance between Tamburlaine and the English. In him, Richmond Barbour suggests, "London's spectators saw themselves" (44). Mary Floyd-Wilson posits an intimate relation between English and Scythian as fellow northerners challenging established hierarchies (89–110).

Tamburlaine's low origins as shepherd stand in contrast to his unbounded imperial ambitions in what I previously called a "model of empire from the periphery" (Ng 215). He is called a "sturdy Scythian thief" and a "paltry Scythian" (*1 Tamb.* 1.1.36, 53), a "thievish villain," "wicked," and a "traitor" (2.2.3, 24, 32). His men are "baseborn Tartars" and "greedy-minded slaves" (2.2.65, 67). Nomadic ethnic identity is associated with thievery. But his conquests push out to the margins of the world. Vowing to "confute those blind geographers," Tamburlaine aims to map regions unknown: "I mean to trace, / And with this pen reduce them to a map" (4.4.79, 81–2). Mapping is a visual form of travel literature's narrative cosmographies. His world conquest is imagined as a march to the South Pole: "We mean to travel to th'Antarctic Pole, / Conquering the people underneath our feet,

/ And be renowned as never emperors were" (4.4.143–5). Rising from the northern peripheries of Scythia, Tamburlaine's renown is secured by extension to the southern peripheries. As explorer, he outlines not the historical Timur's Asiatic conquests but rather Europe's "new discoveries." His identity as a Scythian shepherd, an apparent weakness, in fact gives Tamburlaine the characteristic defining his success: mobility. This mobility stands in contrast to the lassitude of the empires he defeats. Persia is a "maimèd empery" (1.1.126). Her soldiers, rich from war booty, are "Now living idle in the wallèd towns" (1.1.146), such that "the state of Persia droop / and languish" (1.1.155–6).

Tamburlaine's actions belie the name-calling. King Mycetes cowardly tries to hide his crown, acting like a contemptible thief. But Tamburlaine returns the crown to win it on the battlefield. Mycetes marvels, "O gods, is this Tamburlaine the thief? / I marvel much he stole it not away" (2.4.41–2). When Tamburlaine decides to pursue the crown, after helping Prince Cosroe defeat his brother, he does so through warfare: "We will not steal upon him cowardly, / But give him warning and more warriors" (2.5.102–3). The Ottomans' reversal of fortunes is starker. Tamburlaine humiliates Bajazeth, locking him up in a cage and making him pull his chariot. By the end Bajazeth's queen Zabina laments, "Why should we live, oh, wretches, beggars, slaves, / ... That all the world will see and laugh to scorn / The former triumphs of our mightiness / In this obscure infernal servitude?" (5.1.248, 252–4). But if Tamburlaine "Doth teach us all to have aspiring minds" (2.7.20), his successes come with a warning. The deaths of Bajazeth and Zaniba are emblems of "fickle empery" (5.1.353). As model for English Empire, Tamburlaine also serves as warning.

The second part of *Tamburlaine*, however, seems a wholly different play. Tamburlaine is preoccupied with domestic concerns: his wife's death and the fitness of his sons to inherit. His religion now takes center stage. Previously a pagan defender of Christians, he becomes inexplicably a Muslim, swearing at points "by sacred Mahomet" (1.3.109), though at the end he spectacularly burns the Qur'an. Tamburlaine's kingdom comes more to resemble the Islamicate empires he opposes. His sons' weaknesses, echoing Persian royal family squabbles, suggests anxiety over the ability to sustain empire. The model of empire from the periphery, highly effective for conquest, seems insufficiently robust for governance from the center.

2 *Tamburlaine* continues to engage the rhetoric of marginality but also racializes Tamburlaine in Black–white binaries. When a resurgent Ottoman Empire prepares to recontest preeminence, we see a return to the language of "thief of Scythia" (3.1.15). The sequel reiterates the point that status and breeding no longer determine outcomes: "For Tamburlaine came up

of nothing" (3.1.75). However, *2 Tamburlaine* destabilizes the prior valuation of racial characteristics. While a tricolor scheme shapes the action of *1 Tamburlaine*, whereby Tamburlaine successively raises white, red, and black flags to signal the increasing rigor with which he will treat his enemies, in *2 Tamburlaine* that color coding is displaced by a Black–white opposition. Criticizing his sons, Tamburlaine says, "Their hair as white as milk and soft as down – / Which should be like the quills of porcupines, / As black as jet" (1.3.25–7). In *1 Tamburlaine* whiteness signifies northern hardness, but here it is reversed, while Scythians are implicitly blackened. Whiteness is now associated with Christian figures such as Prester John, the mythical priest-king of Asia: Tamburlaine says, "John the Great sits in a milk-white robe, / Whose triple mitre I did take by force" (1.3.188–9). His paean to Zenocrate at her deathbed – "Black is the beauty of the brightest day" (2.4.1) – plays on the paradoxes of sonneteering conventions with all their ambivalences about blackness. Thus, while *1 Tamburlaine* tells of the rise of a figure of northernness, *2 Tamburlaine* refashions Tamburlaine into a Muslim convert who then recants.

Dealing also with Anglo-Persian relations is John Day, William Rowley, and George Wilkins's play, *Travels of the Three English Brothers* (1607), featuring not a Scythian upstart, but English adventurers, the Sherley brothers, Robert, Anthony, and Thomas. Based on Anthony Nixon's pamphlet, the play was commissioned by Thomas to promote his younger brothers' efforts to forge an alliance between Europe and Persia against the Ottomans. While Anthony traveled to European courts as Shah Abbas's ambassador, the youngest, Robert, remained a hostage in Persia. Jonathan Burton calls it a "public relations campaign" (Burton 33). Critics emphasize the contrast between the brothers and their Muslim counterparts. Chloë Houston argues that the propagandistic play fends off the Islamic "threats to gender identity" and "anxiety about the vulnerability of masculinity" by portraying the brothers as representing "a powerful, masculine, Christian Englishness" (223).

Its heroic representation must be read in intertextual engagement with Marlowe's Tamburlaine. The depiction of the Ottoman sultan, the Great Turk, as a ranter is most obviously Marlovian. A reference to a "low and mean-bred Saraber" (11.96), that is, a "Saracen," may recall the Scythian Tamburlaine. Laurie Ellinghause argues that this "'low and mean-bred' figure whose nomadic lifestyle make him an especially dangerous brand of runagate" is Robert's foil (118). However, the notably mobile Sherleys, I argue, resemble the nomadic "Saracen" or Scythian. The low-born itinerant figure is also their mirror. They adopt a rhetoric of marginality and self-professed virtues of Christian humility and meekness. Their Tamburlainian marginality is first geographical. Robert describes Britain as small and remote: "My country's far remote, / An island, but a handful to the world" (i.131–2). The English perform a martial display with only a "small retinue" (i.63). They are also accused of baseness. On the Russian embassy, the Persian courtier Halibeck disparages Anthony for "his low birth, base manner and defects" (iv.14–15), accusing him of being "a fugitive, / A Christian spy, a pirate and a thief" (iv.21–2), recalling both Tamburlaine and Vasco da Gama of Luís Camoës's *Os Lusíadas* protesting that the Portuguese are no spies (2.633–6). The allusion to "wandering Aeneas" (iii.120), also a fugitive, posits a future imperial greatness from obscure origins for Robert, who marries the Sophy's niece.

Underpinned by Christianity, peripheral heroics is embodied in the abject body of the martyred Christ. Halibeck scoffs at English beliefs in Christ: "kneel to one that lived a man and died?" (ii.195). The Sherleys profess Christian humility in performing acts "for honour not to boast" (iii.105). Christian humility also appears as radical equality in Anthony's speech about bodily similitude:

> All that makes up this earthly edifice
> By which we are called men is all alike.
> Each may be the other's anatomy;
> Our nerves, our arteries, our pipes of life,
> The motives of our sense all do move
> As of one axletree, our shapes alike. (i.164–9)

Men are so alike that their body parts are interchangeable, propelled by the same intentions as if wheels on one axle. The differences lie only in "art," in the externalities of how each country "shapes as she best can piece them" (i.173). Forced to land in Ottoman domains, Thomas cheers his sailors up with a speech touting equality: "For me, so you are, so am I a little pile / Of earth, slimed earth, and have no greater style / Than you have, but a man" (vi.32–4). Finally, Robert denies the Sophy's accusations of ambition: "My thoughts are like my fortunes, mean and low" (xi.106). Thus, though termed "Sherley the Great" (vii.66), an epithet fit for a king, he avers that his "humility … / Doth not affect that overdignity" (vii.67–8).

The last scene of the baptism of Robert's child with the Sophy's niece is best read in this context of Christian humility, recalling Jesus's admonition: "Verily I say unto you, Except ye be converted, and become as little children, ye shall not enter into the kingdom of heaven" (Matthew 18:3). The baptism's conjunction with the founding of a church in Persia may be the stuff of pure fantasy, but it reinforces the injunction to convert. It is fitting that the child is Robert's. As the youngest of the Sherleys – "The young'st and meanest spirit speaks in me" (xi.170) – the great Robert demonstrates the Christian paradox of the last being the first, humble to the end as "Low-minded Sherley" (xi.248). The ending shows the Sherleys' meteoric rise from remote Britain to the Persian imperial center.

English weakness is symbolized by gender in Thomas Heywood's *Fair Maid of the West*, with a working-class female protagonist, Bess Bridges, standing in for Queen Elizabeth. As cross-dressing freebooter, she is an "emblem of England," Jean Howard argues, "the exceptional woman [who] transforms the members of a factionalized, strife-ridden community into a harmonious band of brothers" (102, 106). But in setting the first three acts in taverns, this bourgeois play valorizes merchants. Bess is tapstress and then owner of an inn inherited from her upper-class lover Spencer. National valor inheres in business transactions. Its adventure plot, and thus English expansion, is divided between battles against the Spanish and commercial negotiations with Moroccan Fez.

English identity is further destabilized by race. Heywood's representation of Anglo-Moroccan relations is not completely coherent. Moroccans are allies, reflecting Elizabeth I's historical attempts to forge diplomatic ties, but through the kisses exchanged with the King of Fez, Mullisheg, Bess demonstrates white femininity's power to coerce the North African Other into economic submission "in a process of exploitation rather than commerce" (Mendoza 116). Although Bess's black ship, named *The Negro*, has a metonymic relation to Mullisheg, in that both are wholly "dominated" by her, it is also a "conflation between the English and the Moors" revealing their "symbolic closeness" (Barthelemy 165; Fuchs 132). I argue that Bess's rise, however, could be compared to Tamburlaine's. Her peripheral heroics upstage the men's chivalric acts.

Voyaging is first characterized in chivalric terms when Spencer joins the Earl of Essex's project to capture the Azores, known as the Islands Voyage. But the failures of that voyage and Spencer's part in it call gentlemanly chivalry's efficacy into doubt. When his foil Goodlack wonders why a "gentleman of fortunes, means" will "adventure thus / A doubtful voyage" to "pillage" (1.2.4–6, 8), Spencer asserts that his purpose is "for honor; and the brave society / Of all these shining gallants … / No hope of gain or spoil" (1.2.9–12). In fact, he needed to escape England after killing a man in a duel. In the Azores he is seriously injured after intervening in a quarrel between two English captains. Masculine heroism is tainted by self-inflicted violence among the English.

Instead, the play foregrounds Bess's peripheral heroics, marginal in terms of her gender, class, and extraterritorial privateering. The last half pivots to Bess's quest, upon hearing of Spencer's supposed death, to recover his

## 3 Peripheral Heroics on the Renaissance Stage

body. While Bess as a figure for Queen Elizabeth has been widely discussed, less noted are her links to Sir Walter Raleigh, explorer, defender against the Spanish Armada, and participant in the Islands Voyage. Her migration from Plymouth, Devon to Foy, Cornwall, and thence to the open seas parallels Raleigh's career. A native of Devon, he was Lord Lieutenant of Cornwall and explored the Americas in search of gold. Just as Raleigh upstages Essex by landing troops at Fayal before the latter's arrival – alluded to in the captains' quarrel in Act 2.2 that injures Spencer (Publicover 142) – so too Bess's masculine privateering displaces Spencer to take center stage as she achieves the honor of foreign conquests. Emerging from the marginal West Country – she is born in Somersetshire – Bess is given a geographic milieu that suggests a similarly obscure origin. The locations she is associated with – Somerset, Devon, and Cornwall – constitute England's Celtic peripheries, and given the early modern racial link between Celts and Scythians, further suggest a parallel with Tamburlaine. Even the space of Morocco owes something to Marlowe. Heywood's Fez is a place-name from *1 Tamburlaine* when Tamburlaine's friend Techelles becomes King of Fez after victory over Bajazeth. Bess's Tamburlainian rise is measured by her class transformations, beginning as a "trade fall'n tanner's daughter" (3.3.64) who attracts "gallants" and "knights' sons already come as suitors to her" (2.1.4, 11–12). She transcends her class when uprooted from land. As a cross-dressed sea captain, she triumphs over the Spanish with sea fights "gallantly perform'd" (4.4.2). While not gallants by birth, she and her sailors are so by deed. By the end of the play, Bess wins over a crowned monarch, Mullisheg, saving Christians from the galleys.

The Jacobean sequel, *Fair Maid Part II*, repeats tropes from earlier plays, such as accusations of piracy leveled at Tamburlaine – "These English pirates" (3.1.89) – as well as assertions of human sameness from *Travels* in Clem's descriptions of England: "Our countrymen eat and drink as yours do for all the world" (1.1.68–9). Even as the play insists on absolute racial difference, it offers a virtuous Muslim, the bashaw, or high officer, Joffer, as Spencer's worthy rival in noble acts. The men's relationship overshadows the romance plot. While Joffer is prompted by fellow feeling and fully trusts Spencer – "He's gvy'd to me by faith" (3.3.12) – Spencer returns his faith by rescuing Joffer when he is captured by the Italians. Upon discovering the captured bashaw's identity, Spencer comically thrusts Bess aside to embrace his bosom buddy: "Bashaw Joffer? – Leave my embraces, Bess, / For I am of force am cast into his arms. – / My noble friend!" (5.4.155–7).

In *Part II*, Spencer displaces Bess as the protagonist, but his heroism is the sacrificial kind. Rejecting Mullisheg's blandishments, he refuses to give Bess up with a speech that compares the bribes to the temptation of Christ:

"Wert thou the king of all the kings on earth / ... / ... and hadst power to install me / Emperor of th'universal empery, ... / ... I'd die a hundred thousand deaths first" (3.3.87–94). While Spencer escapes death, his tribulation is symbolically imagined as Christ's martyrdom. When rescuing Joffer from the Italians his language is similarly sacrificial – "if myself, ... / May redeem him home, unto my naked skin / I'll sell myself. And if my wealth will not / Amount so much, I'll leave myself in hostage" (5.4.173–6) – recalling the Christian injunction to divest oneself of worldly goods. While Florence praises Bess in the final speech, it is Spencer's avowed atonement that converts Joffer to Christianity. Heroism takes the form of Christian sacrifice.

Heroic martyrdom takes center stage in John Dryden's *Amboyna, or The Cruelties of the Dutch to the English Merchants: A Tragedy* (1673). In this Restoration play, merchants become suitable protagonists. No longer is the mercantile origin of the protagonists obscured by heroic feats of martial valor. Valor is transmuted into passive suffering. As the subtitle suggests, the play dramatizes events of the so-called 1623 Amboyna Massacre, in which English EIC agents were accused of treason by the Dutch with whom they shared a factory in Ambon, Indonesia, and were tried, tortured, and summarily executed. Dryden revived this bitter history, entrenched as the defining narrative of Anglo-Dutch relations in the Indies, to fan the flames of the Third Anglo-Dutch War. Reshaping pamphlet material around a romance plot, his protagonist is the EIC's chief factor, Gabriel Towerson, affianced to the native Amboynan Ysabinda, also loved by the Dutch governor's son, Harman Junior. Rejected by Ysabinda, Harman violently rapes her on her wedding night, but is killed in a duel by an avenging Towerson. The play's Machiavel, the Dutch Fiscal, uses it as a pretext for accusing the English of conspiring with Japanese soldiers to overthrow Dutch rule. Torturing and executing the English, the Dutch wholly engross the spice trade.

Most scholars read Dryden as an apologist of empire, mystifying the profit motive with discourses of honor. The female characters, Ysabinda and Julia, wife of the Spanish captain Perez, symbolize the contested colonies. Variously read as Spanish, *mestizo*, or Native, Julia's comment on her three lovers reinforces the main plot's use of romance as symbolic of European colonial competition: "If my *English* Lover *Beaumont*, my *Dutch* Love the *Fiscall*, and my *Spanish* Husband, were Painted in a piece with me amongst 'em, they wou'd make a Pretty Emblem of the two Nations, that Cuckold his Catholick Majesty in his *Indies*" (2.1.226–30). In this emblem the northern nations destabilize the Iberian dominion. The romance plot suggests a benevolent English Empire. Candy

## 3 Peripheral Heroics on the Renaissance Stage

Schille finds "Dryden's endorsement of the colonial project ... less than wholehearted," with a "simultaneous desire for and contempt for colonial persons and spaces" (para. 5, 13), but Carmen Nocentelli avers that it delegitimizes interracial romance, exposing "cross-racial sexuality as a site of defilement and degeneration" (*Empires* 144).

The play's ambivalences stem from the contradictions of distinguishing English imperialism from Dutch. In the mutual competition, both English and Dutch point out each other's mercantile origins. While the English sneer at the Dutch governor's origins as a "Cooper in his Countrey" (1.1.147), Harman Junior disparages Towerson as merely a Company man, returning to Amboyna only because "proffer'd ... large conditions" (2.1.9–10). Calling Towerson "part Captain, and part Merchant," he scoffs at English national lack of fortune: "his Nation of declining Interest Here" (2.1.22–3). Commenting that the "bearer of English virtue" is a merchant representing the "commercial ethos that Dryden derides," Shankar Raman observes the undoing of the distinction between English ideals of patronage bonds and Dutch self-interest as patronage itself came to be commercialized (191). Dryden's transformation of "abject ... merchants into patriotic heroes," Robert Markley argues, "demonstrates the instabilities within the discourses of nationalism, free trade, and gentlemanly civility" (143–4). Marjorie Rubright contends that ambivalence arises from Anglo-Dutch likeness rather than difference in a "crisis of Anglo-Dutch interchangeability" (192).

In directing its dynamic of emulation and disavowal at the Dutch, *Amboyna* departs from the anti-Spanish tenor of the plays already discussed. The Spanish Perez proves to be rehabilitable, acting with honor in the end. Tracing connections to the Spanish Black Legend, Nocentelli suggests that "Dutch activities" were "analogized to Spanish ones," with the torture scene in Dryden's *Amboyna* a "recycling" from William Davenant's masque, *The Cruelty of the Spaniard in Peru* (1658) ("Dutch Black Legend," 359). The torture scene prompts Towerson's comparison to the Spanish: "*D'Alva*, whom you condemn for cruelty did ne're the like; ... as your Countrey lies confin'd in Hell, just on its Marches, your black Neighbors taught ye, and just such pains you invent on Earth, Hell has reserv'd for you" (5.1.310–17). The Dutch are "blackened" as devils and racialized as "barbarous" (3.3.109, 4.5.228).

Dutch barbarity is contrasted against English weakness, often gendered female. Dryden's wide-ranging use of female characters is symbolically significant. In one scene a rescued English woman denounces Dutch depredations, telling her tale of being ejected from two Indies islands, robbed at sea by a Dutch captain feigning friendship, and finally left to drown. Her speech functions as a proleptic indictment of the torture and execution to come. Towerson's lament underlines English powerlessness: "My Countrey Men opprest by Sea and Land, / And I not able to redress the wrong, / So weak are we, our Enemies so strong" (3.3.161–3). Torture, too, such as Harman's waterboarding, is gendered female: "You shall be muffl'd up like Ladies" (5.1.140). Kristina Bross suggests that the conflation of sexual and other forms of violence fuels anxiety about English unmanning (186–7). However, another proleptic scene – the torturing of two boys and a woman – attests to precocious English fortitude. The boys "indur'd the Water Torment" (5.1.177–8), prompting Harman's comment on their manliness: "you *English* Boys have learn't a trick of late, of growing Men betimes, and doing Mens Work too, before you come to twenty" (5.1.184–6). They are matched by the Englishwoman "of a Courage full as Manly" (5.1.210). The bravery of English boys and women prove the men braver still.

In the climactic torture scene, a tableau shown to Towerson, his emotional distress – his "tears of Blood" (5.1.319–20) – is a display of English humanity contrasted against unfeeling Dutch cruelty. The scene frames weakness as honor. But Dryden's revision of manliness begins early with Ysabinda's definition when rejecting Harman Junior: "you've done a most unmanly and ungrateful part, to court the intended Wife of him, to whom you are most oblig'd" (2.1.14–16). Moreover, even before the torture scene, Towerson learns from her to accept his own bodily frailty and to welcome death as honorable. Turning to the fort as metaphor for the body, he says, "if as a Governor he [God] sets me here, to guard this weak built Cittadel of Life, when 'tis no longer to be held, I may with honour quit the Fort" (4.5.70–2). By analogy, the English's quitting of the Ambon fort, a historical fact, is honorable. If Ysabinda is a type of Lucretia – Towerson alludes to Tarquin (4.5.84) – his embrace of death, leaving life "with no regret" while prophesying vengeance by "An English Monarch with Blood" (5.1.449, 453–4), makes him not so much her avenging kinsmen but rather another Lucretia.

Martyrdom is peripheral heroics taken to its logical end. English adventure plays' glorification of English deeds abroad adopts a Tamburlainian arc of heroic action with unlikely protagonists: women, middle-class adventurers, pirates, and merchants. Such protagonists rise from low social origins to claim a place at imperial centers. They adopt a Christian rhetoric of humility and lowness. British, or northern, remoteness and marginality paradoxically forecast future greatness. But the plays are riven with ambivalences. Even as the voyage drama emerges as a genre of British maritime expansion, a celebratory drama of nation, racialized encounters with Islamic characters abjure the foreign taint, in part by redirecting this taint at European rivals, the Spanish and the Dutch. Through transnational figures with malleable identities, Renaissance drama negotiated English marginality in an interimperial context, exploring through peripheral heroics English desires for and fears of transculturation, their emulation and disavowal of empire.

## Works Cited

Armitage, David. *Ideological Origins of the British Empire*. Cambridge UP, 2000.
Barbour, Richmond. *Before Orientalism: London's Theatre of the East 1576–1626*. Cambridge UP, 2003.
Bartels, Emily. *Spectacles of Strangeness: Imperialism, Alienation, and Marlowe*. U of Pennsylvania P, 1993.
Barthelemy, Anthony Gerard. *Black Face, Maligned Race: The Representation of Blacks in English Drama from Shakespeare to Southerne*. Louisiana State UP, 1987.
Bross, Kristina. *Future History: Global Fantasies in Seventeenth-Century American and British Writings*. Oxford UP, 2017.
Burton, Jonathan. "English Anxiety and the Muslim Power of Conversion: Five Perspectives on 'Turning Turk' in Early Modern Texts." *Journal of Early Modern Cultural Studies*, vol. 2, no. 1, 2002, pp. 35–67.
—. "The Shah's Two Ambassadors: *The Travels of the Three English Brothers* and the Global Early Modern." *Emissaries in Early Modern Literature and Culture: Mediation, Transmission, Traffic, 1550–1700*, edited by Brinda Charry and Gitanjali Shahani. Ashgate, 2009, pp. 23–40.
—. *Traffic and Turning: Islam and English Drama, 1579–1624*. U of Delaware P, 2005.
Camoēs, Luís de. "The Lusiad, or Portugals Historicall Poem." Sir Richard Fanshawe, *The Poems and Translations of Sir Richard Fanshawe*, vol. 2, edited by Peter Davidson, Clarendon P, 1999, pp. 1–330.
Chaudhury, Sushil, and Michel Morineau, editors. *Merchants, Companies, and Trade: Europe and Asia in the Early Modern Era*. Cambridge UP, 1999.
Day, John, William Rowley, and George Wilkins. "The Travels of Three English Brothers." *Three Renaissance English Plays*, edited by Anthony Parr, Manchester UP, 1995, pp. 55–134.
Dryden, John. *The Works of John Dryden: Amboyna, The State of Innocence, Aureng-Zebe*, vol. 12, edited by Vinton Dearing, U of California P, 1994.
—. *The Works of John Dryden. Vol. 5: Poems, The Works of Virgil in English, 1697*, edited by William Frost, U of California P, 1956.
Ellinghausen, Laurie. *Pirates, Traitors, and Apostates: Renegade Identities in Early Modern English Writing*. U of Toronto P, 2017.
Floyd-Wilson, Mary. *English Ethnicity and Race in Early Modern Drama*. Cambridge UP, 2003.
Forman, Valerie. *Tragicomic Redemptions: Global Economics and the Early Modern English Stage*. U of Pennsylvania P, 2008.
Fuchs, Barbara. *Mimesis and Empire: The New World, Islam, and European Identities*. Cambridge UP, 2001.

Furber, Holden. "Asia and the West as Partners before 'Empire' and After." *Journal of Asian Studies*, vol. 28, no. 4, 1969, pp. 711–21.
Greenblatt, Stephen. *Renaissance Self-Fashioning: From More to Shakespeare*. U of Chicago, 1980.
Hakluyt, Richard. *The Principal Navigations, Voyages, Traffiques and Discoveries of the English Nation*, 2nd ed. George Bishop, Ralph Newberie, and Robert Barker, 1599–1600.
Heywood, Thomas. *The Fair Maid of the West, Parts I and II*, edited by Robert K. Turner, Jr., U of Nebraska P, 1967.
—. *If You Know Not Me, You Know No Body, The Second Part*. Nathaniell Butter, 1623.
—. *The Second Part of, If You Know Not Me, You Know No Bodie*. Nathaniell Butter, 1606.
Hollis, Gavin. *The Absence of America: The London Stage, 1576–1642*. Oxford UP, 2015.
Houston, Chloë. "'I wish to be no other but as he': Persia, Masculinity, and Conversion in Early-Seventeenth-Century Travel Writing and Drama." *Gender and Religious Change in Early Modern Europe*, edited by Simon Ditchfield and Helen Smith, Manchester UP, 2017, pp. 216–35.
Howard, Jean. "An English Lass Amid the Moors: Gender, Race, Sexuality, and National Identity in Heywood's *The Fair Maid of the West*." *Women, "Race," and Writing in the Early Modern Period*, edited by Margo Hendricks and Patricia Parker, Routledge, 1994, pp. 101–17.
—. *Theater of a City: The Places of London Comedy, 1598–1642*. U of Pennsylvania P, 2007.
Jowitt, Claire, and David McInnis, editors. *Travel and Drama in Early Modern England: The Journeying Play*. Cambridge UP, 2018.
Kling, Blair B., and Michael Pearson. *The Age of Partnership: Europeans in Asia before Dominion*. U of Hawai'i P, 1979.
Markley, Robert. *The Far East and the English Imagination, 1600–1730*. Cambridge UP, 2006.
Marlowe, Christopher. *Tamburlaine the Great*, edited by Joseph Sandy Cunningham and Eithne Henson, Manchester UP, 1998.
Mendoza, Kirsten N. "Navigating a Kiss in the Racialized Geopolitical Landscape of Thomas Heywood's *The Fair Maid of the West*." *Race and Affect in Early Modern English Literature*, edited by Carol Mejia LaPerle, ACMRS P, 2022, pp. 99–118.
Ng, Su Fang. *Alexander the Great from Britain to Southeast Asia: Peripheral Empires in the Global Renaissance*. Oxford UP, 2019.
Nocentelli, Carmen. "The Dutch Black Legend." *Modern Language Quarterly*, vol. 75, no. 3, 2014, pp. 355–83.
—. *Empires of Love: Europe, Asia, and the Making Early Modern Identity*. U of Pennsylvania P, 2013.
Orr, Bridget. *Empire on the English Stage, 1660–1714*. Cambridge UP, 2001.
Publicover, Laurence. *Dramatic Geography: Romance, Intertheatricality, and Cultural Encounter in Early Modern Mediterranean Drama*. Oxford UP, 2017.
Raman, Shankar. *Framing "India": The Colonial Imaginary in Early Modern Culture*. Stanford UP, 2002.

Rubright, Marjorie. *Doppelgänger Dilemmas: Anglo-Dutch Relations in Early Modern English Literature and Culture.* U of Pennsylvania Press, 2014.

Schille, Candy B. K. "'With Honour Quit the Fort': Ambivalent Colonialism in Dryden's *Amboyna.*" *Early Modern Literary Studies,* vol. 4, 2006, pp. 1–30, http://purl.oclc.org.ezproxy.lib.vt.edu/emls/12-1/schiambo.htm (accessed December 10, 2022).

Vitkus, Daniel. *Turning Turk: English Theater and the Multicultural Mediterranean, 1570–1630.* Palgrave Macmillan, 2003.

# 4

JASON PEARL

# Travel Narratives and the Early Novel

It is well known that the source of *Robinson Crusoe* (1719) was the story of Alexander Selkirk, an actual castaway, whose ordeal on the largest of the Juan Fernández Islands was recounted by Woodes Rogers in *A Cruising Voyage Round the World* (1712).[1] At the time, many writers looked to travelers for exotic settings and compelling situations that might be made use of in fiction. Richard Steele's "Inkle and Yarico" (1711), itself the origin of a comic opera by George Colman (1787), was derived from an anecdote in Richard Ligon's *History of the Island of Barbados* (1657). "Rime of the Ancyent Marinere" (1798), by Samuel Taylor Coleridge, owes its main idea to a passage in George Shelvocke's *Voyage Round the World* (1726). These lines of influence were once a major preoccupation in studies of the novel. Today, we acknowledge that writers took from travelers not just specific details but also general thematic concerns and narrative and descriptive conventions (Adams, *Travel Literature* 81–102; McKeon 100–5; Rennie 55–82). The relationship of fact and fiction was complex and dynamic, exceeding the mere act of borrowing and reusing. Writers of novels assumed poetic license, reworking and expanding suggestive details and exploring implications more or less neglected by the sailors, soldiers, and pirates who first put them to paper. The purpose of travelers, for the most part, was to say what they saw and did. It was the prerogative of writers of fiction to reflect on what it meant.

Travel accounts – factual narratives of journeys beyond England – were themselves quite popular and needed no embellishment. Addison professed, "There are no books which I more delight in than in travels, especially those that describe remote countries" (Addison 2, 321). Anthony Ashley Cooper, the Third Earl of Shaftesbury, affirmed but lamented their popular appeal: "These are in our present days what books of chivalry were in those of our forefathers" (153). The lines of influence went in both directions, in that travelers, though they did not admit it, adopted techniques from fiction, telling tall tales alongside true ones (Adams, *Travelers and Travel*

## 4 Travel Narratives and the Early Novel

*Liars* 105–31). The genre of the voyage in particular was immensely popular; as many as two thousand book-length narratives were published in the eighteenth century (Edwards 2). These works promised stories of adventure and detailed reports of strange new flora and fauna. They brought armchair travelers – imaginatively – to little-known places, giving both entertainment and education to readers of a growing empire. From the writings of William Dampier, the buccaneer turned author, to those of James Cook, the vaunted explorer, accounts of distant journeys offered "marvels" (Greenblatt 16–17) and "wonders" (Campbell 2–9) that defied understanding with a surfeit of novelty. At the same time, a traveler could turn the tables and foist an illusion of knowledge and mastery, adopting the guise of a "modest" or "virtual witness" (Shapin and Schaffer 60–5) and seizing the authority of what Mary Louise Pratt has called a "monarch of all I survey" (201–8). And still, despite their role as agents of empire, travelers wrote, as well, of suffering and captivity, which complicates the presumption of unimpeded conquest (Colley 1–20). Selkirk, marooned on an island the Spanish abandoned, was himself an example of the limits of imperial power.

The lessons of travel, implied or suggested in first-hand narratives, were explored more fully by writers of fiction. Indeed, the novel, as a genre, owes much to accounts of overseas journeys and descriptions of faraway lands.[2] Selkirk's story, in the book by Rogers, runs a handful of pages, whereas Crusoe's is hundreds, with a sequel, *The Farther Adventures of Robinson Crusoe* (1719), and a third volume devoted wholly to commentary, *Serious Reflections during the Life and Surprising Adventures of Robinson Crusoe* (1720). At the end of his account of Selkirk, Rogers gives a few thoughts but then announces, quite abruptly, "I must quit these Reflections, which are more proper for a Philosopher and Divine than a Mariner, and return to my own Subject" (1:132). That is the point where Defoe begins (Pearl, "Woodes Rogers"). There was no agreed-on line between fact and fiction: Defoe and others, from Aphra Behn to Jonathan Swift, insisted their stories were truthful, sometimes ironically. And yet we find in the texts we call novels a deliberate effort to expand and develop, to reflect and conjecture. These narratives too served as imperial propaganda. James Joyce called Crusoe "the true prototype of the British colonist" (24). At the same time, antithetically, Defoe makes a virtue of solitude, extolling a life of withdrawal from worldly concerns. In *Oroonoko* (1688), Behn took issue with the failings of colonial governance. Swift, in *Gulliver's Travels* (1726), offered a number of alternatives – good, bad, or somewhere in between. These novels, and many more, drew on the conventions of literary utopias but reflected more critically on the possibility of ideal societies in the blank spaces of European maps.[3] Other fictions of the time dealt with the perils of courtship, with settings that were narrowly domestic, either in England or on the Continent (Ballaster 31–66). Later in the century, the latter form won out, so that engagement with the wider world – and the building of the British Empire – was mostly pushed to the margins, repressed or neglected altogether in narratives that centered instead on the refinement of national character (Doody 291–3; Siskin 180–7).

## Travel Narratives

Despite a reluctance to indulge in reflection, Rogers, and many others, wrote at length about incidents on the ship, about winds and currents at sea, about faraway lands, and – at least to Europeans – unfamiliar peoples, plants, and animals.[4] For the most part, travelers were known for not brevity but prolixity. In Swift's words, their writing was "too circumstantial"; it was "tedious and trifling" (5, 79). Readers wanted to learn about distant parts of the world, especially the Far East, the center of global commerce (Markley, *Far East*), and the largely uncharted South Seas, now the Pacific Ocean, a space of sporadic exploration and impassioned speculation (Williams 161–74). To solicit this knowledge, the Fellows of the Royal Society issued instructions for travelers that laid out methods of observation; headings and subheadings of information; and specific questions about specific places (Pearl, "Geography and Authority"). Whether or not he knew of the instructions, Dampier promised on the title page of his *New Voyage Round the World* (1697) descriptions of "Soil, Rivers, Harbours, Plants, Fruits, Animals, and Inhabitants." His accounts of strange creatures and hitherto unknown plant life go on for pages and give the impression of rapt observation. The lens of natural history, it turns out, did not contain – instead it accentuated – the wonders of exotic objects and phenomena (Barnes and Mitchell). Lionel Wafer, a shipmate, wrote a book, as well, though he broke up narrative and description into separate chapters, so that the record of natural history seemed separate from – and therefore untainted by – personal experience (Frohock, "Tattoos"). Later in the century, John Hawkesworth, a stay-at-home writer by profession, ran afoul of prevailing conventions, adding novelistic embellishment and exaggeration to the bare journals of Cook and others (Thell 153–87). Cook himself won fame as a man of science, bringing with him on his voyages such naturalists as Joseph Banks and Johann Reinhold and Georg Forster. He charted much of the Pacific and disproved the longstanding myth of a great southern continent, thus closing an important chapter in the history of overseas exploration.

The motive was not disinterested. Cook and the others sought "useful knowledge," theorized by Francis Bacon and pursued by the Royal Society as a means of attaining power over nature (Mokyr 70–98). Science, they knew, would advance the interests of overseas trade and empire, charting new routes to new resources. The complicity of science and empire has been well established and needs little elaboration.[5] Even botany, a seemingly neutral field of study, was implicated in imperial ambitions (Schiebinger 1–22). Drawings and descriptions of flora and fauna put people at home in the position of a vicarious witness. Travelers themselves, as narrators, were often so slight a presence in the text that there was no one in the way, nothing that could block the fantasy of possession from afar. For his part, Dampier professed "a hearty Zeal for the promoting of useful knowledge, and of any thing that may never so remotely tend to my Countries advantage" (1). Wafer and Rogers took part in colonial ventures: Wafer as an advisor to the ill-fated project by Scotland to settle the Darien Isthmus; Rogers as Governor of the Bahamas, which he rid of pirates and defended against the Spanish. Cook, as well, was an agent of empire. For his first voyage, he received two sets of instructions: The first pertained to observing the transit of Venus; the second, kept secret, told him to "take possession of Convenient Situations in the Country [what is now Australia] in the Name of the King of Great Britain" (11). The event of his death, at the hands of Indigenous Hawaiians, has spurred a well-known debate about the limits of what explorers – and even anthropologists – can understand: Was Cook seen as Lono, a deity of the Hawaiians, and killed in a ritual of distinctive religious significance (Sahlins, *Islands of History*)? Is such an explanation symptomatic of ethnocentrism (Obeysekere)? Can scholars from the West enter into non-Western ways of thinking (Sahlins, *How "Natives" Think*)?

Those who survived told stories of hardship and suffering. Some died at sea from maladies such as scurvy, which Jonathan Lamb has dubbed "the disease of discovery" (Lamb, *Scurvy* 6). Others spent years on deserted islands, enduring worse fates than Selkirk (Lamb, *Preserving the Self* 165–99). Still others were held captive in North America (Derounian-Stodola) and the north coast of Africa (Matar). In most cases, the travelers in question cared little to nothing about the misery they inflicted on native populations. It bears emphasis that their personal struggles do not diminish the crimes of imperial conquest. Indeed, the growth of empire was underwritten by narratives of adversity, which hardened readers to the challenges of settler colonialism and reduced non-Europeans to the status of savage others and enemies of Christianity. At the same time, we must not aggrandize the power and influence of Britain, assuming its empire was a foregone conclusion, the result of well-laid plans or confident implementation. The work of travelers was often unsuccessful, unproductive. As Lamb puts it, "To insist that the point of such voyages was exclusively the production of truth for imperial purposes is to ignore ... the confusing and sometimes inexpressible experience of extreme conditions endured by the voyagers themselves" (*Preserving the Self* 7).

## The Early Novel

One of the first novels to feature overseas travel was Behn's *Oroonoko*, which defended the cause of empire but questioned the practices of colonial governance.[6] It seems the author herself went to Surinam, where the story takes place, in the role of a spy for the Crown (Todd 35–66). The novel was subtitled *A True History*, its narrator stating, "I was my self an Eye-Witness," so this fiction was rooted in fact, much like *Robinson Crusoe* (Behn 8). What she did not learn first-hand Behn might have gotten from George Warren's *Impartial Description of Surinam* (1667), which recounts with some candor the brutal plight of enslaved and transported Africans. The novel's first half, set in Coramantien, or modern-day Ghana, draws on the tropes of both French romance and what was then called the "oriental tale."[7] The second half shifts to Surinam, which Behn portrays with much more geographic and historical specificity. There are references to animals such as "a very strange fish, called, a numb eel" – a creature of natural history, rather than myth or romance (46). There are, as well, a number of historical personages, for instance, William Byam, who took the place of the absent governor, Francis Willoughby. And yet, despite the facts, we must accord this text all the subtleties and complexities of fiction. The narrative as a whole pits Old World ideals against New World realities, so that the titular hero, a prince in Africa, is made a slave in Surinam, where he is tortured and executed. Some scholars have read the novel for its reflections on race and slavery (Ferguson; Aravamudan, *Tropicopolitans* 29–70). For others, it is about the status of the monarchy in England and the politics of the Glorious Revolution (Pacheco; Kroll). Still others have read it as a critique of colonial mismanagement (Hoegberg; Frohock, *Heroes* 53–80). On the one hand, Behn endorsed the expansion of empire so long as it was consistent with hierarchies at home. She wrote a poem in praise of the Duke of Albemarle, the short-lived Governor of Jamaica, whom she painted as a chivalric hero. On the other hand, as in *The Widdow Ranter* (1689), Behn saw colonies across the Atlantic as overrun by grasping opportunists. As Elliott Visconsi asserts, "The barbarians are not indigenous peoples but rather the dregs of English culture who find in the Americas free rein for their natural predilections for self-interest, cruelty, mob rule, and lawlessness" (160).

It was, of course, Defoe who wrote the best-known novel of travel, at least in the period under discussion. He too presented his narrative as truthful – it was "a just History of Fact" – and he too explored the theme of colonial failure (3). In this case, though, the hero is a shipwrecked Englishman, whose story offered lessons in both spiritual development and economic individualism. The account of Selkirk, by Rogers, concluded with the maxim that "Necessity is the Mother of Invention" (Rogers 1:130). We find the same moral in *Robinson Crusoe*, where the island, at first a prison, becomes a kind of refuge, a place of escape from worldly vices and temptations. Here, Crusoe declares, "I might be more happy in this Solitary Condition, than I should have been in a Liberty of Society, and in all the Pleasures of the World" (Defoe 89). Many have written on his status as a Christian and the theme of religious improvement (Starr 74–125; Hunter 23–50). For others, the focus of the novel is the pursuit of material wealth: Crusoe, after all, has grown rich when he at last returns to England (Watt 60–92; McKeon 315–37).[8] He gains his wealth by means of colonial settlement (Hulme 175–222) and overseas trade and commerce (Neill 55–76). Defoe himself was a dogged promoter of nascent globalization, believing "every Nation has something to fetch from and something to send to one another" (Defoe, *Selected Writings* 119). Midway through the novel, Crusoe rescues the character he renames "Friday," a Caribbean islander, whom the Englishman, straight away, makes a personal servant. They fight against "savages" and subdue Europeans from Spain and England, so that the island becomes a model for the expansion of the British Empire (McLeod 164–215; Schmigden 32–62). In the sequel, *The Farther Adventures*, the fledgling colony falls apart from both the pressure of invading tribes and the conflicts that arise among the colonists themselves (Markley, "'I Have Now Done'"). Crusoe leaves them behind and continues his travels – to Madagascar, China, and Siberia – committing terrible violence along the way and securing incredible profits, though he waxes nostalgic about the simplicity of his life on the island. In the third volume, *Serious Reflections*, he suggests that the peace of isolation is available to all who would study their thoughts (Pearl, *Utopian Geographies* 75–97). As Crusoe puts it, "A Man under a Vow of perpetual Silence, if but rigorously observ'd, would be even on the Exchange of *London*, as perfectly retired from the World, as a Hermit in his Cell; or a *Solitair* in the Desarts of *Arabia*" (Defoe 6). The three volumes, as a whole, posit a narrative of imperial adventure but also, paradoxically, a moral and spiritual lesson on stasis and withdrawal.

What distinguishes Swift is his complex satire of the genre of travel writing as a whole. He distilled its conventions and blurred the difference between the tall tales of voyagers and the ideals of utopian fabulists, for instance Thomas More, who makes an appearance in part three in *Gulliver's Travels*. Swift included references to actual travelers, naming Dampier as

Gulliver's cousin and hinting at Geoffrey Psalmanazar, a notorious imposter and author of the fraudulent *Description of Formosa* (1704). And yet the satirist went further, using the so-called plain style of writing, a rhetoric of truthfulness, and inserting within it content that was patently fantastical (Smith). He added engravings of his fictitious countries made from maps by Herman Moll, the preeminent cartographer of the time (Bracher). On the basis of its antirealism, *Gulliver's Travels* is sometimes omitted in histories of the English novel, though it engages the nature of novelistic representation itself.[9] Indeed, Swift was critical of the very purpose of overseas travelers, mocking not just their supposed plain-spoken honesty but also their support for imperial endeavors (Hawes 139–68). Throughout the first three voyages – to Lilliput, Brobdingnag, Laputa, and so on – Gulliver is an agent of the empire, or so he thinks, much to the amusement of the author who belittles him – literally in part two, where the hero is one-twelfth the size of a Brobdingnagian. A defender of Ireland, Swift understood the injustices of exploitation by a foreign power (Moore 121–33). At the end of the novel, a wiser Gulliver looks back on his travels and lays bare the brutal pattern of imperial conquest:

> A Crew of Pyrates are driven by a Storm they known not whither ... they see an harmless People, are entertained with Kindness, they give the Country a new Name, they take formal Possession of it for their King.... Ships are sent with the first Opportunity, the Natives driven out or destroyed, their Princes tortured to discover their Gold; a free License given to all Acts of Inhumanity and Lust, the Earth reeking with the Blood of its Inhabitants: And this execrable Crew of Butchers employed in so pious an Expedition, is a *modern Colony*. (Swift 248)

The positive alternative is the Land of the Houyhnhnms, depicted as a place of moral perfection (Pearl, *Utopian Geographies* 115–32). Or are they intolerant of – even genocidal toward – the supposedly savage Yahoos, stand-ins for the Irish (Rawson 1–16)? Either way, Swift revisits and revises the central idea of *Robinson Crusoe*: The Yahoos, after all, are descended from two castaways who do not evolve – but devolve – in isolation, turning into the brutes from whom Gulliver is at pains to distinguish himself. We should look at ourselves, the novel suggests, before looking on the map for new lands to conquer.

Travel, a major theme in the early novel, began to recede, in some measure, as the genre matured. It had driven plots and supplied settings, putting readers in touch with the world beyond Europe. Now, the sphere of action contracted (Moretti 47–57), with an emphasis on the space of the nation (Anderson 22–36), even the drawing room (Armstrong 3–27). As Margaret

Cohen puts it, "the maritime picaresque was abandoned" (100). There were exceptions, of course: Additional novels later in the period about travel and faraway lands, presented more and less realistically (Bannet 1–19; Aravamudan, *Enlightenment Orientalism* 1–30; Pearl, "*Peter Wilkins*"). The fictions of Richardson and Fielding mark a trend in the other direction, one that solidified in the marriage plots of Jane Austen. It is ironic that travel would be less prominent exactly at the time when it was becoming more common, when the British Empire was reaching maturity, having expanded far beyond its extent in the days of Defoe and Swift, despite the loss of the North American colonies. In *Mansfield Park* (1816), the issue of colonial wealth is mostly hushed up, kept at the margins, so that the issue of empire is an absent presence (Said 80–97). Austen's elites owe more than they care to admit to the enslavement of Africans and their forced labor on Caribbean plantations. The wider world, once regarded as filled with possibility, was now a trigger of embarrassment, a reminder of inconvenient truths.

As I have shown, the writings of travelers did much to promote the interests of imperial expansion; the writings of novelists advanced the same cause, though they did so with a sense of critical reflection and even utopian speculation. We should think of these fictions as not just models or blueprints for imperial expansion but also sources of neglected perspectives and possibilities. Like the genre of the literary utopia, the novel was imaginative and exploratory. It surpassed the demands of the British Empire and offered questions and ideals that remain worthy of attention to this day.

### Notes

1. It is likely Defoe had in mind several sources, though he mentioned none explicitly. Hunter calls Selkirk "the direct inspiration for *Robinson Crusoe*" (2). See also Secord (21–111).
2. The question of the novel's origins has been a matter of much debate. See Watt and McKeon. Recent work has shown the influence of transatlantic travel and engagement with the world beyond Europe. See, for instance, Doyle and Cohen.
3. On the influence of utopias on the novel, see Bruce and Pearl, *Utopian Geographies*, 7–11.
4. My focus in what follows is on voyages at sea: long-distance journeys made mostly by men. This type of travel promised the most novelty and exerted the greatest influence on the genre of the novel. For travel within Britain and to the Continent, see Batten. On the Grand Tour, see Chard. For accounts of the Middle East and beyond, see Leask. On narratives by women, see O'Loughlin.
5. See Drayton on the long history science and empire. See Harrison for a survey of the historiography. On science in the Atlantic World, go to Delbourgo and Dew; in the Pacific, go to Lincoln. On shipboard science, see Sorrenson.
6. For Behn's position in the history of the novel, go to Spengmann and Dillon.

7. The genre of the novel subsumed and reworked these and other genres, including utopian literature, as I have claimed. For an account of this heterogeneity, see Bakhtin.
8. It is a common fate in novels by Defoe: His heroes travel the world and amass great riches. See, for instance, *Captain Singleton* (1720), *Colonel Jack* (1722), *Moll Flanders* (1722), and *Roxana* (1724).
9. Watt's criterion of "formal realism" makes Swift's narrative an outlier (9–34). For McKeon, the purpose of the genre was to explore "questions of truth," and, of course, Swift calls into question the kind of testimony that Behn and Defoe deployed less self-reflexively (90–128).

## Works Cited

Adams, Percy. *Travelers and Travel Liars, 1660–1800*. U of California P, 1962.
   *Travel Literature and the Evolution of the Novel*. UP of Kentucky, 1983.
Addison, Joseph. *The Works of the Right Honourable Joseph Addison, Esq. in Four Volumes*. Printed for Jacob Tonson, at Shakespear's-Head, over-against Katharine-Street in the Strand, 1721.
Anderson, Benedict. *Imagined Communities*. Revised ed., Verso, 2006.
Aravamudan, Srinivas. *Enlightenment Orientalism: Resisting the Rise of the Novel*. U of Chicago P, 2014.
   *Tropicopolitans: Colonialism and Agency, 1688–1804*. Duke UP, 1999.
Armstrong, Nancy. *Desire and Domestic Fiction: A Political History of the Novel*. Oxford UP, 1987.
Austen, Jane. *Mansfield Park*, edited by Claudia Johnson, W. W. Norton, 1998.
Bakhtin, Mikail. "Discourse in the Novel." *The Dialogic Imagination*. Translated by Caryl Emerson and Michael Holquist, edited by Michael Holquist, U of Texas P, 1981, pp. 259–442.
Ballaster, Ros. *Seductive Forms: Women's Amatory Fiction from 1684–1740*. Clarendon P, 1992.
Bannet, Eve Tavor. *Transatlantic Stories and the History of Reading, 1720–1810: Migrant Fictions*. Cambridge UP, 2011.
Barnes, Geraldine, and Adrian Mitchell. "Measuring the Marvelous: Science and the Exotic in William Dampier." *Eighteenth-Century Life*, vol. 26, no. 3, 2002, pp. 45–57.
Batten, Charles. *Pleasurable Instruction: Form and Convention in Eighteenth-Century Travel Literature*. U of California P, 1978.
Behn, Aphra. *Oroonoko, The Rover and Other Works*, edited by Janet Todd, Penguin, 2003.
   *To the Most Illustrious Prince Christopher Duke of Albemarle on His Voyage to His Government of Jamaica*. John Newton, 1687.
Bracher, Frederik. "The Maps of *Gulliver's Travels*." *Huntington Library Quarterly*, vol. 8, 1944, pp. 59–74.
Bruce, Susan. "Introduction." *Three Early Modern Utopias*, edited by Susan Bruce, Oxford UP, 1999, pp. ix–xlii.
Campbell, Mary Baine. *Wonder and Science: Imagining Worlds in Early Modern Europe*. Cornell UP, 1999.

Chard, Chloe. *Pleasure and Guilt on the Grand Tour: Travel Writing and Imaginative Geography, 1600–1830*. Manchester UP, 1999.
Cohen, Margaret. *The Novel and the Sea*. Princeton UP, 2010.
Coleridge, Samuel Taylor. *The Rime of the Ancient Mariner*, edited by Paul H. Fry, Bedford/St. Martin's, 1999.
Colley, Linda. *Captives: Britain, Empire, and the World, 1600–1850*. Random House, 2002.
Colman, George. "Inkle and Yarico: An Opera, in Three Acts." *English Trader, Indian Maid: Representing Gender, Race, and Slavery in the New World*, edited by Frank Felsenstein, Johns Hopkins UP, 1999, pp. 167–33.
Cook, James. *The Journals of James Cook*, edited by Philip Edwards, Penguin, 1999.
Cooper, Anthony Ashley. *Characteristics of Men, Manners, Opinions, Times*, edited by Lawrence E. Klein, Cambridge UP, 1999.
Dampier, William. *Memoirs of a Buccaneer: Dampier's New Voyage Round the World, 1697*, edited by Percy Adams, Dover Publications, 1968.
Delbourgo, James, and Nicholas Dew, editors. *Science and Empire in the Atlantic World*. Routledge, 2007.
Defoe, Daniel. *Captain Singleton*, edited by Manushag Powell, Broadview, 2019.
*Colonel Jack*, edited by Gabriel Cervantes and Geoffrey Sill, Broadview, 2015.
*The Farther Adventures of Robinson Crusoe*, edited by Maximillian Novak, Irving Rothman, and Manuel Schonhorn, Bucknell UP, 2022.
*Moll Flanders*, edited by Paul Scanlon, Broadview, 2005.
*Robinson Crusoe*, edited by Michael Shinagel, W. W. Norton, 1994.
*Roxana*, edited by Melissa Mowry, Broadview, 2009.
*Selected Writings of Daniel Defoe*, edited by James Boulton, Cambridge UP, 1975.
*Serious Reflections during the Life and Surprising Adventures of Robinson Crusoe*. W Taylor, 1720.
Derounian-Stodola, Kathryn Zabelle. "Introduction." *Women's Indian Captivity Narratives*, edited by Kathryn Zabelle Derounian-Stodola, Penguin, 1998, pp. xi–xxxv.
Dillon, Elizabeth Maddock. "The Original American Novel; or, The American Origin of the Novel." *A Companion to the Eighteenth-Century English Novel and Culture*, edited by Paula Backscheider and Catherine Ingrassia, Blackwell, 2009, pp. 235–60.
Doody, Margaret. *The True Story of the Novel*. Rutgers UP, 1996.
Doyle, Laura. *Freedom's Empire: Race and the Rise of the Novel in Atlantic Modernity, 1640–1940*. Duke UP, 2008.
Drayton, Richard. *Nature's Government: Science, Imperial Britain, and the "Improvement" of the World*. Yale UP, 2000.
Edwards, Philip. *The Story of the Voyage: Sea-Narratives in Eighteenth-Century England*. Cambridge UP, 1994.
Ferguson, Moira. "Oroonoko: Birth of a Paradigm." *New Literary History*, vol. 23, 1992, pp. 339–59.
Fielding, Henry. *Tom Jones*, edited by John Bender and Simon Stern, Oxford UP, 1996.
Frohock, Richard. *Heroes of Empire: The British Imperial Protagonist in America, 1596–1764*. U of Delaware P, 2004.

"Tattoos and Nose Rings: Lionel Wafer's Immersion in Cuna Culture." *1650–1850: Ideas, Aesthetics, and Inquiries in the Early Modern Era*, vol. 7, 2002, pp. 27–50.
Greenblatt, Stephen. *Marvelous Possessions: The Wonder of the New World*. U of Chicago P, 1991.
Harrison, Mark. "Science and the British Empire." *Isis*, vol. 96, 2005, pp. 56–63.
Hawes, Clement. *The British Eighteenth Century and Global Critique*. Palgrave Macmillan, 2005.
Hawkesworth, John. *An Account of the Voyages Undertaken by the Order of His Present Majesty*. W. Strahan and T. Cadell, 1773, 3 vols.
Hoegberg, David. "Caesar's Toils: Allusion and Rebellion in *Oroonoko*." *Eighteenth-Century Fiction*, vol. 7, 1995, pp. 239–58.
Hulme, Peter. *Colonial Encounters: Europe and the Native Caribbean, 1492–1797*. Methuen, 1986.
Hunter, Paul. *The Reluctant Pilgrim: Defoe's Emblematic Method and Quest for Form in Robinson Crusoe*. Johns Hopkins UP, 1966.
Joyce, James. "Daniel Defoe." Translated by Joseph Prescott, *Buffalo Studies*, vol. 1, no. 1, 1964, pp. 1–25.
Kroll, Richard. "'Tales of Love and Gallantry': The Politics of *Oroonoko*." *Huntington Library Quarterly*, vol. 67, 2005, pp. 573–605.
Lamb, Jonathan. *Preserving the Self in the South Seas, 1680–1840*. U of Chicago P, 2001.
———. *Scurvy: The Disease of Discovery*. Princeton UP, 2017.
Leask, Nigel. *Curiosity and the Aesthetics of Travel Writing, 1770–1840: From an Antique Land*. Oxford UP, 2004.
Ligon, Richard. *A True and Exact History of the Island of Barbadoes*, edited by Karen Ordahl Kupperman, Hackett, 2011.
Lincoln, Margarette, editor. *Science and Exploration in the Pacific: European Voyages to the Southern Ocean in the Eighteenth Century*. Boydell & Brewer, 1998.
Markley, Robert. *The Far East and the English Imagination, 1600–1730*. Cambridge UP, 2006.
———. "'I Have Now Done with My Island, and All Manner of Discourse about It': Crusoe's *Farther Adventures* and the Unwritten History of the Novel." *A Companion to the Eighteenth-Century English Novel and Culture*, edited by Paula Backscheider and Catherine Ingrassia, Wiley-Blackwell, 2009, pp. 25–47.
Matar, Nabil. "Introduction." *Piracy, Slavery, and Redemption: Barbary Captivity Narratives from Early Modern England*, edited by Daniel Vitkus, Columbia UP, 2001, pp. 1–52.
McKeon, Michael. *The Origins of the English Novel, 1600–1740*. Johns Hopkins UP, 1987.
McLeod, Bruce. *The Geography of Empire in English Literature, 1580–1745*. Cambridge UP, 1999.
Mokyr, Joel. *A Culture of Growth: The Origins of the Modern Economy*. Princeton UP, 2017.
Moore, Sean. *Swift, the Book, and the Irish Financial Revolution: Satire and Sovereignty in Colonial Ireland*. Johns Hopkins UP, 2010.

Moretti, Franco. *The Atlas of the European Novel, 1800–1900*. Verso, 1998.
Neill, Anna. *British Discovery Literature and the Rise of Global Commerce*. Palgrave, 2002.
Obeysekere, Gananath. *The Apotheosis of Captain Cook: European Mythmaking in the Pacific*. Princeton UP, 1992.
O'Laughlin, Katherine. *Women, Writing, and Travel in the Eighteenth Century*. Cambridge UP, 2018.
Pacheco, Anita. "Royalism and Honor in Aphra Behn's *Oroonoko*." *Studies in English Literature*, vol. 34, 1994, pp. 491–506.
Pearl, Jason. "Geography and Authority in the Royal Society's Instructions for Travelers." *Travel Narratives, the New Science, and Literary Discourse, 1569–1750*, edited by Judy Hayden, Ashgate, 2012, pp. 71–83.
—. "*Peter Wilkins* and the Eighteenth-Century Novel." *Studies in English Literature, 1500–1900*, vol. 57, 2017, pp. 541–59.
—. *Utopian Geographies and the Early English Novel*. U of Virginia P, 2014.
—. "Woodes Rogers and the Boundary of Travel Facts." *Eighteenth-Century Life*, vol. 33, no. 1, 2007, pp. 60–75.
Pratt, Mary Louise. *Imperial Eyes: Travel Writing and Transculturation*. Routledge, 1992.
Psalmanazar, Geoffrey. *An Historical and Geographical Description of Formosa*. Dan. Brown, G. Strahan, W. Davis, Fran. Coggan, 1704.
Rawson, Claude. *God, Gulliver, and Genocide: Barbarism and the European Imagination, 1492–1945*. Oxford UP, 2001.
Rennie, Neil. *Far-Fetched Facts: The Literature of Travel and the Idea of the South Seas*. Clarendon P, 1995.
Richardson, Samuel. *Pamela: or Virtue Rewarded*, edited by Thomas Keymer and Alice Wakely, Oxford UP, 2008.
Rogers, Woodes. *A Cruising Voyage Round the World*. A. Bell and B. Lintot, 1712, 2 vols.
Sahlins, Marshall. *How "Natives" Think: About Captain Cook, for Example*. U of Chicago P, 1995.
—. *Islands of History*. U of Chicago P, 1985.
Said, Edward. *Culture and Imperialism*. Vintage, 1994.
Schiebinger, Londa. *Plants and Empire: Colonial Bioprospecting in the Atlantic World*. Harvard UP, 2004.
Schmigden, Wolfram. *Eighteenth-Century Fiction and the Law of Property*. Cambridge UP, 2002.
Secord, Arthur Wellesley. *Studies in the Narrative Method of Defoe*. U of Illinois P, 1924.
Shapin, Steven, and Simon Schaffer. *Leviathan and the Air-Pump: Hobbes, Boyle, and the Experimental Life*. U of Chicago P, 1985.
Shelvocke, George. *A Voyage Round the World by Way of the Great South Sea*. T. Combes, J. Lacy, and J. Clarke, 1726.
Siskin, Clifford. *The Work of Writing: Literature and Social Change in Britain, 1700–1830*. Johns Hopkins UP, 1998.
Smith, Frederik. "Scientific Discourse: *Gulliver's Travels* and *The Philosophical Transactions*." *The Genres of Gulliver's Travels*, edited by Frederik Smith. U of Delaware P, 1990, pp. 139–62.

Sorrenson, Richard. "The Ship as a Scientific Instrument in the Eighteenth Century." *Osiris*, vol. 11, 1996, pp. 221–36.
Spengmann, William. "The Earliest American Novel: Aphra Behn's *Oroonoko*." *Nineteenth-Century Fiction*, vol. 38, 1984, pp. 384–414.
Starr, George. *Defoe and Spiritual Autobiography*. Princeton UP, 1965.
Swift, Jonathan. *Gulliver's Travels*, edited by Albert Rivero, W. W. Norton, 2002.
Thell, Anne. *Minds in Motion: Imagining Empiricism in Eighteenth-Century British Travel Literature*. Bucknell UP, 2017.
Todd, Janet. *The Secret Life of Aphra Behn*. Rutgers UP, 1996.
Visconsi, Elliott. *Lines of Equity: Literature and the Origins of Law in Later Stuart England*. Cornell UP, 2008.
Wafer, Lionel. *A New Voyage and Description of the Isthmus of America*. James Knapton, 1699.
Warren, George. *An Impartial Description of Surinam*. William Godbid and Nathaniel Brooke, 1667.
Watt, Ian. *The Rise of the Novel: Studies in Defoe, Richardson, and Fielding*. U of California P, 1957.
Williams, Glyndwr. *The Great South Sea: Voyages and Encounters, 1570–1750*. Yale UP, 1997.

# 5

JAMES MULHOLLAND

# Anglophone Epics and Ruin Poetry in Eighteenth-Century India

Poetry uses ruins to reimagine empire. This has been true for millennia within the Anglophone and European literary traditions, but during the late eighteenth century, when British colonizers were beginning to occupy India in larger numbers, epics, and ruin poetry were important ways for authors to capture the peculiar status of what has been called the Company Raj, the expanding administrative state of the East India Company (EIC or Company) (e.g., Sen xx).

Anglophone epics and ruin poetry in eighteenth-century India drew from the attitudes of Greek and Roman antiquity, but with subject matter, locales, and authorial positions shifted to Asia in formats that were formally quite conventional, even unfashionable by the late eighteenth century, such as heroic couplets. Poetry proved to be especially important for those administrators who sought to understand the relationships between the Company and other European contestants and South Asian sovereignties. Ruin poetry, in particular, could mobilize historical facts within an artistic setting and allow for debates about politics in forums other than the dispatches, consultations, and newspaper essays that were the common venue for assessing Britain's empire.

Atypically for poetry of the imperial state, these poems were tilted toward what Michael Cohen has called "social transmission" rather than fame and posterity, recounting (and often distorting) details about the realities of Asia (Cohen 2008, 13). their authors drew examples from vast political and cultural histories to achieve contemporary relevancy. They demonstrate how poems on affairs of state remained vibrant within Britain's imperial domains, inserting themselves into conversations about governance and adding another attribute to Suvir Kaul's idea that eighteenth-century English-language poetry was a "unique and privileged literary form" to "enunciate the vocabulary of empire" (5). It was a facet of what I have called the "cultural company-state," which used art and literature – printing, artistic patronage, sculpture, painting, and more – as a calculated strategy to expand the political power of the EIC (Mulholland).

Recognizing this strategy requires scholars to adopt new ideas about literature as an exercise of colonial power. Poetry not only engages in the "vocabulary of empire," but it also demonstrates the limits of national identity to create coherence in overseas imperial domains. Instead, Anglophone epics and ruin poetry perform a kind of "verse politics" that combines non-European culture objects, local sovereignties and their histories, and regional languages to explain the shifting position of British imperialism in eighteenth-century Asia. It turns poetry not just into an object influenced by politics, and thus able to be historicized, but a means of advancing the political conditions and assessing the policies upon which colonialism depends.

To capture the verse politics of eighteenth-century Asia, I appeal to the example of Eyles Irwin, an EIC administrator posted to Madras in 1766 who served throughout Asia until the 1790s. Irwin began publishing poetry during the 1770s while residing in India, a decade before the arrival of William Jones (who is often marked as the originator of an Anglophone Indian poetic tradition). I focus in particular on Irwin's lengthy unpublished manuscript poem "The Ruins of Madura, or, the Hindoo Garden" (c. 1785–92) which versifies the holy sites and gardens of an ancient southern Indian city, Madura (Madurai), and the decayed palace of one of its Hindu rulers, Tirumala Nayaka. This two-part poetic epistle catalogs flora, fauna, cuisine, art, architecture, customs, and religion to present "the riches of the Kingdom of Madura under the Hindoo Kings" (Irwin, "Ruins" I. Argument). From these details, and Madura's ruins, Irwin reanimates a South Indian culture and polity.

Irwin's recovery act is not proto-anthropological but is instead artistic and political, poising ruins' reanimated past with questions about present-day British imperial expansion. His poem is an argument for South Asia as a new topic for writerly invention. He combines georgic and epic modes with South Asian myths and supernaturalism and appeals directly to precursor poets and forms, especially the Virgilian career. His efforts accord with his contemporaries, such as William Jones, who planned an epic poem intertwining Britain and India titled *Britain Discovered*; Julius Mickle, who translated *Os Lusíadas*, Luis de Camões's poem of Portuguese contact with India, into English; and William Marsden, who conceived a Sumatran epic, the "Malaiad," while stationed in Sumatra during the 1770s when he was researching the *History of Sumatra* (1783; 1811). Recovering how and why British imperialists valorized particular literary forms (epic; heroic couplets) reintroduces needed historical and imperial dynamics to the poetry of postcolonial studies. It provincializes the Anglo-American literary academy that has focused on what Virginia Jackson and Yopie Prins have called the nineteenth-century lyricization of poetry. Instead, I attend to geographically localized, historically expansive, and multigeneric poems like Irwin's as a formal approximation for the diverse, multifarious identities that occupied eighteenth-century British India and the politics that made their presence possible.

## Haunted by Empire?

In eighteenth-century Anglo-India, the ruin was an imperial assemblage meant to produce active historical juxtapositions. It was a counterpoint to the neoclassical buildings inspired by ancient Greece and Rome that the Company constructed in its Presidency cities, especially Calcutta, when it expanded its administrative scope after the accession to *diwani* status in 1765.[1] The EIC had been active in India for 150 years before it triumphed at the Battle of Plassey (in 1757) and the Battle of Buxar (in 1764), which secured lucrative privileges, including control over taxation in Bengal, a populous province with a large economy.

Even after these successes, British dominion of South Asia was not assured. The EIC competed with other European company-states and with fractured Indigenous polities, such as the Kingdom of Mysore and the Maratha Confederacy, particularly during the 1780s, when Irwin was writing "The Ruins of Madura" and the British Parliament was seeking increased control over the Company through legislation. While Britain made peace with breakaway American settler colonies and witnessed the uprising of French revolutionary sentiment, it inserted itself ever more into EIC oversight, most notoriously with the trial of Warren Hastings and the appointment of Lord Cornwallis to India as Governor-General.

Mediterranean antiquity may have been the primary inspiration for much of British India's art and writing, but it also remixed specific landscapes and political histories of Asia, combining the Hellenistic past with Persia, central Asia, and the multilingualism of South Asia. Mary Ellis Gibson has described British India as a "complex linguistic contact zone" whose multilingualism was defined by translocal and regional awareness (20). Its literary culture was based on socialization among a relatively small community of three to four thousand Europeans that was influenced by but often antagonistic toward metropolitan Britain, changing its fashions and artistic codes to reflect its unique geographical and cultural positions. Late eighteenth-century British India developed a vibrant art world predicated on strategic multilingualism. Elite Orientalists were fascinated with Sanskrit, a regional prestige language, but Anglophone poets also drew from Persian, the official language of Mughal administration, and from localized vernaculars, such as Tamil and Brajbhasha (Mulholland).

Reimagining ruins was one way that Europeans debated art and governance, especially how classical ideas about culture and sovereignty (*translatio studii* and *translatio imperii*) might help them understand modernity's empires.[2] Andrew Hui suggests the European Renaissance was when the ruin became a "distinct category of cultural discourse" and an "inspirational force for the poetic imagination" (2). Renaissance authors sought more "enduring artifacts" than classical ruins by absorbing the past and allowing for its future "appropriation and mutation" (Hui 2). Hui points in particular to the tradition of *spolia* by which ruins provide for materials for newer buildings (3). With adaptation and rebuilding, ruins are "severed from their contexts of production" and so are "formless" without intervention or restoration, Susan Stewart observes (2). For empires, ruins could be a ghostly haunting, spectral but durable (Stoler 10; Keach; Camoglu 146). Anne Janowitz intuits the peculiarity of ruins when she notes how evidence of decay – spoiled cottages and broken castles – could nonetheless become symbols of British national unity (2).

Transporting these dynamics to Asia places Britain in a complex cultural and imperial setting. William Marsden, seeking to capture the "unaccustomed and striking objects" of Sumatra, first thought to "give my sketch the form of a poem, to be denominated the *Malaiad*" – an English-language epic of Sumatran history (21). After he abandoned this project, he turned to a "general account of the island, in a physical, moral, and political view" that became the *History of Sumatra* (Marsden 21). Epic poetry preceded Orientalist treatise. Marsden's pattern is strikingly similar to William Jones, who was already well versed in Arabic and Persian poetics when he sailed for India in 1784 with a plan for a never-completed epic poem called *Britannia Discovered* that told a story of Britain's founding as an *Aeneid*-like quest resisted by Hindu deities. The poem offers political advice throughout its wildly telescoping geographies and temporalities, such as when Jones's nationalist epic suggests that Indigenous Indians should be governed by their own laws, not those of foreigners. Upon arrival in India, Jones maintained his poetry, but he also embarked on a governmental career that included inquiry in the region's legal customs.

Luís de Camões's sixteenth-century epic of Vasco da Gama's journeys, and Portugal's Asian colonies, *Os Lusíadas*, was a significant precursor, and it was translated by Company employee Julius Mickle into "a manifesto for building the right and most moral kind of empire" (DeWispelare 207). Irwin purchased Mickle's translation while in Madras and it served as a model for his poetry.[3] The meaning of ruins remained a live conversation throughout eighteenth-century India – Fort William College, an institution dedicated to the legal and linguistic training of EIC employees, included public debates

## 5 Anglophone Epics and Ruin Poetry in India

on the assertion that antiquities allow the "curious traveller" to "trace the progress of the arts, and the grandeur and declension of empires" (College of Fort William 23). Ruins informed imperial administration in much the same way that epics informed treatises.

Attention to South Asia's ruins undermines the idea that the English merely transported their customs abroad. John Plotz has argued for the "exceptional power" that "discrete objects" of Englishness came to possess overseas and Ian Baucom has argued for how English elements, such as cricket pitches and gothic architecture, literalized otherwise metaphorical national identities (Plotz 20; Baucom 4). But in South Asia these discrete objects and literal architectures were frequently positioned together with the many languages and long histories of Indigenous sovereignties they could not avoid: Cricket whites and gothic architecture receded behind Hindu temples and Mughal fortresses, which were inescapable reminders of forces beyond British imperialism. The EIC frequently compared itself to past empires and ancient Rome-structured "Romantic poetics and theories of the imagination," Jonathan Sachs notes (20). But Rome's classical antiquity was only one element of this contest over expansion and Britain's Asian administrators of empire contended with past and current imperial sovereignties such as the Ottoman, Mughal, and Qing dynasties.

For colonial administrators such as Irwin, ruins were a means of administrative thinking and poetry a coherent expression of imperial policy. Ruins were cautionary governance, not hauntology, and aesthetics responded to crisscrossing sovereignties. The caution of imperial ruins was comparative – at the same time that figures like George McCartney, Irwin's superior in Madras, delivered bold expositions about a "vast empire, on which the sun never sets," others saw fragile interconnected domains in danger of corroding (McCartney 55). Ruins provided material access to otherwise remote histories as reminders of what might be. Ruins were the *memento mori* of empire.

### Eyles Irwin's Ruin Poetry

Ruins as a *memento mori* for empires was an idea inherited from classicism for educated authors such as Irwin, who was born in Calcutta in 1751 to an Irish family that had become associated with the Company. His father, brother, son, and nephew were all employed by the Company at some point in their lives. Irwin was sent to England from Calcutta at a "tender age," where he was educated before returning to India in 1766 as a covenanted "writer" – a scribe/accountant at Fort St. George, Madras (Anon. 179–81).

Figure 5.1. George Willison, *Eyles Irwin*, oil on canvas, c. 1776. This portrait was composed when Irwin was about twenty-five years old and employed in Madras (Archer 106). Private collection © Christie's Images/Bridgeman Images.

He had returned to India at a crucial moment: after the British had captured Bengal and achieved the right to collect taxes, which, in the understated words of one administrative report, showed such an "immense Fortune acquired with such Rapidity" that its consequences could not be ignored (British Library 457). Irwin progressed through the EIC's administrative hierarchy and traveled throughout southern India, four times between Europe and India, and once back and forth to China as part of George McCartney's first British embassy to the Qing Empire (Figure 5.1). He wrote both poetry and prose throughout his extensive administrative career, much of it travel writing that utilizes ruins to assess questions about British colonialism in India.

Proximity was important for his writing and instructive endnotes in his poems were meant to offer authentic knowledge about Asian subjects and places. His ruin poems are akin to a set of antiquities or an archaeological dig, with Irwin collecting a deep past with his verse. His aspiration is temporal as much as spatial: To seize what otherwise might seem transient. Irwin fashions his entire career around the premise that relics can be preserved in acts of writing (and in drawing: He frequently sketched the settings he encountered and had them engraved for his publications, leading a

## 5 Anglophone Epics and Ruin Poetry in India

reviewer for *The Scot's Magazine* to describe one publication as "a poem, a history-piece, and a landscape" [Boswell 600]).

While returning to India from England and Ireland in the early 1780s, Irwin went through Egypt and the Arabian Peninsula and then across the Indian Ocean. He wrote about his encounters with the ruins of Europe and the Levant in his *Occasional Epistles* (*OE*) (1783), a collection of travel poems. Palmyra's ruins were evidence of being previously a "Guardian of the arts, and Freedom's younger child" due to its patronage of the classical philosopher Longinus and its resistance to Rome (Irwin, *OE* III. 79). Baghdad was the Garden of Eden, where "Adam first his blushing consort knew" (Irwin, *OE* III. 13–14) but also a "sad reverse" of this past whose "ruins yield" evidence of "our parents' crime," referring to Adam and Eve (Irwin, *OE* III. 20, 19).

In Greece and Rhodes, "where the Colossus rear'd his tow'ring head, / And where his shatter'd frame the groaning earth o'erspread" (Irwin, *OE* II. 67–8), ruins display the dangers of Muslim empires. Like the Colossus, the "Turk" – that is, the Ottoman Empire – has

> too large a realm embrac'd,
> One foot on Asia, one on Europe plac'd,
> Totters at Destiny's destructive call,
> And strong convulsions indicate his fall.
> 
> (Irwin, *OE* II. 70–4)

Engaging with the Ottoman Empire in art was a "vexed" enterprise because it frequently led to the translation and deformation of otherwise familiar genres (O'Quinn 3). For Irwin, such vexation appears as a verse politics of place, evident in the sedimented ruins that demonstrate how Greece's "former lustre" is "worn away" by Ottoman suppression (Irwin, *OE* II. 78–9). (Unmentioned is the irony of a British colonizer complaining of an empire that spans Asia and Europe.)

The idea that ruins are the worn remains of once-vibrant polities is a common theme among Irwin's poems, arguably learned while he was stationed in southern India at Madras, Tinnelvelly (Tirunelveli), and Madura (Madurai). For a brief period, Irwin was Madura's superintendent of revenue and, while in that area, he perceived contestation between historically Hindu and Muslim states. Despite the EIC in effect acting as an agent of Muslim Mughals, Irwin portrays Muslims as oppressors of Hindus, who in his description were docile and feminine, an "inoffensive race" that "walks thro' life in peace" (Irwin, *OE* II. 154–6).

Irwin was aware of the complicated interactions among the different groups, religious practices, and sovereignties of South Asia. His poetic treatment of Muslims and Hindus simplifies a complex situation to legitimize British imperialism. Irwin, like many EIC administrators, expressed antipathy toward empire while simultaneously regretting its supposed necessity. Like William Jones, Irwin's perception of the relationship between British liberty and colonial exertion was systematic but inconsistent.

Aversion to Islam and fascination with Hinduism are most evident in Irwin's lengthy unpublished poem "The Ruins of Madura, or, the Hindoo Garden." Composed between 1784, when Irwin was stationed in southern India, and 1792 when he traveled to China, it is a generically unusual poem – a supernatural Orientalist epistle set in Asia but written in heroic couplets with pastoral, georgic, and epic modes.[4] Its supernatural elements explain the historical realities of eighteenth-century British sovereignty by appealing to Hindu deities and religious sites. Irwin's verse politics mix his classical education with what he learned about South Asia from colonial administration and personal observation.

"The Ruins of Madura" describes the evocative architecture and once-lush Persian-style gardens of Madura, the capital of the early modern Madurai Nayaka state. The Madurai Nayakas were agents of the larger Vijayanagara, an empire that in the words of Burton Stein changed southern India from "its medieval past to its modern future" through a "segmentary state" system of coherent units bound together by ritual sovereignty rather than through territorial integrity and political singularity, as was the model of European nation-states (Stein, *Vijayanagara* 140; Stein, *Peasant State* 23, 266–75).[5] Sovereignty in these precolonial South Asian states was organized into "concentric layers" from the inner realm of kings and courts out toward the "blurred, chaotic fringe" of volatile border challenges and disputes (Howes 226). Madurai was linked with Vijayanagara first as a subordinate, but then as a successor. What attracted Irwin to its history was the contest between southern Hindu kingdoms and encroaching Muslim states (allied with the Delhi Sultanate in the early modern period and the Mughals after the Delhi Sultanate ceased to exist).

Madura, especially its temple and palace ruins, engrossed British Orientalists, including Colin Mackenzie, who visited early in his Indian career, and Thomas and William Daniell, who produced sketches, paintings, and engravings of the city which they collected in their volumes of *Oriental Scenery*. Adam Blackader, who was surgeon resident at Madura throughout the 1780s, wrote a letter to Joseph Banks and the Society of Antiquaries in London, publicizing Madura's existence and commending the "immense size" and "workmanship" of its architecture (Blackader 449). By the late eighteenth century, decline had eliminated its vibrancy. Thomas and William Daniell captured this decay in their paintings and engravings

## 5 Anglophone Epics and Ruin Poetry in India

Figure 5.2. Thomas Daniell, "Ruins of the Palace, Madura," c. 1790s, hand-colored aquatint on paper. This image was engraved by William Daniell and included in *Oriental Scenery* (1797–98). Courtesy of the President and Fellows of Trinity College, Oxford.

and wrote that the ruins showed "evident marks" of their "former grandeur" (Daniell 10) (Figure 5.2).

Irwin's poem tries to rejuvenate this "former grandeur," and, as in the georgic tradition, to create "harmony" from what was a "land of strife."[6] His goal is to compose "themes fortuitous and wand'ring lays" that prevent Madura "from being forgotten" (Irwin, "Ruins" I. 20). He found evidence of this former grandeur in the Pudu Mandapa, or the "new hall," of the Minakshi Sundareshvara Temple (hereafter Minakshi) and the "Hindoo Garden" that Irwin claims was nearby. Both are described by Irwin as an architectural "eulogy" for "Trimul Naig," referring to Tirumala Nayaka (also known as Tirumalai Nayaka) (r. 1623–1659), the ruler who achieved autonomy for Madurai from the Vijayanagara. The Pudu Mandapa was constructed between 1622 and 1633 with Tirumala's patronage, but the Minakshi temple is much older, built intermittently between the twelfth century and the seventeenth century into a large complex that became a significant Hindu religious site (Bes 450). The new hall exists outside of the temple complex as a place for festive gathering and public performance,

Figure 5.3. "Tremal Naig's Choultry, Madura." Etching and aquatint, drawn by Thomas Daniell and engraved by Thomas and William Daniell, 1798, showing the long hall and succession of Madurai Nayaka rulers. Included in *Oriental Scenery* (1797–98). Courtesy of the President and Fellows of Trinity College, Oxford.

"externalizing" the "previously internal, delimited space" of the temple that was restricted to some caste communities (Fisher 178). Europeans were prevented from entering the temple, so the new hall's numerous pillars that depict holy scenes, mythical animals (*yali*), and the succession of rulers of the Madurai state and their consorts, including Tirumala, was a focus of European fascination (Figures 5.3 and 5.4) (Branfoot 193, 215). The new hall was well documented by Europeans and was considered remarkable because so few temples in southern India had recognizable patrons (Branfoot 215). Being able to identify Tirumala Nayaka's patronage attracted a politically motivated poet like Irwin to the structure.

The architecture of these buildings testifies to Hindu sophistication. While the ruins of the Madura palace possessed "massive columns" of "just Proportion" and "rustic stile" (Irwin, "Ruins" II. 86) that evoked ancient Greece, the new hall's richly intricate statuary reminds Irwin of the "Ruins of Palmyra, Balbec, and Persepolis" (Irwin, "Ruins" II. 65 notes). From these columns and complicated carvings Irwin intuits "a Sever'd Empire"

5 Anglophone Epics and Ruin Poetry in India

Figure 5.4. "Architectural drawing of Tirumala Nayak at Madura," pen and ink on paper, c. 1780s. This drawing, thought to be commissioned by Adam Blackader and drawn by an Indian artist, shows Tirumala Nayaka and his wives on a pillar of the new hall. The writing at the top is in Tamil and includes marks reading "68 N," "68 W," "68 S," and "68 E." © Victoria and Albert Museum, London (AL 7766:87) (Guy 209–10).

akin to the Palmyrene Empire that briefly achieved independence from Rome during the third century CE before falling (Irwin, "Ruins" I. 64). In Madura's ruins, like those of Greece, Irwin intuits lessons, and these lessons are absorbed in the politics of his verse.

Paired with this evocative architecture is the "Hindoo garden" of the poem's title, which Irwin describes as a sumptuous happy valley. Although Irwin never identifies the exact location of this garden, supposedly abandoned and lost, he describes it as a "tuneful grove" and "Sylvan place" away from "hollow Courts" of political power (Irwin, "Ruins" II. 147, 150, 148). He claims it was one of the few examples in India of Persian-style gardens and compares it with "Baug Erim," referring to Bāgh-e Eram, the Eram Garden in Shiraz, which had been cultivated since the eleventh century CE Seljuk Empire and is currently a UNESCO World Heritage site (Irwin, "Ruins" II. 148, 150, 147). In Irwin's telling, the "Hindoo garden" takes on fantastical characteristics and his poem includes long digressions on flora and fauna, including exclamatory descriptions of teak, sandal, bamboo,

87

mango (in which "the Nect'rine and the Peach unite"), jackfruit, pomegranates, guava, plantain, and apples, the "Asian brood" (Irwin, "Ruins" II. 160–70, 176–88). This lush ecology is the setting for the downfall of the Nayaka dynasty, which Irwin attributes to Tirumala Nayaka's mistaken jealousy of his alluring wife, "Castouri" (*kasturi*, a term from many South Asian languages, especially Sanskrit, for a fragrant musk), who had sought refuge in the garden. In Irwin's poem, Tirumala attempts to murder her in a fit of rage, but Castouri is saved by a Hindu deity who transforms her into songbird hiding among the bushes, an Ovidian transformation that reminds listeners of Tirumala's mistakes. (Irwin's tale obscures the fact that the Madurai Nayakas did not collapse until the mid eighteenth century, nearly a century after Tirumala Nayaka's reign.)

Irwin admitted to the novelty of such supernatural episodes and conceded that the foreignness of his settings, characters, and vocabulary might repel many domestic British readers. He affirmed in one letter from 1786 that he expected his poem would meet with "the objection" of critics who would "start [startle] to the barbarous names of Indostan," but he insisted that they were "musical in my ear" (Irwin, Hayley Manuscripts). If his descriptions of the ruins and the gardens of Madura were "devoid of oriental terms," he argued, they might "equally be applied to the ruins and gardens of Europe" (Irwin, Hayley Manuscripts). Being "equally applied to the ruins and gardens of Europe" was not Irwin's goal. The ruins of Madura, and its Hindu stories and fables, offered him an opportunity to recover South Asian architecture, environments, and history and with them to reinject politics into pastoral, georgic, and epic epistolary poetry situated beyond Britain in its overseas empire.

### South Asian History, Politics, and Poetic Invention in the British Empire

Artistic renewal of the type Irwin covets had political consequences for governance. Irwin ultimately wishes for the "Ruins of Madura" to "sustain the Epic theme, / And from the Chaos alien peace redeem" (Irwin, "Ruins" II. 460–1). He hopes that "India's welfare" will "prompt the future Song" with expectation that his poem may "Repress Ambition, quell usurious strife, / And trampeled Nations elevate to life!" (Irwin, "Ruins" II. 528–9, 531–2).

It remains unclear whether the elevated nations include Hindu states. Nonetheless, Irwin sees the possibilities in epics and ruin poetry for a better understanding of British imperial governance. Ruin poetry was meant to corral multi-imperial, ecological, and architectural comparisons that were historically informed yet relevant to the present. Ruin poetry reconciles

## 5 Anglophone Epics and Ruin Poetry in India

obvious oppression of India by the Company with imperial success. Irwin worries that British power is "Convuls'd" by ambition and so "her Bards to Folly's storm submit, / While rivals rob her of the Realms of Wit!" (Irwin, "Ruins" II. 555, 557–8). If Britain does not learn from other empires, he believes, it will fail in its own mission. To misread ruins, and poems about ruins, is to risk losing empire, whose beneficence might rejuvenate Anglophone poetry and liberate Hindus from Muslims (and from other Europeans). It was, and remains, a self-serving contradiction, but among Mediterranean, Near Eastern, and southern Indian ruins, Irwin sees warnings that he transforms into poems. Epics and ruin poetry reimagined writing about empire not as an attempt at personal fame but as an extension of imperial policy. Epic poets, such as Virgil and Camões, were seen to make legitimate contributions to understanding empire and ruin poetry was the Enlightenment's instrument for continuing that tradition.

Recovering how and why British imperialists valorized particular forms (epistle; heroic couplets) and modes (georgic; epic) to advance their politics reintroduces needed historical specificity to analysis of postcolonial literary studies and provincializes the study of eighteenth-century Anglophone literary publics. Scholars of India have shaped the canon of English language verse to the "contours of nationalism," which has caused a "curious dehistoricization" of the "contestation and conversation" that created English-language literary culture in India in the first place (Gibson 2, 4). Rosinka Chaudhuri similarly notes that English-language poetry of India has had a "beleaguered and secret existence" (5), while attention to imperial assemblages and artifacts have focused on their appropriation by colonizers with less attention as to why. Emphasis on the imitation of British national traditions abroad has caused scholars to overlook how southern Indian politics influenced the arts and governance of imperial administrators such as Irwin.

We should reconsider the extent to which British colonialism was easily agreed upon in the late eighteenth century through a unified (even if contentious) national identity that could be projected seamlessly across the globe. Instead, the verse politics of epics and ruins debate the future of the British Empire by appealing to the relics of the Near East and Asia. Such broad comparison was not just aesthetic Orientalism but also attempts at policymaking. Poetry brings the past into contact with the administration of empire, something that scholars have forgotten as the quotidian elements of empire have disappeared into our desire for more systematic models of how imperialism created the modern world on a global scale. Ruins remind us to historicize the immediate contests among competing polities in South Asia and, in that way, epics and ruin poetry disrupt literary criticism that remains dependent on unified nations to make sense of the vast changes brought about by empire. Verse politics is one of the most effective ways to bring poetry back into the realm of relevancy by reattaching it to an urgent sense of history and government.

## Notes

1. On neoclassical architecture and British Empire see Hoock; *diwani* refers to the EIC's assumption of tax collection in Bengal and Bihar on behalf of the Mughal Empire.
2. On this relationship see Curtius.
3. Irwin's name is listed incorrectly under the subscribers with a surname beginning with "J" rather than "I."
4. The poem is housed at Yale University's Beinecke Library as Osborn c234. It is perhaps a fair copy for publication, which never occurred, it may have been part of the William Hayley papers sold in the nineteenth century. Special thanks to the Beinecke for digitizing Osborn c234.
5. On the Vijayanagara state and *nayaka*, or warrior rulers, see Dirks 45–9. On the ambiguity of the term *nayaka*, see Talbot, 58.
6. Irwin, "Ruins" II. 467–8. Subsequent references refer to epistle and line numbers. Quotations from unpaginated endnotes also refers to the corresponding epistle and line numbers which organize the notes.

## Works Cited

Anon. "Memoirs of Eyles Irwin, Esq." *European Magazine*, vol. 15, March 1789, pp. 179–81.
Archer, Mildred. *India and British Portraiture 1770–1825*. Sotheby Parke Bernet, 1979.
Baucom, Ian. *Out of Place: Englishness, Empire, and the Locations of Identity*. Princeton UP, 1999.
Bes, Lennart. *The Heirs of Vijayanagara: Court Politics in Early Modern South India*. Leiden UP, 2022.
Blackader, Adam. "XL. Description of the Great Pagoda of Madura, the Choultry of Trimul Naik, in a Letter from Mr. Adam Blackader." *Archaeologia, or, Miscellaneous Tracts Relating to Antiquity*, vol. 10. Printed by John Nichols, 1792, pp. 449–59.
Branfoot, Crispin. "Tirumala Nayak's 'New Hall' and the European Study of the South Indian Temple." *Journal of the Royal Asiatic Society Series 3*, vol. 11, no. 2, 2001, pp. 191–217.
British Library. India Office Records (IOR) E/4/863.
Boswell, James[?]. *The Scot's Magazine*, vol. 45, Jan. 1783, p. 600.
Camoglu, Arif. "'Supreme in Ruin': Empire's Afterlife in Romantic Encounters with Imperial Ruins." *European Romantic Review*, vol. 32, no. 2, 2021, pp. 145–61.
Chaudhuri, Rosinka. "Introduction." *A History of English Poetry in India*, edited by Rosinka Chaudhuri, Cambridge UP, 2016, pp. 1–17.

Cohen, Michael C. "Peddlers, Poems, and Local Culture: The Case of Jonathan Plummer, a 'Ballad-Monger' in Nineteenth-Century England." *ESQ: A Journal of the American Renaissance*, vol. 54, nos. 1–4, 2008, pp. 9–32.

College of Fort William. *Essays by the Students of the College of Fort William In Bengal*. Honorable Company's Press, 1802–04.

Curtius, Ernst Robert. *European Literature and the Latin Middle Ages*. 1953. Translated by Willard R. Trask, Princeton UP, 1990.

Daniell, Thomas et al. *Oriental Scenery: Twenty-Four Views in Hindoostan, Taken in the Year 1792*. Published as the Act directs by Thos. Daniell, Howland Street, Fitzroy Square, 1797

DeWispelare, Daniel. *Multilingual Subjects: On Standard English, Its Speakers, and Others in the Long Eighteenth-Century*. U of Pennsylvania P, 2017.

Dirks, Nicholas B. *The Hollow Crown: Ethnohistory of an Indian Kingdom*, 2nd ed. U of Michigan P, 1993.

Fisher, Elaine M. *Hindu Pluralism: Religion and the Public Sphere in Early Modern South India*. U of California P, 2017.

Gibson, Mary Ellis. *Indian Angles: English Verse in Colonial India from Jones to Tagore*. Ohio UP, 2011.

Guy, John. "Tirumala Nāyak's Choultry an Eighteenth Century Model." *Makaranda: Essays in Honour of Dr. James C. Harle*, edited by Claudine Bautze-Picron, Sri Satguru, 1990, pp. 207–33.

Hoock, Holger. *Empires of the Imagination: Politics, War, and the Arts in the British World, 1750–1850*. Profile, 2010.

Howes, Jennifer. *The Courts of Pre-colonial South India: Material Culture and Kingship*. RoutledgeCurzon, 2003.

Hui, Andrew. *The Poetics of Ruins in Renaissance Literature*. Fordham UP, 2016.

Irwin, Eyles. Hayley Manuscripts XI Letter 53, Oct. 20, 1786, Fitzwilliam Museum.
 *Occasional Epistles. Written during a Journey from London to Busrah, in the Gulf of Persia, in the Years 1780 and 1781*. Printed for J. Dodsley, 1783.
 "The Ruins of Madura, or, the Hindoo Garden," unpub. manuscript, Beinecke Library, Yale University, Osborn c234.

Janowitz, Anne. *England's Ruins: Poetic Purpose and the National Landscape*. Basil Blackwell, 1990.

Kaul, Suvir. *Poems of Nation, Anthems of Empire: English Verse in the Long Eighteenth Century*. UP of Virginia, 2000.

Keach, William. "The Ruins of Empire and the Contradictions of Restoration: Barbauld, Byron, Hemans." *Romanticism and Disaster*, edited by Jacques Khalip and David Collings. *Romantic Circles*, January 2012, web publication, https://romantic-circles.org/praxis/disaster/keach (accessed April 28, 2025).

Marsden, William. *A Brief Memoir of the Life and Writings of the Late William Marsden, Written by Himself*. J. L. Cox and Sons, 1838.

[McCartney, George]. *An Account of Ireland in 1773*. 1773.

Mickle, Julius. *The Lusiad; or, The Discovery of India, An Epic Poem*. Jackson and Lister, 1776.

Mulholland, James. *Before the Raj: Writing Early Anglophone India*. Johns Hopkins UP, 2021.

O'Quinn, Daniel. *Engaging the Ottoman Empire: Vexed Mediations, 1690–1815*. U of Pennsylvania P, 2019.

Plotz, John. *Portable Property: Victorian Culture on the Move.* Princeton UP, 2008.
Sachs, Jonathan. *Romantic Antiquity: Rome in the British Imagination, 1789–1832.* Oxford UP, 2010.
Sen, Sudipta. *Distant Sovereignty: National Imperialism and the Origins of British India.* Routledge, 2002.
Stein, Burton. *The New Cambridge History of India.* Part 1, vol. 2: *Vijayanagara.* Cambridge UP, 1989.
    *Peasant State and Society in Medieval South India.* Oxford UP, 1980.
Stewart, Susan. *The Ruins Lesson: Meaning and Material in Western Culture.* U of Chicago P, 2020.
Stoler, Ann Laura. "Introduction 'The Rot Remains': From Ruins and Ruination." *Imperial Debris: On Ruins and Ruination*, edited by Ann Laura Stoler, Duke UP, 2013, pp. 1–35.
Talbot, Cynthia. *Precolonial India in Practice: Society, Region, and Identity in Medieval Andhra.* Oxford UP, 2001.

# 6

NICOLE N. ALJOE

# The Black Atlantic, Slave Narratives, and Empire

Published narratives of the experiences of enslavement are often associated with the US and narrators such as Frederick Douglass and Harriet Jacobs, as well as with US abolitionist publishers in the Northeast, such as Isaac Knapp in Boston. However, a significant number of slave narratives, about one-half of those produced before the 1860s, were created and published in the UK. Narratives of the lives of enslaved Black people throughout the Black Atlantic have been written and dictated by a number of Black people in Britain, both those born in Britain or its colonies, as well as visitors to the island. This chapter will examine the range of these texts produced over the course of the long eighteenth century – the period between 1688 and 1838 that is associated with the rise, consolidation, and cessation of British participation in African Atlantic slavery. These texts by or about the experiences of enslaved Africans showcase how Black Atlantic slave narratives participated directly and dynamically within discussions of identity, nation, and spirituality, as well as discussion of slavery and abolition – all elements critical to the foundation of the British Empire. In addition to exploring the poignant role of slave narratives in conversation with British discursive systems, the chapter will also offer close readings of six texts – "A Speech Made by a Black of Guardaloupe [sic], at the Funeral of a Fellow-Negro" (1709), "The Speech of Moses Bon Sàam" (1735), "The Speech of Mr. John Talbot Campo-Bell" (1736), *Joanna: A Female West Indian Slave* (1820), "Narrative of the Enslavement of Ottobah Cugoano, a Native of Africa; Published by Himself on the Year 1787," and *The History of Mary Prince, a West Indian Slave* (1831). Each of these texts illuminates questions of form and notions of voice – the key discourses that the slave narratives were in conversation with – as well as the key tropes of the genre. Ever since the appearance of one of the first texts about the life of an enslaved man, *Oroonoko* by Aphra Behn in 1688, narratives by or about the enslaved published in Britain before the end of formal slavery in most British colonies in 1838 have been in implicit and explicit conversations with notions of empire.

93

I want to begin this chapter with a summary of the conversations scholars and critics have had regarding these texts about the lives of enslaved Black people in the British Empire. The earliest critical discussions of Black British writing that did not immediately dismiss or denigrate the narratives often discussed the texts as historical documents and as offering evidence of the existence of Black British history rather than highlighting their literary import. These engagements frequently did not distinguish amongst the writings by Black people in Britain, and texts by enslaved people were often discussed without differentiation alongside texts by Blacks who either were born free or whose exact status was unclear. Additionally, early employment of the term "Black" in the UK context was often intended to include not only African-descended people, but also South and East Asians.[1] Texts such as Edward Scobie's *Black Britannia* (1972), as well as Folarin Shyllon's texts *Black Slaves in Britain* (1974) and *Black People in Britain 1555–1833* (1977) offer some of the earliest engagements with early Black British histories and texts that highlight the manner in which African-descended authors and narrators participated in British society. Building on such work, historians like Peter Fryer brought to bear the theoretical and sociological work of Black scholars from the Caribbean and Africa who were educated in England, like Stuart Hall, Folarin Shyllon, and Eric Williams, to offer new perspectives on the necessity of the inclusion of Black British experiences within the broader umbrella of general British history. These efforts culminate in recent work by Miranda Kaufman, Michael Ohajuru, and David Olusoga, which has brought more of the complexities of Britain's Black history to the fore through the venues of popular history, TV documentaries, and other media. Literary critics have contributed to these conversations begun by historians by highlighting the significance and participation of Black British writing with the forms and aesthetics of literary discourses. Scholars such as Ziggi Alexander, Joan Anim-Addo, 2004 Paul Edwards, and Victor Mtubani, writing in the 1980s and 1990s, drew upon these foundational historical studies and brought more critical literary analysis to the texts in order to create what we might call genealogies of Black British writing. Such work acknowledges the multiplicity of early Black writing, which more recent work, such as that by Ryan Hanley, also takes up: "writing produced by [B]lack people during this period reflected not a homogenous [B]lack perspective but a staggering *diversity* of views and experiences" (7). Such perspectives offer a welcome expansion of the literary discursive contexts within which we can consider Black writing by articulating the myriad discourses with which Black British writing conversed. More recent scholarly engagement continues to complicate our understanding of early Black British writing. For example, the recent republication of Gretchen Gerzina's book, *Black England*, is notable for the way in which Gerzina joins historical specificity with literary analysis. Like Hanley's text, Gerzina's close focus on the British context of early Black Atlantic writing shifts the focus from US exceptionalism and notions tied to the progressive narrations of the "American Dream" to highlighting the multiplicity of diaspora and the Black Atlantic.

Shifting our perspective of the slave narrative from a US to a transnational, Black Atlantic frame, in addition to allowing us to explore other discourses that the narratives were in conversation with, and broader international contexts, as well as notions of empire and movement, also will enable us to consider questions about the naming of the genre.

Elsewhere, I've made the argument that our understanding of the genre "slave narrative" has been significantly constrained, informed, and overly determined by the explosion of the genre in the US during the mid nineteenth century with the advent of popular narratives by Frederick Douglass, William Wells, Brown, Harriet Jacobs, Mrs. Keckley, and others. Moreover, the term itself is contradictory since the concepts of "enslavement" and "narrative" are distinct. Does it make sense to call the narratives by enslaved Africans and African-descended people "slave narratives"? Are these texts instead "slave's narrative" as the volume by Davis and Gates suggests? Are they auto/biographies, abolitionist propaganda, spiritual conversion narratives, or captivity narratives?

Relatedly, scholars such as P. Gabrielle Foreman have advocated for a change in terminology away from the use of the word "slave" to "enslaved person." The impetus for this replacement is the fact that the term "slave" connotes the notion that the individual is a special kind of person and distances them from other "normal" individuals under the umbrella of humanity and evacuates any semblance of nuance. The term "enslaved person," however, highlights the process of enslavement – and the fact that this process is something that is done to "normal" human beings, rather than a characteristic of their humanity – enslavement happens to persons – as Frederick Douglass illuminates in his narrative with the infamous phrase: "You have seen how man is turned into a slave, now you will see how a slave is turned into a man" (76). Given this change in terminology and nomenclature, how should we refer to the narratives produced by these narrators about their experiences of enslavement? This has been a debate almost from the very beginning. As numerous scholars have pointed out, this "new" genre came into being by appropriating elements from various genres, such as spiritual and conversion narratives, captivity narratives, picaresque adventure tales, the early novel, witness testimony, reportage, and others (Fisch). In one of the earliest analyses of the genre, American clergyman Ephraim Peabody referred to these texts as "pictures of slavery." It has been referred to as "slave testimony." Historian Marion Starling referred to them as "slave narratives," and Charles Davis and Henry Louis Gates Jr. referred to the texts as "the slave's narrative" in the title of their edited, field-defining volume on the genre. They have also been referred to as "slavery narratives." Other scholars have referred to these texts as "enslaved narratives," "narratives of the lives of the enslaved," and "narratives of enslavement" (Noel). So how should we refer to these texts? Foreman and others point out that the language and terminology we use to describe and define these texts are essential. Indeed, when I was first asked to write this chapter, I asked the editor to change the title from "enslaved narratives" to "slave narratives." Part of my reasoning was because the term "enslaved narrative" does not seem to describe the variety of texts under this rubric adequately. Moreover, the syntax of the term "enslaved narrative" seems to suggest that it is the narratives themselves that are/were enslaved rather than the fact that the narratives were focused on the reflections and testimonies of the experiences of enslavement. Consequently, I feel that the terms "slave narratives" or "slavery narratives" offer a more expansive umbrella for the inclusion of a greater variety of texts.

\*\*\*

The default to broader inclusion in terms of generic nomenclature also reflects that, as Hanley and others note, the earliest iterations of the genre were not always explicitly tied to notions of abolitionism. Instead, these foundational texts often drew from a variety of paratexts and other types of texts that were intended to provide vivid "pictures" and representations of the experiences of enslavement for European readers who had not traveled to or had experiences with the locations of enslavement in the Caribbean and Africa. The generic variety of these texts reveals their various discursive influences and conversations reflected by the tremendous rise of print culture that occurred over the course of the eighteenth century. For example, texts such as *Oroonoko* (1688), "The Speech by a Black of Guardaloupe [sic]" (1709), the "Memoirs of Job Ben Solomon" (1730), and Ukawsaw Gronniosaw's *A Narrative of the Most Remarkable Particulars in the Life of James Albert Ukawsaw Gronniosaw, an African Prince* (1770) all draw heavily on the forms and rhetorics of reportage associated with the eyewitness report. Each of these texts paints a vivid picture of the narrative occasion: Behn provides specific details about the landscape, flora, and fauna of Africa and the Caribbean, and the speech from Guadeloupe provides specifical details about the funerary experiences of the island's enslaved and maroon populations,[2] and Job Ben Solomon and Gronniosaw provide dynamic details about their experiences of being born in freedom in cosmopolitan nations in western Africa.

Through highlighting a variety of voices and experiences of enslavement, these early texts are remarkable in their formal and aesthetic diversity – Behn's text draws more heavily on fictionalizing elements, the Guadeloupe and Bon Sàam texts emphasize recorded speech, and Diallo's and Gronniosaw's texts recount their "interesting" life experiences. And, though offering a variety of perspectives and formally differentiated, these early texts are also remarkable in their similar efforts to emphasize and draw attention to the voices of the enslaved. The most affecting aspects of Behn's text are the various speeches by Oroonoko and his wife Imoinda; similarly, Gronniosaw and Diallo's life narratives are framed as spoken narratives. Though grounded in the rhetorics of reportage, this focus on notions of "voice" also places the enslaved narrators in conversation with the rhetorics of the "essay" and its intended goal of persuasion.

Some of the earliest writings about slave experiences are presented as transcriptions of overheard speeches; for example, "The Speech of a Black at Guardaloupe [sic]," "The Speech of Moses Bon-Sàam," and "The Speech of John Talbot Campo-Bell." All three speeches encourage readers to reconsider the capabilities of enslaved Africans by connecting to and drawing upon notions of voice. Each text represents a specific voice recounting a particular experience and making a separate argument. And though it is possible that each text might not have actually been written by or transcribed from a real enslaved person, the fact remains that each text is explicitly presented as such, which relies upon the assumption that such a text could, in actuality have been produced by an enslaved person. While space prohibits a thorough examination of each speech, a cursory articulation of how each narrative is in conversation with notions of speech can be helpful here. "The Speech of a Black at Guardaloupe [sic]" was supposedly recorded after the writer heard a funeral oration of an enslaved man. It mainly draws upon the rhetoric of the humanity of enslaved Africans. And while it might be a ventriloquization, it is also possible that there might have been elements of truth in the speech. In addition to asserting the humanity of Africans, the speeches also draw upon political rhetoric. "The Speech of Moses Bon Sàam" offers engagement with political rhetoric, though historian James Greene initially asserted that the narrative must have been a fabrication because he felt it was unlikely that an enslaved person would have known natural philosophy. However, given what we know about the complexity of the experiences of the enslaved, it is also within the realm of possibility that the speaker could have been familiar with philosophy. This speech offers a clear anti-slavery argument and articulates what we might call an early version of pro-Black messaging: "What Preference, in the Name of that *mysterious God*, whom these Insulters of our *Colour* pretend to worship;

what wild imaginary Superiority of dignity has their pale sickly *Whiteness* to boast of, when compared with our *Majestick Glossiness!*" (Anon., "The Speech of Moses Bon Sàam" 103). The purported speaker raises his voice to "enumerate [the] *Miseries*" communicated in a "lamentable *Howl*" (Anon., "The Speech of Moses Bon Sàam" 105) and advocates for his audience to find refuge in the "*Fastness* of these *inaccessible Mountains*" from which they can "continue on the *Defensive*, [...] make[ing] *Incursions*, thereby weakening at once our Enemy" (Anon., "The Speech of Moses Bon Sàam" 105–6). Published soon after the Bon Sàam speech, "The Speech of John Talbot Campo-Bell" is one of the few narratives of the lives of the enslaved that is couched in proslavery terms. And while it is possible that the proslavery slant might suggest that the narrative was ventriloquized, and indeed, James Tobin includes the speech in a list of texts written by the proslavery Reverend Robert Robertson of Nevis (108), it is also possible the text could represent the beliefs of some of the enslaved who were invested in the stability often associated with social status quo. Regardless of whether the text is invented or not, the speaker articulates a nuanced proslavery argument, blaming metropolitan bankers and insurers for the slave trade, and further characterizes it as a necessary evil and argues that to end it would be to "destroy that general Balance of Trade (and, by Consequence, of Power) which wise Me think out to be maintained in the World" (Anon., "The Speech of John Talbot Campo-Bell" 120).

Intended as a direct response to Moses Bon Sàam's speech, alongside which it was published, the speaker calls on his audience not to join the maroon rebels and instead to "make ourselves, and all you are concern'd with, as easy as possible" (Anon., "The Speech of John Talbot Campo-Bell" 140). In addition to offering key engagements with notions of voice, these texts, like *Oroonoko*, which preceded them, also combined eyewitness descriptions with fictional discourses of romance and sentiment – a characteristic that would repeatedly appear in the genre. Indeed, Campo-Bell's speech is "authorized" by a sentimental portrait of his own experience of enslavement that precedes his argument. The characteristics of the portrayal of Campo-Bell's life experiences of enslavement seem very similar in terms of sentimental rhetoric to the descriptions of enslaved characters in *Oroonoko*. The speaker describes his capture in a war between the kings of Angola and Congo, a futile shipboard rebellion, and eventual enslavement in Jamaica and England, where he accompanied his enslaver while he was educated in Yorkshire and eventually Oxford. And he finally claims, "Had I not been sold from *Africa* myself, I should have been undone! Whereas now the Reverse is happily my lot!" (Anon., "The Speech of John Talbot Campo-Bell" 136).

The intimate, often sentimental portraits of these early Black Atlantic writings consequently have a great deal in common with the fictionalizing and imaginary techniques associated with the coterminous genres of allegory and the early novel. And like the early novel, early slave narratives such as "A Speech Made by a Black of Guardaloupe [sic]" (1709) and the "The Speech of Moses Bon Sàam" (1735) "worry the line" between fiction and history (Ward). Like the early novels, these early slave narratives claim to be "history" yet draw extensively upon fictionalizing techniques such as sentimental tropes and reconstructed scenes and conversations. The ambiguity of the relationships between fiction and history is particularly highlighted when one considers the narratives mentioned here alongside more explicitly fictional representations of the slave narrative, such as Aphra Behn's proto-novel, *Oroonoko*, and the likely fictionalized slave narrative, "The Speech of Mr. John Talbot Campo-Bell." What becomes clear is that the early narratives also participate in the novel's efforts to provide iconic images of particular types of humanity. For example, the Campo-Bell narrative spend a great deal of time characterizing Bon Sàam as an example of the "*black Creole* tyrants" that are "Monsters in Wickedness, Devils incarnate, Murders, Ravishers, [and] Robbers" in contradistinction to the "Gentleman who governs this island, and [...] most of the whites" who will forgive those who rebel if they submit (Anon., "The Speech of John Talbot Campo-Bell" 140, 121). The focus on characterization and stereotype, as well as numerous instances of recreated dialogue, ultimately reveals that the "novelization of genre" that William Andrews illuminates as a central feature of the paradigmatic narratives of later nineteenth-century narratives of William Wells Brown, Frederick Douglass, and Harriet Jacobs is, in fact, apparent in the earliest narratives as well.

One of the more compelling texts that engage with the boundary between fiction and history that would characterize the genre is the story of Joanna. Initially appearing in John Gabriel Stedman's military narrative, Joanna's narrative was one of the more popular sections of Stedman's narrative. It was so popular that it was eventually excised and twice published as its separate text, once in the UK in 1820 and then again in the US in 1838. Joanna's text, though mediated through Stedman, is one of the few representations of the experiences of an enslaved West Indian woman. In representing Joanna, Stedman combined the descriptions of his real experiences with Joanna with the discourses of the prevailing ideology of the day – sentiment.

In Stedman's published memoir and as well in the two excisions, Joanna is portrayed as a sentimental heroine. When we are first introduced to her, Stedman draws heavily on rhetorics associated with the heroines of eighteenth-century literary fiction – Joanna is idealized and associated with the domestic, providing Stedman and us, as readers, with a representation of European female domesticity, but transposed to the Caribbean. Joanna is characterized as beautiful, accomplished, and an appropriately gracious hostess. She nurses Stedman from illness, takes care of his fellow mercenaries, and is consistently portrayed as bringing him sustaining food. Moreover, when she is described as preferring to remain in Suriname rather than return with Stedman to the UK, this seems in line with fictional representations of European sentimental heroines who remain in the domestic space. The fictionalizing is manifest when one examines the presentation of Joanna in Stedman's unedited diaries. The diaries highlight the primarily transactional nature of Stedman's relationship with Joanna – in exchange for sex and keeping his house, Joanna and her mother earn money, access to power, and protection. This is at odds with the image in the published memoir, suggesting a kind of fictionalization. It is important to pay attention to the distinction between the image of Joanna in the diaries and that in the published memoir, because as some have argued, it might have been an effort by Stedman to situate his relatively unusual narrative of Joanna within a discourse that would be legible to his European readers.

***

And yet, despite, or maybe because of, the often wholesale appropriation of fictional strategies and techniques, the narratives would go on to play a key role in developing abolitionist discourses. The engagement with fiction, at first blush, seems a contrary fit, especially because questions of authenticity and authority were so crucial within the narratives of enslaved peoples associated with the abolitionist movement. And indeed, scholars have focused on how narratives of the lives of the enslaved, commonly understood as "slave narratives," engaged with explicit claims to authenticity and authority as distinct from those of the novel genre that developed simultaneously. These questions of authenticity are often connected to the discursive foundations and frameworks of abolitionism. To solely focus on whether or not a narrative is a "true or authentic" reflection of experiences of enslavement is to accept that narratives of the lives of the enslaved can only ever be ethnography. However, enslaved and free Black narrators and their publishers drew heavily upon engagements with notions of subjectivity and social action that appeared in other genres, such as epistolary forms and poetry, as well as the novel. And so, consequently, rather than understanding the slave narrative as a genre that is focused solely on the institutions of enslavement and abolition, we have instead a genre that is in dynamic conversation with other discourses and genres.

## 6 The Black Atlantic, Slave Narratives, and Empire

And while the early novel, fiction, sentiment, and the related questions of authority and authority had a significant impact on the form, another of the key discourses that had an impact was that of the spiritual and conversion narrative. Many of the early narratives, including that by Gronniosaw, Equiano, and Mary Prince, are all explicitly engaged, in various ways, with experiences of spirituality and, specifically, Christianity. On the one hand, this is a reflection of the fact that the earliest abolitionist societies began within spiritual organizations such as the Quakers and Methodists in the UK. The connection to evangelical Christianity is also grounded in the proselytizing that would become a significant component of the abolitionist movement. But on the other hand, one can also read the engagements with Christianity as a translation or palimpsestic articulation of their ancestral spiritualities.

Indeed, one of the first explicitly abolitionist slave narratives published in England, Ottobah Cugoano's *Thoughts and Sentiments on the Evils of Slavery* (1791) draws very heavily upon the rhetoric of the spiritual conversion narrative and ties it to abolitionist messaging: "the incumbent duty of all men of enlightened understanding, and of every man that has any claim or affinity to the name of Christian, that the base treatment which the African Slaves undergo, ought to be abolished" (3). Cugoano narrates how though "[b]rought from a state of innocence and freedom, and in a barbarous and cruel manner, conveyed to a state of horror and slavery" (10), that "it was what the Lord intended for [his] good" (7). As one of the first texts to offer these links, it also provides a template for how abolitionist texts manifest their own kind of conversion, encouraging their readers to move from the position of unknowing about the importance of abolitionism to engaging in the political action of anti-slavery. Cugoano's text aligns abolitionism with Christian morality and evangelism, which would become a model for texts such as Mary Prince's narrative, which was published in London fifty years later in 1831.

Though discussion of Prince's narrative often focuses on the representation of gender and sexuality, and certainly, her narrative is important for offering another perspective from an enslaved Caribbean enslaved woman, as Sue Thomas and others have highlighted, Prince's narrative can also be read as a record of her spiritual development because of the ways it appropriates elements of the spiritual conversion narrative. The connections between abolitionists and organized religion are key, particularly in the UK. The Quakers created the earliest anti-slavery group and many members of the later societies for the prevention of slavery were members of the various dissenting religions, such as Methodists and Moravians. Given the long history of autobiographical writing as an important aspect of recounting and validating spiritual engagements, it should be no surprise that its formats should have been taken up by the early abolitionist movement. Spirituality and spiritual discourses proved popular and valuable – indeed, before the mid nineteenth century, most writing that people encountered was in the form of Bibles and/or religious texts. The evangelical aspects of abolitionism provided a welcome pattern for the life writing of the enslaved. We see this in Prince's narrative. Prince represents her life in sin, her recognition of God, her backsliding, and then her eventual sanctification with freedom in the UK. However, her narrative not only records Christian spirituality but also seems to encode another story of spirituality that might have been grounded in the cultures of Africa. Her description of Mrs. I- has a lot in common with West African spiritualities like Vodun, which is grounded in beliefs about the divinity of the earth (Aljoe *Creole Testimonies*). The representation of the land and weather as being invested in the life experiences of the enslaved and on their side also seems connected to iconographies associated with Vodun gods and goddesses like Sakpata, god of the earth, Hevioso, god of thunder, and Jo, god of the air. And indeed, even Prince's decision to speak can be attributed to these spiritualities and the connection possibly to West African traditions of the griot.[3] Although the African slave trade had been outlawed, particularly in the Caribbean, where absentee rather than settler ownership characterized the islands, African retentions had more of an opportunity to survive not only amongst the fugitive maroons but also within the creole traditions of the enslaved decedents of Africans.

Another of the most intriguing aspects of some of these narratives is their engaging and specific portraits of Africa and the Caribbean. While some, indeed those specifically about the Caribbean, infrequently participated in notions of the "Caribbean picturesque," which provided often romanticized representations of Edenic precolonial or pre-enslavement experiences, the narratives of Africa also drew upon the rhetorics and descriptions associated with reportage and eyewitness accounts in providing specific details about West African societies and cultures (Thompson).

Representations of African culture and the transatlantic movement are other aspects of these narratives. Many of the narratives, while not always describing the details of the Middle Passage, often discuss movement in some way, shape, or form. Prince records her movements across the islands of the Caribbean. Cugoano records his movements; even the speeches are connected to Africa and notions of the griot. Joanna's narrative is one of the few that does not explicitly record movement – though Joanna and Stedman's son supposedly joins the Navy, where he perished at sea. Joanna refuses to move with Stedman to the UK and remains in the Caribbean, where she dies, supposedly poisoned by jealous enslaved people. Ayuba Ben

Solomon's was one of several texts which described the life of an African prince. Like Oroonoko, he presented the life experience of a special individual. His narrative records many movements across the ocean. He eventually returns to Africa.

*** 

These seemingly simple narratives tell surprisingly complex stories and reflect the dynamism of the experiences of the enslaved. Though frequently dismissed as litanies of spectacular violence, these texts draw inspiration from and appropriate countless discourses. This rich and diverse tapestry of voices highlights the importance of these texts as repositories of historical, cultural, and social details that communicate the syncretism of Black Atlantic cultures. As Paul Gilroy's field-defining book of the same name argues, the notion of the Black Atlantic is not about the singularity of the Black experience but, instead, its inherence, multiplicity, and movement. Such dynamism was necessary to combat the many-headed hydrae of racism and disempowerment that accompanied the African Atlantic slave trade across the global reach of the British Empire. These texts convey not only the humanity of these individuals but also their resolve to assert and claim their own identities. Finally, focusing on the significance of Black Atlantic narratives of enslavement enables a deeper understanding of the diverse cultures, traditions, and histories that contributed to British cultural traditions.

## Notes

1. Indeed, as late as 2000, collections such as *Writing Black Britain* included writing by South Asians.
2. The term "maroons" describes groups of unenslaved Africans, which often included born-free, as well as emancipated and fugitive people, who formed their own settlements on many of the Caribbean islands. In Jamaica in the early eighteenth century they constantly and violently challenged the presence of the British colonizers on the island, and in 1738 the British were forced to sign a peace treaty to end the constant hostilities.
3. Griots are associated with West African cultures. They are usually an individual or group who is/are responsible for speaking, sharing – often through storytelling – and retaining traditions and histories.

## Works Cited

Alexander, Ziggi. "Preface." *The History of Mary Prince, a West Indian Slave.* (Edited by Thomas Pringle, 1831), edited by Moira Ferguson, U of Michigan P, 1987, pp. 55–6.

Aljoe, Nicole. *Creole Testimonies*. Palgrave/Springer, 2012.

Aljoe, Nicole, and Ian Finseth. *The Journeys of the Slave Narrative*. U of Virginia P, 2014.

Anim-Addo, Joan "Sister Goose's Sisters: African-Caribbean Women's Nineteenth-Century Testimony." *Women: A Cultural Review*, vol. 15, no. 1, 2004, p. 37.

Anon. "A Speech Made by a Black of Guardaloupe [sic], at the Funeral of a Fellow-Negro," 1709. *Caribbeana*, edited by Thomas Krise, U of Chicago P, 1999, pp. 93–100.

Anon. *Joanna: A Female West Indian Slave. Founded on Stedman's Narrative of an Expedition against the Revolted Negroes of Surinam*. Printed for Lupton Relfe; Constable and Co.; and R. Millikin, 1824.

Anon. "The Speech of Moses Bon Sàam," 1735. *Caribbeana*, edited by Thomas Krise, U of Chicago P, 1999, pp. 101–7.

Anon. "The Speech of Mr. John Talbot Campo-bell," 1736. *Caribbeana*, edited by Thomas Krise, U of Chicago P, 1999, pp. 108–40.

Behn, Aphra. *Oroonoko*. 1688. Penguin Edition, 2003.

Cugoano, Ottobah. "Narrative of the Enslavement of Ottobah Cugoano, a Native of Africa; Published by Himself on the Year 1787." *The Negro's Memorial, or, Abolitionist's Catechism; by an Abolitionist*, edited by Thomas Fisher. Printed for the Author and Sold by Hatchard and Co., 1825.

Davis, Charles, and Henry Louis Gates, Jr. *The Slave's Narrative*. Oxford UP, 1991.

Douglass, Frederick. *The Narrative of the Life of Frederick Douglass*. Penguin P, 2002.

Edwards, Paul. *Unreconciled Strivings and Ironic Strategies: Three Afro-British Authors of the Georgian Era: Ignatius Sancho, Olaudah Equiano, Robert Wedderburn*. Edinburgh UP, 1991.

Equiano, Olaudah. *The Interesting Narrative of the Life of Olaudah Equiano, or Gustavus Vassa, the African. Written by Himself*. Printed for the Author, 1789, 2 vols.

Fisch, Audrey, editor. *The Cambridge Companion to the African American Slave Narrative*. Cambridge UP, 2007.

Foreman, P. Gabrielle. "Writing about Slavery/Thinking about Slavery: A Community-Sourced Document," www.pgabrielleforeman.com/writing-about-slavery-guide. Accessed February 28, 2025.

Fryer, Peter. *Staying Power: The History of Black People in Britain*. Pluto P, 1984.

Gerzina, Gretchen. *Black England: A Forgotten Georgian History*. John Murray Publishers, 2022.

Gilroy, Paul. *The Black Atlantic: Modernity and Double Consciousness*. Verso, 1993.

Greene, Jack. "'A Plain and Natural Right to Life and Liberty': An Early Natural Rights Attack on the Excesses of the Slave System in Colonial British America." *The William & Mary Quarterly*. Third Series, vol. 57, no. 4, 2000, pp. 793–808.

Gronniosaw, James Albert Ukawsaw. *A Narrative of the Most Remarkable Particulars in the Life of James Albert Ukawsaw Gronniosaw, an African Prince*, edited by Walter Shirley, S. Hazzard, 1770.

Hall, Stuart. "Black Diaspora Artists in Britain: Three 'Moments' in Post-War History." *History Workshop Journal*, vol. 61, Spring 2006, pp. 1–24.

Hanley, Ryan. *Beyond Slavery and Abolition: Black British Writing c.1770–1830*. Cambridge UP, 2019.

Jacobs, Harriet. *Incidents in the Life of a Slave Girl*. Harvard UP, 1987.

Kaufman, Miranda. *Black Tudors: The Untold Story*. Oneworld Publications, 2017.

Noel, Carlos. "More Than a Slave: Embedding Dimension into Enslaved Narratives." *Tropics of Meta: Historiography for the Masses*, Jan. 4, 2023, https://tropicsofmeta.com/2023/01/04/more-than-a-slave-embedding-dimension-into-enslaved-narratives. Accessed Feb. 28, 2025.

Ohajaru, Michael. *The John Blanke Project*, http://JohnBlanke.com. Accessed Feb. 28, 2025.

Olusoga, David. *Black and British: A Forgotten History*. Picador, 2016.

Prince, Mary. *The History of Mary Prince, a West Indian Slave*. (Edited by Thomas Pringle, 1831), edited by Moira Ferguson, U of Michigan P, 1987.

Richardson, Alan, and Debbie Lee. *Early Black British Writing: Equiano, Mary Prince, and Others*. Houghton Mifflin, 2004.

Scobie, Edward. *Black Britannia*. Johnson P, 1972.

Shyllon, Folarin. *Black People in Britain*. Institute for Race Relations, 1977.

*Black Slaves*. Institute for Race Relations, 1974.

Starling, Marion. *The Slave Narrative: Its Place in American History*. Howard UP, 1988.

Tobin, James. *Cursory Remarks upon the Reverend Mr Ramsay's Essay on the treatment and conversion of African Slaves in the Sugar Colonies. By a friend to the West India Colonies and their inhabitants*. 1785.

Thomas, Helen. *Romanticism and Slave Narratives*. Cambridge UP, 2000.

Ward, Candace. *Crossing the Line: Early Creole Novels and Anglophone Caribbean Culture in the Age of Emancipation*. U of Virginia P, 2017.

Williams, Eric. *Capitalism and Slavery*. 1944. U of North Carolina P, 2021.

PART II

# Entanglements of Prose, Poetry, and Empire: 1800–1900

# 7

ARIF CAMOGLU

# Romantic Orientalist Poetry and the Spectacle of Revolution

> No century has ever elapsed in which Asia has not
> produced some Buonaparte of its own.
> Southey, "Review"

It was with such historical determinism that Robert Southey opined on the prospect of Indian self-determination. His reflections echo the tired but enduring Orientalist conviction that counterhegemonic initiatives in Asia are doomed to undo themselves in indefinite perpetuity, bookended typically by the return of a tyrannical ruler. Whereas the image of revolution in the West was only recently disfigured by Buonaparte, Asia seems to have long been a witness to its ever-recurring horrors, according to Southey. Indeed, the so-called Orient, not only in Southey's immodest proposals but also in the poetic works of his numerous contemporaries, corresponds to an imaginary zone wherein both the promises and perils of revolution could be eyed from a safe distance. This chapter examines the affinity between the British Empire and the poetry of the Romantic period through the Orientalist poetics of revolution. The cluster of poems studied here, authored by Southey, Felicia Hemans, Lord Byron, Percy B. Shelley, and Thomas Moore, utilizes the Orient to craft a spectacle of revolution which prophesies at once a relief from imperially established power structures and their eventual recovery. Staged in these texts is a struggle for a new world order sabotaged by Napoleonic monstrosities (i.e., a gruesome reverting back to a previous state of subjugation) that are deemed intrinsic to non-Western geographies. Hence, what readers discover in these cultural productions is, to use Nigel Leask's incisive phrasing, "a discourse of revolution which admits that it is also a discourse of domination" (119).

The Orientalist poetry of the Romantic era creates a venue for negotiations with the threat posed by revolution to the British Empire by associating its terrors with places and peoples regarded culturally and historically alien to Western consciousness. This poetic tendency undermines the historical immediacy and cultural relevance of revolutionary efforts taking place within and outside the British Empire. The spectacle of revolution configured in Romantic Oriental poems, accordingly, spares (if not directly serves) empire by aesthetically displacing and dehistoricizing the anti-imperialist imagination.

While revolution, both as an aesthetic and political concept, operates as a metonym for the Romantic era, it does so with a historically untenable fixation on France and North America. After all, the late eighteenth and early nineteenth centuries saw collectivized demands for structural changes across the planet, not exclusively within the West. From India to Haiti, communities brutalized by colonialism, slavery, and the slave trade formed solidarities in search of liberty and equality. In India, to recall, there was a series of "insurrections" against the East India Company which were vigorous enough to alarm even "European observers" with "rumors that Hastings had been killed" (Marshall 265). In Haiti, revolts of enslaved individuals generated an avalanche of reactions on both sides of the Atlantic, which, as Marlene Daut has argued, "were incessantly narrated in a particularly 'racialized' way" (3). Recent scholarship on the Romantic period has uncovered the fact that global counterhegemonic uprisings cannot be reduced to "a tributary of the French Revolution," each being catapulted by and answering to its own immediate cultural and political ecology (Kuiken and White 4). This renewed evaluation of the roots and perimeters of the revolutionary spirit of the age signals, in Manu S. Chander's words, "a new means of theorizing subjectivity and intersubjectivity in the Romantic era," one that commits to unearthing racially and ethnically marginalized imaginaries of dissent and reform (11).[1] Thanks to emergent conceptualizations such as "Black Romanticism," to name but one of them, critics now more perceptively gauge how non-Western subjects "aspired to the kind of total revolution that interested transatlantic radicals" as well as their comrades in the Global South "since the 1790s" (Sandler 23).

Although Romantics were not oblivious to the global scale of revolutions at the turn of the century, their worries, Marilyn Butler claims, were rather local: "Whether they envisage the monstrous fall of the state, or the fall of the monstrous state, the topic is most dreadful because it implies the rejection and the imagined dismemberment of their own community" (135). For Leask, implications of a revolution gushing forth elsewhere, especially the ones located "in the East," were rather positive since those faraway radical enterprises could also denote "a cure for vitiated European nerves" (109). Irrespective of one's standpoint, it is wise to bear in mind the caveat underlined by Saree Makdisi: "[T]he Orient cannot be divorced from related shifts in both colonial and mercantile/industrial networks and paradigms

## 7 Romantic Orientalist Poetry and Revolution

and the role that various Eastern colonial and semi-colonial spaces and societies played in the British empire in the early nineteenth century" (22). Put otherwise, it is worth reconsidering the extent to which colonially manufactured hierarchies could impact the British attitude toward revolutions and revolutionaries in the Orient. As Edward W. Said suggested more than once, ethnoracial stratifications rebrand political violence as a problem endemic to societies in the Global South, thereby mystifying the infrastructures of Western colonialism (261). Then, although Romantics occasionally used the Orient as "a setting in which to explore and critique" domestic British politics, their poetry also commodified the revolts sweeping across otherized lands and cultures (Warren 2).

Revolution in its global manifestations, as David Armitage and Sanjay Subrahmanyam point out, encompasses a "variety of overlapping, backward-looking, and forward-tending" incentives (xvi). Attuned to its competing significations, this chapter treats revolution as an event of systemic renewal that is not bound to a universalizable moral or political teleology and yet is tightly entangled with imperial power structures. Indeed, contemplating revolution entails dealing with empires, but not always in antagonistic ways. Many British Romantics – being well versed in historiographies and cultural-aesthetic discourses of the rise and fall of imperial states – were sufficiently aware of this ambivalent relationship. Popular treatises such as Edward Gibbon's *The History of the Decline and Fall of the Roman Empire* (1782) and Constantin François de Chassebœuf, comte de Volney's *Les ruines, ou méditation sur les révolutions des empires* (*Ruins: Or, Meditations on the Revolutions of Empires*) (1796) helped nurture a widely embraced Romantic thinking about empire wherein revolutions, erupting almost principally in the Orient, signify not an irrevocable demise but a complex revolving of leaderships.[2]

Gibbon stresses in his prefatory remarks to his chronicles that the Roman Empire's end was sealed by the unrest in the Islamic East; comprehending which, he adds, may shed light on the present instabilities in the West: "the conquests of the Mahometans will deserve and detain our attention, and the last age of Constantinople (the Crusades and the Turks) is connected with the revolutions of Modern Europe" (viii). According to Gibbon, there is an obvious parallelism between what is going on in contemporary Europe and what transpired in Islamic states centuries ago, which reaffirms the Orient's value as a model for assessing the before and after of revolutions. Likewise, Volney, while sojourning through the Ottoman Empire, cogitated extensively on what the Orient could teach Western civilizations in terms of political livelihood. He bemoans the "fatal revolutions" that eradicated "what Egypt and Syria had once possessed," but is relieved "to find in Modern Europe the departed splendor of Asia" (24–5). Moreover, Volney forecasts that even those revolutions which have not yet come to pass will first ruin the Orient, expediting the "dissolution," for instance, of the Ottoman Sultanate: "the people of the empire, loosened from the yoke which united them, shall resume their ancient distinctions, and a general anarchy shall follow" (64).

### Revolutions without Ends: Southey, Hemans, and Byron

An understanding of revolution as a sociopolitical disruption which is not anti-imperial by default was thus spreading its roots in the early nineteenth-century Orientalist literary engagements with empire. In Southey's poetry this intricate view of revolution becomes pronounced in metaphysically coded rivalries. Consider *Thalaba the Destroyer* (1801) and *The Curse of Kehama* (1810) in which the poet draws on Islamic and Hindu belief systems to allegorize interventions into the exercise of power. In the former, a group of sorcerers set out to murder Thalaba in order to nullify the prophecy that he would "do the will of Heaven" as he defends the lineage of Muslims against demonic conspirators (Southey, *Thalaba* 231). While the witches succeed in killing his family, Thalaba survives their schemes, rising at the end above those who "serve the cause of Eblis, and uphold / his empire true in death" (323). Undoubtedly, the macrocosmic clash between good and evil in *Thalaba the Destroyer* is by no means a purely metaphysical issue: It is simultaneously a political conflict. The fight between the sacred and the infernal is at the same time a battle that determines whose "empire" should prevail. In this light, the poem's devilish assassins resemble the agents of a botched revolution, much like Napoleon and his disciples, while Thalaba the "destroyer" emerges in the finale as a restorer of the social equilibrium.

*The Curse of Kehama* adopts a similarly circular approach in its dramatization of the craving for supreme authority. Kehama, a Brahmin priest, aspires to achieve immortality by defeating Yamen, the deity of death. Overcome by his hunger for interminable dominance, Kehama dares transgress cosmic–religious boundaries to obtain nothing more than an existence of endless torment, "Doom'd thus to live and burn eternally" (Southey, *Curse* 615). Even as a mortal, on the other hand, Kehama is in possession of an extraordinary authority, which is likened in the poem to a "dominion," "sway," and "reign" (585). With its repeating use of the language of imperial sovereignty *The Curse of Kehama* makes clear that its theme is as political as mythological. After all, Kehama's striving toward eternal strength is also a plotting against the hierarchies of both being and governance. And yet, the revolution Kehama designs hardly accomplishes such

## 7 Romantic Orientalist Poetry and Revolution

goals. Far from disrupting the standing political-metaphysical edifice, the poem concludes with its reinstitution as Kehama's defiance earns him nothing but increased misery. Kehama, a version of an "Indian Buonaparte," to use D. S. Neff's phrase, personifies not only the tragic self-forgetfulness of revolutionary pride but also its presupposed Oriental character (391). As such, he can be said to stand in for a larger correlation which subsumes an entire continent and contracts it to a topography of fruitless rebellions.

While in *The Curse of Kehama* it is South Asia which exemplifies how the Orient is home to disappointing uprisings, in *Thalaba the Destroyer* it is the Middle East. The homogenizing gaze of Orientalism reduces vast and culturally varied geographies to interchangeable locales that are by design expected to produce a spectacle of revolution. This expectation occupied many minds in the nineteenth century, including Felicia Hemans. With clear nods to Gibbon, Volney, and Southey, Hemans masterfully instrumentalized the tropological representations of the South Asia and the Middle East in her verse. For example, her poem, "The Indian City," inspired by James Forbes's *Oriental Memoirs*, fabricates a city adorned with a "crown of domes," "leaves of gold," and "genii gardens" (253). Juxtaposed with these mystifications is the neatly delineated story of "a nobel Muslim boy" who is murdered by "the children of Brahma" (253–4). The historical and geographic vagueness that envelopes India in the poem contrasts sharply with the specificity of its theme, that is, the Hindu–Muslim schism. Its tale of vengeance caricaturizes the Orient as a site of unbridgeable political divides. Like Southey, Hemans privileges interfaith tensions in her Oriental verse as a key factor for sociopolitical bifurcations, which readers can trace in her portrayals of other non-Western regions, stretching from India to the Islamic Spain.

In "The Abencerrage" (1819), for which she consulted Ginés Pérez de Hita's *Historia de las guerras civiles de Granada*, Hemans recounts the war between the Zegries and Abencerrages (two prominent factions during the Muslim rule in fifteenth-century Granada) and Ferdinand V of Castile. At the heart of this triangulated confrontation is Hamet, an Abencerrage, who aids Christian conquerors to dethrone Abdali, the leader of the Zegries. Although, as Tricia Lootens observes, the poem praises "the courage of Crusaders and of the Arab opponents," it centers attention on fissures within the Muslim communities (239). Labeled in the poem "apostate" multiple times, Hamet comes forth as a traitor and rebel simultaneously, despised by his Zegri lover Zayda for spearheading the revolt against a Muslim ruler. At last, if momentarily, Hamet becomes a victor after "Moslem tribes" are "Borne down by numbers, and o'erpower'd by toil / Dispersed, dishearten'd ..." (Hemans, "Abencerrage" 28).

Whereas it facilitates a momentous transfer of power, Hamet's revolution also culminates in nothing but further anguish for him. He is punished with the unyielding scorn of Zayda and finds peace only in death, buried next to her. Like Kehama, Hamet paves the road to his demise with epic willpower. He revolutionizes the order of things for no tangible outcome other than the trading of one master for another without any justification. That is, "The Abencerrage" leaves readers perplexed as to the motives behind the dispute between the "Moslem" groups. It is not easy at all to glean from the text what sets the Abencerrages apart from Zegries. The "factionalism" pictured in the poem, as Nanora Sweet notes, "makes a distinction without a difference" (186). As such, what Hamet catalyzes is an uprising that does not differentiate itself on counterhegemonic grounds: It triggers but a rotating of the arms that consolidate authority, not a farewell to them.

"The Abencerrage" does not explicate the rationale behind the ethnoreligious frictions in Granada, but it does clarify whom they impact the most. The Islamic Spain fades away in the oscillations of regimes. Amplified in the poem's indulgence in what Diego Saglia phrases as "alhambraism" is an imagery of civilizational expiration that concerns most overtly the Islamic world (17): "Here Moslem luxury, in her own domain, / Hath held for ages her voluptuous reign / 'Midst gorgeous domes, where soon shall silence brood, / And all be lone – splendid solitude" (23). Revolution is converted into an omen of a spectacular downfall in the poem's Orientalist political economy. If there is a prophecy of a magnificent defeat, however, it is addressed loudly to the Orient. It is the Islamic, not Christian, Spain that supplies the screen for a viewing of states getting overturned on end. The Orient satisfies the curiosity for a spectacle of revolution wherein hegemony is contested and yet shortly thereafter recovered, time and again.

Such curiosity seized not only Hemans and Southey but also rather well-traveled figures like Byron who boasted first-hand knowledge of the Orient. Mocking Southey, Coleridge, and Wordsworth in *Don Juan* for not having abandoned their "lakes for ocean" (i.e., for being too provincial in their poetics and politics), Byron thought he distinguished himself from the rest by venturing into the Iberian Peninsula and the Mediterranean by less figurative means, partaking in revolutionary undertakings both literarily and literally (599).

As was the case with many writers of his day (e.g., Walter Savage Landor, Leigh Hunt, and Percy B. Shelley), Byron was partial to the cause of Greek liberation which he proudly fought for. In his poetry, Byron ruminates frequently on the conditions of the liberation of Greece, imploring Greeks and their proponents fervently to overthrow the Ottoman rule. He expresses in his *Turkish Tales* a nostalgic plea for an idealized past alongside a frustration with the state of the contemporary Greece. In *The Giaour* (1813), he mourns the "Shrine of the mighty" that Greece was once believed to be, whose "remains" are far from matching its ancient glory (74). Nor could Greeks, despised by Byron as "servile offspring of the free," live up to the legends of the old day (74). Still, Byron does not succumb to complete despair as he, even if contemptuously, goes on to provoke to action the "craven crouching slave," alluding to those whom he deems inured to the Ottoman oppression (74). The country still belongs to Greeks, he insists, only if they show the courage to "Arise, and make again your own / Snatch from the ashes of your Sires" (74). The transformation Byron anticipates in Greece, on the other hand, is to arrive from the past: It is an event of recurrence with radical consequences. Revolution, Byron tells Greek patriots, can only be made "again," announcing not a hitherto unseen future but the return of familiar bygones. As such, the political-cultural rewriting Byron summons in the Orient is an instance of a reclamation of power, not its rejection.

The cyclical dimension of dealing with power is not lost on Byron at all. He reiterates such a Volneyesque conception of revolution explicitly in second canto of *Childe Harold's Pilgrimage* (1812): "Religions take their turn: / 'Twas Jove's – 'tis Mahomet's – and other Creeds / Will rise with other years ..." (26). Greece is not immune to the fact that sovereignties come and go. Whether monotheistic or pagan, the control over Greece will ineluctably change hands, which, according to Byron, is a blessing and a curse at the same time. For what this logic implies is that revolution is always about to bloom and yet it is already doomed. "The city won for Allah from the Giaour / the Giaour from Othman's race again may wrest," Byron surmises confidently at first (35). His optimism quickly withers when he ponders that which awaits Greece farther in time: "But ne'er will Freedom seek this fated soil / But slave succeed to slave through years of endless toil" (35). The horizon of liberty for Greece is in sight, but so is the disappearance of its treasured majesty. Greece, Byron hopes, could be revived by the revolution; still, its grandeur would not survive long.

Whereas Greece was fantasized to be a cradle of the Western civilization in the nineteenth century, it was nevertheless part of the Ottoman Empire. The prospect and the pursuant demise of revolution Byron scrutinize in Greece is thus an inherently Oriental phenomenon. Engulfed by the Orient, Greek counterhegemonic actions are stuck in the gyre of budding and vanishing states. Hence, in their poetic enactments within Orientalist texts such as *The Giaour* and *Childe Harold*, revolutions manifest as futile attempts to alter the course of history: They occur not to stop the wheel of power but to certify that it is to stay unbroken.

## Defeated Revolutionaries: Moore and Shelley

Byron's investment in the Orient, as is well known, paid off handsomely and his commercial triumph persuaded him that romanticization of sociopolitical conflicts afflicting (only) certain parts of the world could profit other aspiring Orientalists too. In an 1813 letter to Thomas Moore, Byron allegedly gave his notorious advice: "Stick to the East.... The North, South, and West, have all been exhausted; but from the East, we have nothing but Southey's unsaleables" (*The Works of Lord Byron* 255). Later, Moore's *Lalla Rookh* (1817) also became a bestseller and went on to ignite interest in Britain and Europe for decades to come. Following the same old recipe used in its less lucrative precedents (like Southey's "unsaleables") *Lalla Rookh* visualizes skirmishes between religious groups in Persian and Arab lands. In Moore's adaptation, however, the theme of Oriental revolution features an arresting twist. Moore declares in his foreword that "the spirit that had spoken in the melodies of Ireland soon found itself at home in the East," which is an unsubtle admission of his wish to approximate the contested hegemonies of the Orient to the British Empire (x).[3] Taking this parallelism at face value, Jeffrey W. Vail conjectures that Moore's "work as a whole condemns the injustice of autocratic power and colonialism and affirms the heroism of colonized peoples who revolt against their oppressors" (3). *Lalla Rookh* does broadcast a politics of disobedience which might have been intended to touch British nerves. Nonetheless, it is hard to deny that the situational alikeness drawn between the Irish and Oriental politics grows less and less determinable in the ambiguous space and time of the poem. In the section titled "Veiled Prophet of Khorassan," the naming of "Persia," "Yemen," and "Kathay" (China) concurrently obscures "each Land" as interchangeable signs for a "fair young Nursery for Heaven" (Moore 13–14).

Spatiotemporal unclarity is not the sole reason why the anti-imperial tenets of Moore's text can be deemed questionable. As *Lalla Rookh* participates in the political revival of romance in the early nineteenth century, it deploys the tropes of the genre – for example, feminine idealization of liberty – not so much "to glamorize the ideas and actions of the French revolution" as critique it (Duff 35). This critique, on the other hand, hinges on a spectacle that negates revolution not once but twice in the poem. First to appear on the battlefield is Mokanna, a Napoleonesque commander, literally veiled as a divine representative of an unmatched reform who later degenerates into an "impostor" manipulating "the vast multitude" (Moore 76). Then comes his opponent, Azim, with his "graceful gratitude of power," keen to re-revolutionize the Orient while hoping to reunite with his beloved Zalika who has been abducted by the false prophet (80). Mokanna and Azim are

## 7 Romantic Orientalist Poetry and Revolution

seen to emulate each other as they both vie over absolute leadership rather than conspire against it. Mokanna "the down-fall'n Chief" lures his followers to their death only to be vanquished at the end (82). Azim's victory is tainted irreparably when he tragically kills his lover Zalika, mistaking her for Mokanna himself as she wears the "Veil" to terminate her captivity by getting immolated (101). Hence, the finale of *Lalla Rookh* conveys a sense of dismay, not festivity, with revolution and restoration becoming almost indistinguishable from one another.

Not all Oriental romances, with their portrayals of a world shaken by revolutions, appealed to the public in the gentle way *Lalla Rookh* did. Percy B. Shelley's *Laon and Cythna*, printed the same year as Moore's poem and hastily withdrawn on grounds of its atheistic and incestuous content, is one such example. Set in "Constantinople and Modern Greece" and framed as "a tale illustrative of such a Revolution as might be supposed to take place in European nation," *Laon and Cythna* was revised and republished under the curious title of *The Revolt of Islam* (Shelley, "From Shelley to Godwin" 239). With this modification – despite his reluctance to delve into a "minute delineation of Mahometan manners" – Shelley conceded to a rather targeted advertising of his poem, one that trimmed its geocultural relatability by toning down its allusions to Christian European states ("Shelley to an Unknown Publisher" 238).

The revolution Shelley conjured up in the Middle East with a proclaimed "tendency to awaken public hope" was ironically also a catastrophic letdown (*Laon and Cythna* 41). Laon and Cythna, the chosen protagonists of an unparalleled resistance against an Ottoman autocrat, characterize a nonviolent revolutionary subjecthood in which the French ideals of equality, liberty, and fraternity would be actualized without their attendant carnage. The Greek heroes manage to emancipate the Orient for a fleeting moment, as they dethrone the sultan by assembling "a nation / Made free by love; – a mighty brotherhood / Linked by a jealous interchange of good" (120). For some, "*The Revolt*'s pacifism reflects Shelley's avowed goal of depicting the 'ideal' revolution and his adherence to the self-image of radicals as placid petitioners" (Cohen-Vrignaud 76). However, a radical twist in the narrative occurs when Laon is captured by the soldiers of the bloodthirsty monarch. Being imprisoned takes its toll on Laon's capacity for peaceful world building, clouding his judgment enough that he attacks his guards whom, he laments, he "murdered ... as they did sleep" (Shelley *Laon and Cythna* 119). Laon's resort to "brute force" reads as a harbinger of a reversal of roles between the tyrant and the rebel in the poem. The line between the revolutionary and the sovereign is irremediably blurred once they are both implicated in the same violent rehearsal of power regardless of their intentions.

Still, Shelley insists that the end does not justify the means when revolution is at stake, which he ensures is lucidly communicated in the poem through a disheartening reestablishment of the sultanic regime. The scales of social justice abruptly tip the other way and those who were once united in peaceful protests morph into a "multitude of moving heartless things" (*Laon and Cythna* 192). Disowned by the crowds they themselves galvanized, Laon and Cythna flee the scene of tumult, transported miraculously right before their execution to a paradisal island. Their absurd dematerialization amplifies the gap between the self-appointed liberators and their devotees which, readers realize, was never genuinely bridged in the poem. Along with them, revolution is further removed in time and space, deferred to what resembles a prelapsarian existence that is out of reach for everyone except for Laon and Cythna, the revolutionaries dispossessed of a revolution.

Even though, as highlighted by Cian Duffy, Shelley's poem sets out "to relocate the apparent catastrophe of the Revolution with a long-term and explicitly *natural* economy of hope," it digresses drastically from this mission in its closure (127). The revolutionary vitality of the masses in *Laon and Cythna* deteriorates into a fatalistic readiness to obey a dictator, which forwards a commentary on the political destiny of the Orient itself. After all it is "Indian breezes" and "Idumea's sand" where "strange natures made a brother of ill" in order to curtail the movement of a systemic change (192). Subtle cartographic insertions like these invoke the Middle East and South Asia as landscapes of immanent corruption, acclimatizing readers further to the already prevalent misconception that revolution's fate in the Orient is a hopeless one. Through its Orientalist dramatization of an unrealized structural transformation, Shelley's text also risks accustoming readers to the conservative equation of revolution with political futility, or worse, deadly social volatility.

Laon and Cythna relinquish the reigns at last to Othman, a despot whose return seems no less predictable than his preliminary defeat.[4] In spite of his plans to distribute an uplifting message, Shelley joins a sizeable chorus of poets in singing the familiar song of a failed revolution. Like Southey, Hemans, Byron, and Moore, he attests in his verse to the spectacular stifling of voices that demand change and the ensuing reconstruction of hegemony in the Orient. To this list can be added many others, including Walter Savage Landor and Thomas Love Peacock, whose poems – respectively, *Gebir* and *Ahrimanes* – analogously romanticize the cycle of upheavals permeating Oriental realms.[5] In Romantic Orientalist poetry, therefore, one is struck by the ubiquity of the spectacle of disappointing uprisings, which in effect puts into question the very realizability of revolution.

## 7 Romantic Orientalist Poetry and Revolution

Although, as Priyamvada Gopal has insightfully argued, "awareness of rebellion and resistance in the colonies, and in due course contact with anticolonial figures shaped British domestic criticism of empire," the counter-hegemonic vision derived from the Orient is also seen to place the idea of revolution at a distance (7). The fruitless political struggles in Romantic fabulations of the Middle East, North Africa, and South Asia reinforce the colonialist association of the Orient with unending sociopolitical violence; they also obfuscate the historical and geographic proximity of revolutionary undertakings to the British Empire itself. In this peculiar poetics of revolution, collective struggles for structural change are relegated to a spatiotemporally vague imagination where they are occurring in loop for no good. The sensational Orientalist spectacle places empire at a safe distance, removed from the reach of eruptions of dissidence.

### Notes

1. One must also keep in mind the fact that the much-romanticized cult of revolutionary subjecthood was not a quintessentially Western invention. See Omar Miranda, for instance, on how the Venezuelan author, Francisco de Miranda, prefigured the Byronic hero.
2. See Camoglu for a discussion of the ways in which empire incorporates the imaginaries of its own ruination into its affective realm of sovereignty.
3. On the presence of Orientalist discourses in British depictions of Ireland, see Lennon.
4. For a detailed study of how the Ottoman Empire inflected British political and aesthetic debates over imperial vitality in the nineteenth century, see Turhan.
5. Landor's *Gebir* (1798) set a precedent for long Orientalist poems authored by Southey, Byron, and others in its transportation of grotesque power struggles to non-Western geographies. Likewise, Peacock's *Ahrimanes*, despite being unfinished, left a mark on Romantic poetry about the revolutionary Orient, serving as a template for Shelley's *Laon and Cythna*.

### Works Cited

Armitage, David, and Sanjay Subrahmanyam, editors. *The Age of Revolutions in Global Context, c.1760–1840*. Palgrave Macmillan, 2010.

Butler, Marilyn. "Plotting the Revolution: The Political Narratives of Romantic Poetry and Criticism." in *Romantic Revolutions: Criticism and Theory*, edited by Kenneth R. Johnson et al., Indiana UP, 1990, pp. 133–57.

Byron, George Gordon, Lord. *Childe Harold's Pilgrimage*, in *The Works of Lord Byron: Complete in One Volume*, edited by Thomas Moore, et al., D. Appleton & Company, 1851, pp. 11–71.

*Don Juan*, in *The Works of Lord Byron: Complete in One Volume*, edited by Thomas Moore, et al., D. Appleton & Company, 1851, pp. 588–771.

*The Giaour, a Turkish Tale*, *The Works of Lord Byron: Complete in One Volume*, edited by Thomas Moore, et al., D. Appleton & Company, 1851, pp. 72–86.

*The Works of Lord Byron: Letters and Journals*, edited by Rowland E. Prothero, vol. 2, John Murray, 1898.

Camoglu, Arif. "'Supreme in Ruin': Empire's Afterlife in Romantic Encounters with Imperial Ruins." *European Romantic Review*, vol. 32, no. 2, 2021, pp. 145–61.

Chander, Manu S. *Brown Romantics: Poetry and Nationalism in the Global Nineteenth Century*. Bucknell UP, 2017.

Cohen-Vrignaud, Gerard. *Radical Orientalism: Rights, Reform, and Romanticism*. Cambridge UP, 2015.

Daut, Marlene. *Tropics of Haiti: Race and Literary History of the Haitian Revolution in the Atlantic World, 1789–1865*. Liverpool UP, 2015.

Duff, David. *Romance and Revolution: Shelley and the Politics of a Genre*. Cambridge UP, 1994.

Duffy, Cian. *Shelley and the Revolutionary Sublime*. Cambridge UP, 2005.

Gibbon, Edward. *The History of the Decline and Fall of the Roman Empire*. Methuen, 1897.

Gopal, Priyamvada. *Insurgent Empire: Anticolonial Resistance and British Dissent*. Verso, 2019.

Hemans, Felicia. *The Abencerrage*, in *The Poetical Works of Felicia Dorothea Hemans*, edited by Humphrey Milford. Oxford UP, 1914, pp. 1–34.

*The Indian City*, in *The Poetical Works of Felicia Dorothea Hemans*, edited by Humphrey Milford. Oxford UP, 1914, pp. 253–8.

Kuiken, Kir, and Debora Elise White. "Introduction." in *Haiti's Literary Legacies: Romanticism and the Unthinkable Revolution*, edited by Kir Kuiken and Deborah Elise White, Bloomsbury, 2021, pp. 1–24.

Leask, Nigel. *British Romantic Writers and the East: Anxieties of Empire*. Cambridge UP, 1992.

Lennon, Joseph. *Irish Orientalism: A Literary and Intellectual History*. Syracuse UP, 2004.

Lootens, Tricia. "Hemans and Home: Victorianism, Feminine 'Internal Enemies,' and the Domestication of National Identity." *PMLA*, vol. 109, no. 2, 1994, pp. 238–53.

Makdisi, Saree. *Romantic Imperialism*. Cambridge UP, 1998.

Marshall, P. J. *The Making and Unmaking of Empires: Britain, India, and America c. 1750–1783*. Oxford UP, 2005.

Miranda, Omar F. "The Celebrity of Exilic Romance: Francisco de Miranda and Lord Byron." *European Romantic Review*, vol. 27, no. 2, 2016, pp. 207–31.

Moore, Thomas. *Lalla Rookh, an Oriental Romance*. Longman, Brown, Green and Longmans, 1849.

Neff, D. S. "Hostages to Empire: The Anglo-Indian Problem in *Frankenstein*, *The Curse of Kehama*, and *The Missionary*." *European Romantic Review*, vol. 8, no. 4, 1997, pp. 386–408.

Saglia, Diego. *Poetic Castles in Spain: British Romanticism and Figurations of Iberia*. Rodopi, 2000.

Said, Edward W. *Culture and Imperialism*. Vintage, 2012.

Sandler, Matt. *The Black Romantic Revolution: Abolitionist Poets at the End of Slavery*. Verso, 2020.

Shelley, Percy B. "From Shelley to Godwin." in *Laon and Cythna, or The Revolution of the Golden City: A Vision of the Nineteenth Century*, edited by Anahid Nersessian, Broadview Press, 2016, pp. 239–40.
  *Laon and Cythna, or The Revolution of the Golden City: A Vision of the Nineteenth Century*, edited by Anahid Nersessian, Broadview Press, 2016.
  "Shelley to an Unknown Publisher." in *Laon and Cythna, or The Revolution of the Golden City: a Vision of the Nineteenth Century*, edited by Anahid Nersessian, Broadview Press, 2016, pp. 237–8.
Southey, Robert. *The Curse of Kehama*, in *The Complete Poetical Works of Robert Southey*. D. Appleton & Company, 1846, pp. 565–646.
  "Review of Periodical Accounts Relative to the Baptist Missionary Society," in *Quarterly Review I*, John Murray, 1809, pp. 193–226.
  *Thalaba the Destroyer*, in *The Complete Poetical Works of Robert Southey*. D. Appleton & Company, 1851, pp. 224–325.
Sweet, Nanora. "Gender and Modernity in *The Abencerrage*: Hemans, Rushdie, and 'the Moor's Last Sigh.'" in *Felicia Hemans*, edited by Nanora Sweet, et al., Palgrave Macmillan, 2001, pp. 181–95.
Turhan, Filiz. *The Other Empire: British Romantic Writings about the Ottoman Empire*. Routledge, 2003.
Vail, Jeffrey W. "'The Standard of Revolt': Revolution and National Independence in Moore's *Lalla Rookh*." *Romanticism on the Net*, vol. 40, 2005, pp. 1–30.
Volney, Constantin François. *Volney's Ruins: or, the Mediation on the Revolutions of Empires*. Translated by Count Daru, Josiah P. Mendum, 1869.
Warren, Andrew. *The Orient and the Young Romantics*. Cambridge UP, 2014.

# 8

IAN DUNCAN

# The Historical Novel and Nineteenth-Century Empire

## The "Classical Form of the Historical Novel"

The historical novel was always about empire. Walter Scott established "the classical form of the historical novel" (Lukács 60) at the close of the Napoleonic Wars, which secured worldwide British naval and commercial dominance. Scott's novels address the integration of Scotland into the modern, multinational Anglo-British state (*Waverley*, 1814), the relation of Great Britain's internal formation to imperial adventures abroad (*Guy Mannering*, 1815), and the colonial origins of England itself in ancient waves of conquest and settlement (*Ivanhoe*, 1820). Adapting the stadial historiography of the Scottish Enlightenment, Scott made the novel historical, attuned to dynamic change at all levels – economic, social, political, cultural – of collective life. The "Waverley Novels" provided a template not only for nineteenth-century realism (as novelists from Balzac to George Eliot adapted their techniques to the representation of contemporary life) but also for late Victorian adventure fiction or imperial romance (Green 99, 128; Bruzelius 23–33). Flourishing in the era of the "New Imperialism," in the new demographic markets – including children's literature – opened following the 1870s Education Acts, imperial romance converted national history into global geography and historical difference into anthropological or biological difference, drawing upon the scientific racism that relegated non-European peoples to an essential condition of primitive or savage life (Dentith 13–15; Hensley 235–7). Meanwhile the historical novel itself, although also increasingly tagged as juvenile reading (Maxwell 233–4, 252–4), remained a powerful medium for the imaginative exploration of relations between empire and nation, history and modernity, individual agency and impersonal forces of determination: more critically for readers in the British colonies and dominions, arguably, than for their metropolitan counterparts. The present essay tracks the historical novel across the transimperial arena (Banerjee 925–8) of nineteenth-century literary production,

## 8 The Historical Novel and Nineteenth-Century Empire

from Scottish origins through the English core to the very different cases of Canada, a white settler colony, and India, a historical palimpsest of imperial civilizations.

Imperial romance's geographical and anthropological conversions of historical difference reversed the ideological operation that critics have ascribed to Scott's historical fiction: the plotting of spatial distance from the metropolis along the temporal axis of Enlightenment stadial history (Trumpener xii–xiii, 128–57: summarized as follows). That plotting recodes ethnic and cultural variations within the British Isles, in Ireland and Scotland (the so-called Celtic fringe), as early stages – archaic or primitive – in an evolutionary progression of social states, from hunting clans to modern commercial society. Scott's novels, ideological instruments in a long process of "internal colonialism," complete the political subjection of Scotland in the British Union with its cultural absorption. *Waverley* adapts the allegory of union pioneered in the Romantic Anglo-Irish National Tale, where the marriage between an English visitor and an Irish heiress supplies the moral and libidinal content of the political union between nations. Sydney Owenson's prototype *The Wild Irish Girl* (1806) imagines a union of equals, in which the bride-to-be schools her suitor in a classical – that is, timeless – Irish culture before he can be worthy of her hand. *Waverley*, set during the 1745 Jacobite rebellion, consigns Highland clan society to the past. The English visitor's journey through Scotland takes him to an archaic anthropological world, glamorous but doomed to vanish, as the exiled old regime harnesses its residual energies in a failed attempt to regain the British throne.

Scott's historical novels afford an extended, experimental recombination and reimagining of the genre's thematic and technical capacities, unmatched in British fiction; it would require the remainder of this chapter to do justice to them. Instead, I will focus on the schema that Victorian historical novels of empire adapted from Scott to their different geopolitical situations. Two formal innovations are critical for this imperial legacy. Together, they constitute a symbolic system which sublimates the violence of national formation into a secular providential history. Historical progress, decoupled from divine guidance, is manifest in an advance from simpler to more complex states, according to scientific laws that are immanent to social and economic organization (the division of labor) and, after 1800, to organic life itself (the *Bildungstrieb* or developmental drive). Its political theme is union: an imperial synthesis dialectically produced through a succession of ethnic, dynastic, and religious conflicts (see Koditschek 37–52). Hence Scott's choice of civil war, the crucible of modern state formation, as the topos of historical fiction (Mufti 63–79). Internal antagonisms are not erased but transubstantiated, from politics to culture, and ancient ethical virtues (courage, honor, loyalty) salvaged as aesthetic values in the media of art and memory (Lincoln 47–63). Correlatively, Scott's novels absorb the literary forms of superseded historical stages – romance, epic, ballad, folktale, lyric – into their heterogeneous technical apparatus. The qualities digested into modernity remain (thus) immanent to it, still available – in a radical potential taken up later – for political reactivation.

Scott's second, much discussed innovation is a new kind of protagonist. Adapted from the contemporaneous (German) *Bildungsroman* or novel of development, this is the soft, "mediocre" or "middling," "never heroic 'hero'" (Lukács 32–3), whose apparent weakness, a deficit of the will-to-action, turns out to be a secret strength, since it releases him from political commitment and ensures his survival amid the clash of historical forces. Key to the character type is the moral disconnection from purpose, which instead belongs – with the burden of epic and tragic violence – to the scientific laws of historical progress. The Hegelian "world-historical individual" or man of destiny who makes a charismatic claim on historical purpose (Napoleon is his modern archetype) warps into the figure of the fanatic or tyrant, an anachronistic menace to civil society.

The protagonist's infirmity of purpose and the purposive strength of impersonal historical process thus regulate one another. However, the protagonist's political ambivalence – his well-noted propensity to waver between allegiances – also marks the disruptive potential of an instability, at once deficit and surplus, that threatens to undo the providential scheme. That potential becomes overt in Victorian-era historical fiction, when the instability shifts from political allegiance to essentialized categories of sexuality and race, as these become the biological drivers of historical process. Scott's novels, already alert to the risk, defuse this destabilizing polyvalency by flanking the protagonist with antagonists and doubles, who convert his lack of purpose into a fatal excess. The charismatic fanatic may appear as an enemy (who must be defeated) or as a friend, more dangerous because attractive (and who must be sacrificed: the Jacobites Fergus and Flora MacIvor, in *Waverley*). The most complex and poignant case of the latter is the Jewess Rebecca, in *Ivanhoe*, whose uncompromising claim upon a recognizably modern, liberal, cosmopolitan ethics issues in her exile from the prototypical English community – a union of the white Christian races, Saxon and Norman – forged at the novel's end. The *Waverley* hero's wavering tropism, meanwhile, is charged with purpose by opportunistic tricksters and shapeshifters, who likewise may imperil the hero (Donald Bean Lean, in *Waverley*) or assist him (Rob Roy, in *Rob Roy*). These figures siphon off the disruptive energy inherent in the protagonist's inconstancy, his ready adaptability to chance and change. Their presence underscores, nevertheless, the mutability at the core of Scott's historical scheme, haunted by the shadows of those whose exclusion guarantees its consummation.

### Greater Britain: *Westward Ho!*

Celebration of English geopolitical expansion is overt in Charles Kingsley's *Westward Ho!* (1855), the novel that decisively repurposed Scott-style historical fiction for Victorian imperial romance. Written to boost patriotic spirits during the Crimean War, popular well into the twentieth century (Sutherland 117–22), *Westward Ho!* became a boy's book by the 1880s, when it spawned other juvenile adventure tales, notably those by the prolific G. A. Henty: *Under Drake's Flag: A Tale of the Spanish Main* (1883) follows the plot of *Westward Ho!* from Devon to New Spain (and beyond); *With Clive in India: The Beginnings of an Empire* (1884) visits a more recent stage of English imperial formation.

The true subject of *Westward Ho!* is empire, the authentic – organic, expansive – condition of national life. Kingsley dedicated the novel to Sir James Brooke, the "White Rajah" of Sarawak, and George Augustus Selwyn, the first Anglican bishop of New Zealand, as modern types of English heroic virtue. Brooke had just survived a Commission of Inquiry (1854) into allegations of excessive use of force against native populations, ostensibly to combat piracy; dismissal of the charges against him fell far short of a vindication. Selwyn acted as an enlightened ally of the Māori, at least until his involvement in the bloody invasion of the Waikato in 1863–64. Kingsley invokes epic as the proper genre of imperial history: "if now and then I shall seem to warm into a style somewhat too stilted and pompous, let me be excused for my subject's sake, fit rather to have been sung than said, and to have proclaimed to all true English hearts, not as a novel but as an epic" (Kingsley 1: 3). *Westward Ho!* glorifies the origins of English ascendancy in the Elizabethan-era conflict with Spain. The contrast between enlightened, liberty-promoting Protestantism and despotic, fanatical Catholicism, an eighteenth-century commonplace, undergirds the modern antithesis between an alien evil empire (here, Spanish; elsewhere, as in Rudyard Kipling's *Kim*, Russian, or Portuguese, or Belgian) and the benign British version. "It is as if Kingsley is producing a counterfactual account of the British Empire" (Freedgood 390), in which slavery and genocide, like the Inquisition, are other nations' crimes.

Having the Spanish Armada furnish his story's epic climax, Kingsley casts the English as heroic opponents of invasion and conquest – not *conquistadores* themselves. The defeat of the Armada inspires "a shout of holy joy" across Protestant Europe, "the prophetic birth-paean of North America,

Australia, New Zealand, the Pacific Islands, of free commerce and free colonization over the whole earth" (3: 334–5). Thirteen years before Charles Wentworth Dilke would promote the idea of a "Greater Britain," befitting "the grandeur of our race, already girding the earth, which it is destined, perhaps, eventually to overspread" (Dilke vii), *Westward Ho!* enlarges the political figure of union to a global scale. Kingsley urges our admiration of his English adventurers: "a nobler company you will seldom see. Especially too, if you be Americans, look at their faces, and reverence them; for to them and to their wisdom you owe the existence of your mighty fatherland" (2: 222). Later, Sir Walter Raleigh invites the novel's hero, Amyas Leigh, to lead the second expedition to colonize Roanoke, "which if he had done, perhaps the United States had begun to exist twenty years sooner than they actually did" (3: 245). "Through America," Dilke confirms in *Greater Britain*, "England is speaking to the world" (viii).

Amyas embodies this national-imperial spirit. He is "a symbol, though he knows it not, of brave young England longing to wing its way out of its island prison, to discover and to traffic, to colonize and to civilize, until no wind can sweep the earth which does not bear the echoes of an English voice" (Kingsley 1: 18). With this brawny blond savage, an English Siegfried or Achilles, Kingsley regresses the Waverley protagonist to a primitive epic archetype, taken up in later imperial romances (cf. Sir Henry Curtis in H. Rider Haggard's *King Solomon's Mines*, 1885). Gold is displaced by sex and then race, biological imperatives, as the object of the imperial adventure – and driver of the historical purpose (English expansion) Amyas unknowingly incarnates. He and his friends dedicate their expedition to Devonshire beauty Rose Salterne, with whom they are all in love, until Rose elopes with a Spanish suitor to the New World, where she suffers a grisly comeuppance – tortured and burnt by the Inquisition. The violation of Anglo-Saxon racial and sexual purity, inflaming Amyas with a fanatical hatred of Spaniards, provides the story's deep motive. Amyas leads his crew into the Amazon hinterland in a delusive quest for the fabulous El Dorado. The real treasure he brings back – redeeming Rose's erotic treason – is a woman: the mysterious foundling Ayacanora, whose "white skin" and "delicate beauty" prompt the local Indians to "[worship] her as a god" (3: 71). Amyas wonders whether she might be "one of the lost Inca race" (3: 69), superior to the degenerate savages she lives among. "I am a daughter of the Sun," Ayacanora upbraids her adoptive tribe, "I am white; I am a companion for Englishmen! But you! your mothers were Guahibas, and ate mud; and your fathers – they were howling apes!" (3: 79). Set apart from one alien race, Ayacanora falls into another, when Amyas learns she might be Spanish. Eventually Ayacanora turns out to be of good English stock, from Amyas's own village, so she can safely take her place as Rose's substitute. The solution at once anticipates and short-circuits the fantasy of lost white indigeneity, justifying the European dispossession of actual, historical natives that recurs in imperial romance (a lost civilization, in Rider Haggard's *Allan Quatermain*, 1887; a last survivor, in W. H. Hudson's *Green Mansions*, 1904).

Ayacanora is the wild card in the game of national historical formation. Her slide across the racial spectrum accompanies a flamboyant performance of savage Amazonian prowess – leaping into torrential rapids, shooting and stabbing dastardly Spaniards. Scrambling the repertoires of sex and gender as well as race, Ayacanora takes over the mutable character of Scott's wavering protagonist (displaced from Kingsley's male hero by his epic hardening) and unleashes it as a volatile, turbulent force that upsets the biological categories at stake in the story. Her role is settled in the aftermath of the climactic fight with the Armada. Amyas curses God for thwarting his revenge (his enemy is drowned before he can catch up with him) and is struck blind by a lightning bolt. The novel closes with Ayacanora tending the disabled hero, like Jane Eyre with Mr. Rochester; she has found a properly feminine vocation, at last, and he a measure of spiritual peace. The epic struggle over, both primitives are domesticated – tamed – for a new English order, purged of the violence of its making.

### Settler-Colonial Romance: *Les anciens Canadiens*

Three years after *Westward Ho!*, W. M. Thackeray's *The Virginians* (1858) interweaves an English family history with the Greater British history of North American colonization and nation formation. In a variant of the "two friends" plot pioneered by Scott, brothers find themselves on opposite sides in the American War of Independence. The loyalist Henry averts a fratricidal clash by resigning his commission and lives to acknowledge the providential outcome: "it was ordained by Heaven, and for the good, as we can now have no doubt, of both empires, that the great Western Republic should separate from us" (2: 352). By the last decades of the nineteenth century, the vision of a global federation of English-speaking states and colonies had achieved quasi-official currency, thanks in part to J. R. Seeley's *The Expansion of England* (1883), "the most influential account of colonial unity in the late Victorian age" (Bell 16). Arthur Conan Doyle, who prized his historical novels above his other works (including the Sherlock Holmes tales), dedicated *The White Company* (1891) – "a little chronicle of our common ancestry" set during the Hundred Years' War – to "the hope of the future, the reunion of the English-speaking races" (iii). Expansion and diaspora, issuing in worldwide union: The vision persisted well into the next century, in Sir Oswald Mosley's *The Greater Britain* (1932), Sir Winston Churchill's *History of the English-Speaking Peoples* (1956–58), and John Tyndall's Greater Britain Movement (1964), inspired by Mosley's Union of British Fascists – white company indeed.

Not all historical novels of the Age of Empire endorsed it. Robert Louis Stevenson's *The Master of Ballantrae* (1889) revisits the terrain of Scott's historical fiction to unmake the fantasy of Scotland as original Romantic homeland, a moral anchor for national memory and adventure overseas. The House of Durrisdeer is fatally split by the family's opportunistic accommodation to the 1745 Jacobite Rising. In a parodic inversion of the "two friends" plot, fraternal antagonists take opposite sides in the conflict, replacing the single protagonist who wavers between allegiances. The story is dispersed across the Atlantic and South Asian theatres of empire until the warring brothers perish in the North American wilderness, united in a common grave: Extinction, not synthesis, awaits on the colonial frontier.

Transplantation of the historical novel to the imperial peripheries put the genre under maximum pressure. The British Conquest of New France (1759–60), the first decisive clash between ascendant European powers, supplies the historical theme of Philippe Aubert de Gaspé's *Les anciens Canadiens* (1863), a settler-colonial adaptation of *Waverley* (Trumpener 259–73; McNeil 70–2). (General Wolfe's 1759 campaign furnishes a key episode in *The Virginians*.) Published in the Francophone enclave of Quebec at the centenary of the Treaty of Paris, *Les anciens Canadiens* resumes the plot of providential union. Assimilation of the French Canadians into a prospective Greater Britain will overcome the trauma of conquest (and avert the worse trauma of domestic revolution):

> The cession of Canada was, perhaps, a blessing in disguise; for the horrors of '93 failed to touch this fortunate colony which was protected by the flag of Britain. We have gathered new laurels, fighting beneath the banner of England; and twice has the colony been saved to England by the courage of her new subjects…. For a century have you struggled, O my countrymen, to preserve your nationality, and you behold it yet intact. (Aubert de Gaspé 168–9)

Aubert de Gaspé cultivates this providential history by memorializing old French-Canadian ways and manners, much as Scott had done for Scotland – "preserving nationality" as a distinctive cultural heritage within the political framework of union (McNeil 75–83).

The historical dialectic is mediated through another "two friends" plot. The affection that binds Jules d'Haberville, son of the seigneur of Port-Joly, and Archibald Cameron of Lochiel, fictional scion of a (historical) Jacobite chieftain exiled after the 1745 Rising, is sorely tested when the former school friends find themselves on opposite sides in the British invasion of New France. Now an officer in the Imperial Army, Archie is given orders to burn French settlements, among them the d'Haberville estate. The deed reprises the atrocities inflicted upon his own people by government forces after Culloden. Eventually Archie is reconciled with the family; but the plot of marital union, which cements political union in the Anglo-Irish National Tales and in *Waverley*, fails to take hold (Cabajsky 32–3). The Haberville daughter, with whom Archie is in love, rebuffs his suit: "Is it now you make me such a proposal, when the flames that you and yours have lighted in my unhappy country are hardly yet extinguished? Is it now, while the smoke yet rises from our ruined homes, that you offer me the hand of one of our destroyers?" (Aubert de Gaspé 245). The conquest has been too violent, the memory of British oppression too bitter, for wounds to have healed. Archie settles in Canada, while Jules returns from France and pledges allegiance to the British Crown, with his father's blessing: "His dearest interests are here where he was born. Canada is his true fatherland. He cannot have the same affection for the land of his ancestors" (239). Settlers become natives, even under a change of regime, as the new country finds room for those who have no place in the old.

The category of "native" further vexes this resolution. As the novel's Waverley-type protagonist, caught between organic, private loyalty to his friends and the impersonal – categorical – imperative of loyalty to the state, Archie becomes the unstable figure that troubles the providential scheme. Parsing the friendship between Jules and Archie, the narrator draws an early equivalence between French settlers and Scottish Highlanders: Both are subjects of Anglo-British conquest and eventual imperial integration. The equivalence falters when Archie becomes the agent of state violence against his friends. At this critical juncture, the narrative undoes the binary equivalence between French and Scots by inserting a third term – the Indians. True natives of the land, the original subjects of conquest, they remain excluded from the plot of providential union, unpacified and unreconciled. Authentic primitives, they also share heroic virtues of honor and bravery with the Scottish Highlanders. This new equivalence, coming into focus when Archie is taken prisoner by Indian allies of the French, displaces the prior equivalence with the French Canadians. "The prisoner is not an Englishman, but a Scotchman, and the Scotch are the savages of the English," explains Dumais, one of the French settlers, to Archie's captors (Aubert de Gaspé 185). He bolsters the claim with a pastiche epic narration, Indian-style, of the exploits of Scots patriot William Wallace:

> "Houa!" cried Grand-Loutre, "they are men these Scotch."
>
> "The Scotch had a great chief named Wallace, a mighty warrior. When he set out for war the earth trembled under his feet. He was as tall as yonder fir-tree and as strong as an army ..." (187)

Persuaded of this heroic affinity, the Indians connive in Archie's escape.

At the same time, the Indians are scapegoats for the cruelty of empire. When Archie expresses remorse for the severity of military discipline that ordered the burning of French settlements, Dumais tells him of far worse crimes against humanity:

> I have seen these barbarians burn an English woman. She was a young woman of great beauty. I still see her tied to the stake, where they tortured her for eight mortal hours. I still see her in the midst of her butchers, clothed, like our first mother, in nothing but her long, fair hair. I shall hear forever her heart-rending cry of "My God! my God!" (Aubert de Gaspé 195)

(As in *Westward Ho!*, the torture of a beautiful young woman serves as pornographic topos of alien barbarism.) The "savage" atrocities of the Indians trump anything committed by the British. They represent an unassimilable residue of colonial violence, only to be erased, presumably, when they are. Indigenous extinction enters the equation as the negative condition of imperial union, underwriting the British and French settlers' achievement of their joint new identity as Canadian natives.

## Uprising: *Anandamath*

"The colonies and India are in opposite extremes," J. R. Seeley observes in *The Expansion of England*: "In the colonies everything is brand-new. There you have the most progressive race put in the circumstances most favourable to progress. There you have no past and an unbounded future. Government and institutions are all ultra-English. All is liberty, industry, invention, innovation, and as yet tranquillity." India, conversely, mired in superstition, fanaticism, despotism, and other retrograde habits now obsolete in civilized Europe, "is all past and, I may almost say, has no future" (176). Let alone tranquility: Badly shaken by the Rebellion of 1857, British imperial rule confronted a tide of resistance movements, culminating in the founding of the Indian National Congress in 1885. The major literary figure associated with the cause was Bankim Chandra Chatterjee (Chattopadhyay), the so-called Scott of Bengal, whose romance of anticolonial resistance *Anandamath* (1882) provided the cause with its unofficial anthem, the poem "Vande Mataram."

## 8 The Historical Novel and Nineteenth-Century Empire

The historical topic of *Anandamath* is a popular uprising led by *santans*, devotees of an ascetic order (*sannyasi*), during the Bengal famine of 1770. (This was the first in a historical succession of famines exacerbated by imperial misrule. As Deputy Magistrate and Deputy Collector of Jessore, Bankim would have witnessed firsthand the effects of the 1873–74 famine in Bengal.) The targets of the uprising are ostensibly the country's Muslim overlords, rather than the British who will succeed them, although the novel makes it clear that the former are East India Company (EIC) clients. Bankim reiterates the imperial theme of union: Once the Mughals are cleared out, British rule may be good for India, a necessary stage in its historical evolution. In a "Notice" to the second edition, he cites a newspaper review of *Anandamath*:

> The leading idea of the plot is this – should the national mind feel justified in harbouring violent thoughts against the British Government? Or to present the question in another form, is the establishment of English supremacy providential in any sense? Or to put it in a still more final and conclusive form, with what purpose and with what immediate end in view did Providence send the British to this country? ... We may state it in this form: India is bound to accept the scientific method of the west and apply it to the elucidation of all truth. (Chatterji 127–8)

No doubt Bankim was seeking to reassure British censors his work was not seditious. The thesis is expounded in the novel by the mysterious guru of the insurgent Brotherhood:

> The outward knowledge no longer exists in this land, and there's no one to teach it.... So we must bring in the outward knowledge from another country. The English are very knowledgeable in the outward knowledge, and they're very good at instructing people. Therefore we'll make them king. And when by this teaching our people are well instructed about external things, they'll be ready to understand the inner. Then no longer will there be any obstacles to spreading the Eternal Code, and the true Code will shine forth by itself again. And till that day comes – so long as the Hindu is not wise and virtuous and strong once more – English rule will remain intact. (Chatterji 229)

Once again, we read the dialectical logic of union: India will be strengthened by the synthesis of British practical and scientific knowledge with Hindu spiritual wisdom. But the present affirmation inverts the imperial hierarchy, putting practical knowledge, a means to an end, at the service of spiritual wisdom, an end in itself. Unstated but clearly implicit is a historical future in which Indians will be able to assume full nationhood once they have learnt Western techniques of governmental and economic management. From a staple of liberal imperialism, the theme would become a staple of

Indian nationalist discourse, affirming an "interior" domain of anticolonial sovereignty during British rule (Koditschek 269–85; P. Chatterjee 6). *Anandamath* bristles with fierce rhetoric about ridding India of the degenerate Muslims; at the same time, in a series of epic battle scenes, Bankim casts EIC soldiers and sepoys as the enemy – narrating with bloodthirsty relish the feats of the *santan* warriors as they stab, spear, and shoot down "whiteskins" (*Gōrā* / গোরা).

"For the novel to flourish in India, it needed to be rendered in indigenous terms that could translate and adapt the British model to Indian needs"; accordingly, Bankim combines themes and tropes of Scott-style historical fiction with those of Hindu mythology and epic (Joshi 170, 154). His is a more audacious solution to the relation between human agency and national destiny, a crux of the historical novel, than Kingsley's reversion of the protagonist to swashbuckling action hero. The men in *Anandamath* are all pretty much alike, indistinguishable and interchangeable; instead, the role of epic hero, bearer of historical purpose, is filled by a communal agent, the *santan* Brotherhood. *Anandamath* exalts the revolutionary dynamism that the "classical form of the historical novel" worked hard to defuse, the realization of a general will in collective action. Scott's decisive treatment of revolutionary collective action, in *Old Mortality* (1816), brands it with fanaticism – doomed to escalate into genocidal millenarianism. Bankim's *santans*, like Scott's Covenanters, are textbook fanatics, as (no doubt) the bearers of historical destiny must be. They shift the work's formal center of gravity away from the conventions of the (Western) novel, with its focus on personal, individual agency, toward nonnarrative genres, such as the ritual catechism (as in Mahendra's initiation into the Brotherhood) and the choric ode or anthem – the soon-to-be-famous "Bande [Vande] Mataram":

> I revere the Mother! The Mother
> Rich in waters, rich in fruit,
> Cooled by the southern airs,
> Verdant with the harvest fair. (Chatterji 144)

The Brotherhood gives voice to its communal identity (dissolving constituent individual identities) as "the Mother's Children" (146) in the hymn to a generic, transcendent maternal figure.

Meanwhile it is the actual women characters, Shanti and Kalyani, who rescue *Anandamath* for novelistic values; who, by virtue of lively individuation, ensure it stays interesting as a novel. Each acts out the role of dutiful wife to a subversive extreme: self-sacrifice (she literally dies and returns to life) in Kalyani's case, and its contrary, a polymorphous free-spiritedness, in Shanti's. Shanti is the novel's wild card, the bearer of existential excess.

## 8 The Historical Novel and Nineteenth-Century Empire

Brought up among men, she chooses to dress in men's clothes and likes nothing better than to wander off into the jungle by herself, even after her marriage. When the uprising breaks out, she joins the *santan* order "in the guise of a boy-ascetic" under the name Nabinananda. Shanti/Nabinananda outdoes her comrades in prowess, deftly switching roles between male warrior and female temptress, outwitting and overpowering British soldiers. She encounters the English officer Captain Thomas in the forest, disarms him, and doffs her boy-ascetic guise to reveal "a woman's form of wondrous beauty!" (Chatterji 192). Smitten, the Captain asks Shanti to come away with him:

> "As your concubine, I suppose!"
> "You can live as my wife, but I shan't marry you."
> "Well, I have something to ask you too," said Shanti. "We had
>   a red-faced monkey at home; it's dead now, and its hutch is empty.
>   If I tie a chain around your waist, will you live in that hutch?
>   We've got lovely bananas in our garden." [...]
> "It's a fine thing to eat bananas," said the Captain. "Do you have some?"
> "Here," said Shanti with contempt. "Here's your gun. There's
>   no point in talking to savages like you." (192)

The scene reprises Amyas's jungle encounter with Ayacanora, in *Westward Ho!*, only to have the alluring nymph fling the racialized language of imperial dominance at the English intruder.

"Shanti occupies an ambivalent status, not indeed of being half-woman and half-man (*ardhanarisvara*), but of being, in a sense, fully woman-and-man," explains the novel's modern editor: "This liminal existence symbolizes her transformation, at the end of the action, into one kind of new woman Bankim envisaged for Mother-India-as-she-would be" (Chatterji 13). (Bankim advocated education and equal rights for women in modern India: B. C. Chatterjee 54–68; Koditschek 280–1.) Shanti's path through *Anandamath* veers wide of any ideological script, however. She comes to life as an embodiment of wild exuberant playfulness, a consummation of the historical novel's trickster-shapeshifter. Wavering not between allegiances but between sexes, Shanti's polyvalent – queer, trans – amplification of the trickster function energizes a utopian swerve from the plot of national destiny. She acts out the evasion of laws and categories that was always latent in the wavering protagonist's disconnection from historical purpose. At the end of the novel, unsettling the *santan* leader's nomination of her as incarnation of the national "Mother," Shanti and her husband Jibananda (whom she has brought back from the dead) renew the *santan* vow of celibacy and go off as wandering pilgrims – withdrawing from the arena of history to the timeless horizon of legend:

> Then both rose up, and hand in hand were lost to view in the boundless expanse of the moonlit night.
>   Alas, Mother, will they ever return? Will you ever again bear in your womb a son like Jibananda and a daughter like Shanti? (Chatterji 228)

As with the exile of Rebecca in *Ivanhoe*, a melancholy yearning toward those lost to history – too great for its worldly settlements – overcasts the novel's resolution.

## Works Cited

Aubert de Gaspé, Philippe. *The Canadians of Old*. Translated by Charles G. D. Roberts, Appleton & Co., 1867.
Banerjee, Sukanya. "Transimperial." *Victorian Literature and Culture*, vol. 46, nos. 3/4, 2018, pp. 925–8.
Bell, Duncan. *The Idea of Greater Britain: Empire and the Future of World Order, 1860–1900*. Princeton UP, 2007.
Bruzelius, Margaret. *Romancing the Novel: Adventure from Scott to Sebald*. Bucknell UP, 2007.
Cabajsky, Andrea. "The National Tale from Ireland to French Canada: Putting a Generic Incentive into a New Perspective." *Canadian Journal of Irish Studies*, vol. 31, no. 1, 2005, pp. 29–37.
Chatterjee, Bankim Chandra. *Equality (Samya)*. Translated by Bibek Debroy, Liberty Institute, 2002.
Chatterjee, Partha. *The Nation and Its Fragments: Colonial and Postcolonial History*. Princeton UP, 1993.
Chatterji, Bankimcandra [Bankim Chandra Chatterjee]. *Anandamath, or The Sacred Brotherhood*. Translated by Julius J. Lipner, Oxford UP, 2005.
Dentith, Simon. *Epic and Empire in Nineteenth-Century Britain*. Cambridge UP, 2006.
Dilke, Charles Wentworth. *Greater Britain: A Record of Travel in English-Speaking Countries in 1867 and 1868*. Macmillan, 1868, 3 vols.
Doyle, Arthur Conan. *The White Company*. Smith, Elder, 1909.
Freedgood, Elaine. "The Novel and Empire." *The Oxford History of the Novel in English*. Vol. 3: *The Nineteenth-Century Novel 1820–1880*, edited by John Kucich and Jenny Bourne Taylor, Oxford UP, 2012, pp. 377–91.
Green, Martin. *Dreams of Adventure, Deeds of Empire*. Routledge & Kegan Paul, 1983.
Hensley, Nathan K. *Forms of Empire: The Poetics of Victorian Sovereignty*. Oxford UP, 2016.
Joshi, Priya. *In Another Country: Colonialism, Culture, and the English Novel in India*. Columbia UP, 2002.
Kingsley, Charles. *Westward Ho! Or, The Voyages and Adventures of Sir Amyas Leigh, Knight of Burrough, in the County of Devon, in the Reign of Her Most Glorious Majesty, Queen Elizabeth*. Macmillan, 1855, 3 vols.
Koditschek, Theodore. *Liberalism, Imperialism, and the Historical Imagination: Nineteenth-Century Visions of a Greater Britain*. Cambridge UP, 2011.

Lincoln, Andrew. *Walter Scott and Modernity*. Edinburgh UP, 2007.
Lukács, Georg. *The Historical Novel*. Translated by Hannah and Stanley Mitchell. U of Nebraska P, 1983.
Maxwell, Richard. *The Historical Novel in Europe, 1650–1950*. Cambridge UP, 2009.
McNeil, Kenneth. *Scottish Romanticism and Collective Memory in the British Atlantic*. Edinburgh UP, 2020.
Mufti, Nasser. *Civilizing War: Imperial Politics and the Poetics of National Rupture*. Northwestern UP, 2017.
Seeley, J. R. *The Expansion of England: Two Courses of Lectures*. Macmillan, 1883.
Sutherland, J. A. *Victorian Novelists and Publishers*. Athlone P, 1976.
Thackeray, W. M. *The Virginians: A Tale of the Last Century*. J. M. Dent, 1911, 2 vols.
Trumpener, Katie. *Bardic Nationalism: The Romantic Novel and the British Empire*. Princeton UP, 1997.

# 9

CHRISTINA MORIN

# Gothic Plots and the Nineteenth-Century Irish Novel

In Catherine Cuthbertson's prolix gothic novel *Romance of the Pyrenees* (1803), the long-suffering heroine, Victoria, is frequently defended by Hippolyto, a sympathetic Black man who has ostensibly been enslaved by Victoria's abductor, Don Manuel. Although Victoria describes Hippolyto simply as "a gentleman" (Cuthbertson 1: 269), those around her repeatedly register either racist disgust at his skin color or surprise at the apparent disjunction between his character and his appearance: "although nature drew Hippolyto in shade, he is one of the noblest works her hand ever pourtrayed" (Cuthbertson 1: 330). Teased about her affection for Hippolyto, Victoria insists that she could never love him, not because of "the colour of his complexion" (Cuthbertson 2: 261), but because she believes herself to be in love with another man: "to give my heart to Hippolyto," she declares, "would surely be so very contrary to Nature's dictates, that I must ever consider it an utter impossibility" (Cuthbertson 2: 251). Victoria nevertheless eventually marries Hippolyto, having been manipulated into understanding that doing so is the only way to rescue him from death, and thereby invites the horror of those around her. As Victoria's companion, Roselia, observes, "the dreadful idea of her beautiful, accomplished, and high-born lady becoming the wife of an obscure negro" could not be borne (Cuthbertson 2: 278). The threatening specter of miscegenation is neatly avoided when Hippolyto's blackness is revealed to be a ruse, cleverly fabricated with dye to produce "a disguise so secure that no danger of detection could possibly be apprehended" (Cuthbertson 4: 164). This disclosure offers a convenient way of squaring Hippolyto's heroism with his appearance at the same time that it gestures toward the literary gothic's use of racial others and otherness "to shore up the normative 'human as white, male, middle class, and heterosexual at times when the desired certainty of this standard was being called into question by rapid changes'" (Wester 157).[1] Hippolyto turns out, in fact, to be a white European aristocrat – Orlando – who had earlier fallen in love with Victoria on a chance encounter at a masquerade ball and who had later infiltrated her prison in his improbable disguise in order to effect her escape.

Cuthbertson's flirtation with interracial marriage in *Romance of the Pyrenees* calls to mind numerous other Irish gothic fictions of the Romantic period, discussed in further detail later in this chapter, and highlights Irish Romantic writers' deployment of the gothic mode to explore, in Laura Doyle's terms, "the contradictory practices and racial ideologies of British empire" (526). In its figuring of Hippolyto as at once an abhorrent, subjugated Other and an innately noble, civilizing force possessing the necessary masculine power to rescue the heroine once and for all, the novel invites readers to question the real source of villainy in the narrative as well as the period's colonial dichotomies of savagery and civilization, premodernity and modernity. Moreover, while *Romance of the Pyrenees* is not itself concerned with Irish subject matter, it gestures toward contemporary Irish gothics that are, and in which questions of empire and race become much more obviously linked to Irish national identity in the years surrounding the 1798 Rebellion, the Act of Union (1800) and resulting Anglo-Irish Union (1801), and Robert Emmet's 1803 Rebellion. More than that, it speaks to the manner in which Irish literary treatments of issues such as slavery, empire, and Orientalism are so often read as being in some way allegorical, the racialized others and exotic locales of texts such as *Romance of the Pyrenees* understood as "contrivance[s]" by which to explore Ireland's own colonial history and condition (Rajan, qtd. in Wright, "Introduction" 19).[2] Such readings frequently sidestep Irish involvement in the British imperial project and,[3] as John Brannigan suggests, falsely exonerate Ireland from racism:

> [O]ne reason why racism in modern Irish culture has largely been ignored by contemporary cultural critics is because of the tendency to explain racism as the product of colonialism. As a correlative to that argument, or perhaps as an alternative formulation, it might be said that the association of racism and nationalism is obscure in the Irish situation, since Irish nationalism is often seen as a movement of liberation from colonialism and therefore from the racist ideologies underpinning colonialism. (10)

Brannigan's focus in his study is on literary and cultural production in Ireland from the foundation of the Free State in 1922 to the 1980s, but his arguments are relevant to the present discussion, not least because of Irish Romanticism's adoption and promotion of cultural nationalism during a period in which an independent Irish political identity seemed out of reach. Turning to a selection of what Franz Potter terms "trade Gothic" (1) alongside more well-known Irish gothics – Cuthbertson's *Romance of the*

*Pyrenees*, Regina Maria Roche's *The Children of the Abbey* (1796), Maria Edgeworth's *Castle Rackrent* (1800), the anonymously published *Amasina; or the American Foundling* (1804), Sydney Owenson, Lady Morgan's *The Wild Irish Girl* (1806), Henrietta Rouvière Mosse's *Arrivals from India* (1812), and Charles Robert Maturin's *Melmoth the Wanderer* (1820) – this essay investigates early nineteenth-century Irish fiction's use of gothic plots to explore and represent Ireland's relationship to empire and linked discourses of racial hierarchies. Taken together, these works provide valuable insight into the at times contradictory approach to questions of empire, relative civilization/barbarity, and ethnographies of race adopted by Irish Romantics.

## Race, Empire, and Romantic Gothic in Ireland

Much has been written about race and processes of colonization and anti-colonialism in *fin-de-siècle* Irish gothic, in particular Sheridan Le Fanu's *Carmilla* (1872) and Bram Stoker's *Dracula* (1897),[4] and, indeed, about what Patrick Brantlinger has compellingly termed "imperial gothic" more widely (227). As Brantlinger posits, imperial gothic emerges in the final decades of the nineteenth century as a response to Victorian imperialism, a function of the anxieties inherent to "the climax of the British Empire" (227–8). However, it is worth remembering here that gothic literary production had been invested in questions of empire from its beginnings in the latter half of the eighteenth century, as is perhaps most evident in Oriental or "quasi-Oriental" gothic works such as William Beckford's *Vathek, An Arabian Tale* (1786), Matthew Lewis's *The Castle Spectre* (1797), and Robert Southey's *Thalaba the Destroyer* (1801).[5] In these works, Oriental and gothic modes combine to differentiate England from the East and colonized or soon-to-be colonized territories by depicting the latter as all that which England is not – barbaric, uncivilized, irreligious, and oversexed. Although distinct in many ways from other areas of the British Empire, Ireland operated in the English cultural consciousness in a very similar manner to "the East," and had done so long before Ireland was legislatively incorporated into Great Britain in 1801 with the enactment of the Anglo-Irish Union and the associated establishment of the Kingdom of Great Britain and Ireland. Approved in the traumatic wake of the 1798 Rebellion, the Union spelled the end of the free Irish parliament established in 1782 by Henry Grattan and rendered Ireland, as William Drennan famously put it, "A nation of abortive men, / That dart – the tongue; and point – the pen" (13). Drennan may have lamented the exchange of military and political might for mere discursive power, but Irish literary production very quickly

## 9 Gothic Plots and the Nineteenth-Century Irish Novel

and purposefully addressed itself to the task of (re)defining Ireland by way of its literary and cultural heritage. As Katie Trumpener, Ina Ferris, Claire Connolly, and others have so usefully demonstrated, Irish Romantic writers and the forms with which they became associated, particularly the regional novel, the national tale, and the historical novel, were heavily invested in defining and defending Ireland against longstanding English stereotypes of the country as uncivilized and barbaric.

Conventionally, the gothic, in this scenario, has been read as outdated and unhelpfully complicit with the negative stereotypes that branded Ireland "[an] atavistic [zone] of the irrational populated by primitive monsters" (Killeen 3). With the Union requiring new, more concerted attention to overturning depictions of a gothicized Ireland, the literary gothic necessarily made way for regional and national forms at the turn of the century, or so the traditional arguments suggest. In countering derogatory colonial views of Ireland, however, Irish writers both drew upon gothic modes and plots in their fictions and deployed what H. L. Malchow calls "a 'racial gothic' discourse" to distinguish Ireland and the Irish from more inherently uncivilized peoples elsewhere (2). Far from being seen as racist, this use of racialized discourse by Irish Romantics has frequently been understood as simply a reaction to Ireland's own experience of colonization. Responding to Luke Gibbons's arguments about Irish gothic as a function of the racialization of the Irish within empire and their concurrent equation with other "primitive cultures or 'doomed races'" (13), Brannigan suggests that while research has ably traced the manner in which "theories of racial inferiority were used by British imperial powers to consolidate colonial rule over the Irish," less attention has been paid to "the adoption of racial theories within Irish nationalist discourse [as] anything other than a knee-jerk reaction to colonial racism" (14 note 17). Such blindness to Irish cultural racism has arguably contributed to the still current misconception that the Irish cannot themselves be racist because they, too, were subject to racist behavior, including enslavement, in the past – an idea forcefully opposed by, for instance, the recent protests against asylum seekers' accommodation in East Wall, Dublin (2022), and reactions to the death of George Nkencho at the hands of Gardaí in 2021.[6] However, what the works discussed here underline are the difficulties and complexities inherent to writing from a marginal position within the British Empire while negotiating Ireland's place within and alongside it. In fact, Irish Romantic writers are often complicit in racial ideologies about other colonized people as they seek to promote the civilization of the Irish and/or the country's significance to Britain. In this, Irish Romantics might be said to share in what Manu Samriti Chander identifies as the hallmark of being a "brown Romantic": a "state of in-betweenness" marked by a "desire to be part of the dominant culture ... coupled with a desire to resist that very culture" (107).

The conflict Chander ably traces is evident, for instance, in *Romance of the Pyrenees*. While Cuthbertson seems to push against the "cliché of racist writing" noted by Malchow, namely "[t]he threat that white women might be brutalized by oversexed black men of great strength and size" (25), her novel ultimately abandons any anti-racist agenda it might seem to espouse as its gothic plot comes to an end with a series of deaths and revelations that legitimize and almost literally whitewash Victoria's marriage to Hippolyto. A similar movement of resistance to stereotypes followed by apparent support for the systems that uphold them is registered in the anonymously published *Amasina; or the American Foundling* (1804). Late in the narrative, the novel builds a shared sympathy between Irish, English, and Native American characters when the hero, Delwick, is captured by "a group of savages" while campaigning with the British Army in South Carolina during the Revolutionary War (Anon. 2: 305).[7] Delwick seems destined to be slain by the so-called "queen of Carolina" in revenge for the murder of her son, "the noble prince Auzolettee Shela," killed in leading an "attack [on] the invaders of liberty" (Anon. 2: 306). He is rescued, however, by Zorayandee, Auzolettee's sister, on vowing never to enact violence "against a savage of America" again (Anon. 2: 310). Her compassion is lauded as defying racial stereotypes: "Was this European goodness, or American barbarism? Answer, ye philanthropists, and with justice acknowledge, there blooms a female Howard [presumably a reference to philanthropist and penal reformer, John Howard (1726?–1790)], in a world where we have been taught to expect only vice, cruelty and murder" (Anon. 2: 311). Yet, while Zorayandee functions as an ultimately empathetic character, she also draws attention to what the novel depicts as truly gothic behavior – the revolutionary zeal of the patriots fighting for independence from Britain. Delwick's involvement in what appears to be the siege of Charleston (1780) specifically denigrates the Revolutionary War and neatly sidesteps the very recent history of Irish rebelliousness, namely Emmet's 1803 Rebellion, producing a kind of colonial national tale, whereby Ireland can grow out of its gothic identity through participation in the British Empire (Morin, "Bildungsroman" 77–8).

As in later national tales, the integration of Ireland into Britain and British concerns is symbolically suggested in *Amasina* by marriage between the Irish heroine and the English Delwick. However, the use of gothic elements – and specifically an aborted wedding scene that will be repeated in both Sydney Owenson's *The Wild Irish Girl* (1806) and Charles Maturin's *Melmoth the Wanderer* (1820) – conveys significant doubt about the future

## 9 Gothic Plots and the Nineteenth-Century Irish Novel

of this relationship. Just as Amasina is about to marry another man, convinced that Delwick is dead, her former lover reappears:

> She faultered; the deep blush that had mantled her cheek undividedly vanished; the sacred, unalterable, only death-dissolving affirmative hovered on her trembling lips; when all attention was attracted by an impetuous trampling up the avenue; a superb equipage drawn by six horses, covered entirely with foam by the velocity of their motion, stops at the gate, and almost instantly the drawing-room door bursts open, and an elegant young man reeling frantically in, views the groupe before him, and exclaiming, in a voice nearly indistinct by agitation, "Am I too – too late?" staggers a few paces forward, and drops in an agony at Amasina's feet. (Anon. 2: 301)

As the narrator reports, those gathered soon recognize the stranger as "the dead – the buried – the lamented DELWICK!!" (Anon. 2: 301). The curious juxtaposition of past and present tenses in this passage suggests that time is out of joint and, while the marriage of Amasina and Delwick is soon after celebrated with joy, apparently vanquishing the ghosts of the past once and for all, uncertainty lingers, as it does in Owenson's later *The Wild Irish Girl*, very often understood as the first Irish national tale. Like *Amasina*, *The Wild Irish Girl* features, as its title suggests, an Irish heroine and envisions a meeting of representative Irish and English characters on Irish soil. This narrative of encounter depends, in the first instance, on a belief in the intrinsically gothic nature of Ireland and its people. Indeed, having been exiled from England by his father, Horatio Mortimer travels to Ireland, expecting to find himself surrounded by cannibalistic "*Esquimaux*" (Owenson 13). His prejudiced thinking reflects his grounding in the work of Fynes Moryson (1565/6–1630) – Horatio recounts "meeting somewhere with the quaintly written travels of *Moryson* through Ireland" (Owenson 13) – but also, more widely, contemporary depictions of the colonial Other as defined by a "cannibal impulse" that cements its gothic and "monstrous" nature (Malchow 41). As Horatio becomes acquainted with the Irish princess, Glorvina, and her family, the gothic otherness of Ireland begins to wane and the narrative itself transitions from a plot of gothic encounter to a sentimental romance, as Horatio and Glorvina fall in love (Matthews-Kane 13–14). By the end of the novel, it is suggested, Horatio has undergone a complete cultural conversion that culminates in his engagement to Glorvina – moments after he, like Delwick, appears almost supernaturally to interrupt a wedding ceremony between Glorvina and Horatio's own father – and a future marriage which, it is hoped, will be "prophetically typical of a national unity of interests and affections" between England and Ireland (Owenson 250). Yet, as Bridget Matthews-Kane suggests, the heavy use of gothic tropes and conventions in the closing scenes of the novel, including the abortive wedding, transforms sentimental romance back into a gothic one and emphasizes Owenson's unease with the Act of Union as just the most recent iteration of a long history of Irish subjugation (Matthews-Kane 14).

Uncertainty is a key idea in Maria Edgeworth's *Castle Rackrent* (1800), too, where racial stereotyping and contemporary understandings of the term gothic are combined to equate the feckless Rackrent landlords with racial others elsewhere. Notably, Sir Kit's Jewish wife is dismissed as "little better than a blackamoor" (Edgeworth 25). Against racial stereotyping of the Black female body as physically other and sexually excessive – ideas powerfully demonstrated by the near contemporary exhibition of the body of Saartjie Baartman, the so-called Hottentot Venus – Sir Kit's wife is completely subjugated by her abusive husband, who, unhappy with her refusal to relinquish her diamond cross, imprisons her in her bedroom and serves her pork. She thus becomes the victim of a plot of domestic confinement and male violence familiar from near contemporary gothic fictions, including those by Ann Radcliffe (1764–1823), Regina Maria Roche (1763/4–1845), Clara Reeve (1729–1807), and other prominent practitioners of what Ellen Moers would later instrumentally term "female gothic" (90). As such, Sir Kit's wife functions as a largely sympathetic character, despite being imaged as the villain of the piece by the Rackrent family retainer, Thady: "Her diamond cross was, they say, at the bottom of it all; and it was a shame for her, being his wife, not to show more duty, and to have given it up when he condescended to ask so often such a bit of a trifle in his distresses" (Edgeworth 36).

Edgeworth's use of a gothic plot of female detention and male violence, and the resulting contradictory construction of the racialized Other, is of a piece with depictions of non-Europeans in late eighteenth and early nineteenth-century English gothics and Oriental tales. Think, for instance, of the violent yet heroic characterization of the enslaved men, Hassan and Saib, in Lewis's *The Castle Spectre* (1797), or the eponymous antihero of Charlotte Dacre's Oriental gothic tale, *Zofloya; or, The Moor* (1806), in which, as Peter Kitson argues, "the hyper-Orientalised body of the Arab male ... is viewed as a site of both desire and danger" (180). These works clearly respond to the anti-slavery debate of the late eighteenth century – Lewis famously inherited a sizeable estate in Jamaica – as well as to the Haitian Revolution (1791–1804). However, while it would be tempting to read *Castle Rackrent*'s racialized female character as a plea for manumission, in anticipation of the 1833 abolition of slavery in Britain, we would do well to remember Edgeworth's emphasis on what is truly gothic in her tale: "the race of the Rackrents" (Edgeworth 4). I have argued elsewhere that Edgeworth's title purposely constructs her novel as a gothic romance, despite

## 9 Gothic Plots and the Nineteenth-Century Irish Novel

the exclusion in the narrative of conventional gothic imagery and tropes, in particular, the use of the supernatural (Morin, *Novel* 98). Edgeworth's tale further insists throughout on the Rackrents as being "long since extinct" (Edgeworth 4); they represent a gothic past that must and, indeed, as her paratext frequently suggests, had already been relinquished by the time of publication, in order for modern Ireland to take shape. Despite her sympathetic appeal, therefore, Sir Kit's wife is shown to be no better, if also no worse, than her husband in their shared gothic identities. She is gothicized – made to seem uncivilized and barbaric – by her racially othered body, he by his attachment to arcane ways and identities, including, most notably, a native Catholic Irishness that continues to contaminate and delegitimize the Rackrent family's claim to its titles and estates. Much as Edgeworth would suggest in her later short story, "The Grateful Negro" (1804), and in her national tales of the first two decades of the nineteenth century, the key to dealing with both enslaved peoples and the native Irish population is a conservative paternalism that maintains hierarchical distinctions between the rulers and the ruled.[8]

A similarly conservative message that applauds British paternalism is delivered in Henrietta Rouvière Mosse's *Arrivals from India* (1812), which begins with the apparently spectral return to England of "lord Riverston himself, risen, as it were, from the dead" (1: 59). It turns out that Riverston is not a ghost, but his arrival on "the fleet" in place of the anticipated "baubles" for a "grand gala" initiates a tale of intrigue in which both race and class signify otherness and potential threat to the nation (Mosse 1: 3). Riverston has been absent from England for over twenty years, having sailed on "the Bengal fleet" shortly before his father dies, his beloved sister Adelaide is disowned and subsequently driven to her death in mysterious circumstances, and a merchant upstart who had ingratiated himself with the then Lord Riverston, Sir James Stretton, takes possession of his estate and wealth (Mosse 1: 59). When it is understood that Riverston is alive and well, comments focus on his corporeal appearance as well as that of his companions:

> Riverston himself, to be sure, is an European – but, good Lord! for his tawny children, and party-coloured household – our table will look like the halt of a caravan by the side of a spring – how I hate this yellow generation of the desert! (Mosse 1: 70).

Although Fanny Stretton has no objection to having "black attendants," as, she says, "it's style," other characters are actively hostile to Riverston's party (Mosse 1: 70). Fanny's lady's maid, for instance, expresses the hope that "my lady won't ask me to wait upon Miss What's-her-name, the filthy black *creeter*; I would not dress her for the world; she'd soil my fingers" (Mosse 1: 115).

The suntanned looks of Riverston and his family – all white Europeans by birth – set them apart, as do their attitudes toward the colonial project. Despite traveling to India as a British military officer, Lord Riverston understands British rule there to have gone awry; it is, he suggests, "the unprincipled usurpations of mercantile ambition" (Mosse 1: 245). Riverston distances himself from this corruption by way of his paternalistic stance to the Indian people; he is described in Edgeworthian terms as a humane and compassionate colonial figure who has attained his wealth honestly and who is regarded with affection by the native people. Indeed, the narrative pairs Riverston and his family with the Indian people in describing them as victims of a kind of gothic commercialism that cares only for wealth and status. The socially destabilizing effects of personal greed and an economic order based on consumerism fed, at least in part, by the colonies, is apparent in the second half of the novel, which unravels a gothic plot of haunted houses, insane mothers, adopted babies, and disguised identities that eventually reveals the real villainy of the tale: The monstrous greed and ambition of Stretton and his "new" money. He dies in a scene familiar from Radcliffean gothic tales of the 1790s and early 1800s when the apparently dead Adelaide appears before him as "a tall majestic female, in flowing robes of white," bringing on both a paralytic fit and a deathbed confession in which he acknowledges that the former Lord Riverston had not, in fact, cursed his daughter (Mosse 4: 236).

## Conclusion

Locating gothic monstrosity within England and subjecting to scrutiny the motivations behind colonialism, *Arrivals from India* nevertheless suggests that colonialism itself is acceptable if operated on the basis of benevolent paternalism. More than that, its emphasis on the circulation of goods – the "baubles" from India that Miss Stretton so anxiously awaits and repeatedly comments upon in the opening sections of the book – gestures toward the material culture and economic systems of empire. A similar prominence is accorded to colonial trade in many of the texts discussed here and in early nineteenth-century Irish gothic plots more widely. In *Amasina*, for instance, Delwick is rescued by Mr. Mercer, a wealthy Irish merchant, after his ship from America to England is wrecked off the Bahamian coast. Assisting Delwick to return home and clothing him in his own luxurious "mantle" (Anon. 2: 315), Mr. Mercer signifies the financial success of the Irish abroad and their contribution, by way of mercantilism, to the wider colonial project (Morin, "Bildungsroman" 75). In Maturin's *Melmoth the Wanderer* – not discussed in detail earlier in this chapter but arguably the single most well-known Irish gothic novel of the Romantic period – a cataclysmic shipwreck early in the tale serves to introduce the narrator, John Melmoth, to his spectral ancestor, the eponymous Wanderer, near his former home in County Wicklow, Ireland. Echoed repeatedly throughout the novel's nested tales, and calling to mind the Delwick's experiences in *Amasina*, the opening shipwreck invites us to consider the active role that Irish ports played in the international movement of peoples and goods in the nineteenth century. Extra-diegetically, it reminds us that the success of these novels was very often dependent on the global circulation of goods represented in their pages – a fact that frequently becomes reflected narratologically within their plots. Indeed, as I have argued elsewhere, Irish gothic of the Romantic period often exhibits an acute cartographic consciousness by which it both considers Ireland's global positioning and identity and seeks to situate itself in a global literary marketplace. In the case of Regina Maria Roche, for instance, author of the bestselling gothic novel *The Children of the Abbey* (1796), this manifests itself in narratives focused on "bookish characters that trace the trade routes by which [Roche's] novels [themselves] were consumed by a worldwide readership"; Roche's fiction thus "comment[s] shrewdly on the central position occupied by Irish gothic fiction in the transnational expansion of the Romantic-era book trade" (Morin, *Novel* 157).

Further consideration of this element of the gothic plots of nineteenth-century Irish fiction is, unfortunately, beyond the scope of this essay. It is notable, however, that all of the texts considered here were published in London or Edinburgh by Irish writers who were either emigres from Ireland or who, in the years immediately surrounding the Union, found publication by an Irish publisher untenable. While this reflects the cultural migration of Irish literature in the late eighteenth and early nineteenth centuries, as traced very ably elsewhere, it also speaks to the wider context of the newly emerging transnational literary marketplace and its imbrication within systems of colonial power and empire. In their use of gothic plots and narrative tropes to explore questions of otherness, race, and empire, then, the texts considered here present a nuanced and layered exploration of the realities of the expanding colonial project and Ireland's relationship to it. Investigating the use of gothic conventions and "a 'racial gothic' discourse" in the works discussed here helps us to understand how Irish Romantic writers deployed racist stereotypes to resist but also, at times, implicitly to valorize empire and to create a unique position for Ireland within it. At the same time, this analysis points to the intrinsic connectedness of the literary marketplace and colonial order, suggesting the importance of scholarly attention to the global circulation, impact, and reception of Irish gothic fiction in the long nineteenth century. Success in the global literary arena was enabled to a large extent by the networks, routes, and activities of colonialism, creating a kind of gothic feedback loop, recognition of which may help to elucidate the contradictory depictions of race and empire in Romantic-era Irish gothic literature.

## Notes

1. Wester is quoting Hogle (205).
2. Rajan is speaking specifically about Sydney Owenson's *The Missionary* (1811), but the idea is frequently extrapolated to Irish Romantic fiction more broadly.
3. Daniel Sanjiv Roberts cogently observes: "While Irishmen and Irish goods circulated freely in the empire, strengthening imperial growth in proportion to its massive population and large-scale production of raw materials and agricultural products for Britain, Ireland itself, on account of restrictive trading laws and political subservience to Westminster during this period, is often under-represented in the narrative of British empire, apart from the relatively small numbers of elite voices of political ascendancy" (135).
4. See, for instance, Arata, Gibbons, Malchow, Valente, and Warren.
5. Makdisi uses the term "quasi-Oriental" to suggest the ways in which much of the literature that emerged from British Orientalism in the eighteenth century had little to do "with actual Arabic or Persian cultural or literary forms" (62).
6. Recent work on the so-called Irish slave myth is invaluable here. See, for example, Hogan, McAtackney, and Reilly.
7. I discuss the anachronism of Delwick's involvement in the Revolutionary War in "The Gothic Bildungsroman" (Morin 77 note 63).
8. For a consideration of "The Grateful Negro" and its anti-abolitionist message, see Boulukos and Murphy.

## Works Cited

Anon. *Amasina; or, the American Foundling*. Minerva P, 1804, 2 vols.

Arata, Stephen D. "The Occidental Tourist: *Dracula* and the Anxiety of Reverse Colonization." *Victorian Studies*, vol. 33, no. 4, 1990, pp. 621–45.

Boulukos, George E. "Maria Edgeworth's 'Grateful Negro' and the Sentimental Argument for Slavery." *Eighteenth-Century Life*, vol. 23, no. 1, 1999, pp. 12–29.

Brannigan, John. *Race in Modern Irish Literature and Culture*. Edinburgh UP, 2009.

Brantlinger, Patrick. *Rule of Darkness: British Literature and Imperialism, 1830–1914*. Cornell UP, 1988.

Chander, Manu Samriti. *Brown Romantics: Poetry and Nationalism in the Global Nineteenth Century*. Bucknell UP, 2017.

Connolly, Claire. *A Cultural History of the Irish Novel, 1790–1829*. Cambridge UP, 2012.

Cuthbertson, Catherine. *Romance of the Pyrenees*. G. & J. Robinson, 1803, 4 vols.
Doyle, Laura. "At World's Edge: Post/Coloniality, Charles Maturin, and the Gothic Wanderer." *Nineteenth-Century Literature*, vol. 65, no. 5, 2011, pp. 513–47.
Drennan, William. *Fugitive Pieces, in Verse and Prose*. Belfast, 1815.
Edgeworth, Maria. *Castle Rackrent*. 1800. Edited by George Watson. Introduced by Kathryn J. Kirkpatrick. Oxford UP, 1999.
Ferris, Ina. *The Romantic National Tale and the Question of Ireland*. Cambridge UP, 2002.
Gibbons, Luke. *Gaelic Gothic: Race, Colonization, and Irish Culture*. Arlen House, 2004.
Hogan, Liam, Laura McAtackney, and Matthew Reilly. "The Irish in the Anglo-Caribbean: Servants or Slaves?" *History Ireland*, March–April, 2016, pp. 18–22.
Hogle, Jerrold E. "The Gothic Crosses the Channel: Abjection and Revelation in *Le fantôme de l'Opéra*." *European Gothic: A Spirited Exchange, 1760–1960*, edited by Avril Horner, Manchester UP, 2002, pp. 204–29.
Killeen, Jarlath. *The Emergence of Irish Gothic Fiction: History, Origins, Theories*. Edinburgh UP, 2014.
Kitson, Peter J. "Oriental Gothic." *Romantic Gothic: An Edinburgh Companion*, edited by Angela Wright and Dale Townshend, Edinburgh UP, 2015, pp. 167–84.
Makdisi, Saree. "Literature, National Identity, and Empire." *The Cambridge Companion to English Literature, 1740–1830*, edited by Thomas Keymer and Jon Mee, Cambridge UP, 2004, pp. 61–79.
Malchow, H. L. *Gothic Images of Race in Nineteenth-Century Britain*. Stanford UP, 1996.
Matthews-Kane, Bridget. "Gothic Excess and Political Anxiety: Lady Morgan's *The Wild Irish Girl*." *Gothic Studies*, vol. 5, no. 2, 2003, pp. 7–19.
Moers, Ellen. *Literary Women*. The Women's P, 1977.
Morin, Christina. "The Gothic Bildungsroman." *The Irish Bildungsroman*, edited by Gregory Castle, Sarah L. Townsend, and Matthew Reznicek, Syracuse UP, 2025, pp. 60–83.
  *The Gothic Novel in Ireland, c. 1760–1829*. Manchester UP, 2018.
Mosse, Henrietta Rouvière. *Arrivals from India; or, Time's a Great Master*. Minerva P, 1812, 4 vols.
Murphy, Sharon. *Maria Edgeworth and Romance*. Four Courts P, 2004.
Owenson, Sydney, Lady Morgan. *The Wild Irish Girl*. 1806. Edited by Kathryn Kirkpatrick. Oxford UP, 1999.
Potter, Franz J. *The History of Gothic Publishing, 1800–1835: Exhuming the Trade*. Palgrave, 2005.
Rajan, Balachandra. *Under Western Eyes: India from Milton to Macaulay*. Duke UP, 1999.
Sanjiv Roberts, Daniel. "A 'Teague' and a 'True Briton': Charles Johnstone, Ireland and Empire." *Irish Fiction, 1660–1830*, special issue of *Irish University Review*, vol. 41, no. 1, 2011, pp. 133–50.
Trumpener, Katie. *Bardic Nationalism: The Romantic Novel and the British Empire*. Princeton UP, 1997.

Valente, Joseph. *Dracula's Crypt: Bram Stoker, Irishness, and the Question of Blood.* U of Illinois P, 2002.

Warren, L. S. "Buffalo Bill Meets Dracula: William F. Cody, Bram Stoker, and the Frontiers of Racial Decay." *American Historical Review*, vol. 107, no. 4, 2002, pp. 1124–57.

Wester, Maisha. "The Gothic and the Politics of Race." *The Cambridge Companion to the Modern Gothic*, edited by Jerrold E. Hogle, Cambridge UP, 2014, pp. 157–73.

Wright, Julia M. "Introduction," in Sydney Owenson, Lady Morgan, *The Missionary*, edited by Julia M. Wright, Broadview P, 2002, pp. 9–57.

# 10

AVIVA BRIEFEL

# The Victorian Industrial Novel and the Working Classes

The industrial novel, also termed the "social problem" or "condition of England" novel, emerged on the Victorian literary scene in the early 1840s. This subgenre of realist fiction was informed by increasing middle-class awareness of – and anxiety about – the condition of the working classes, particularly following the passage of the Poor Law in 1834 and the emergence of the Chartist movement in 1838.[1] Amanda Anderson argues that the industrial novel's primary objectives were to address "conditions and crises occasioned by the Industrial Revolution in Britain, including the discontent and misery of the working classes; the negative effects of a world increasingly dominated by machinery, alienated labor, and the profit motive; and, not least, the impact of worker uprisings, strikes, and violence" (79). The most influential industrial novels include Frances Milton Trollope's *The Life and Adventures of Michael Armstrong, the Factory Boy* (1840), Benjamin Disraeli's *Sybil* (1845), Elizabeth Gaskell's *Mary Barton* (1848) and *North and South* (1854), Charles Kingsley's *Alton Locke* (1850), Charles Dickens's *Hard Times* (1854), and George Eliot's *Felix Holt* (1866).

Industrial narratives had a difficult task. Intended primarily for a middle-class readership, they attempted to draw attention to the plight of the working classes, particularly factory and mill laborers, but without undermining capitalist structures by endorsing widespread infrastructural change or revolution (Lesjak 3). Novelists' attempts to achieve this delicate balance have led some scholars to critique the genre for not going far enough, for laying aside political reform in favor of eliciting emotional responses, such as sympathy, from their readers. As Carolyn Betensky writes, "Nineteenth-century social-problem novels are largely responsible for the idea that it *matters* how I feel about poverty, whether or not I do anything more than care about it" (1, emphasis in original).

Along with anxieties about working-class revolt, these novels confronted another challenge: How (or whether) to represent the extent to which

British imperialism fueled industrialism's dehumanization, violence, and "ecological degradation" (Hensley and Steer, "Introduction" 2). Sven Beckert traces this network of connections in *Empire of Cotton* (2014), arguing that "slavery and land expropriation on a continental scale created the expansive, and elastic, global cotton supply network necessary for the Industrial Revolution" (92). Sukanya Banerjee urges us to identify these linkages in reading Victorian novels, including industrial fiction, by taking on a "transimperial analytic framework ... by continually questioning the discrete solidities of the (British) nation and placing it in an inexhaustible relation of continuity and interconstitutiveness with the empire 'out there'" ("Transimperial" 925). We should, for example, recognize that the cotton industry depicted in Gaskell's *Mary Barton* was shaped by Britain's campaign to dismantle India's systems of textile production beginning in the eighteenth century, as well as the ecological and humanitarian impacts caused by this campaign, including overproduction and famine (Banerjee, "Ecologies of Cotton"). These crucial connections are lost when the industrial novel's representations of class and gender difference are considered outside the contexts of race and imperialism. As Carolyn Lesjak argues, "The crisis of industrialism, the industrial novel's raison d'être, and its connected attempt to understand the newly emerging experience and processes of modernity cannot be understood outside the context of English nationalism and empire" (25).

Illuminating such networks is an essential aspect of the work that Ronjaunee Chatterjee, Alicia Mireles Christoff, and Amy Wong have termed "undisciplining Victorian studies," in order to understand "how race and racial difference subtend our most cherished objects of study, our most familiar historical and theoretical frameworks, our most engrained scholarly protocols, and the very demographics of our field" (370). Their piece responds to the marginalization of race and empire in Victorian criticism, despite crucial interventions by scholars including Edward Said, Gayatri Spivak, Gauri Viswanathan, and Anne McClintock. In this chapter, I discuss two of the ways in which the industrial novel compels us to make (and, in some cases, overlook) connections between its stated concern with the "condition" of England and how that condition was informed by imperial and racial structures. In the first section, "Working-Class Identities," I examine literary representations of British factory workers in terms that evoke transatlantic slavery and imperial otherness. In the second, "Spaces and Commodities," I turn to British spaces and colonial objects – the imported shawls, calicos, and rugs populating Victorian fiction – that call forth the imperial stories and identities often suppressed in industrial novels.

## Working-Class Identities

In *The Condition of the Working Class in England* (1845), Friedrich Engels compares industrial workers to enslaved peoples:

> The worker is, in law and in fact, the slave of the property-holding class, so effectually a slave that he is sold like a piece of goods, rises and falls in value like a commodity.... The only difference as compared with the old, outspoken slavery is this, that the worker of today seems to be free because he is not sold once for all, but piecemeal by the day, the week, the year, and because no one owner sells him to another, but he is forced to sell himself in this way instead, being the slave of no particular person, but of the whole property-holding class. (91)

Engels deploys an analogy made by earlier critics of industrialism, including the Tory reformer Richard Oastler, who, in an October 16, 1830 letter to the *Leeds Mercury*, contended that Yorkshire factory workers "are at this very moment existing in a state of Slavery, *more horrid* than are the victims of that hellish system – '*Colonial Slavery*'" (qtd. in Gallagher 3, emphasis in original). Catherine Gallagher clarifies that such comparisons were not always intended to condemn slavery but could be used with the intent to "discredit the leaders of the antislavery movement" (5).[2] Nonetheless, the bringing up of slavery in the context of British cotton manufacturing threatened to expose their interconnectedness. The supply of cotton that enabled the Industrial Revolution in Britain depended on multiple strains of oppression, beginning with "slaves in the southern United States growing cotton on land expropriated from Native Americans" (Beckert 85). These systems are a component of "racial capitalism," the idea that structures of racism are "outgrowths of particular models of capitalist development" (Levenson and Paret 333).

We find extensive use of the analogy between factory workers and the enslaved in what is often identified as the first major industrial novel, Frances Trollope's *Michael Armstrong*. Centered on the plight of its titular factory child worker, the novel turns to the language of slavery in appealing for industrial reform: "Woe to those who supinely sit in contended ignorance of the facts ... while thousands of helpless children pine away their unnoted, miserable lives, in labour and destitution, *incomparably more severe*, than any ever produced by negro slavery" (186, emphasis in original). Trollope incorporates characters who are involved in anti-slavery campaigns and deliver "benevolent lamentations over the sable sons of Africa," but who ignore the plight of workers at home (150). This critique is not an indictment of transatlantic slavery per se, but draws on the assumption that British readers would already be outraged by the abuses of slavery – particularly after the recent passage of the Slavery Abolition Act of 1833 – and should now turn to dehumanizing conditions within England. At the same time, repeated analogies to slavery in a novel about British textile production might compel readers to think about the instrumental link between the two. As Lucy Sheehan argues, "Trollope invites us to read the resulting mimesis of slavery and industrialism as evidence of a causal connection that links the factory system backward to the slave trade" (522).[3]

Trollope includes another way in which white workers might become racialized: through the cruelty and degradation of factory labor. Joseph Bizup writes that references to the "'savage' manners and appearance" of laborers in Victorian writings "gave expression to an anxiety that the factory system itself was contributing to the apparent degeneration of the working classes" (85). A character in Trollope's novel remarks that Michael has a "vulgar dark complexion" that sets him apart from upper-class children: "'Tis Africa and Europe.... I should not be at all surprised to find, when the march of philosophy has got a little farther, that the blackamoor look comes along with the condition, and, that the influence of wealth and consequence is ... quickly shown upon the external appearance of men, women, and children" (55–6). Class difference produces racial difference. In his *Artisans and Machinery* (1836), Peter Gaskell describes the negative effects of the "heated atmosphere" of the factory on mill girls, who become a kind of "exotic species": "The female population engaged in mill labour, approximates very closely to that found in tropical climates; puberty, or at least sexual propensities, being attained almost coeval with girlhood" (qtd. in Marshall, 63). For their part, coal miners, especially female miners, came to be "represented as a 'race' apart, figured as racial outcasts, historically abandoned, isolated and primitive" (McClintock 115). Indeed, Nasser Mufti argues that in the first half of the nineteenth century, writers of industrial fiction often depicted the struggle between classes as a "race war" (23–4).

With the character Tom Gradgrind in *Hard Times*, Dickens suggests that a rigid adherence to capitalist and industrial values can provoke the racial transformation of members of the privileged class. Subjected to his father's utilitarian upbringing, Tom undergoes an ethical and moral degradation, which the novel expresses in racist terms. After committing a bank robbery, he hides out in Sleary's Circus – a realm of play that had been closed off to him as a child – and uses minstrel makeup to disguise himself. His father and sister find him "with seams in his black face, where fear and heat had started through the greasy complexion daubed all over it; ... his hands, with the black partly worn away inside, looking like the hands of a monkey" (Dickens 261, 262). Marc Muneal contends that the son's transformation manifests his father's dehumanizing social philosophy: "His own self, his own name, his own humanity has been reduced to blackness, his son's blackened skin a recognizable symbol of an enslaved mind and body in their social context" (96). In yet another acknowledgment that Tom has forsaken his place in white middle-class society, he is expelled from England – presumably to an imperial territory – where he dies before he can return home.[4]

There was one category of British laborer who was frequently marked by racial difference: Irish workers, many of whom had immigrated to English industrial towns as a result of the Great Famine of 1845–49 (Cammack 116). Patrick Brantlinger explains that by the Victorian period, there was a "widespread view in England of the Irish or Celtic 'race' as brutes, savages, degenerates" (136). In *The Condition of the Working Class in England*, Engels egregiously reinforces these stereotypes, describing Irish workers as "little above the savage" for their alleged dirtiness, poor working habits, and alcoholism, adding that "even if the Irish … should become more civilized, enough of the old habits would cling to them to have a strong degrading influence upon their English companions in toil, especially in view of the general effect of being surrounded by the Irish" (104). Extending his racial references, Engels adds, "The Irishman loves his pig as the Arab his horse" (103). Amy Martin elucidates that Engels's view of Irish immigrants reflects a widespread belief that they were "the source of the economic, cultural, and racial degeneration that has in turn engendered class consciousness and working class radical politics" (85).[5]

Gaskell devotes a substantial section of her industrial novel *North and South* to English perspectives on Irish workers. To counter the strike organized against his cotton mill in Milton – a fictional northern town modeled on Manchester – John Thornton brings in a group of Irish workmen. The English workers were

> surprised and indignant at the poor Irish, who had allowed themselves to be imported and brought over to take their places. This indignation was tempered, in some degree, by contempt for "them Irishers," and by pleasure at the idea of the bungling way in which they would set to work, and perplex their new masters with their ignorance and stupidity, strange and exaggerated stories of which were already spreading through the town. (Gaskell 228)

Despite acknowledging that these stories were "exaggerated," Gaskell's narrator implies that there is some truth to them, given the "daily annoyance" of "the incompetence of the Irish hands, who had to be trained to their work, at a time requiring unusual activity" (318). These imported workers are also "characterized in terms of weakness and fear" and "need to be soothed, protected, and comforted," ensuring that, ultimately, they do not pose a real threat to the social hierarchy of the novel (Bhowmik 128). Susanne Cammack contends that we should also consider the significance of Gaskell's rare centering of the "Irish Question" in her novel, which places "Irish characters and concerns at the heart of industrial – and likewise, national – concerns" (122). While reinforcing certain stereotypes about Irishness, Gaskell implicates the British industrial system's mistreatment of its Irish workforce.

There is one strain of *North and South* that unexpectedly weaves together themes of racial difference, slavery, and revolt: the story of Frederick Hale, brother to the novel's heroine, Margaret. Frederick and other crew members of the ship *Avenger*, tasked with tracking down slave ships, had mutinied to overthrow its unjust captain. In the aftermath of this revolt, newspapers depict Frederick as a "'traitor of the blackest dye,' 'a base, ungrateful disgrace to his profession'" (Gaskell 108), and he is forced to exile himself to South America and then to Spain. When Margaret meets her brother after a long separation, she notices a new "swarthiness of his complexion" and a "ferocity of expression that comes over the countenances of all natives of wild or southern countries" (Gaskell 247). Despite his racialization and the fact that his mutiny parallels the violent strike directed against Thornton's mill, Frederick is exonerated by his sister and, by extension, the world of the novel. As Margaret tells him, "You disobeyed authority – that was bad; but to have stood by, without word or act, while the authority was brutally used, would have been infinitely worse" (Gaskell 259). Her sympathy, a valued affect in the Victorian novel, redeems the mutiny as a justified revolt, in contrast to the injustices of the mill strike, during which Margaret had been injured. As Julia Sun-Joo Lee contends, Frederick's rebellion and racialization bring together thematic strains that would otherwise remain invisible. His escape and subsequent racialization lends his story a "formal contiguity to the American slave narrative" (99), signaling yet another instance of the industrial novel's transatlantic mapping of the story of cotton.

## Spaces and Commodities

The fictional settings of the industrial novel are also marked by the global forces that shaped British capitalism. We can locate these traces in Trollope's descriptions of the deplorable conditions of the cotton factory in which Michael Armstrong works, whose overseers and systems of corporal punishment (including lashings) recall slave plantations (Sheehan 529). In *Hard Times*, Dickens famously evokes the exoticism of imperial spaces in describing the fictional Coketown's factories as "melancholy mad elephants" (106), perhaps, as Tamara Ketabgian suggests, to associate British capitalist practices with the supposed injustices of "Asiatic despotism" (59). Jesse Oak Taylor argues that this colonial imagery, along with the description of the novel's setting as "a town of unnatural red and black like the painted face of a savage" (Dickens 26), brings to mind the "imperial encounters undertaken to characterize and subjugate modernity's outsiders" (Taylor 48). Colonial spaces can likewise manifest themselves in the air or atmosphere, as when the heroine Caroline Helstone in Brontë's *Shirley* becomes infected with a disease resembling cholera, which the narrator describes as "the yellow taint of pestilence, covering white Western isles with the poisoned exhalations of the East, dimming the lattices of English homes with the breath of Indian plague" (392).[6]

The most pervasive representations of an imperial presence in the industrial novel are found in the foreign objects scattered in its domestic spaces. In her field-defining book *The Ideas in Things*, Elaine Freedgood urges us to trace the "fugitive meanings" of objects depicted in Victorian narratives, to undertake "metonymical readings" in which an "object is investigated in terms of its own properties and history and then refigured alongside and athwart the novel's manifest or dominant narrative" (12). Using this method, Freedgood analyzes the calico checked curtains found in the working-class home of the heroine of Gaskell's *Mary Barton*. At once conveying the "coziness" and domesticity of a home that is otherwise beset by poverty, the presence of these calico curtains also invokes the "history of the deindustrialization of the Indian textile manufacture, and the rise to dominance of British cotton production.... The blue and white curtains that promise protection at key narrative moments have been purchased at the expense of the laborers who make them in England, and the laborers who no longer make them in South Asia" (Freedgood 57). In addition, the check pattern on these curtains "are associated with the African-Caribbean slave trade, and … the slave trade is in turn associated with Indian calico" (Freedgood 63). The network of connections generated by a seemingly innocuous decoration positions the curtains as "veils that hide and attempt to replace a traumatic loss or lack" (Freedgood 70).[7]

Another thing – or, in this case, substance – that ties this novel to the traumas caused by British imperialism is the opium to which Mary's father, John, becomes addicted. Granting him a dangerous and temporary "forgetfulness" (Gaskell 149) from his difficult life, the drug also captures the cultural amnesia that allows readers to overlook the histories of colonization and enslavement fueling industrialization. Writing about the significance of John Barton's addiction, Liam Corley argues that "Gaskell's choice to set *Mary Barton* during the Opium War [the First Opium War of 1840–42] not only associates the economic violence of the industrialists against the working class with British imperialism in China, it also highlights the metaphoric possibilities of the economic interdependence of the cotton and opium trade" (5). To each imperial thing featured within the pages of the industrial novel is attached a proliferation of associations that disrupt the genre's ostensibly nationalist concerns.

In *North and South*, Gaskell focuses on the significance of Indian shawls, items that were rife with imperial meaning in the mid Victorian period. Margaret Hale poses with a number of these items in one of our first encounters with her:

> Margaret went down laden with shawls, and snuffing up their spicy Eastern smell.... Margaret's tall, finely made figure, in the black silk dress which she was wearing as mourning for some distant relative of her father's, set off the long beautiful folds of the gorgeous shawls.... Occasionally, as she was turned round, she caught a glimpse of herself in the mirror over the chimney-piece, and smiled at her own appearance there – the familiar features in the usual garb of a princess. She touched the shawls gently as they hung around her, and took a pleasure in their soft feel and their brilliant colours, and rather liked to be dressed in such splendour. (9)

This passage interweaves images of British domesticity, gender identity, and imperial commodification. Margaret is introduced to the reader as a young and white English woman admiring her beauty, enhanced by the smell and touch of the Indian things she wraps around her, at the center of her middle-class home.[8] Suzanne Daly explains that Indian shawls served as recurring signifiers of class and gender status in Victorian novels including Charlotte Brontë's *Villette* (1853), Gaskell's *Cranford* (1853), and Elizabeth Braddon's *Lady Audley's Secret* (1862). In *North and South*, an industrial novel about the production of cotton, the presence of these shawls draws attention to histories of production and imperial oppression. While the novel suggests that the shawls worn by Margaret are authentic Indian products, imbued with that "spicy Indian smell," imitation Indian shawls were also being mass-produced in Manchester factories by the time of the novel's publication. Daly argues that Margaret's marriage to Thornton, the Milton cotton-mill owner, at the end of the novel, "serves to valorize Manchester and an industry whose remarkable expansion, commonly attributed to advances in machine technology, was in reality driven by the increase in markets brought about by the expansion of the empire" (32). Ultimately, *North and South* seems to replicate Britain's systematic dismantling of the Indian cotton industry.[9]

Margaret's self-display while wearing the shawls magnifies the fact that her identity as a British domestic woman is shaped by imperialist structures. As Anne McClintock reminds us, imperialism "com[es] into being through *domesticity*" (32, emphasis in original). Like many other industrial novels,

## 10 The Victorian Industrial Novel and Working Classes

*North and South* eventually turns to the marriage plot – Margaret accepts Thornton's proposal – possibly to distract from pressing social and political concerns. Nathan Hensley and Philip Steer argue that Gaskell's narrative "deploys romance to offer its recuperative response to the social and economic forces unleased by the steam-driven economy: the erotics of the marriage plot wrest from this chaos a fantasy of the racially pure, harmonious, and future-oriented nation" ("Signatures of the Carboniferous," 71). While the marriage plot may serve as a distraction in this and other industrial novels, the connections that emerge in these narratives often push against the expected closure of romance. Anderson, for instance, invites us to explore the ways in which "plot tensions and shifting modes can be seen to stage the specific challenges of politics and to register forces that exceed its realm" (84). However they might blend into domestic space, the imperial commodities of the industrial novel insistently ask us to think about their own origin stories, which disrupt the sense of their inherent belonging in England.

In closing, I turn to another image of an imperial commodity, whose out-of-placeness signals the possibility of disruption. In Dickens's *Hard Times*, Josiah Bounderby, whom Raymond Williams describes as the "embodiment of the aggressive money-making and power-seeking ideal which was a driving force of the Industrial Revolution" (93), tries to persuade a visitor about the benefits of Coketown. After arguing that the smoke that pervades the environment is "the healthiest thing in the world in all respects, and particularly for the lungs" (Dickens 119), Bounderby expounds on the ideal conditions in the mills: "It's the pleasantest work there is, and it's the lightest work there is, and it's the best-paid work there is. More than that, we couldn't improve the mills themselves, unless we laid down Turkey carpets on the floors" (Dickens 120). Bounderby's defense of the mills is as blatantly implausible as his argument about the salutary effects of factory smoke. But his reference to the preposterousness of placing Turkey carpets on the factory floor also has the unwanted effect of making the reader imagine *how* these things are related to each other. An imperial commodity fetish par excellence, the Oriental rug appeared in British homes and collections and "elicited the fantasies, fears, and pleasures associated with gaining and losing imperial possessions" (Rappaport 290).[10] The imagined presence of the rug in a factory uncomfortably situates colonial conquest at the heart of British industrial production. In addition, the fact that such a rug would generally appear within a bourgeois household collapses the barriers that middle-class Victorians tried to construct between the private and public, the domestic and political. The carpet in the factory is thus at once completely incongruous and fully logical, signaling the cycles of concealment and exposure that characterize the nineteenth-century industrial novel.

## Notes

1. See Vargo for a discussion of Chartism and its relationship to the social problem novel.
2. Cunliffe explains that these comparisons were sometimes informed by the spurious "argument that, at least on the plantations of the American South, black slave families were relatively well cared for" (15).
3. See also Zlotnick's discussion of the novel.
4. Using Tom's expulsion as an example, Said writes, "Outlying territories are available for use, at will, at the novelist's discretion, usually for relatively simple purposes such as immigration, fortune, or exile" (74).
5. Beatty offers another perspective on Engels and Marx's representations of the Irish by arguing that they also saw them as "a people from the precapitalist past whose supposed communalism simultaneously signposted the socialist future" (844).
6. Torgerson clarifies that the "Asiatic cholera" had reached Western Europe in 1831 and 1848. Because *Shirley* is set in the past, in 1811–12, Brontë alludes to this disease without referring to it by name (Torgerson 3–4).
7. See also Banerjee's discussion of the novel's "ecologies of cotton" and its relationship to the *swadeshi* movement in India in the late nineteenth and early twentieth centuries.
8. Puri writes that the shawls, as "desirable, almost titillating, Indian objects facilitate the performance of a middle-class femininity, ... while themselves becoming unevenly domesticated in the process" (3).
9. Bhowmik also addresses the history of Indian shawls and their significance as "imperial commodities" in Gaskell's novel. For a discussion of the British appropriation of shawls and other Indian commodities, see Chaudhuri.
10. See Moallem and Spooner for the imperial history and significance of this commodity.

## Works Cited

Anderson, Amanda. *Bleak Liberalism*. U of Chicago P, 2016.

Banerjee, Sukanya. "Ecologies of Cotton." *Nineteenth-Century Contexts*, vol. 42, no. 5, 2020, pp. 493–507.

———. "Transimperial." *Victorian Literature and Culture*, vol. 46, nos. 3/4, 2018, pp. 925–8.

Beatty, Aidan. "Marx and Engels, Ireland, and the Racial History of Capitalism." *Journal of Modern History*, vol. 91, no. 4, 2019, pp. 815–47.

Beckert, Sven. *Empire of Cotton: A Global History*. Vintage, 2014.

Betensky, Carolyn. *Feeling for the Poor: Bourgeois Compassion, Social Action, and the Victorian Novel*. U of Virginia P, 2010.

Bhowmik, Urmi. "Empire and the Industrial Novel: Imperial Commodities and Colonial Labor in Elizabeth Gaskell's *North and South*." *Nineteenth-Century Studies*, vol. 26, no. 1, 2012, pp. 117–34.

Bizup, Joseph. *Manufacturing Culture: Vindications of Early Victorian Industry*. U of Virginia P, 2003.

Brantlinger, Patrick. *Taming Cannibals: Race and the Victorians*. Cornell UP, 2011.
Brontë, Charlotte. *Shirley*. Penguin, 2006.
Cammack, Susanne S. "'You Have Made Him What He Is': Irish Laborers and the Preston Strike in Elizabeth Gaskell's *North and South*." *New Hibernia Review*, vol. 20, no. 4, 2016, pp. 113–27.
Chatterjee, Ronjaunee, Alicia Mireles Christoff, and Amy R. Wong. "Introduction: Undisciplining Victorian Studies." *Victorian Studies*, vol. 62, no. 3, 2020, pp. 369–91.
Chaudhuri, Nupur. "Shawls, Jewelry, Curry, and Rice in Victorian Britain." *Western Women and Imperialism: Complicity and Resistance*, edited by Nupur Chaudhuri and Margaret Strobel, Indiana UP, 1992, pp. 231–46.
Corley, Liam. "The Imperial Addiction of *Mary Barton*." *Gaskell Society Journal*, vol. 17, 2003, pp. 1–11.
Cunliffe, Marcus. *Chattel Slavery and Wage Slavery: The Anglo-American Context, 1830–1860*. U of Georgia P, 1979.
Daly, Suzanne. *The Empire Inside: Indian Commodities in Victorian Domestic Novels*. U of Michigan P, 2011.
Dickens, Charles. *Hard Times*. Oxford UP, 2006.
Engels, Friedrich. *The Condition of the Working Class in England*. Oxford UP, 1993.
Freedgood, Elaine. *The Ideas in Things: Fugitive Meaning in the Victorian Novel*. U of Chicago P, 2006.
Gallagher, Catherine. *The Industrial Reformation of English Fiction: Social Discourse and Narrative Form, 1832–1867*. U of Chicago P, 1985.
Gaskell, Elizabeth. *Mary Barton*, edited by Thomas Recchio, Norton, 2008.
—. *North and South*. Oxford UP, 1998.
Hensley, Nathan K. and Philip Steer. "Introduction: Ecological Formalism; or, Love among the Ruins." *Ecological Form: System and Aesthetics in the Age of Empire*, edited by Nathan K. Hensley and Philip Steer, Fordham UP, 2019, pp. 1–18.
—. "Signatures of the Carboniferous: The Literary Forms of Coal." *Ecological Form: System and Aesthetics in the Age of Empire*, edited by Nathan K. Hensley and Philip Steer, Fordham UP, 2019, pp. 63–82.
Ketabgian, Tamara. *The Lives of Machines: The Industrial Imaginary in Victorian Literature and Culture*. U of Michigan P, 2011.
Lee, Julia Sun-Joo. *The American Slave Narrative and the Victorian Novel*. Oxford UP, 2010.
Lesjak, Carolyn. *Working Fictions: A Genealogy of the Victorian Novel*. Duke UP, 2006.
Levenson, Zachary and Marcel Paret. "The Three Dialectics of Racial Capitalism: From South Africa to the U.S. and Back Again." *Du Bois Review*, vol. 20, no. 2, 2022, pp. 333–51.
Marshall, Bridget M. *Industrial Gothic: Workers, Exploitation and Urbanization in Transatlantic Nineteenth-Century Literature*. U of Wales P, 2021.
Martin, Amy E. "Blood Transfusions: Constructions of Irish Racial Difference, the English Working Class, and Revolutionary Possibility in the Work of Carlyle and Engels." *Victorian Literature and Culture*, vol. 32, no. 1, 2004, pp. 83–102.
McClintock, Anne. *Imperial Leather: Race, Gender and Sexuality in the Colonial Contest*. Routledge, 1995.

Moallem, Minoo. *Persian Carpets: The Nation as a Transnational Commodity*. Routledge, 2018.

Mufti, Nasser. *Civilizing War: Imperial Politics and the Poetics of National Rupture*. Northwestern UP, 2018.

Muneal, Marc. "Charles Dickens, Harriet Beecher Stowe, and Tom: The Real Culprit's Name in *Hard Times*." *Nineteenth Century Studies*, vol. 25, no. 1, 2011, pp. 87–100.

Puri, Tara. "Indian Objects, English Body: Utopian Yearnings in Elizabeth Gaskell's *North and South*." *Journal of Victorian Culture*, vol. 22, no. 1, 2017, pp. 1–23.

Rappaport, Erika. "Imperial Possessions, Cultural Histories, and the Material Turn: Response." *Victorian Studies*, vol. 50, no. 2, 2008, pp. 289–96.

Said, Edward W. *Culture and Imperialism*. Vintage, 1993.

Sheehan, Lucy. "'Fraud, Fun, and Feeling': Slavery, Industrialism, and the Mother-Machine in Frances Trollope's Fiction." *Victorian Literature and Culture*, vol. 48, no. 3, 2020, pp. 519–50.

Spooner, Brian. "Weavers and Dealers: The Authenticity of an Oriental Carpet." *The Social Life of Things: Commodities in Cultural Perspective*, edited by Arjun Appadurai, Cambridge UP, 1986, pp. 195–235.

Taylor, Jesse Oak. *The Sky of Our Manufacture: The London Fog in British Fiction from Dickens to Woolf*. U of Virginia P, 2016.

Torgerson, Beth. "Ailing Women in the Age of Cholera: Illness in *Shirley*." *Victorian Review*, vol. 30, no. 2, 2004, pp. 1–31.

Trollope, Frances. *The Life and Adventures of Michael Armstrong, the Factory Boy*. Henry Colburn, 1844.

Vargo, Gregory. *An Underground History of Early Victorian Fiction: Chartism, Radical Print Culture, and the Social Problem Novel*. Cambridge UP, 2018.

Williams, Raymond. *Culture and Society: 1780–1950*. Columbia UP, 1983.

Zlotnick, Susan. *Women, Writing, and the Industrial Revolution*. Johns Hopkins UP, 1998.

## 11

PHILIP STEER

# Victorian Liberalism, Settler Character, and Literary Form

> I never yet could get the proper knack of telling a story. Here I am now ... talking of ... things belonging to the new and deplorable state of affairs which began when this country became "a British colony and possession," and also "one of the brightest jewels in the British crown." I must go back.
>
> F. E. Maning, *Old New Zealand, a Tale of the Good Old Times*

The settler invasions of Australia and New Zealand, along with those of Canada and Southern Africa, were celebrated in Britain throughout the nineteenth century as the positive face of imperialism. "It was in the settler colonies," Duncan Bell argues, "that many liberals found the concrete place of their dreams" (33). Those "dreams" were predicated upon the destruction of Indigenous lifeways and ecosystems. By the turn of the twentieth century, when Australia's settlers numbered around 3,800,000, the Indigenous population had been decimated by an estimated two thirds, to perhaps 90,000; at the same point, there were around 770,000 settlers in New Zealand, while the number of Māori had almost halved to 46,000 (Australian Bureau of Statistics; Jackson and Pool). The demographic and economic growth of these settler polities was hailed by metropolitan commentators as evidence of their world-historical importance as white realms of civilizational progress. In the lectures published as *The Expansion of England* (1883), liberal historian J. R. Seeley influentially asserted the settler colonies' ontological difference, due to their perceived modernity, from India and the so-called dependent empire: "There you have the most progressive race put in the circumstances most favourable to progress. They have no past and an unbounded future. Government and institutions are all ultra-English. All is liberty, industry, invention, innovation, and as yet tranquillity" (176). The entanglement of the liberal rhetoric of settler modernity with racial violence was made more explicit in another lecture, this time delivered in New Zealand in 1869, where the naturalist W. T. L. Travers argued that the attainment of "a populous country, with the arts and letters, the matured policy, and the ennobling impulses of a free people" was ample justification for "the extinction of a people which, in the past had accomplished so imperfectly every object of man's being" (313). Seeley and Travers's willingness to look past or even embrace the genocidal consequences of colonization signals the outer boundaries of the nineteenth-century liberal imagination, which were narrowly drawn around the nature and destiny of the settler populations.

Literary responses to liberalism's "ultra-English" logic of settlement concentrate typically on whether the settler subject matches up to what Stefan Collini terms the period's "ideal of character" (94). Informed by John Locke's *Second Treatise on Government* (1689) and eighteenth-century stadialist history, nineteenth-century economists and political theorists postulated the individual's cultivation of the soil as the origin of private property, commerce, sovereignty, and social contract. In the colonies, this narrative of possessive individualism "provid[ed] the painter, the poet and the explorer with a rhetoric with which to announce the imperial destiny of a young nation" (Dixon 3). The developmental framework that posited settled agriculture as the threshold of civilized modernity justified dispossession, deforestation, and wetland drainage as inevitable stages in human progress, while dismissing Indigenous populations, their forms of land tenure, and their environmental interactions as meaningless, outmoded, or unproductive. Aileen Moreton-Robinson (Goenpul) points out the enduring legal status of this distinction: "Indigenous communal property rights are never accorded equal value because ontologically white possession requires that Indigenous people are not perceived as being out of a state of nature" (121). These racialized parameters of stadialist thought delimited literary conceptions of civilization and sociability in the settler colonies, and within those bounds prose writers concentrated on the conceptual linkages between settled society and settled character. Collini's analysis of the political import of Victorian ideals of character stresses "the assumption that the possession of settled dispositions indicated a certain habit of restraining one's impulses" (97). The mid-century British novels most prominently associated with colonial themes – Edward Bulwer-Lytton's *The Caxtons: A Family Picture* (1849), Charles Dickens's *David Copperfield* (1850) and *Great Expectations* (1861), Charles Kingsley's *The Recollections of Geoffry Hamlyn* (1859) – tend to affirm this view with little hesitation, celebrating Australia as a place for the "secular rebirth" of metropolitan subjects, where they might recapitulate stadial progress through the disciplined and restorative labor of colonial pastoralism or the slightly more dubious route of digging for gold (Brantlinger 123). Our understanding of nineteenth-century liberalism's relation to settler colonialism can be productively broadened, however, by turning from these familiar reflections conceived at a distance to narratives actually written in the colonies.

Britain and its settler populations comprised a transnational public sphere, centered in London, which paradoxically strengthened throughout the course of the century even as the colonies increasingly conceived of themselves as independent nations. "Books, news, mail, and the like were the nervous system of Greater Britain," James Belich argues, with London its "cultural and economic capital" (461). British book publishers came to dominate the colonial trade and colonial periodicals struggled against metropolitan titles that were "rapidly and cheaply imported, often selling for less than their Australian imitators" (Webby 19). Consequently, settler authors often wrote with a dual colonial and metropolitan audience in mind and this chapter accordingly focuses on works that attained critical recognition and commercial success in Britain. Although critics of Australian and New Zealand literature have in the past tended to associate such metropolitan entanglements with aesthetic failure, due to their apparent inability to articulate a distinctively national sense of place or identity, more recent accounts have begun to explore ways that they be seen not as "reactionary ambivalence" but as "an enabling cultural tension" (Shannon 206). Indeed, the transnational cultural networks that spanned the Victorian settler empire impacted not only colonial culture but also metropolitan society, through an "inconsistent yet disproportionately significant effect on how British political identity and society was defined and demarcated" (Steer 34). I begin to chart the settler empire's literary networks of liberal thought by addressing two contrasting narratives of cultural contact: Arthur Phillip's official account of establishing the colony of New South Wales, *The Voyage of Governor Phillip to Botany Bay* (1789), and Frederick Maning's fictionalized memoir, *Old New Zealand, a Tale of the Good Old Times* (1863). I then turn to several Australian novels that thematized settler criminality: Marcus Clarke's *His Natural Life* (1870–72), Rolf Boldrewood's (Thomas Alexander Browne's) *Robbery under Arms* (1882–83), and Fergus Hume's *The Mystery of a Hansom Cab* (1886). I conclude with two short story collections exploring settler identity, and especially gender roles, in frontier environments: Australian author Barbara Baynton's *Bush Studies* (1902), and *Sons o' Men* (1905) by New Zealand author G. B. Lancaster (Edith Lyttleton). The broad aim of focusing on a range of narratives that are rarely if ever discussed within the context of Victorian studies is to suggest the inadequacy of limiting the discussion to metropolitan texts that treat settler colonialism as little more than a thought experiment and to instead highlight the necessity of considering how liberalism was actively construed and reconfigured by writers on the settler periphery.

The expanded literary horizon advanced here thus seeks to bring to greater visibility the "intrinsically transnational discursive constellation" of nineteenth-century liberalism (Goodlad 110). On the one hand, our understanding of that "discursive constellation" can be extended by highlighting the diversity of narrative genres employed by settler writers to articulate and explore liberal thought in colonial territory: from prosaic forms such as government dispatches and memoir, to short fiction, to varieties of the novel ranging from realism to detective fiction and the imperial romance. Collectively, these narratives underscore the important role played by literary characterization – and related techniques of perspective and voice – in examining the claims being made for "the most progressive race" by liberal thinkers, by focusing attention both on individual settler character and on the nature of settler polities. On the other hand, foregrounding histories of imperial literary circulation and reception can complicate our sense of the "intrinsically transnational" nature of liberalism by drawing attention to the variety of settler voices that were heard in Britain. This activity in the literary sphere parallels the degree of political innovation shown by colonial legislatures towards the end of the century. As the settler politician and commentator William Pember Reeves observed, "Though the colonial Progressives have transplanted much from the mother country and something from America, their needs, their aims, their methods, and their reasoning, are chiefly the result of their environment and local experiences" (1: 69–70). This suggests that the liberal framing of settlement was subjected to more sustained scrutiny than is evidenced by the smaller number of novels written on the subject by British authors. Ultimately, however, I shall argue that such literary self-examination was intense but uneven: In general, although settler writers placed significant pressure on ideas of individual and societal improvement, they largely left unchallenged underlying developmental assumptions about race, civilization, and modernity.

## Liberalism and Settler Empire

Narratives of the earliest encounters between settlers and Indigenous peoples in Australia and New Zealand illuminate the formal challenge of aligning those experiences with the liberal understanding of societal development. Arthur Phillip's dispatches on the establishment in 1788 of the first penal colony in Australia, at Warrane/Sydney Cove, were quickly edited (and rewritten in the third person) before being published in Britain as *The Voyage of Governor Phillip to Botany Bay* (1789). Phillip's actions and

## 11 Victorian Liberalism, Settler Character

observations testify to the foundational assumption that the colonial instantiation of liberal modernity hinged on the introduction of agriculture. The "accommodations of civilized life" that he imagines offering to the Eora people include "the means of procuring constant and abundant provision" through agriculture (141), while the draining of "swamps and marshes" is presented as evidence of "the great improvement which may be made by the industry of a civilized people in this country" (98). The form of the journal – linear, episodic, one-sided – appears well suited to this drive for change. An entry that has been described as "one of the founding passages of Australian history" (Carter 304) implicitly aligns the creation of such a regular narrative with a modernizing imperative to reorganize the landscape:

> There are few things more pleasing than the contemplation of order and useful arrangement ... and perhaps this satisfaction cannot any where be more fully enjoyed than where a settlement of civilized people is fixing itself upon a newly discovered or savage coast.... [B]y degrees large spaces are opened, plans are formed, lines marked, and a prospect at least of future regularity is clearly discerned[.] (Phillip 122–3)

At the same time, Phillip's records of his interactions with the Eora work against such straightforward assertions of settler order and "future regularity." He had hoped "to bring even the native inhabitants of New South Wales into a voluntary subjection; or at least to establish with them a strict amity and alliance" (68). Instead, his encounters are often inconclusive or uncertain, with the Eora's "very extraordinary shyness" often meaning Phillip simply cannot find them when he wants to (136). After six months of noncontact, he speculates, "They think perhaps that we cannot teach them anything of sufficient value to make them amends for our encroachments upon their fishing places" (139). Nevertheless, even as these acts of resistance and refusal evade the colonizers' desire for Indigenous consent, *The Voyage of Governor Phillip* remains overdetermined by the language of development as a self-evident justification for that colonial intrusion.

The temporal structure of development was engaged more self-consciously, even extravagantly, in the most notable account of colonial encounter to emerge from New Zealand, Frederick Maning's *Old New Zealand, a Tale of the Good Old Times* (1863). Written under the name of "A Pakeha Maori," or a settler who lives as Māori, *Old New Zealand* is a fictionalized memoir of Maning's experiences after arriving in the north of New Zealand in 1833 to establish himself as a timber trader. One reviewer in Britain found it "improbable in the extreme" that Maning might have had such an experience and yet "lose nothing of his mental cultivation and literary tastes" (Anon., "Review" 668). *Old New Zealand* foregrounds the stadialist distinction between the "old" world dominated by Māori – "before Governors were invented, and law, and justice, and all that" (A Pakeha Maori 1) – and the new dispensation of settler modernity, yet it also complicates this contrast through irony and digressions. Maning's first-person voice is central to his ironic coloring of imperialism's rhetoric, as evidenced by the opening chapter's lengthy description of arrival and disembarkation: He recounts dressing in formal clothes, "such as I calculated would 'astonish the natives,' and cause awe and respect for myself individually and the British nation in general," only to ignominiously fall into the sea while being carried ashore (9–10). In contrast to the Eora refusal to engage with the invading settlers, Maning describes his growing realization that he is regarded as a possession of the *iwi* (people) he is living among, not so much a self-governing subject as "a part, and by no means an inconsiderable one, of the payment for my own land" (141). The balance of power between Māori and settler populations had changed considerably between Maning's arrival and when he published his memoir, which coincided with the outbreak of wars in the Taranaki and Waikato regions. Yet even in discussing the likelihood of conflict, Maning's text struggles against the binary opposition that its title ostensibly espouses: "I get so confused, I feel just as if I was two different persons at the same time. Sometimes I find myself thinking on the Maori side, and then just afterwards wondering if 'we' can lick the Maori" (180). From the distance of Britain, though, the formal complexities of *Old New Zealand* were viewed as little more than comic gestures, and it was read primarily as an ethnographic text. Upon being reprinted in 1876, it was praised as "the best book ever written about a savage race," offering "the best picture of a state of society and of a people which both have all but passed away, and which will soon be gone" (MacColl 653). In this light, the liberal account of development and modernity, and its concomitant expectation of Indigenous extinction, can also be seen to assist a metropolitan process of interpretative simplification that imposes stability upon unruly settler narratives.

## The Novel and Criminality

Even as British commentary on settlement in the last quarter of the nineteenth century emphasized its value for individual and societal improvement, the Australian settler writing receiving most attention was focused on criminality. Marcus Clarke's *His Natural Life* – later retitled *For the Term of His Natural Life* – was first serialized at enormous length in Melbourne in 1870–72, before being radically abridged for publication in London in 1875 (Wilding 137–8). The novel tells of a young member of English society's

## 11 Victorian Liberalism, Settler Character

upper echelons who, under the assumed name of Rufus Dawes, is wrongly convicted and transported to Australia, where he is moved through its most notorious penal colonies before meeting his death without ever gaining his freedom. Clarke explores claims of colonial progress at an individual level through characters who pose the question of whether criminality is inherent or a consequence of social factors. At one extreme is Dawes, degraded by the system that ensnares him, of whom the narrator asks whether it is "possible to imagine, even for a moment, what an innocent man, gifted with ambition, endowed with power to love and to respect, must have suffered during one week of such punishment?" (1: 217). At the other extreme is another convict, Matthew Gabbett, whose innate bestiality is exemplified by acts of cannibalism and who appears so "horribly unhuman, that one shuddered to think that tender women and fair children must, of necessity, confess to fellowship of kind with such a monster" (1: 204). More broadly, *His Natural Life* also presents the institution of the penal colony as a profound challenge to ideas of progress and liberty by stressing its foundation of metropolitan criminality: "Oh, how strangely must the world have been civilised, that this most lovely corner of it must needs be set apart as a place of banishment for the monsters that civilization had brought forth and bred!" (2: 215). Writing in *The Athenaeum*, John Monsey Collyer reflected that "though we would never willingly read the book again, we recognize some tragic force in the method of its writing" (436). Yet even though the "tragic force" of Clarke's novel is directed toward querying liberal assertions of development and improvement, it focuses narrowly on the social world that Britain is making rather than on the underlying colonizing impulse.

Whereas *His Natural Life* locates colonial crime in the convict past, Fergus Hume's *The Mystery of a Hansom Cab* (1886) sets its transgressions within a colonial city, Melbourne, portrayed as thoroughly modern. The self-published novel was a surprise literary sensation for its novice author, and its success in Australia led to its republication in England, where a combination of low pricing and canny marketing sold more than 340,000 copies in its first year (Sussex 160). The novel describes its protagonists' efforts to solve a murder, which requires them to traverse the full range of Melbourne's social strata. The detectives' mobility reveals the inequalities of settler society, where streets that "correspond … to New York's Broadway, London's Regent Street and … the Boulevards of Paris" (Hume, 59–60) coexist cheek by jowl with grinding poverty and urban squalor that leaves them "wonder[ing] how human beings could live in them" (103). Those contradictions are also shown to be manifested in settler character. The perpetrator of the crime, Mark Frettlby, is an archetype of Lockean colonial success: his "great perseverance and never failing luck" as a pastoralist means that "now at the age of fifty-five he did not himself know the extent of his income" (34). Yet this appearance of propriety is belied by his behavior years earlier, amid the "riotous, feverish Melbourne life" brought about by the gold rushes, when he had secretly married and had a child with an actress who later fled to England with another lover (216). Believing that she had died, Frettlby remarried and had another child, only to discover that he was a bigamist; the man he murders was attempting to blackmail him with this "disagreeable reminder of the past" (219). The novel concludes with Frettlby's illegitimate daughter leaving the colony for "the old world and the new life," with her departing steamship appearing to be "making its way through a sea of blood" (230). With its portrait of staggering inequality and uncontrolled desires, *Mystery of a Hansom Cab* differs from *His Natural Life* in offering a critique of settler improvement that concentrates on the internal workings of the new society more than on how that society has been shaped by Britain.

A third prominent novel of settler criminality and character offers yet another variation on the theme by turning to the subject of outlaw "bushranging." Rolf Boldrewood's *Robbery under Arms* was first serialized in Australia in 1882–83, before achieving commercial success when it was abridged for Macmillan's Colonial Library in 1891 – some 46,000 copies were printed for the British market and 52,000 for the colonies by 1896 and subsequent cheaper reprints sold in even larger numbers (Eggert 82–3). The novel is narrated retrospectively by Jim Marston, who had formed a criminal gang with his father and brother under the leadership of a charismatic gentleman outlaw known only as Starlight. The Marstons' nomadic lifestyle and escalating crimes – from cattle stealing through to armed robbery – are contrasted with the steady commercial success of their neighbor, George Storefield, whose name indicates the agricultural basis of his fortune and character. Storefield displays the idealized traits of liberal character, notably a consistent work ethic and a willingness to defer pleasure: "He'd worked early and late, always been as steady as a rock, and had looked ahead instead of taking his pleasure straight off when he got the first few hundred pounds together" (Boldrewood 364). In contrast to this exemplar of improvement, the novel's dramatic and emotional energies are fully invested in the romance of its outlaw characters. "Men like us, that don't know what's to happen to them from one day to another," Marston reflects, "often have more real pleasure in the bit of time they have to themselves than many a man has in a year that has no call to care about time or money or be afraid of anybody" (318). *Robbery under Arms* also problematizes character by questioning whether criminality is destined or a matter of choice, with the narrator entertaining both possibilities within the space of a few pages. First, he acknowledges the role of "luck and chance" in shaping the individual's life: "How men were not let do what they knew was best for 'em ... but something seemed to drive 'em farther and farther along the wrong road, like a lot of stray wild cattle that wants to make back to their own run" (254). At the same time, however, he also asserts that "men and women grow up as they are intended to from the beginning" and society has little or no ability to shape their character: "All the same as a tree from seed. You may twist it this road or that ... but you won't alter the nature of that tree or the fruit that it bears" (255). One British reviewer reflected this tension in confessing to "a feeling of sympathy for the high-spirited Dick and his brother, with their perverted fine natures, and their capacities for different and better things" (Sergeant 253). *Robbery under Arms* queries the progressiveness of the settler colony by allocating its sympathies to an avowedly criminal protagonist even as it pays lip service to the prosaic developmental logic of settled labor.

## The Short Story and Identity

From the 1890s, a number of settler writers began to explore aspects of empire and identity through the more compressed and fragmentary narrative form of the short story. The commercial success of G. B. Lancaster, penname of the New Zealand author Edith Lyttleton, began with her first collection, *Sons o' Men* (1905), which was published in London with very few copies reaching the colonies (Sturm 71). *Sons o' Men* offers a series of loosely linked tales concerning the male workforce of a vast southern sheep station and it romanticizes the idea of a rugged colonial masculinity forged out of the encounter with "savage mountains and scarred flats" (Lancaster 1). In a review for the *Daily Telegraph* (London), W. L. Courtney noted the collection's "particular charm" in "presenting us with new human types," specifically the "strong, hard pieces of masculinity, very crude, very direct" produced by settler colonialism: "There must be something rough, acrid, untamed about the people who succeed on this difficult soil" (6). At the same time, a "dark undercurrent of violence, defeat, madness and death" in the stories also highlights the multiple ways in which that male settler identity is strained or fractured (Sturm 59). One of the stories in *Sons o' Men*, "Without Proof," describes the mental deterioration of a solitary worker, tasked with poisoning rabbits in a far corner of the property, who becomes convinced that the landscape is talking to him. The narrator describes the self-policing that other characters undertake to manage the threat this poses to their own subjectivities: "Walt met the terrified soul that looked out of Tommy's eyes, and laughed at it. For it was necessary" (Lancaster 44).

Another story, "On Bassett's Camp," is set amongst a group of tree fellers, where an exhausted young man, Muller, is bullied until he attempts to kill his main tormentor and then holds the rest of the workforce at bay with a rifle. Immediately prior to the attack, the narrator observes that a narrow view of gender is inadequate for comprehending the pressures of settler life: "It needs a strong mind to recognise the woman that is in every man, and to give it its due regard…. The woman in Muller clutched his throat hysterically; the man part made him drunken with rage" (251). While Lancaster's emphasis on capable men ultimately affirms a normative account of colonial masculinity and their Lockean possession of the soil, this is not the case with her Australian peer, Barbara Baynton.

Barbara Baynton's only collection of short stories, *Bush Studies* (1902), presents an unrelentingly naturalistic account of rural settler society defined by male self-interest and sexual predation. As Leigh Dale puts it, one of Baynton's main themes is "a woman's voice which cannot be heard, women's words which are stopped up, thrown back, misrecognized or mocked" (372). Silencing is central to "Squeaker's Mate," which presents the indolent Squeaker and his unnamed hardworking wife, who is regarded by other men in the region as "the best long-haired mate that ever stepped in petticoats" (Baynton 15). After she is paralyzed by a tree she is felling – she "silently went down under it" (17) – she watches on, "silent always," while her partner squanders her earnings and installs a new mistress in her place (32). "Billy Skywonkie" tells of a woman's arduous journey into the drought-stricken outback, first by train and then twelve miles by cart, to take up a position as a housekeeper at a sheep station. On the train she overhears "obscene jokes, and … snatches of lewd songs" (82) and is then harassed as she is driven across the "sun-smitten treeless plain" (89), only for her employer to dismiss her from her role early the next day, with the implication that the position was dependent on her attractiveness and sexual availability. "The Chosen Vessel" describes the fate of a "young, very young" mother (146), left alone with her baby while her dismissive husband is away working, who is sexually assaulted and murdered by a man with "cruel eyes, lascivious mouth, and gleaming knife" (148). While some Australian reviewers welcomed Baynton's realism, others were appalled by the view that it offered of the colony, with the *Sydney Mail* asserting that the stories' "danger" lay in being "taken for a fair presentment of Australian country life, and not, as we know them to be, merely of the darker side of it" (Anon., "Literature" 211). Such anxieties were not misplaced, for the anonymous reviewer for the *Daily Telegraph* (London) found that *Bush Studies* "represents the bush as peopled with a set of white savages so callous and brutal that the wild animals at the Zoo would be infinitely preferable as next-door neighbours" (Anon., "Notes" 12). In contrast to Seeley's claims of "the most progressive race put in the circumstances most favourable to progress" (176), Baynton employs character to present the colony as a space riven with inequalities of power that are unable to be stabilized or restrained by agricultural labor, let alone improved.

## Conclusion

The settler writing that circulated in Britain during the nineteenth century, preoccupied with criminality, violence, mental strain, and sexual threat, amounts to a sustained literary examination of liberalism's justification of colonization as a means of civilizational progress and improvement. At the same time, settlement's racialized foundations of possessive individualism remained in plain sight without being meaningfully questioned. One of the most intriguing outliers in this regard is Maning's *Old New Zealand*, whose narrator places "the proper knack of telling a story" at an ironic distance from the "state of affairs which began when this country became 'a British colony and possession'" (A Pakeha Maori 67). These "difficulties in telling his own history," Alex Calder suggests, "are prophetic of everything that makes this country unsettled about settlement" (71). By contrast, most settler writers were unwilling or unable to extend the fullest powers of characterization outside the bounds of British subjectivity. This self-imposed limit on liberalism's "transnational discursive constellation" both reflects and reinforces its theorization of a fundamental incompatibility, originating in its stadialist underpinnings, between settler and Indigenous populations. To trouble that developmental logic, after all, would bring to light the dilemmas of settlement's ethical and political illegitimacy that Anthony Trollope had laid out in his eyewitness account, *Australia and New Zealand* (1873):

> [H]ad the first English settlers any right to take the country from the black men who were its owners, and have the progressing colonists who still go westward and northward in search of fresh lands the right to drive the black men back… ? If they have no such right, – that is, if they be morally wrong to do it, – then has the whole colonizing system of Great Britain been wrong, not only in Australia, but in every portion of the globe…. Should we have abstained when we found it was peopled, – and, so to say, already possessed? (1: 74–5)

Trollope's response to his own question is to simply turn away: "It is their fate to be abolished; and they are already vanishing" (1: 75). Settler novels and short stories likewise furthered the tale of Indigenous "vanishing," even at the cost of claims of liberal progress, by asserting that colonialism's most calamitous and consequential forms of violence are those the settlers directed against themselves.

## Works Cited

A Pakeha Maori [F. E. Maning]. *Old New Zealand, a Tale of the Good Old Times; and a History of the War in the North against the Chief Heke, in the Year 1845.* Bentley, 1876.

Anon. "Review of *Old New Zealand: Being Incidents of Native Customs and Character in the Old Times*. By a Pakeha Maori." *John Bull*, vol. 43, no. 2236, 1863, p. 668.

Anon. "Literature: Books We Read." *The Sydney Mail and New South Wales Advertiser*, Jan. 28, 1903, p. 211.

Anon. "Notes and Reviews." *Daily Telegraph*, Apr. 24, 1903, p. 12.

Australian Bureau of Statistics. "Historical Population." *Commonwealth of Australia*, www.abs.gov.au/statistics/people/population/historical-population/latest-release. (accessed Dec. 2, 2022).

Baynton, Barbara. *Bush Studies*. Duckworth, 1902.

Belich, James. *Replenishing the Earth: The Settler Revolution and the Rise of the Anglo-World, 1783–1939*. Oxford UP, 2009.

Bell, Duncan. *Reordering the World: Essays on Liberalism and Empire*. Princeton UP, 2018.

Boldrewood, Rolf. Thomas Alexander Browne. *Robbery under Arms*. Macmillan, 1891.

Brantlinger, Patrick. *Rule of Darkness: British Literature and Imperialism, 1830–1914*. Cornell UP, 1988.

Calder, Alex. *The Settler's Plot: How Stories Take Place in New Zealand*. Auckland UP, 2011.

Carter, Paul. *The Road to Botany Bay: An Exploration of Landscape and History*. U of Minnesota P, 2010.

Clarke, Marcus. *His Natural Life*. Bentley, 1875.

Collini, Stefan. *Public Moralists: Political Thought and Intellectual Life in Britain, 1850–1930*. Clarendon P, 1991.

Collyer, John Monsey. "Review of *His Natural Life*. By Marcus Clarke." *The Athenaeum*, no. 2501, 1875, pp. 435–6.

Courtney, W. L. "Books of the Day." *Daily Telegraph*, Oct. 19, 1904, p. 6.

Dale, Leigh. "Rereading Barbara Baynton's *Bush Studies*." *Texas Studies in Literature and Language*, vol. 53, no. 4, 2011, pp. 369–86.

Dixon, Robert. *The Course of Empire: Neo-Classical Culture in New South Wales, 1788–1860*. Oxford UP, 1986.

Eggert, Paul. "The Bibliographic Life of an Australian Classic: *Robbery under Arms*." *Script & Print: Bulletin of the Bibliographical Society of Australia & New Zealand*, vol. 29, 2005, pp. 73–92.

Goodlad, Lauren M. E. "Liberalism and Literature." *The Oxford Handbook of Victorian Literary Culture*, edited by Juliet John, Oxford UP, 2016, pp. 103–23.

Hume, Fergus W. *The Mystery of a Hansom Cab*. Hansom Cab Publishing, 1887.

Jackson, Natalie and Ian Pool. "Population Change – Key Population Trends." *Te Ara – The Encyclopedia of New Zealand*, Manatū Taonga Ministry for Culture and Heritage, https://teara.govt.nz/en/graph/28720/new-zealand-population-by-ethnicity-1840-2013 (accessed Dec. 2, 2022).

Lancaster, G. B. [Edith Lyttleton]. *Sons o' Men*. Melrose, 1904.
MacColl, Norman. "Review of *Old New Zealand, a Tale of the Good Old Times. By a Pakeha Maori*." *The Athenaeum*, no. 2560, Nov. 18, 1876, pp. 653–4.
Moreton-Robinson, Aileen. *The White Possessive: Property, Power, and Indigenous Sovereignty*. U of Minnesota P, 2015.
Phillip, Arthur. *The Voyage of Governor Phillip to Botany Bay: With an Account of the Establishment of the Colonies of Port Jackson & Norfolk Island*. Stockdale, 1789.
Reeves, William Pember. *State Experiments in Australia and New Zealand*. Richards, 1902, 2 vols.
Seeley, John R. *The Expansion of England: Two Courses of Lectures*. Macmillan, 1883.
Sergeant, Lewis. "Novels of the Week." *The Athenaeum*, no. 3174, Aug. 25, 1888, p. 253.
Shannon, Mary L. "Colonial Networks and the Periodical Marketplace." *Journalism and the Periodical Press in Nineteenth-Century Britain*, edited by Joanne Shattock, Cambridge UP, 2017, pp. 203–23.
Steer, Philip. *Settler Colonialism in Victorian Literature: Economics and Political Identity in the Networks of Empire*. Cambridge UP, 2020.
Sturm, Terry. *An Unsettled Spirit: The Life and Frontier Fiction of Edith Lyttleton (G. B. Lancaster)*. Auckland UP, 2003.
Sussex, Lucy. *Blockbuster! Fergus Hume and* The Mystery of a Hansom Cab. Text, 2016.
Travers, W. T. L. "On the Changes Effected in the Natural Features of a New Country by the Introduction of Civilized Races." *Transactions and Proceedings of the New Zealand Institute*, vol. 2, 1869, pp. 299–330.
Trollope, Anthony. *Australia and New Zealand*. 2nd ed., Chapman & Hall, 1873, 2 vols.
Webby, Elizabeth. "Australia." *Periodicals of Queen Victoria's Empire: An Exploration*, edited by Rosemary VanArsdel and J. Don Vann, U of Toronto P, 1996, pp. 19–58.
Wilding, Michael. *Marcus Clarke: Novelist, Journalist and Bohemian*. Australian Scholarly Publishing, 2021.

## 12

SANDEEP BANERJEE

# The Imperial Romance
## Colonialism in Ritual Form

Forged in the crucible of colonial modernity during the long nineteenth and twentieth centuries, the imperial romance emerged as a key literary genre and a crucial site for the articulation and performance of the ideology of English imperialism. This essay delineates the formal specificity of the imperial romance and reads it as a *colonial scripture*, that is, a ritualized site for the performance of colonial ideology. It focuses on Philip Meadows Taylor's "mutiny novel" *Seeta* (1872) and Henry Rider Haggard's *King Solomon's Mines* (1885) to illustrate how these texts rearticulate categories of "good" and "evil" besides resolving colonial anxiety around racial miscegenation to perform their ritual (and utopian) function that reaffirms and perpetuates colonial ideology.

My formulation of the imperial romance as a colonial scripture draws on Northrop Frye, who memorably characterizes the romance as a secular scripture that was "a verbal imitation of ritual or symbolic human action" (*Secular* 55). Frye suggests that romances are "nearest of all literary forms to the wish-fulfilment dream," and elaborates on its ritualistic form and function in *Anatomy of Criticism*:

> The complete form of the romance is ... the successful quest, and ... has three main stages: ... of the perilous journey and the preliminary minor adventures; the crucial struggle, usually some kind of battle in which either the hero or his foe, or both, must die; and the exaltation of the hero.... Thus the romance expresses more clearly the passage from struggle through a point of ritual death to a recognition scene.... A threefold structure is repeated in many features of romance – in the frequency, for instance, with which the successful hero is a third son, or the third to undertake the quest, or successful on his third attempt. It is shown more directly in the three-day rhythm of death, disappearance and revival which is found in the myth of Attis and other dying gods, and has been incorporated in ... Easter. (186–7)

Moreover, for Frye, romances allow readers to confront, and negotiate, ideas of the good and evil. In romances, he writes, heroes and villains exist primarily to symbolize the contrast between two worlds, one above the level of ordinary experience, the other below it. There is, first, a world associated with happiness, security, and peace ... *the idyllic world*. The other is a world of exciting adventures, but adventures which involve separation, loneliness, humiliation, pain and the threat of more pain ... *the demonic on night world*. (*Secular* 53, emphasis mine)

Frye's elaboration, then, provides us with the most exhaustive delineation of the genre's structural features. Romances express a desire for wish fulfillment that is articulated, typically, through the trope of the quest that makes the form inherently transformative and utopian in addition to aligning it to symbolic human action, that is, ritual performance. Furthermore, in presenting a contrast between the "idyllic" and "demonic" worlds and their inhabitants, it provides readers with an aesthetic education about the categories of good and evil.

In his project of historicizing literary form and criticism, Fredric Jameson takes up the romance and, unsurprisingly, engages Frye's insights from a historical materialist vantage. Frye offers, Jameson notes, a "positive hermeneutic" that stresses "the affinity between the cultural present of capitalism and the distant mythical past of tribal societies" as well as a "sense of the continuity between our psychic life and that of primitive peoples" (*Political* 117). A "negative hermeneutic," Jameson insists, would underline "our sense of historical difference, and ... stimulate an increasingly vivid apprehension of what happens when thought falls into history, so to speak, and enters the force field of the modern societies" (*Political* 117). Jameson's peculiar use of "history" warrants clarification: He is not suggesting that premodern societies were worlds inhabited by people, so to speak, without history; rather, his is a more constrained usage where history is synonymous with capitalist modernity. The issue of capitalist modernity is underlined further when he writes that

> the persistence of romance as a mode is that of *substitutions, adaptations, and appropriations*, and raises the question of what, *under wholly altered historical circumstances*, can ... replace the raw materials of magic and Otherness ... [found in] medieval romance.... A history of romance as a mode becomes possible ... when we explore the substitute codes and raw materials, which, in the increasingly secularized and rationalized world that emerges from the collapse of feudalism, are pressed into service to replace the older magical categories of Otherness... (*Political* 117, emphasis mine)

The "wholly altered historical circumstances" in Jameson's comment is no doubt an allusion to the development of the capitalist mode of production. It enables us to think of the "substitutions, adaptations, and appropriations" in the romance thereby historicizing Frye's insights. But despite this significant intervention, Jameson's engagement with the question of historical (and formal) difference remains limited to the *diachronic* axis and draws attention to the reconstitution of romance, a precapitalist form, under capitalism. In so doing, Jameson overlooks the *synchronic* axis of historical difference: our one and uneven world shaped by colonial capitalist modernity.

This is a crucial consideration for thinking about the imperial romance for, as Gayatri Spivak cautions us, it "should not be possible to read nineteenth-century British literature without remembering that imperialism, understood as England's social mission, was a crucial part of the cultural representation of England to the English" (243). But despite proffering a positive hermeneutic, it is Frye who alludes to the question of colonial difference. In a throwaway remark of sorts, he notes that the romances of Henry Rider Haggard, John Buchan, and Rudyard Kipling are "adventure stories ... [that] incorporate the dreams of British imperialism" and are symptomatic of the "process of ... 'kidnapping' romance ... [and] absorbing ... it into the ideology of an ascendant class" (*Secular* 57). Frye's use of the term "kidnapping" is insightful as it situates this corpus – the authors mentioned signal, quite precisely, the form of the imperial romance – as distinct from the norm and an expression of generic alterity.

Any consideration of the form and function of the imperial romance as distinct from the modern romance as such requires the fact of generic alterity be read in relation to actually existing historical difference *at the synchronic level*, that is, with respect to colonial difference fashioned by that ensemble of political, economic, and cultural practices we call colonialism. Raymond Williams, always keen to ground literary and cultural forms in material practices, reminds us of the capitalist constitution of colonial difference in *The Country and the City*. He notes that "the 'metropolitan' states, through a system of trade, but also through a complex of economic and political controls, dr[ew] food and, more critically, raw materials from these areas of supply, this effective hinterland, that is also the greater part of the earth's surface ... [with] the great majority of its people" (Williams 279). This process, Williams insists, produced the "'metropolitan' societies of Western Europe and North America ... [as] the 'advanced,' 'developed,' industrialised states; centres of economic, political and cultural power. In sharp contrast with them ... [were] societies ... [considered] 'underdeveloped': still mainly agricultural or 'under-industrialised'" (279). The ideological implication of this global unevenness is what Edward Said termed "orientalism," one instance of which was characterized as a "style of thought based on the ontological and epistemological distinction made between 'the Orient' and ... 'the Occident'" (2). But it is ultimately Williams who is singularly helpful for thinking about the historical conditions of possibility for the emergence and consolidation of the imperial romance. Williams writes that the

> history of the extension of the dominant model of capitalist development to include other regions of the world ... was not ... a case of "development" here, "failure to develop" elsewhere. What was happening in ... the "metropolitan" economy was determined by what was made to happen in the "country"; first the local hinterland and then the vast regions beyond it, in other people's lands. What happened in England has since been happening even more widely, in new dependent relationships between all the industrialized nations and all the other "undeveloped" but economically important lands. Thus one of the last models of "city and country" is the system we now know as imperialism. (279)

Readers will note just how central the category of colonial difference is for Williams even as he details the development of global capitalism. Williams's theorizations thus enable us to ground Frye's comments about the "kidnapping" of romance in the force field of colonial history to illuminate it as a displacement of generic norms and a literary form of exception. From this perspective, Frye's abstract (though astute) characterizations of the "idyllic" and "demonic" realms of the romance become the concrete spaces of the metropole and colony respectively. Likewise, the struggle between heroes and villains – and the good–evil dichotomy – now appears as enchanted renditions of the moral distinction between the colonizer and the colonized. Furthermore, the genre's alignment with the "wish-fulfillment dream" becomes a symbolic articulation of colonial capitalist desire for ceaseless profit and the ejection of the colonized from their lands. In effect, the imperial romance emerges as a symbolic form gesturing toward the reconstitution of the world from one marked by diverse ways of being into one structured by hierarchical difference – or, as Frantz Fanon put it succinctly, into a "world divided into compartments ... cut in two ... [as if] inhabited by two different species" (39–40). This is particularly evident in the romances of Meadows Taylor and Rider Haggard where notions of "good" and "evil" as well as racial anxieties, especially around the issue of miscegenation, are articulated and performed.

## Narrativizing Ritual, Ritualizing Narrative

A critical aspect of the colonial quest for profit worldwide was the recoding of human alterity into a hierarchy of races – an imperial world picture as it were – that posited the identities of "European" and "white" at its apex with the racialized "others" ordered beneath. While this process posited races as bounded categories, it also produced the concomitant anxiety of the breaking of such boundaries that were typically centered around fears of racial miscegenation. Imperial romances served as a key site for the articulation of such anxieties and their eventual neutralization, typically through narrative closures that expelled the "evil" (read "nonwhite") subject/s from their narrative worlds. Such closures effect imaginary resolutions of narrative crises in the symbolic realm (see Jameson *Political*; Jameson "Reification"; Girard). More properly put – and to reformulate Jameson for my purposes – these narratives offer symbolic resolutions of real contradictions of *colonial life* (see Jameson *Political*). In so doing, they not only inscribe colonial difference into symbolic human action but also serve as sites for *the ritualized performance of colonial ideology* to reaffirm it. In sum, the form and function of the imperial romance underline it as a colonial scripture that illuminates the ideology of the colonial aesthetic.

Philip Meadows Taylor's "mutiny novel" *Seeta* (1872) provides a powerful illustration of the imperial romance as a colonial scripture. The "mutiny novel" was a specific kind of sensational fiction that emerged in the aftermath of the 1857 Uprising against the East Indian Company that the British termed the "Sepoy Mutiny" (hence the "mutiny" in the form's appellation).[1] Structured as prose romances, these texts were immensely popular on publication and influential in molding British public opinion against the Uprising and the Indians. They depicted the rebels as irredeemably evil and sexually depraved while positing the colony as "mired in changeless patterns of superstition and violence which can be dominated but not necessarily altered for the better" (Brantlinger 200). The narrative of *Seeta* revolves around the love between the novel's eponymous heroine and the colonial official Cyril Brandon. The prime antagonist is Azrael Pande who murders Seeta's husband and child during a robbery at the start of the narrative. Subsequently arrested and tried by Brandon, Seeta's testimony at the trial convicts Pande but he manages to escape, vowing vengeance. Pande attacks Seeta at her house once again, but Brandon saves her though he is himself injured in the fight. As Seeta nurses him back to health they fall in love and this inaugurates the narrative's explicit interracial romantic plot that makes the text singular. Over time, Brandon marries Seeta – the interracial marriage, and in particular, the possibility of a biracial child, provokes anxiety in many of the British and the Indian characters. Pande, in time, stirs up troubles as the 1857 Uprising breaks out across North India. With the English crushing the rebellion, Pande goes into hiding with the rebels but reappears with his band to attack the house where the British were celebrating their victory. In the fighting, Seeta dies protecting Brandon who, now freed from his marital obligation, marries an English woman Grace Mostyn, thus reestablishing the colonial norm in the diegetic universe.

## 12 The Imperial Romance

The narrative of *Seeta* lays out, in the most unexceptional of ways, the clash between the categories of good and evil. Pande embodies unalloyed evil, who, Taylor notes in his introduction, came out of his attempt to "depict the character of the rebel and treasonable emissaries of the time. Malignant and persistent, they were led on by blind hatred and religious fanaticism, to the instigation and commission of crimes at which humanity shudders" (ix). The character's villainy is further underlined by the author's decision to name him Azrael Pande. Shuchi Kapila draws attention to the name, noting that "Azrael is the formidable and ruthless angel of death in Christian, Jewish, and Islamic literature. It is unlikely that Pande, a Brahmin, would have [such] a first name" (117). However, this incongruity is moot: While "Azrael" would conjure for Taylor's European readers the figure of the angel of death, "Pande" would evoke the figure of Mangal Pande, the "sepoy" of the 34th Bengal infantry who is traditionally depicted as the person who started the troubles outside Calcutta that snowballed into the 1857 Uprising. Mangal Pande, moreover, was the inspiration behind the term "pandy" (plural, "pandies"), the typical British term for the mutineers, and a word Taylor uses throughout the text. In addition, as if to ensure this connection is not lost on his readers, Taylor depicts Azrael as Mangal Pande's uncle in the narrative.

If Pande is the epitome of evil, Brandon, not surprisingly, is the paragon of good. He is described as not just "tall, extremely well made, and graceful in his movements" but also, blazon-like, as someone with a "broad, white forehead, over which his glossy brown hair clustered in heavy waves, strong eyebrows, with very clear, earnest blue eyes, shaded by long dark eyelashes, a pleasant mouth, a bright complexion, very white teeth, with a full chin" (Taylor 69). But most significantly, he is presented as a *good* colonial official, someone whose efforts

> to soften down the hard mechanical actions and rules of official life – had won him ... more than ordinary popularity.... [With each passing year] the fine qualities of his character ... became more and more appreciated.... [Many] a dame ... repeated his name with that of her household gods each night, as she lighted the lamp before the simple shrine of her faith, and taught her children to say it. (Taylor 69)

Brandon's idealization in this passage gestures toward the imperial romance articulating the "political fantasy of creating through a process of benevolent rule, native subjects acculturated to European values who welcome colonial rule and ally themselves with British interests" (Kapila 3). The novel also presents Seeta as another version of goodness, which is best encapsulated in Brandon's first encounter with her:

> The large dewy eyes were soft and pleading ... her features were ... very sweet and full of expression; her eyes were large and soft, of that clear dark brown which, like a dog's, is always so loving and true.... For a native woman, Cyril Brandon had never seen any one so fair or of so tender a tone of colour. (Taylor 61)

In depicting Seeta's physical features, the narrator describes her eyes twice: "large dewy eyes" that are "soft and pleading" and, then again, "dark brown" eyes that are "large and soft" and, "like a dog's ... always so loving and true." The use of the dog simile is illuminating – it not only evokes notions of fidelity and tameness but also signals the imperial romance ritualistically illuminating colonial heterosexual desire where "docility represents political subservience" (Kapila 3).

But the crucial site for the narrative's ritual performance is around the anxiety about Seeta's status as the Brandon's wife and the prospect of children from this union. As Mrs. Pratt tells Seeta, by "English law and Christian custom, if you had a son as you are, he could not inherit except what was specially given him. He would have no rank and no name ... [and] be illegitimate" (Taylor 374). Seeta is further told that while she is indeed married to Brandon, it is by Hindu rites that "English law does not recognize," and the Christian minister could not marry them as long as she remained a Hindu (Taylor 374). This "problem" is helpfully resolved with Pande's attack on the English. As Brandon tries to lead Grace Mostyn and Seeta to safety, he is attacked by Azrael Pande. Brandon is overpowered by Pande who "drew back his ... [spear] to strike" when Seeta rushes in front of him and receives the "the blow in her breast," sacrificing herself to save Brandon (Taylor 377). Pande too is killed in the melee, thus effecting a purging of evil from the world of the narrative. The imperial romance gestures toward its function as ritual here in several ways. It provides an imaginary resolution of real crises in colonial life that is represented, foremost, by Seeta – the nonwhite wife of a colonial British official – who by virtue of the heterosexual union holds up the possibility biracial children and, thus, racial miscegenation. It also solves the crisis represented by Pande, the "evil" native who simply refuses to be colonized – a recalcitrance that undoubtedly shapes the narrative's view on his character. Significantly, Seeta and Pande, the twin sources of narrative anxiety, cancel out each other. To put this another way, the narrative instrumentalizes "nonwhite" life by making it a means of "white" salvation, a process that also extinguishes the "nonwhite" life. This is arguably the most crucial way in which imperial romance signals itself as a form of colonial ritual. I will return to this ritualistic aspect of the imperial romance to discuss it further after examining another imperial romance with similar characteristics: Henry Rider Haggard's *King Solomon's Mines*.

## 12 The Imperial Romance

Supposedly written out of a bet with his brother to "do a 'thriller' as successful as [Robert Louis Stevenson's] *Treasure Island*," *King Solomon's Mines* was published in 1885 and became the best seller for that year (Monsman 11). In the process, Haggard's novel inaugurated the immensely popular "Lost World" genre, whose narratives all follow conventions of the romance. Writers and exemplars from this tradition include, but are not limited to, Rudyard Kipling (*The Man Who Would Be King*, 1888), Arthur Conan Doyle (*The Lost World*, 1913), Edgar Rice Burroughs (*The Return of Tarzan*, 1913; *The Land That Time Forgot*, 1924), James Hilton (*The Lost Horizon*, 1933), and H. P. Lovecraft (*At the Mountains of Madness*, 1936). *King Solomon's Mines* narrates the journey of Allan Quatermain, Sir Henry Curtis, and Captain Good to the unexplored interior of Africa to find Curtis's brother who had traveled there in search of the fabled mines of King Solomon. The entourage cross a desert and a mountain range to enter Kukuanaland, which is ruled by the "evil" king Twala with the old woman Gagool as his advisor. In time, the servant of the entourage Umbopa is revealed to be Ignosi, the true heir to the throne of the Kukuanas. The English depose Twala in battle and install Ignosi on the throne. Good and a Kukuana woman, Foulata, become romantically attached while she nurses the former back to health after the battle. Readers will no doubt notice the similarity with *Seeta* here. Gagool, who is captured by the English, reluctantly leads them to the fabled mines but tries to sneak out and lock them in. She is stopped by Foulata and in the scuffle Gagool fatally stabs her before being crushed to death by the stone door (notice, once again, the similarity with *Seeta*). The travelers remain stuck in the dark chamber for a few days before they manage to find a route to escape – a moment in the narrative that Anne McClintock in her remarkable reading of the romance calls "an extraordinary fantasy of male birthing, culminating in the regeneration of white manhood" (248). The narrative concludes with a wish fulfillment that befits the rapaciousness of colonial capitalist modernity as well as the homosocial and familial patriarchal order of English imperialism. The Englishmen not only bring back some of the diamonds from the mine but also succeed in finding Curtis's brother during their journey back. A letter from Curtis to Quatermain at the end of the narrative confirms the diamonds' monetary value besides suturing class mobility and homosociality with an imperial utopianism. Curtis tells Quartermain that the diamonds have been assessed and are "of the finest water, and equal in every way to the best Brazilian stones" (Haggard 318). He then asks Quartermain to return to England with these words: "I want you to come home, my dear old comrade, and to buy a house near here. You have done your day's work, and have lots of money now" (Haggard 319).

*King Solomon's Mines* sets up, as in *Seeta*, the ideas of "good" and "evil" in sharp contrast. Twala, for instance, is described as an "enormous man with the most entirely repulsive countenance ... [and with] lips [as] ... thick as a negro's, the nose was flat, he had but one gleaming black eye, for the other was represented by a hollow in the face, and his whole expression was cruel and sensual to a degree" (Haggard 141). He is also depicted as someone who ascended the throne with help of Gagool for which he took his brother "by the hair, [and] stabbed him through the heart with his knife" (Haggard 124). Gagool is another figure of evil who is introduced as "a withered-up monkey, wrapped in a fur cloak ... [that] crept on all fours" (Haggard 140). Unsurprisingly, the imperial romance devises strategies for the ejection of these characters from its diegetic universe, the most crucial of which is the moment involving the deaths of Gagool and Foulata. As the explorers hear Foulata's cry, they rush to her to find the "door of rock ... closing down slowly; it is not three feet from the floor. Near it struggle Foulata and Gagool. The red blood of the former runs to her knee, but still the brave girl holds the old witch, who fights like a wild cat" (Haggard 280). The narrative recounts this climactic scene with verve:

> Foulata falls, and Gagool throws herself on the ground, to twist like a snake through the crack of the closing stone. She is under – ah! God! too late! too late! The stone nips her, and she yells in agony. Down, down, it comes, all the thirty tons of it, slowly pressing her old body against the rock below. Shriek upon shriek, such as we never heard, then a long sickening *crunch*, and the door was shut just as, rushing down the passage, we hurled ourselves against it.
> 
> It was all done in four seconds. (Haggard 280)

This moment in the narrative is another instance of the "good nonwhite" sacrificing herself to prevent the "evil nonwhite" from wreaking havoc in the diegetic universe of the narrative. In fact, Foulata's sacrifice is anticipated in the novel by the sacrifice of the Zulu servant Khiva. When Good slips and falls in front of an elephant during a hunt, the narrator writes that

> Khiva, the Zulu boy, saw his master fall, and brave lad as he was, ... turned and flung his assegai [spear] straight into the elephant's face. It stuck in his trunk.
> 
> With a scream of pain, the brute seized the poor Zulu, hurled him to the earth, and placing one huge foot on to his body about the middle, twined its trunk round his upper part and *tore him in two* ...
> 
> We rushed up mad with horror, and fired again and again, till presently the elephant fell upon the fragments of the Zulu.
> 
> As for Good, he rose and wrung his hands over the brave man who had given his life to save him ... (Haggard 62, emphasis in original)

This is an anxious moment in the narrative that emerges from the threat to "white" life from an aberrant nonhuman, the elephant. And in a move that is structurally similar to *Seeta*, the narrative once again underlines its ritualistic function by making the "nonwhite" an instrument of "white" salvation while extinguishing it in that process. Notice how the passage begins with calling Khiva a "Zulu boy" but describes him as "the brave man" after his death. It is as if his instrumentalization – ritualistic sacrifice – to save and perpetuate "white" life enables him to gain age and stature in the eyes of the "white" narrator.

While the narrative is not marked by the anxiety of racial mixing at the time of Khiva's death, Foulata's, on the other hand, becomes an occasion for making a statement against interracial romance. As she lies dying, Foulata says: "Say to my lord … that – I love him, and that I am glad to die because I know that he cannot cumber his life with such as I am, for the sun may not mate with the darkness, nor the white with the black" (Haggard 281). Haggard underlines this further, when the narrator Alan Quatermain notes that Foulata's death was indeed

> a fortunate occurrence, since, otherwise, complications would have been sure to ensue. The poor creature was no ordinary native girl, but a person of great, I had almost said stately, beauty, and of considerable refinement of mind. But no amount of beauty or refinement could have made an entanglement between Good and herself a desirable occurrence; for, as she herself put it, "Can the sun mate with the darkness, or the white with the black?" (Haggard 300)

*Seeta* and *King Solomon's Mines*, then, underline the use of death as a narrative strategy in the imperial romance: "nonwhites" are either sacrificed to perpetuate "white" lives as well as to remove them from the narrative universe to resolve anxieties about racial mixing. Simple and formulaic though this may seem, the situation is a tad more complex.

In *Seeta*, the good "white" character (Brandon) is threatened by the evil "nonwhite" (Pande) and the latter's threat is neutralized by the sacrifice of the good "nonwhite," Seeta. To put this differently, Seeta is not just an object of sacrifice – a *scapegoat* in the traditional and ritualistic sense of the term – but also the *remedy* to the *poison* that is Pande. The narrative structure of *King Solomon's Mines* is also quite similar where the threat to the good "white" characters (Quartermain, Curtis, and Good) comes from the "evil nonwhite" (Gagool), which is neutralized through the sacrifice of the "good nonwhite," Foulata. And here again, Foulata is not just an object of sacrifice, she is also the *remedy* to the *poison* that is Gagool. However, the narrative situation looks somewhat different from the vantage of racial purity: Seeta and Foulata now become threats to the colonial world order – as Brandon's wife and as Good's lover and possible wife, respectively, they have the ability to upend the racialized ordering of the colonial world. From this view, Pande and Gagool become *remedies* – and indeed sacrificial *scapegoats* – to the *poison* signified by Seeta and Foulata and the threat to the purity of the colonial racial universe. I use the words "scapegoat," "poison," and "remedy" not without reason but to allude to the category of the *pharmakon* (φάρμακον) that signifies all three of these terms, the first deriving from the *pharmakos* ritual of human sacrifice in Greece and the latter two terms from toxicology. Jacques Derrida has famously discussed writing as a *pharmakon*, to underline the three meanings as well as the philosophical notion of indeterminacy in "Plato's Pharmacy." For my purposes, significantly, the "nonwhite" characters of the imperial romance serve as *pharmakoi* – indeterminate in their position as either "scapegoat," "poison," or "remedy" even as they are deployed ritualistically to transform the narrative universe.

This transformation of the narrative universes in *Seeta* and *King Solomon's Mines* gesture toward the symbolic resolution of real crises of colonial life. And though such a formulation recalls Jameson, these resolutions are – this is crucial to note – significantly different from what he outlines in his discussion on the romance genre. For Jameson, the form of the romance effects a kind of "semic evaporation" where the category of evil represented through, for instance, a figure such as the hostile knight asks for mercy when defeated and is eventually "reinserted into the unity of the social class" (*Political* 105). However, in the context of the imperial romance where the racial divide underwrites the rule of capital and class antagonisms, characters such as Seeta, Pande, Foulata, and Gagool are not reinserted into the social structure but killed off and *removed* from the narrative world. Their deaths effect a resolution that is not so much a *semic evaporation*, as Jameson suggests, but a symbolic and *ritualistic ejection* from the symbolic order and indeed the real world.[2] This signals a more violent desire to remove the natives from their lands and reinscribe the fantasy of *terra nullius* on to the narrative world. This sentiment underwrites the settler colonies across the globe but finds a succinct expression in a letter (from October 4, 1857) by Charles Dickens to Angela Burdett Coutts in the aftermath of the 1857 Uprising. Dickens writes:

> I wish I were Commander in Chief in India. The first thing I would do to strike that Oriental race with amazement ... I should do my utmost to exterminate the Race upon whom the stain of the late cruelties rested; and that I was ... now proceeding, with ... merciful swiftness of execution, to blot it out of mankind and raze it off the face of the Earth. (Qtd. in Brantlinger 206–7)

Dickens's sentiment is given its most terse, if fever-crazed, expression by Kurtz in his pithy exclamation: "Exterminate all the brutes!" (Conrad 62).

### Notes

1. For studies on the 1857 Uprising, see Ashraf and Joshi, Stokes and Bayly, Bates and Carter. For a study on the British imagination of the 1857 Uprising, see Chakravarty.
2. In "Reification and Utopia in Mass Culture" Jameson reads the death of Quint as an allegory for "the twofold symbolic destruction of an older America ... of small business and individual private enterprise [and] ... the America of the New Deal and the crusade against Nazism, ... of the depression and the war and of the heyday of classical liberalism" (*Signatures* 38). This does not, however, take away from my larger point about the narrative resolution in the imperial romance.

### Works Cited

Ashraf, Mohammad, and Puran Chandra Joshi, editors. *Rebellion, 1857: A Symposium*. People's Publishing House, 1957.

Bates, Crispin, and Marina Carter, editors. *Mutiny at the Margins: New Perspectives on the Indian Uprising of 1857*. Vol. 3: *Global Perspectives*. SAGE Publications, 2013.

Brantlinger, Patrick. *Rule of Darkness: British Literature and Imperialism, 1830–1914*. Cornell UP, 1988.

Chakravarty, Gautam. *The Indian Mutiny and the British Imagination*. Cambridge UP, 2005.

Conrad, Joseph. *Heart of Darkness*, edited by Robert Hampson, Penguin, 2007.

Derrida, Jacques. "Plato's Pharmacy." *Dissemination*, translated and edited by Barbara Johnson, Athlone P, 1981, pp. 65–171.

Fanon, Frantz. *Wretched of the Earth*. Translated by Constance Farrington, Grove P, 1963.

Frye, Northop. *Anatomy of a Criticism*. 1957. Princeton UP. 1990.

—. *The Secular Scripture: A Study of the Structure of Romance*. Harvard UP, 1976.

Girard, René. *Deceit, Desire, and the Novel: Self and Other in Literary Structure*. Johns Hopkins P, 1965.

Haggard, Henry Rider. *King Solomon's Mines*. Cassel & Company, 1886.

Jameson, Fredric. *The Political Unconscious: Narrative as a Socially Symbolic Act*. 1981. Routledge. 2002.

—. *Signatures of the Visible*. Routledge, 1990.

Kapila, Shuchi. *Educating Seeta: The Anglo-Indian Family Romance and the Poetics of Indirect Rule*. Ohio State UP, 2010.

McClintock, Anne. *Imperial Leather: Race, Gender, and Sexuality in the Colonial Contest*. Routledge, 1995.

Monsman, Gerald. "Introduction." *King Solomon's Mines*, by Henry Rider Haggard, Broadview, 2022, pp. 9–31.

Said, Edward W. *Orientalism*. Vintage Books, 1994.

Spivak, Gayatri Chakravorty. "Three Women's Texts and a Critique of Imperialism." *Critical Inquiry*, vol. 12, no. 1, 1985, pp. 243–61.
Stokes, Eric, and Christopher A. Bayly. *The Peasant Armed: The Indian Revolt of 1857*. Clarendon P, 1986.
Taylor, Philip Meadows. *Seeta*. C. Kegan Paul & Co., 1880.
Williams, Raymond. *The Country and the City*. Oxford UP, 1973.

PART III

# Figures, Movements, and Histories: 1900–1945

# 13

DOMINIC DAVIES

# Unraveling Adventure Fictions
## *Modernist Compressions and Anti-imperial Connections*

### Introduction: Unraveling Adventure Fictions

The arrival of the twentieth century in Britain brought the era of "New Imperialism" to an end. In the final decades of the nineteenth century, adventure fictions by authors such as H. Rider Haggard had boomed, their linear plots registering this moment of imperial confidence. But in the first decades of the twentieth, these were undermined by slowing economic growth, eugenicist fears of racial contamination and degeneration, broadening awareness of the violent brutalities of imperialism, and the rise of anti-imperial movements that drew advocates from both metropolitan and colonized territories (see Boehmer; Gopal). It is perhaps Fredric Jameson who most famously identified the pressures placed by this imperial overreach on the shape and structure of literary form. "The hypothesis suggested here," wrote Jameson in a short pamphlet in 1988, was that there existed material connections "between the emergence of a properly modernist 'style' and the representational dilemmas of the new imperial world system" (Jameson 59). For Jameson, the narrative hallmarks of modernism – circular and nested narratives, a refusal of realism's representational confidence, an emphasis on the lumpiness of space-time – gave formal shape to the disjunctions and displacements of Britain's imperial economy. While Jameson was concerned primarily with what he called "First World modernism," including novels by Virginia Woolf and James Joyce, he suggested these contortions might be especially evident in literature written not in Europe, but in the fraught context of the colonial encounter, where "the face of imperialism is brute force, naked power, [and] open exploitation" (59).

Since Jameson's "Modernism and Imperialism" essay, the shifting conjunction between imperial formations and modernist forms in British literature has been debated and nuanced, but its existence powerfully confirmed (see Gikandi; Booth and Rigby; Childs; Esty; Cleary). Some of this work has focused on the ways in which adventure fictions specifically were unraveled by the adoption of modernist styles among writers of empire.

Several authors frequently appear in these discussions: Joseph Conrad's many stories and novels; Rudyard Kipling's formal innovations in *Plain Tales from the Hills* (1888); E. M. Forster's *Passage to India* (1924), with its unrepresentable Marabar caves; and Olive Schreiner's remarkable 1883 novel, *A Story of An African Farm*, which evokes and then breaks the romance's linear structure with narrative fragments, dreams, and allegories. However, this chapter turns its attention to literary texts of the early twentieth century that are not so often discussed by critics in this light, yet which are equally powerful in their revelation of modernism's fraught origins on the peripheries of empire, rather than merely in its metropoles. This is important, I argue, not only because this narrative material shows how modernism compressed the zealotry of the New Imperialist phase, or how aspects of the romance endured. It also registers structural tensions in the imperial world, including the emerging threat of interimperial rivalries that would lead to two World Wars and a growing network of nationalist and anti-imperial movements.

The sections that follow will look at two authors of colonial fiction written between 1900 and the 1930s: First, John Buchan, an arch-imperialist and politician whose well-known Richard Hannay series of spy thrillers compresses adventure fiction with modernist forms; and second, Edward John Thompson, a friend of Gandhi and translator of Tagore, whose Indian novels connected the generic residues of the romance with emerging anti-imperial resistance. Forster, an interlocutor of Thompson's, will also be discussed. By juxtaposing these different examples, the chapter aims for a broader view of the different ways in which adventure fictions were unraveled through the final decades of Britain's formal empire than is usually discussed.

### John Buchan: Modernist Compressions

John Buchan was a Scot who spent much of his life at the heart of Britain's political establishment, both at home and overseas. After graduating from the University of Oxford, where he had been president of the Union for a short time, he traveled to South Africa to work as a colonial administrator in the Land Settlement Department of Alfred Milner's "kindergarten," the imperial project designed to transform South Africa into a "thoroughly British" domain in the immediate aftermath of the Anglo-Boer War (Meredith 365–7). Working as Milner's "fixer" between 1901 and 1903, it was Buchan's job to ride across the South Africa "Highveld" – a large inland plateau that reminded Buchan of his own Scottish Highlands – to reclaim land formerly promised to Boer farmers for settlement by incoming British colonists

(Redley 68). Buchan developed a powerful attachment to the landscape that was only intensified by his early dismissal from Milner's government. When a local company launched a legal complaint against the resettlements that Buchan had been tasked to enforce, he was cut off by Milner as a convenient scapegoat in the midst of potentially career-ruining public criticisms. Returning prematurely to Britain, Buchan pursued a different though equally elite career, becoming a Tory MP, editor of *The Spectator*, and eventually the 15th Governor-General of Canada, then one of the Empire's dominions. But he never forgot his time on the South African Highveld, and while his fiction drips with nostalgia for a romanticized frontier, his practical experience of the dirty land politics of colonization also contorts their imperial confidence, leading to narrative insecurities and generic fragmentations.

Buchan's *political* interest in the Empire's frontiers – first in South Africa and later in Canada – was widely held among the British ruling class. He saw the "vast spaces" of the Highveld as "England, richer, softer, kindlier … waiting for a human life worth of such an environment" (Buchan, *African* 126), imaginatively emptying them of their native inhabitants. It was not only that these "empty" frontiers were in need of hardworking Britons; just as importantly, the British working class were also in need of what Buchan came to describe as the redemptive power of the frontier. "These new countries give a man a horizon and an ideal which he may not be able to find at home," Buchan remarked. "It is as the residuary remedy for social disorders that we must advocate it, and it is a remedy which must be increasingly used if both the Mother Country and the outlying Empire are to remain in social and economic health" (Buchan, *Comments* 127–8). The function of the frontier as a pressure valve for the contradictions of British capitalism underpins the imaginative power of the frontier for politicians like Buchan and it found literary expression in the genre of the imperial romance. Yet just as the shipping of prisoners, veterans, and vagrants out to the frontiers of empire never completely relieved Britain of its internal social tensions, Buchan's romances and spy thrillers remain haunted by the brute fact of imperialism's geographic and economic interconnections, where they find expression as modernist compressions.

These contradictions are least obvious in Buchan's first novel, *Prester John* (1910), perhaps the most conventional of his romances. Set on the South African Highveld, it tells a predictable story of white, male imperialists using their ingenuity and pluck to single-handedly subdue an uprising of Black Africans who have rebelled under the leadership of Prester John, a sharply racialized priest. Although it entertains the prospect of imperial instability and incorporates Black agency into its plot, its ending is profoundly conservative: Prester John is killed, sealed in a cave in the African interior, while his once rebellious followers, when deprived of their leader, are easily assimilated into the settler colony as a passive labor force. In its final chapters, *Prester John* resolves white anxieties around racial purity and economic pressures on capitalist reproduction, anticipating the ideology that would find concrete expression in the later South African government's policy of apartheid (see Davies 165–79).

It is in his Hannay novels, and especially *The Thirty-Nine Steps* (1915) – the first of the series, made famous by Hitchcock's 1935 film adaptation – that the ideological integrity of Buchan's romances begins to break down. Written and published in the run-up to the First World War, and set in Britain rather than South Africa, the novel does not at first glance appear to have much to do with the romance of the imperial frontier. In his Hannay novels, Buchan seems more concerned to demonize German militarism and stoke nationalist feeling among British readers (he would go onto write for the British War Propaganda Bureau during the war). Yet despite this agenda, *The Thirty-Nine Steps* still registers Buchan's personal connections with the South African frontier, global shifts in Britain's political hegemony, and endemic crises in the imperial-capitalist system. As a consequence, the narrower British geography of the novel is broken apart by anxieties that are inextricably bound up with the loss of empire.

To begin with, though technically British by birth, Richard Hannay himself is a frontiersman recently returned from South Africa. We learn early on that Hannay has been working in Bulawayo as a mining engineer and has accumulated a modest "pile – not one of the big ones, but good enough for me" (Buchan, *Complete* 13). Beginning with his return to London, the novel therefore inverts the imperial romance, starting at the point at which the genre usually concludes (Jones 418). But perhaps for this very reason, the whole narrative is powered forward by a fear that the prospects of the frontier and its associated romance might be over and done with. It quickly becomes clear that Hannay does not want to settle down with his cash, as he sets about searching for another adventure. Walking from the wealthy neighborhoods of north London to the "slums and mean streets" of the East End, Hannay begins to feel "my restlessness was growing worse" (Buchan, *Complete* 76), as though London's deep inequalities are propelling the narrative outwards to a new frontier. In its basic geography, *The Thirty-Nine Steps* not only suggests itself as a romance, but meta-textually implies its own adventurism as effective treatment for Britain's socioeconomic tensions.

The novel's plot takes off when Hannay comes across the eponymous "thirty-nine steps" (an indecipherable code) on the body of a murdered man who has been sheltering in his apartment. Indicatively, Hannay interprets the murder through his experience of frontier warfare: "I had seen men die violently before; indeed, I had killed a few myself in the Matabele War; but this cold blooded indoor business was different" (Buchan, *Complete* 22). Pursued by hostile German spies, Hannay flees London and leaps aboard a train heading north to the Scottish Highlands, aware that he'll be able to put his frontier skills to use in that terrain. As he rides northwards, he puzzles over the "thirty-nine steps" to decipher the meaning of the code, just as we readers lean into the novel to decipher the meaning of the plot. Again, Hannay's frontier experience comes in handy, allowing the narrative to progress: "I did a bit [of code-cracking] myself once as intelligence-officer at Delagoa Bay during the Boer War" (27). Throughout the novel, the romanticized frontier functions as a stable reference point that *enables* Buchan's plot by resolving moments of tension and catapulting it forward.

This continues when Hannay steps off the train in Scotland: "I felt just as I used to feel when I was starting for a big trek on a frosty morning on the high veld" (Buchan, *Complete* 28). Yet the freedom and exhilaration of this new frontier barely lasts: He soon finds himself visible to "espionage from the air," pursued across the Highlands by an airplane flying overhead (32). Perhaps the novel's – certainly the film's – most iconic scene, this steady enclosure of the frontiersman from above might be read as a registration not only of Buchan's personal exile from South Africa, but of Britain's declining hegemony in the region. Afraid to lose Britain's colonies as a redemptive socioeconomic force, Buchan repeatedly compares the Highlands to the Highveld in an attempt to produce a new frontier *within* the nation-state. But in so doing, he breaches exactly the imaginative divisions between homeland and frontier that the romance was designed to police. With this uneasy suturing of peripheral into metropolitan geographies, *The Thirty-Nine Steps* scrambles the romance's generic architecture and registers imperialism's "time-space compression" (Harvey 240) in a form that begins to look, on occasion, distinctly modernist.

This shift, from the romance's abstraction of colonial space into an accessible site of accumulation to modernism's insistence on subjective insecurity and narrative collapse, comes to a head in the climactic scene of *The Thirty-Nine Steps*. Here, Hannay has tracked down the spies to their lair and arrives to make an arrest. But to his bewilderment, he discovers his German spies dressed up as three middle-class English gentlemen. "A man of my sort, who has travelled about the world in rough places, gets on perfectly well with two classes, what you may call the upper and the lower," Hannay explains. "But what fellows like me don't understand," he continues, "is the great comfortable, satisfied middle-class world, the folk that live in villas and suburbs" (Buchan, *Complete* 91). Where his experience of the frontier has hitherto *enabled* Hannay's investigation and allowed the narrative to progress, this confrontation with a materially unproductive bourgeois class utterly confounds his powers of sight (see Trotter). Looking at the spies around him, he realizes that while there "was nothing in their appearance to prevent them being the three that had hunted me in Scotland," there was also "nothing to identify them" (Buchan, *Complete* 94). To his frustration, Hannay "simply can't explain why [...] I, who have a good memory and reasonable powers of observation, could find no satisfaction" (94). In its most climactic moment, it is not only Hannay's "powers of observation" that are undermined, but the descriptive capacity of narrative itself.

The romance emerged as a genre that was able to resolve the sharp contradictions of imperial extraction through the production of the frontier as a space of economic opportunity – at least, for its white male protagonists. But it did this by concealing the capitalist class who, divorced from the dirty work of colonial settlement, extracted their wealth from unproductive assets. When *The Thirty-Nine Steps* comes face to face with this class and the economic disjunctions of empire it represents, its form submits to modernism's representational crisis. As though panicked by his own revelation, Buchan quickly interrupts his story with three stars, marking a scene change and clean narrative break. When it resumes, so does the romance's confidence. Hannay notes that "something awoke in me" and the narrative shifts from visual obscuration to re-recognition: "The three faces seemed to change before my eyes and reveal their secrets.... The plump man's features seemed to dissolve, and form again, as I looked at them" (Buchan, *Complete* 95). Without any satisfactory explanation, Hannay is suddenly able to identify these men as the German spies they have been all along, resolving the crisis that temporarily interrupted the narrative. Yet what we see on the page is the narrative manufacturing its ideological resolution, as it works to override the modernist compressions it has inadvertently incorporated by returning awkwardly to the safe structures of the romance. Little wonder, then, that the novel's ending is "astonishingly abrupt" (Riach 174), drawing to a close just a couple of pages later: At this historical juncture of imperial crisis, the novel reaches for but is no longer able to sustain the ideological resolution that the genre of the romance had once provided.

## Edward Thompson: Anti-imperial Connections

If the threat of a rising German Empire turns up in Buchan's adventure fiction through these strange modernist compressions, then it is Edward

Thompson's Indian novels, and especially *An Indian Day* (1927), that navigate the challenge posed by more explicitly *anti*-imperial connections to the genre of the imperial romance. It is not widely read today, overshadowed by E. M. Forster's slightly earlier *A Passage to India* (1924). Yet *An Indian Day* was actually intended by Thompson as a "counterblast" to Forster's novel, which in his view erased the rich detail of Indian life by projecting symbolic concerns onto topographies that were at once modernist and romanticized. *A Passage to India* begins in the fictional town of Chandrapore, but it is based on Bankipore in Bihar, where Forster had spent just three weeks in January 1913 (see Forster, *Passage* 344). Forster did return again in 1921 for a brief stay, bringing some early drafts of *Passage* with him. But as he later remembered, when these descriptions "were confronted with the country they purported to describe, they seemed to wilt and go dead and I could do nothing with them.... The gap between India remembered and India experienced was too wide. When I got back to England the gap narrowed, and I was able to resume" (Forster, *Hill* 153). While *Passage* is rightly read as an indictment of empire and a foreshadowing of its decline, for a reader as embedded in Bengal and its anti-imperial networks as was Thompson, it came across not as resistant to but derivative of the romance.

Thompson first arrived in Bengal in 1910 as a Methodist minister to teach English literature at the Wesleyan College (his parents had served as Wesleyan missionaries in South India). He served as an army chaplain between the Tigris and Euphrates through the First World War, for which he was honored with a Military Cross. In 1919, he published a memoir and celebrated collection of poetry, *The Mesopotamian Verses*. As a recognized poet who spoke Bengali, he became close friends with Rabindranath Tagore, the polymath who would become such a vocal critic of the British Empire. They corresponded for nearly three decades, Thompson making clear his distaste for the romanticized view of India in a letter from 1935: "the outside world's opinion about India is a chaos – baroque art and gigantic monstrous images, rajas, elephants, tigers, Brahmins, untouchables," he remarked, confident that "this will be understood some day. After all, you [Tagore] have educated a lot of typical John Bulls like myself" (Das Gupta 187–8). Reading Tagore's poetry in the original Bengali, Thompson objected to its Orientalist reception in Britain, though eventually even Tagore himself became frustrated by Thompson's various hypocrisies and tendency to self-righteousness. Perhaps Thompson's most successful attempt to break open the romance's view of India came neither in fiction nor poetry, but a nonfiction study entitled *The Other Side of the Medal* (1925), which challenged hegemonic understandings of the widespread 1857 Uprising against

British rule as little more than a "Mutiny" (Thompson 10). By identifying the legitimacy of rebels' grievances and showing how imperialism had materially altered Indian lives, Thompson so effectively challenged a dominant perspective in colonial discourse that the essay became "something of a classic amongst British writings on India" (Parry, *Delusions* 177).

In *An Indian Day*, the first of five novels he was to set in India, Thompson continued this project of riposte, taking Forster's *Passage* as his target. Like Buchan's Hannay novels, *An Indian Day* was the first in a series that would recycle the same characters, address questions of fragmenting imperial power, and probe the inadequacy of adventure fiction's depictions of the colonial world. Unfortunately, however, and as Thompson's biographer notes, while "Thompson knew his India better," it was Forster who "wrote the better novel" (Lago 225). Writing of India at some remove, Forster was able to distil and subvert many key tropes of the imperial romance, from its heteronormative agenda and linear plot to its colonizing, cartographic gaze. Thompson, meanwhile, sought to capture the realities of colonial life as it rubbed up against actual anti-imperial politics on the ground, but as a consequence his novel often descends into dry *tête-à-tête*'s between pro- and anti-imperial characters who function little more than mouthpieces for different ideological positions (see Parry, *Delusions* 201). Yet rather than cast it aside as a "bad" novel, it is worth pursuing *An Indian Day*'s narrative limitations, which broaden our view on the different ways in which adventure fiction unraveled.

To begin with, *An Indian Day* nuances the seemingly obvious relationship between an author's geographic and cultural proximity to the realities of empire, on the one hand, and the reproduction or subversion of the romance, on the other. For writers like Schreiner, the imperial romance was a genre "best written in Piccadilly or in the Strand … untrammelled by contact with any fact" (Schreiner xxix–xl). But for Thompson, it is paradoxically his detailed knowledge of the anti-imperial movement that *prevents* his novel from gaining persuasive narrative momentum. This is due to Thompson's ambition to reject the romanticization of the colonial landscape, but it also reflects the ambivalence of his personal politics. In addition to exchanging letters with Tagore, Thompson was a close friend of Jawaharlal Nehru's and acted as "an anxious and persistent courier between the Government of India and the Indian nationalists" for more than a decade (Das Gupta 6). He was also known to Gandhi during this time, with the Mahatma's incisive description of Thompson as "India's prisoner" – he abandoned the nationalist cause in frustration on numerous occasions, before repeatedly returning to it – capturing his indecision on the question of Indian independence. While Thompson protested the Raj's use of force against nationalists, befriended the movement's leaders, and repeatedly critiqued romanticized and Orientalized accounts of the subcontinent, he was never able to fully commit to the practical withdrawal of British rule and the reality of Indian self-government. Administering famine relief in rural areas, he remained imprisoned in the liberal and proto-humanitarian ideologies of what Pablo Mukherjee has termed the Raj's "palliative imperialism" (Mukherjee 18). His death in 1946 meant that Thompson just missed the eventual dissolution of the Raj. But his strange mix of strong anti-imperial connections and nationalist aspirations, combined with a fundamental inability to shake himself free of imperial hegemony and concede an independent India, makes for a confused and revealing application of the romance's generic structures and forms.

It is by reading *An Indian Day* through *Passage to India* that we can most clearly track these developments. Numerous critics have read Forster's Marabar caves as a "symptom of what the novel is unable to comprehend" (Parry, "Materiality" 185). As Debrah Raschke (11) suggests, the caves' Platonic allusion invokes the romance's projection of an idealist realm that is then rejected by the material topography of the Indian landscape. Even Aziz, Forster's protagonist, realizes that the English heroine Adela Quested's "pose of 'seeing India' ... was only a form of ruling India; no sympathy lay behind it" (Forster, *Passage* 291–2), while her name, "Quested," suggests that the quests of adventure fictions are over, in the past tense (Davidis 266). In Haggard's archetypal romance, *King Solomon's Mines*, written some forty years before, the white male protagonists pass through the explicitly sexualized "bowels" of an underground cave. While their passage is fraught, they do eventually escape with their plunder of diamonds and gold. Meanwhile, rather than the figurative rape of the colonial landscape by buccaneering imperialists, Forster's caves lead to an echo chamber in which white fears of "mutineering" Indians instill in Adela a conviction that it is *she* who has been assaulted.

Building on these composite images, *An Indian Day* follows a group of colonial officers – Findlay, Nixon, Hamar, and Alden (possibly a coded reference to Forster's Adela) – as their administration of famine relief in remote rural India leads them to discover a terrorist cell operating on behalf of the nationalist movement. Prior to the discovery of this anti-imperial activity, the novel sets up the landscape as ancient and unchanging, outside of capitalist development. The subcontinent and its inhabitants are at once unknowable, troubling the generic structures of the romance, while at the same time effectively evacuated of historical agency. The novel takes place on the outskirts of Vishnugram, a fictional Bengali location described as "not a great city, but just an entirely typical provincial town – the capital of an area of perhaps a thousand square miles" (Thompson, *Indian* 5–6). Addressing an implied male reader directly, the novel's anonymous narrator assures him that "he will not be far wrong if he imagined that the conditions and circumstances" of Vishnugram "are essentially the same in thousands of Indian provincial cities, of which the tourist necessarily knows nothing" (5–6). This colonial gaze is combined with the ideology of palliative imperialism: as Findlay later remarks, "in this land there was always famine somewhere. There was always disease and suffering" (61). Sniping at writers such as Forster, who swing through India and write a bestseller, Thompson implies that his own proximity to Indian life authorizes his more expert novelistic view. And yet, even as he does so, he flattens the very same topography into a static and unchanging landscape perpetually in need of the Raj's "humanitarian" intervention. While at one level the generalizations of the romance are refuted in *An Indian Day*, at another its generic processes endure.

It is all the more revealing, then, that at the center of Thompson's novel is Trisunia, "a hill outcropped from the thickest of the wilderness on the Orissa borders [that] humped itself to a height of a thousand feet above the surrounding plain" (Thompson, *Indian* 149). As civil unrest begins to circulate through the famine-stricken region, Nixon decides that this hill must be the source of dissent: "Nixon, scanning his reports and seeking for some focus to all this wide-wining rumour, some place to search for a definite foe to strike at, settled on Trisunia" (149). The narrative gives no reason for Nixon's apparently arbitrary decision, beyond his intuition. It is doubly curious, then, that just a few pages later, we learn Trisunia has "a rocky surface pitted with caves and cracks.... One of the caves went deep into the hill. No one had ever been interested or hardy enough to explore it" (153). It transpires that a strange noise has been emerging from this cave: "It was from the unknown heart of this cave that Hara Deva the Destroyer was now roaring. Terrified crowds had heard him, at the spring festival; but the rumour had died away, only to be revived as the miseries of famine grew to their height" (153). Attempting to diagnose the meaning of this strange noise, Alden reflects that he "read something some time ago, about what seditionists had been doing in the Philippines. It seems they had a cave of sorts there also; and they fixed it up with a whopping megaphone. It was a place with magnificent echoes" (156).

In this weird compression of genre and geography, *An Indian Day* combines the cavernous diamond mines at the center of Haggard's romances with Forster's modernist reinterpretation of those same landscapes in the Marabar caves. This topographical amalgamation of romanticized and modernist styles is then triangulated with anti-imperial connections. When

Alden and his men eventually "penetrate" the cave it turns out to be empty, creating a profound anticlimax in the narrative: "there was an easy way out to an opening in an unpathed tract of the forest. There had been cooking and sleeping and habitation in the cave. This they discovered, beyond a peradventure; but the rest was guess-work" (Thompson, *Indian* 158). On the one hand, there are no treasures to be seized, nor indeed are there any rebels to arrest: The novel defies adventure fiction's generic securitization of the imperial imaginary. But on the other, these caves are not entirely indecipherable, as were Forster's. There is nothing either romantic *or* modernist in this scene. Instead, all they find is evidence that members of the underground movement exist, and that they have escaped arrest. Moreover, the caves are very easy to escape from: There is little that is hair-raising or adventurous or confounding about them. They are simply holes in the landscape and nothing more.

Given how quickly the caves become redundant to the narrative after this scene, we might also be tempted to read them as holes in the plot – but more interesting interpretations are available. For Benita Parry, these hills may have a "more circumscribed function" than Forster's "multi-symbolic caves," but they do nonetheless announce "the unrelenting presence of an India immensely old, remote from the British and the modern world, and contemptuous of its works" (Parry, *Delusions* 187). In my reading, Thompson's cave marks a new turn in adventure fiction, one that registers the continued fragmentation of imperial power by an insurgent nationalist movement. His imperial characters are aware of the anti-imperial presence, connected to it through the ephemeral echoes emerging from the cave. Yet when they attempt to thwart nationalist activities, that same presence becomes impossible to pin down. This is a redirection of Forster's amorphous modernist compressions to a more emphatically anti-imperial statement of defiance. Like Thompson himself, the novel is not able to countenance the actual end of British rule and his colonial administrators remain mostly in place as a benevolent force as *An Indian Day* comes to a close. But when we read Thompson's novel at the level of genre and form, there is a revealing historicity that points to the end of the British Empire and with it, the unraveling of British adventure fiction.

## Works Cited

Boehmer, Elleke. *Empire, the National, and the Postcolonial, 1890–1920: Resistance in Interaction.* Oxford UP, 2005.

Booth, Howard, and Nigel Rigby. *Modernism and Empire: Writing and British Coloniality, 1890–1940.* Manchester UP, 2000.

Buchan, John. *The African Colony: Studies in Reconstruction.* William Blackwood & Sons, 1903.
    *Comments and Characters*, edited by W. Forbes Gray, Thomas Nelson & Sons, 1940.
    *The Complete Richard Hannay Stories.* Wordsworth Editions, 2010.
    *Prester John.* House of Stratus, 2008.
Childs, Peter. *Modernism and the Post-Colonial: Literature and Empire, 1885–1930.* Continuum International Publishing Group, 2007.
Cleary, Joe. *Modernism, Empire, World Literature.* Cambridge UP, 2021.
Das Gupta, Uma, editor. *A Difficult Friendship: Letters of Edward Thompson and Rabindranath Tagore, 1913–1940.* Oxford UP, 2003.
Davidis, Maria. "Forster's Imperial Romance: Chivalry, Motherhood, and Questing in *A Passage to India*." *Journal of Modern Literature*, vol. 23, no. 2, pp. 259–76.
Davies, Dominic. *Imperial Infrastructure and Spatial Resistance in Colonial Literature, 1880–1930.* Peter Lang, 2017.
Esty, Jed. *Unseasonable Youth: Modernism, Colonialism, and the Fiction of Development.* Oxford UP, 2011.
Forster, E. M. *The Hill of Devi.* Penguin Books, 1963.
    *A Passage to India.* Penguin Classics, 2005.
Gikandi, Simon. *Maps of Englishness: Writing Identity in the Culture of Colonialism.* Columbia UP, 1996.
Gopal, Priya. *Insurgent Empire: Anticolonial Resistance and British Dissent.* Verso, 2020.
Haggard, H. Rider. *King Solomon's Mines.* Oxford World's Classics, 2008.
Harvey, David. *The Condition of Postmodernity: An Inquiry into the Origins of Cultural Change.* Wiley-Blackwell, 1991.
Jameson, Fredric. "Modernism and Imperialism." *Nationalism, Colonialism, and Literature*, edited by Terry Eagleton, Fredric Jameson, and Edward Said. U of Minnesota P, 1990, pp. 43–66.
Jones, Susan. "Into the Twentieth Century: Imperial Romance from Haggard to Buchan." *A Companion to Romance*, edited by Corinne Saunders. Blackwell Publishing, 2004, pp. 406–23.
Kipling, Rudyard. *Plain Tales from the Hills.* Oxford World's Classics, 2008.
Lago, Mary. *India's Prisoner: A Biography of Edward John Thompson, 1886–1946.* U of Missouri P, 2001.
Meredith, Martin. *Diamonds, Gold, and War: The Making of South Africa.* Pocket Books, 2008.
Mukherjee, Upamanyu Pablo. Natural Disasters and Victorian Empire: Famines, Fevers, and the Literary Cultures of South Asia. Palgrave Macmillan.
Parry, Benita. *Delusions and Discoveries: Studies on India in the British Imagination, 1880–1930.* The Penguin P, 1972.
    "Materiality and Mystification in *A Passage to India*." *NOVEL: A Forum on Fiction*, vol. 13, no. 2, 1998, pp. 174–94.
Raschke, Debrah. "Forster's *Passage to India*: Re-Envisioning Plato's Cave." *The Comparatist*, vol. 21, 1997, pp. 10–24.
Redley, Michael. "John Buchan and the South African War." *Reassessing John Buchan: Beyond the Thirty-Nine Steps*, edited by Kate Macdonald. Pickering & Chatto, 2010, pp. 65–76.

Riach, Alan. "John Buchan: Politics, Language, and Suspense." *Reassessing John Buchan: Beyond the Thirty-Nine Steps*, edited by Kate Macdonald. Pickering & Chatto, 2010, pp. 171–82.
Schreiner, Olive. *The Story of an African Farm*. Oxford World's Classics, 2008.
Thompson, Edward. *An Indian Day*. Penguin Books, 1940.
*The Other Side of the Medal*. Harcourt, Brace, & Company, 1927.
Thompson, Edward. *The Other Side of the Medal*. The Hogarth Press, 1930.
Trotter, David. "The Politics of Adventure in the Early British Spy Novel." *Intelligence and National Security*, vol. 5, no. 4, 1990, pp. 30–54.

# 14

PAUL STASI

# Poetic Accumulation, Modernist Verse, and Imperial Capital

C. L. R. James's *Letters from London* – which gathers together a series of articles he wrote for the *Port of Spain Gazette* in 1932 just after he arrived in the imperial capital – seems, at first glance, a curious departure from the more decidedly anticolonial work for which he is best known. For though the letters make repeated oblique mention of his anticolonial work, James is more interested in displaying how well he fits, "both by instinct and by training," into the Bloomsbury intellectual milieu that is their most sustained focus than he is in denouncing the racism he also encounters there (54). The reason for this is relatively clear: James is positioning himself as the legitimate heir of British culture. We see a striking, if paradoxical, confirmation of this in the publication of his pamphlet *The Case for West Indian Self-Government* by Virginia and Leonard Woolf's Hogarth Press in 1933. The most visible sign of James's ability to fit into Bloomsbury, then, is its dissemination of his case for leaving it.

Nevertheless, despite the absence of any sustained argument about empire, James's letters offers us a relatively damning portrait of the British capital that, inevitably, reads back onto the imperial relation. Beginning at the Victoria and Albert Museum, he asks a simple, if central, question: "Why haven't we got such a place at home?" (3). What begins as a kind of rapture about the opportunities available in London quickly shifts into praise for the ingenuity of the citizens of his native land, who are deprived of such luxuries:

> When you move around this place and see the opportunities the people have … and then stop and think for a minute of the conditions in the West Indies, Trinidad and poor Barbados, the wonder is not that the creoles do so little but that they do so well. All that any middle-class Englishman needs is a little ambition. If he has that, the way to achievement and success is wide open. (11)

Despite having "nearly a thousand years of uninterrupted opportunity … millions of these people are still mentally adolescent" (122). Amidst this critique of British immaturity, James offers a kind of skeletal version of

Andre Gunder Frank's argument about the "development of underdevelopment." The absence of opportunity in Trinidad is somehow related to its abundance in London.

But London's development also offers something to the people of Trinidad, or at least those able to make the journey: Access to those same imperial spoils. James's *Letters* thus set out the contradictory process by which empire, in part, created the conditions for its dissolution. For James is just one of the many imperial subjects who made their way to London in the early twentieth century, making the capital, as writers such as Minkah Makalani, Priyamvada Gopal, and Anna Snaith, among many others, have argued, a "key crucible for anti-colonialism" (Snaith 84). Karl Marx's ringing opening to *The Eighteenth Brumaire* – "Men make their own history, but not of their own free will; not under circumstances they themselves have chosen but under the given and inherited circumstances with which they are directly confronted" – aptly sums up this process by which the new emerges directly through the transformation of historical constraints (146).

What I would like to track, in this essay, is the ways in which the accumulation of value in the imperial metropole produces a poetic analogue: The investment of many of the immigrant writers in early twentieth-century London in the construction of a cross-cultural dialogue between East and West, one that gradually diminishes in the postcolonial period. Poetry, in the modernist period, dismantles the simple binary between authenticity and derivation that has blinded us from seeing these poets as participating in a common enterprise, even as we can observe the ways in which this enterprise registered differently for poets on either side of the imperial relation.

## Imperial Culture

Literary history, of course, has tended to see a strong divide between the formally dense poetry of writers such as T. S. Eliot or Ezra Pound and the more directly political poetry of figures such as Una Marson or Sarojini Naidu. Naidu's poetry, "seen as sentimental, derivative and backward-looking, sits awkwardly alongside her feminist anti-colonialism" (Snaith 69). Similarly, Marson's poetry has been taken to task for "its reliance upon British models and its lack of experimentation and 'authenticity'" (Donnell, "Contradictory" 45). The keynote here is derivative, which either means an anti-modern attachment to older forms or a failure to speak from some imagined authentic anticolonial subject position. Without ignoring the formal differences between, say, *The Waste Land* and the lyrics of Rabindranath

Tagore, there are a few important points to make. The first is that those two pejoratives supposedly marking colonial verse – derivative, inauthentic – fall apart under the barest of scrutiny: Modernism rests precisely on a transvaluation of the very idea of the derivative. "We dwell with satisfaction upon the poet's difference from his predecessors," Eliot famously wrote in "Tradition and the Individual Talent," "Whereas if we approach a poet without this prejudice we shall often find that not only the best, but the most individual parts of his work may be those in which the dead poets, his ancestors, assert their immortality most vigorously" ("Tradition" 4). "We *know* so much more" than the dead writers, Eliot continues, "and they are that which we know" – (6). Key modernists such as Yeats, Pound, and Eliot often wrote direct imitations of older verse forms as "part of a wider late-nineteenth and early-twentieth century quest for various alternatives to capitalist, imperialist modernity," a quest that included many poets from the empire and might itself be considered the most characteristic modernist structure of feeling (Snaith 77).

At the same time, how exactly are we to assess the authenticity of a Trinidadian subject, like C. L. R. James, educated under colonialism, who was a lifelong cricket fan and whose favorite author was Thackeray? Is Eliot an authentic Englishman because he worked tirelessly to transform himself into one? Without ignoring aesthetics, then, we can nevertheless historicize the poetic production of the early twentieth century as emerging from a situation James Clifford has named *ethnographic modernity*: "ethnographic because [the poet] finds himself off center among scattered traditions; modernity since the condition of rootlessness and mobility he confronts is an increasingly common fate" (3). The governing structure of this ethnographic modernity is imperialism, creating both the rootlessness and the longing for stability that is its most obvious result.

That modernist writing is tied to empire is by now a relatively uncontroversial fact. Writing in 1989, Edward Said remarked that "the fundamental historical problem of modernism" is that "the subaltern and the constitutively different suddenly achieved disruptive articulation" into European consciousness (223). The breakdown of canonical literary forms typically associated with modernism is due, in part, to this awareness of alterity. Writing at roughly the same time as Said, Raymond Williams offered a more sustained historicization of modernism's relation to "the magnetic concentration of wealth and power in imperial capitals and the simultaneous cosmopolitan access to a wide variety of subordinate cultures" (*Modernism* 44). The ability of "small groups in any form of divergence or dissent" to "find some kind of foothold" in the capital, along with the increased "opportunities of patronage" drew a large immigrant population to the capital (45), which, in turn, created a decidedly new aesthetic: "Liberated or breaking from their national or provincial cultures ... encountering meanwhile a novel and dynamic environment from which many of the older forms were obviously distant, the artists and writers and thinkers of this phase found the only community available to them: a community of the medium; of their own practices" (45). That old chestnut of ahistorical modernist criticism – the exploration of the properties of the medium – finds, here, its proper historical context.

This idea of cross-cultural exchange – often reduced to a binary opposition or synthesis of "East and West" – is, in fact, one of the great themes of the period, even if the terms of the encounter are always unequal. An obvious effect of this unevenness is the modernist penchant for reading colonial writers through an Orientalizing lens. Thus, we have Tagore, "a modernizing poetic force in his native Bengal," seen primarily as a mystic (Boehmer 225). If, as Auritro Majumder has argued, Tagore is "a philosopher of the modern, someone who insists on the need to engage with the world as it exists," his spiritualism is, perhaps, best understood as one of those repositories of alternative values with which the modernists tended to confront their fallen world (7). Indeed, Yeats found in Tagore "an interlocutor on shared questions of cultural revival and spiritual renewal, which for Yeats was never merely a Eurocentric project" (Boehmer 229). For his part, Tagore "did not come to England in 1912 as either a proselytizer for India or a supplicant before the west.... Rather it was as a sophisticated advocate of what he himself in 1907 called visva-sahitya or 'world literature' ... that he made his journey" (Boehmer 231). Naidu's poems too "are not merely a retreat to a 'pure' and 'essential' India, or the wholesale ventriloquizing of a British romantic tradition" but rather "the product of the negotiation of multiple, competing influences" (Snaith 72). What distinguishes these writers, then, and part of what makes them difficult to assimilate to our late twentieth- and twenty-first-century sense of national specificity, is their investment in a form of universal humanism, what Majumder calls, in relation to Tagore's work, the "development of humanity-in-common ... a 'union of its particular humanness with all humanity'" (4).

We might find here an ironic echo of the humanism supposedly undergirding the colonial mission. As Jed Esty writes: "colonial discourse of the nineteenth and early twentieth centuries tended to view colonized territories as the originary locations of modern European civilization. According to this rhetoric, thoroughly documented by Edward Said in *Orientalism*, modern Europe had reconnected, through conquest, with the primary sites of its Judeo-Christian, Indo-European, Greco-Roman heritage" (41). Colonialist rhetoric, that is to say, tended to hide the interests of capital under a veneer of cosmopolitanism. What I would like to suggest here, is that though these cross-cultural encounters are, necessarily, tied at all points to empire, they are not reducible to it. For the constitutive background of ethnographic modernity generated a series of literary projects which sought to find meanings in common across cultures. Eliot's *Waste Land*, for instance, tries to find the "roots that clutch" among a sea of competing poetic traditions, while Pound maintained a lifelong interest in the project of cultural comparison (Eliot, *Poems* 53). The early twentieth century, then, was dominated by the possibility of cross-cultural contact and by an ideal shared across the colonial divide that some greater cultural wholeness might be attained through the combination of different cultures. A shared humanity was both the idea undergirding this project but also something to be achieved. Situating the work of Tagore or Naidu in this context allows us to perceive further common ground between their poetry and the modernists to which they often seem opposed.

Of course, this project is laced with pitfalls and blind spots, marked, as we are more and more acutely aware, by the power relations that the supposedly autonomous realm of art wishes to keep outside its purview. The colonizer's desire to know the colonized is, as Said has taught us, intimately tied to its economic and political rule, and the knowledge it produces is often partial, incomplete, or outrightly ideological. Meanwhile, the colonized of this moment often seem to our twenty-first-century ears too marked by their allegiance to the colonized to be truly speaking as themselves. What we need, though, is to replace these relatively crude judgments with something like the more "nuanced and complex vocabulary," Santanu Das outlines in his effort to understand the loyalty of Indian soldiers serving in the British Army in the First World War (29). I turn then, first, to the poetry of the early twentieth century before, briefly, discussing the shift in registers in the immediate postwar period.

## Imperial Subjects

We can see the relation between poetic innovation and imperial spoils reflected, more or less directly, in the work of the modernists. Pound's early poem "Epilogue," for instance, explicitly metaphorizes his poetic discoveries as "spice and robes" and "spoils" he has brought back as gifts from "exile" (209). The imperial analogy here reads across Pound's career, describing the groundbreaking, polyglot, and multicultural *Cantos* as much as his early imitations of Provençal poetry and medieval verse forms. *The Waste Land* can also be read through this lens, for though one of the poem's speakers famously claims "I can connect / Nothing with nothing," the poem itself

## 14 Poetic Accumulation

makes numerous connections across various poetic traditions, constellating Elizabethan lyric, Baudelairean ennui, Shackleton's voyage to Antarctica, and *The Upanishads* into a new poetic whole, even if one that remains fragmentary (Eliot, *Poems* 64). The accumulation of culture characteristic of the modernist poem is, in large part, due to the accumulation of wealth in the imperial metropolis.

But, of course, neither Pound nor Eliot are, or were at the time at least, British. Indeed, if we think of the dominant poetic voices of the early twentieth century – Eliot, Pound, but also Yeats, and even Rudyard Kipling – all are marked by empire and emigration, Kipling having been born in Bombay. And yet all resided, at least for a time, in London, along with intellectuals and writers such as Naidu, Marson, Tagore, George Padmore, Eric Waldron, Mahatma Gandhi, C. L. R. James, and Claude McKay, to name only a few. Imperialism, again, is the context for thinking of all of these writers together. And if imperialism brought these writers to London, it also provided them the resources to produce their critiques of empire. This point is not new; nationalism has famously been described, by Partha Chatterjee, as a derivative discourse. But to critique nationalism for its reliance on the empire it would overthrow risks romanticizing the idea of rupture, imagining that something new can emerge untainted by the older forms it wishes to displace. Rather, the new always emerges as a recombination of what already exists: The older poets are what we know. Poetic imitation, then, is never only imitation; the transformed circumstances in which imitations occur produce new readings of the forms that are imitated. Concepts are changed by their contexts.

Consider, in this light, Peter Kalliney's recent account of the ways in which colonial intellectuals "were strongly attracted to the modernist idea of aesthetic autonomy" (5). Kalliney outlines this position by analogy with James's reading of the political importance of cricket:

> Black and colonial subjects could compete on equal terms in sport, as in the arts, even if they could do so nowhere else. Yet for precisely this reason, sport and the arts could be charged with a form of racial significance otherwise stifled by political inequalities. This bubble of autonomy invests these particular forms of activity with special political meaning. (26)

Colonial investment in aesthetic autonomy is something more than mimicry, as colonial subjects took up the idea because it might be a way round "the political inequities and racial injustices of the imperial situation" (6). Immediately, however, there is a dialectical reversal, as one's ability to participate in the apolitical realm of aesthetics takes on a political valence, due to the structural position one occupies *outside* the supposedly disinterested realms of sport or art.¹ From this angle, the "cultural collecting and agglomeration" in *The Waste Land* might seem less the confident poetics of someone saturated with "the mind of Europe," than the most visible sign of the author's Americanism, which is to say precisely his position *outside* of Europe, even as the poem asserts an American's ability to claim that heritage as his own (Cleary 135).²

This last idea comes from Joe Cleary's *Modernism, Empire, World Literature*, which reads modernism as the cultural analogue to capital's migration from London to New York in the early part of the twentieth century. Crucially, this shift was initiated by writers from the semi-periphery: Eliot and Pound as well as the Irishmen Yeats and James Joyce. Modernist literature, then, in its most canonical articulations, was tied both to a shift in the structure of empire and to the immigration that empire made possible. Turning to Pound's early writings on America, Cleary articulates the links between "the languages of metropolitan decline and decadence and those of peripheral renaissance and rejuvenation" which "dialectically provoke each other" (96). "The emergence of a school of self-assured West Indian writers," the *Times Literary Supplement* argued in 1962, "can thus be related to the composition of *The Waste Land*" (qtd. in Kalliney 12). When things fall apart, others can emerge. The inward turn of English verse in the 1930s and 1940s – what Esty has called *The Shrinking Island* – is itself the cause and result of the irruption of the colonial alterity noted by Said.

We can observe something of this dual process in a striking poem by the Jamaican poet Claude McKay called "America," written just before his first trip to London. Though focused on the United States, the poem resonates across several of the more properly London-based poems I will discuss. Here is McKay:

> Although she feeds me bread of bitterness,
> And sinks into my throat her tiger's tooth,
> Stealing my breath of life, I will confess
> I love this cultured hell that tests my youth.
> Her vigor flows like tides into my blood,
> Giving me strength erect against her hate,
> Her bigness sweeps my being like a flood.
> Yet, as a rebel fronts a king in state,
> I stand within her walls with not a shred
> Of terror, malice, not a word of jeer.
> Darkly I gaze into the days ahead,
> And see her might and granite wonders there,
> Beneath the touch of Time's unerring hand,
> Like priceless treasures sinking in the sand. (Ramazani et al. 1: 503)

McKay, here, transforms the traditional rhetoric of the sonnet structure he inhabits. In place of the cruel or indifferent beloved we find the "cultured hell" of the United States which, nevertheless, is also the source of the poet's resistance, allowing him to position himself in that quintessentially American role of the rebel against monarchy. And yet what is most striking about the poem is its attachment to English poetic traditions: its use of the sonnet form and its echo of Shelley's "Ozymandias." For McKay's poem gazes "darkly" into a future where America's "wonders" sink into the sand just like Shelley's famous statue.

We can set this poem next to its near-contemporary, Yeats's 1921 lyric "The Second Coming," which imagines the ruins of culture giving birth, again in darkness, to a "rough beast" (187). A similar image appears in Tagore's 1922 text "Creative Unity," where he has "the vision of a huge demon, which had no shape, no meaning, yet had two arms that could strike and break and tear," an image that emerges from the "battlefields of France," but which is immediately tied to "the effect of the West upon Eastern life" (531–2). What reads as "mere anarchy" from one position, might be an opportunity from another; the beast threatening Western culture might actually emerge from within (Yeats 187).

A similar set of ideas are surprisingly present in the work of that arch-imperialist Kipling, in poems from his 1906 prosometric work *Puck of Pook's Hill*. This text is a kind of historical fantasy, narrating scenes from England's past to two contemporary children through the figure of Shakespeare's Puck, who either tells the stories himself or conjures people from the past to tell them. The stories, not surprisingly, tend to reinforce Kipling's great theme of the duty to empire, as in those about a Roman soldier in conquered Britain, but interlaced with these stories are poems, which often undermine the stories' confident tone.

Take, for instance, the poem "A Pict Song," which voices the complaints of "the Little Folk" upon whom Rome's "heavy hooves," always fall (Kipling 44). The poem ends with a stanza that reads as a weaker version of McKay's conclusion:

> No indeed! We are not strong,
> But we know Peoples that are.
> Yes, and we'll guide them along,
> To smash and destroy you in War!
> We shall be slaves just the same?
> Yes, we have always been slaves,
> But you – you will die of the shame,
> And then we shall dance on your graves! (44)

What is almost entirely missing from the Roman stories in the book – the sense, as in *Heart of Darkness*, that "this also has been one of the dark places in the earth," and, therefore, that there might be some kinship between contemporary African's experiences of empire and that of the ancient Britons – is here given voice, as Kipling imagines the resistant consciousness of an imperial subject, something he was unable to do in *Kim*, or indeed much of his other work (Conrad 5). Here, though, there appears to be another side to the imperial story; within Kipling's tales of imperial duty, then, there emerges a form of resistance that runs entirely counter to Kipling's aims.

A strikingly similar poem was written by the Indian feminist anticolonial intellectual Sarojini Naidu following the Jallianwala Bagh (Amritsar) Massacre, in which the British Army, whose troops were largely South Asians themselves, fired on peaceful protestors, an action which Kipling famously defended. Estimates of the carnage are uncertain, but somewhere between 400 and 1,500 people were killed, with another 1,200 injured. Here is Naidu's poem, "Panjab, 1919":

> How shall our love console thee or assuage
> Thy piteous wounds? How shall our grief requite
> The hate that scourges and the hands that smite
> Thy loveliness with rods of bitter rage?
> Lo! let thine anguish be our battle-gage
> To wreck the terror of the tyrant's might
> That mocks with ruthless scorn thy tragic plight,
> And mars with shame thine ancient heritage!
> O beautiful! O broken and betrayed!
> Endure thou still, unconquered, unafraid,
> O mournful queen! O martyred Draupadi!
> The sacred rivers of thy stricken blood
> Shall prove the five-fold stream of Freedom's flood,
> And guard the watch-towers of our Liberty.

As with McKay's "America," the poem is a sonnet, literalizing the form's rhetoric of love and tyranny for political ends. Addressed to those who lost their lives in the massacre, Naidu suggests that the love the speaker feels must be transformed into anticolonial resistance, drawing on the main heroine of the Hindu epic *Mahabharata* as a figure for an unconquered India. Western and Eastern traditions meet, as the poem presents two distinct forms of temporality: one the transformation of colonial violence into anticolonial resistance, the other the "ancient heritage" of Indian Liberty which persists into the present.

But if Naidu manages to smuggle resistance into a largely imitative verse form, the work of Marson illustrates the way these cross-cultural exchanges can produce seemingly opposed views in one intellectual career. We are used to excusing the reactionary political views of aesthetically innovative authors. Similarly, we often excuse the traditional aesthetics of writers whose verse presents positions we find politically amenable. Marson offers us an odd spin on these familiar problems, for her poetry tends both to be written in what was, by the 1930s, an old-fashioned style, even as it also fails to provide us with the political positions we might expect from this notably anticolonial feminist author. If "the opposing ideologies of racism and Pan-Africanism that Marson had encountered in Britain led her to work through a new political identity and agenda for social justice," we find little of this in her poetry, which consistently articulates a vision of self-sacrificial love, often, startlingly enough, through the figure of the slave (Donnell, "Feminism" 126).

Here, for instance, is the opening of the sonnet "In Vain":

> In vain I build me stately mansion's fair,
> And set thee as my king upon the throne,
> And place a lowly stool beside thee there,
> Thus, as thy slave to come into my own. (Marson 45)

For Donnell, this poem "articulate[s] a space in which the subject can position itself even within the structure of slavery," which seems, partly, right ("Contradictory" 55). It's also possible to hear in the poem the presentation of an imperial subject in thrall to the motherland who consistently misrecognizes tyranny for love. If it is true that Marson, "like many colonial writers, gained from, but also generated, the city's modernity by creating a symbiotic relationship between colony and metropole," we might see these poems as encoding this same relationship as one of violence and dispossession, as the metaphor of distant king and waiting slave outstrips its rhetorical context when spoken by a Jamaican poet living under the reign of George VI (Snaith 174). But Marson does not seem entirely in control of this register of the poem and it appears only sporadically within the sonnet sequence. More consistent, if also more direct, is Marson's rewriting of "If," which, as Donnell argues, turns Kipling's paean to imperial masculinity – "If" you can control yourself, then, "Yours is the Earth and everything that's in it" (469) – into a portrayal of "the domestic obstacle course which faces a prospective bride," and, in doing so, exposes the "cultural politics" of "the mother tongue" (Donnell, "Contradictory" 55, 45, 45). A similar process occurs in the poem "In Jamaica," which contrasts the "wonderful life" of the tourist with the "dreary life" of "the beggars" in the "large slums" (Marson 78). In each of these works, mimicry or imitation is, in part, transvalued.

And yet it is hard to read these poems and not see a disconnect between Marson's politics and aesthetics, even if we can observe a somewhat increased attention to politics as her poetic career progresses. Returning to Kalliney, we might say that Marson values autonomy, the ability to write in a poetic tradition without the burden of representing her culture. What is most striking about these poems, though, is the way the political seeps through them. Metaphors of slavery insist on being read as political, while the closing stanzas of the Jamaica poem – where the speaker insists on her attachment to Jamaica no matter what – remain haunted by the brief glimpse of lives typically hidden from view and only fleetingly seen in Marson's own verse. If Kipling seemed unaware of the anti-imperial subtext of "A Pict Song," we might say something similar about Marson; in each case the poetry seems to outstrip the most obvious intentions of the writers themselves, itself an apt figure for the ways in which empire generates its own negations and dialectical reversals.

## Coda: Colonization in Reverse

By the mid-1930s, the situation was already starting to change. The Italian invasion of Ethiopia in 1935 galvanized the anticolonial resistance centered in London. At the same time, the modernists, as Esty has shown, began the long process of "translating the end of empire into a resurgent concept of national culture" (2). The defining emblem of this trajectory is, for Esty, Eliot's *Four Quartets*, which mark a shift from *The Waste Land*'s investment in "meaning's travel across cultures" to "meaning ... within the fixed bounds of a given tradition" (137).

This process only accelerates in the postwar period, as a new generation of colonial subjects, themselves typically less privileged than the writers I've been tracking, arrive in England. Sam Selvon's 1956 *The Lonely Londoners*, which "represents the disconnection between black London and white London as an obvious fracture in the idea of shared imperial subjecthood," is the crucial document here (Esty 202). The distance from his fellow Trinidadian's *Letters from London* couldn't be starker. What is most striking about Selvon's work, though, is not only its content but its form: the creolized English that narrates the experiences of its hero Moses. Crucially this narration is in the third person. Selvon is not, here, representing the subjective English of Moses so much as transforming the objective means of representation itself. Omniscience might also be West Indian. A similar idea is taken up by Louise Bennett's "Colonization in Reverse," published the year after Selvon's novel:

14 Poetic Accumulation

> Wat a joyful news, miss Mattie,
> I feel like me heart gwine burs
> Jamaica people colonizin
> Englan in reverse.
> ...
> What a islan! What a people!
> Man an woman, old an young
> Jus a pack dem bag an baggage
> An tun history upside dung! (Ramazani et al. 2: 173)

Selvon and Bennett here stand in for a number of writers of their generation, for whom the imitation of metropolitan forms was no longer viable and whose literary work would increasingly move away from the synthesis of East and West often imagined in early twentieth-century verse to a development of the particularity of their own national and regional identities.

The English, for their part, would follow suit, particularly if we consider the verse of figures such as Philip Larkin, Stevie Smith, or even the more obviously ambitious poetry of W. H. Auden, whose move to America is generally taken to correspond with an increased sense of poetry's inability to effect political change. Esty gives us two remarkable examples. The first is from Maynard Keynes, arguing in 1932 that England must "let goods be homespun" (qtd. in Esty 179). The second is Raymond Williams's suggestion that, in his early work, he sought to allow England "to persist in its own terms" (*Politics* 72).

\* \* \*

Snaith's discussion of Naidu closes with an anecdote that aptly characterizes the oddity of a British culture seemingly now in imitation of its former territories: "I went to a 'British Fair,'" Naidu writes, "and laughed till I cried – it was the replica of our Swadeshi exhibitions, with just the same eagerness to show off the homespuns, the glassware, the beads and trinkets ... and boost them" (Naidu, *Selected* 265–6). No longer universal, British culture had become just one national project like any other.

### Notes

1. The same situation arises in Das's survey of Indian's relationship to the First World War, where "imperial war service becomes a route to its opposite, national autonomy" (316).
2. The phrase "The mind of Europe" comes, of course, from Eliot, "Tradition," 6.

## Works Cited

Boehmer, Elleke. *Indian Arrivals 1870–1915: Networks of British Empire*. Oxford UP, 2015.
Chatterjee, Partha. *Nationalist Thought and the Colonial World: A Derivative Discourse*. 1986. U of Minnesota P, 1993.
Cleary, Joe. *Modernism, Empire, World Literature*. Cambridge UP, 2021.
Clifford, James. *The Predicament of Culture: Twentieth-Century Ethnography, Literature, and Art*. Harvard UP, 1988.
Conrad, Joseph. *Heart of Darkness*. 1899. 5th ed., W. W. Norton, 2006.
Das, Santanu. *India, Empire, and First World War Culture: Writings, Images and Songs*. Cambridge UP, 2018.
Donnell, Alison. "Contradictory (W)omens? Gender Consciousness in the Poetry of Una Marson." *Kunapipi*, vol. 17, no. 3, 1995, pp. 43–58.
———. "Una Marson: Feminism, Anti-Colonialism and a Forgotten Fight for Freedom." *West Indian Intellectual in Britain*, edited by Bill Schwarz. Manchester UP, 2018, pp. 114–31.
Eliot, Thomas Stearns. *Collected Poems, 1909–1962*. Harcourt, Brace & World, 1963.
———. "Tradition and the Individual Talent." *Selected Essays*, Harcourt, Brace & World, 1964, pp. 3–11.
Esty, Jed. *A Shrinking Island: Modernism and National Culture in England*. Princeton UP, 2004.
Frank, Andre Gunder. "The Development of Underdevelopment." *Monthly Review*, vol. 18, no. 4, 1966, pp. 17–31.
Gopal, Priyamvada. *Insurgent Empire: Anticolonial Resistance and British Dissent*. Verso, 2020.
James, Cyril Lionel Robert. *Letters from London*. Prospect P, 2003.
Kalliney, Peter J. *Commonwealth of Letters: British Literary Culture and the Emergence of Postcolonial Aesthetics*. Oxford UP, 2013.
Kipling, Rudyard. *The Complete Verse*. Kyle Cathie, 2006.
Majumder, Auritro. *Insurgent Imaginations: World Literature and the Periphery*. Cambridge UP, 2021.
Makalani, Minkah. *In the Cause of Freedom: Radical Black Internationalism from Harlem to London, 1917–1939*. UNC P, 2014.
Marson, Una. *Selected Poems*. Peepal Tree, 2011.
Marx, Karl. "The Eighteenth Brumaire of Louis Bonaparte." Translated by Ben Fowkes. *Marx's Political Writings*. Vol. 2: *Surveys from Exile*, edited by David Fernbach. Verso, 2010, pp. 143–249.
Naidu, Sarojini "Panjab." *Young India*, May 24, 1919.
———. *Selected Letters 1890s to 1940s*, edited by Makarand Paranjape. Kali for Women, 1996.
Pound, Ezra. *Collected Early Poems*, edited by Michael King. New Directions, 1976.
Ramazani, Jahan, Richard Ellmann, and Robert O'Clair, editors. *The Norton Anthology of Modern and Contemporary Poetry*. 3rd ed., W. W. Norton, 2003, 2 vols.
Said, Edward. "Representing the Colonized: Anthropology's Interlocutors." *Critical Inquiry*, vol. 15, no. 2, Winter 1989, pp. 205–25.

Selvon, Sam. *The Lonely Londoners*. Penguin, 2021.
Snaith, Anna. *Modernist Voyages: Colonial Women Writers in London, 1890–1945*. Cambridge UP, 2014.
Tagore, Rabindranath. "Creative Unity." *The English Writings of Rabindranath Tagore, Plays, Stories, Essays, Volume 2*, edited by Sisir Kumar Das. Sahitya Academy, 1996.
Williams, Raymond. *Politics and Letters: Interviews with New Left Review*. Verso, 1981.
   *The Politics of Modernism: Against the New Conformists*. 1989. Verso, 2007.
Yeats, W. B. *The Complete Poems*. Collier Books, 1989.

## 15

SONITA SARKER

# Modernist Women, Technologies of Whiteness, and Undoing Empire

Every historical period is definitively designated as such only in retrospect; as a daily experience, a period is a series of ruptures or a gradual transition from one to the next, depending on the perspective. While early twentieth-century Western European and North American modernism has been characterized as a rupture, a revolution, a shock, its reverberations pulled the effects of the past in the wake of the new, differentially, depending on one's circumstances in early twentieth-century global modernity.[1] This chapter discusses how, in that rupture/transition from the "traditional" to the "modern," the passages of Elizabeth Bowen, Pauline Smith, Dorothy Livesay, Katherine Mansfield, and Jean Rhys into and out of British imperial metropole London, in the "Mother Country" (England), reveal their self-conscious adaptations of modernist technologies that both un-do some imperial trappings as well as re-do prevailing imperial-patriarchal structures of value and status to which they claim membership or to which they aspire. Writing from her Regent's Park home in London, the Anglo-Irish Bowen records how her surroundings "were repeatedly and heavily blasted by V1s, which shattered not only the inside part of the house but [my] writing routine" (*Weight* 12).[2] I would venture to say that the technologies of the Second World War (the V-1 bombs) disrupt not only Bowen's domestic and writerly life but become one of the factors, along with the other social and political revolutions of the times, that impacts aesthetic form and function. Other technologies, such as the telephone, had already fractured experience and meaning in new ways; Mansfield writes on May 21, 1918: "I positively feel, in my hideous modern way, that I can't get into touch with my mind. I am standing, gasping in one of those disgusting telephone boxes and I can't 'get through'" (*Diaries* 247).

As with the period marked as modernism, so with the figure of the New Woman – she appears in clear and sharp relief, in retrospect, on urban cultural landscapes but is, in the moment of emergence, made mobile across the thresholds between cultural and technological traditions and innovations.

## 15 Modernist Women

To the extent that Bowen, Smith, Livesay, Mansfield, and Rhys are figurations of the New Woman, they are, more accurately, versions of what might be dubbed the New-Woman, where the hyphen conveys their transient as well as transitional status. Generally, "technology" refers to the material infrastructure of modernity that the women authors encountered and adapted; in this essay, it refers more specifically to "tékhnē," the craft or skill that these writers display in their diaries, which are the closest but also inexact guides to their experiences as authors and women. Furthermore, "technology" derives from "teks," the fabric woven to convey the intangible but felt experience (the traces) of being-in-empire.

As women traveling to and from the perceived "periphery" to the "center" (the "Mother Country"), the authors enter the modern, and by extension, modernism, by adopting and negotiating both "new" and "old" machinic and aesthetic technologies.[3] I have selected Bowen, Smith, Livesay, Mansfield, and Rhys for their heritages in British settler-colonial outposts; these geographical peripheries had Dominion status (except for the Caribbean), which meant that White "citizens" benefited from a racialized privilege.[4] The gendered connotation of the "Mother Country" inflects this privilege for all the women writers and becomes integral to their personae and productions, as is evident across their careers.[5] These writers, all émigrés-become-residents in British imperial metropoles, perform the paradoxical rhetorics of empire–democracy in texts in which they un-do form, the only aesthetic means to generate meaning and convey its effects, while they also struggle to retain some semblance of belief in the (White) liberal humanist subject/author captured in the figure of the New-Woman. Their techniques retain the vestigial Victorian subject and aesthetics, specifically White, but rarely named as such. The traces of racialized others who are formative in their own settler-colonial histories appear visibly in their early journal, diary, and autobiographical entries, and then gradually vanish from view as they strive to present the authorial self, the (White) modernist woman writer who negotiates "old" and "new." I argue that the aesthetic modes through which traces of the native and Indigenous dis/appear in their hybrid technologies illuminate the authors' own understanding of their place as modern, White women writers in imperial metropoles.

### The Technology of the Modernist Missive

These authors, positioned as they are in terms of their heritages, places of origin, and education, claim their cultural traditions to be the literary heritages of Western Europe, primarily England and France, and North America, and not the traditions of Aotearoa or Zulu or other Indigenous lineages that each lists in her diaries. Imbibing the history of European and North American literatures, for instance, is itself a technology through which they understand their artistic heritages. Their standards of achievement, of "good" and "bad" writing, derive from this "education," and inform their own compositions as well as the means to assess/review other publications. These structures of value are inevitably coded in terms of race, nationality, and gender.[6]

In the foreword to *Tomato Cain and Other Stories* by Nigel Kneale, Bowen draws attention to the form and technology of the short story, observing that now there are "genuinely interested" readers "who *value* craftsmanship and react to *originality*" (*People*, 250, emphasis mine).[7] She comments approvingly that Kneale is "not dependent on regionalism ... but ... draws strength from it" and that "his work at its *best* has the flavour, raciness, 'body' that one associates with the *best* of the output from Ireland, Wales, Brittany, and the more remote, untouched and primitive of the States of America" (Bowen, *People* 251, emphasis mine). Bowen continues on to mention Maupassant, Kipling, Wells, Saki (H. H. Munro), and Maugham as frames of reference. She adopts the urbane, cosmopolitan, hegemonic gaze in delineating the geographical and artistic standards which establish value; there appears to be a word missing in the phrase "primitive of the States of America," perhaps "regions," and the import of the observation is the relationship between "regionalism" and the local or the "primitive."

Mansfield, from a different margin of the British Empire, expresses on December 21, 1908, a strong desire to write

> much in the style of Walter Pater's "Child in the House." About a girl in Wellington; the singular charm and barrenness of that place, with climatic effects – wind, rain, spring, night, the sea, the cloud pageantry. And then to leave the place and go to Europe, to live there a dual existence – to go back and be utterly disillusioned, to find out the truth of all... (*Notebooks* 1: 111)

The model presented by English literary heritage (Pater) will frame a picture of Wellington (the local, the regional, the natural); her destination is, naturally, Europe and the anticipation of "dual existence" and disillusionment is prescient, illuminating the relationship between aesthetic technologies and cultural traces that arise for all the modernist authors in their connection to the British Empire. For Rhys, the "dual existence" similarly allows her to claim an intimate knowledge about her "native" regions, like Mansfield, but also becomes the basis to critique the "center." This current discussion focuses on the authors' nonfictional work but Rhys's *tour de force*, the novel *Wide Sargasso Sea*, bears mention here. Across a prolonged period (1957 to 1966), Rhys writes to various correspondents, expressing shock and annoyance at Brontë's depiction of the first Mrs. Rochester in *Jane Eyre*, because it is "only one side – the 'English side,'" and deferring the question of whether she herself had any "right" to tackle the representation.[8] Despite this implied doubt about her place and legitimacy, Rhys is "fighting mad to write *her* story," that is, the story of "that particular mad Creole [who] ... is cold ... fire [being] the only warmth she knows in England" (emphasis in original).[9] However, this "Indigenous" persona is, as clearly indicated, Creole, not Black, Arawak, or Carib.

The diaries of Rhys, Mansfield, Bowen, Livesay, and Smith, as means of expression and confession, are sites of negotiation in which the "traditional" form and structure of descriptive narrative and realist chronicle merge with "new" scattered sketches of moments. In "World's End and a Beginning," Rhys describes filling three and a half "exercise books" at the age of twenty, taking them with her whenever she moves, but does not make them the foundation of a linear narrative, for she "never looked at them again for seven years" (*Smile Please* 105). Pauline Smith's letters are self-conscious contemplations on her literary technique, containing both direct statements on politics in South Africa as well as disjunctures and discontinuities, of the kind that Mansfield experiences about being on the phone. Smith writes to "Sarie" (a correspondent who requests anonymity) on November 17, 1946: "I have never myself been able to learn *how* to write – I do only what I *can* – never what I *ought* by rule or art" ("Letters" 33, emphasis mine) and again to the same addressee on April 18, 1948: "I'm afraid my letter is worse written than ever – .... But I write too much, & too badly" (Smith, "Letters" 48). Here, Smith reveals an awareness of unspoken standards of value ("ought") and evaluates her writing negatively in implicit comparison to "good writing."

## The Vanishing Indigene

The title of this section is a version of the "Vanishing Indian," a common myth perpetuated in the US of the gradual disappearance of Native American peoples, and a cruel gloss on the systematic cultural and physical genocide that settler colonials committed. The response from Native peoples in North America is: "We're still here." I do not intend to draw a straight line from that reference, which occurred later in US history than the era being discussed here, to these modernist writers. Rather, I draw attention to the fading presence of Indigenous peoples in the authors' textual praxes.

As depicted in the previous section, the diaries are intentional technologies of remembrance and record, penned by women whose Whiteness, implicitly or explicitly, becomes an indelible marker of their claims to belonging in the imperial metropole's cultural scene. Flashes of their "native" cultures, strong at first when they are in their homelands, begin to vanish from their chronicles as the authors travel to the "Mother Country" (England, and that Mother is White), which supplants their homelands as the place of their rebirth and homecoming.[10] As the bonds that tie them to their homelands become frayed, and the Indigenous vanishes, seemingly so does the part of them that is connected to those formative influences. In this way, the Indigene vanishes twice – the actual people whom they lived alongside and the elements of their past that they retained prior to their passages to England.

How does the Indigene appear as trace and then vanish without a trace? In *Beginnings*, Livesay depicts the Indigenous at Indian Point as "half-naked, tousled ... children [scampering] away, like ants scuttling into cracks"; the foreigner (Polish) Anna, their maid, is thought to have joined the "Indians" (51). Thus, native and foreigner are dispensed with in Livesay's record of her early life and replaced by Gina, the main character in the only chapter in *Journey with My Selves* in which the subject is addressed as "you"; this technique gives her individuality and breaks the mold of the memoir to simulate the mode of the letter. The Indigene is resurrected in Gina's nickname ("Cherokee") but simultaneously sublimated and disappeared completely in Livesay's activities with Gina. Together, the young Dorothy and Gina memorize Shakespeare, Marvell, and de la Mare, learn English, French, and Latin, and study Horace, Virgil, Dryden, and, later, H. D., Pound, and Amy Lowell, among others. Mansfield, in 1907, describes her passion for a Māori school friend Maata Mahupuku: "I want Maata ... as I have had her – terribly. This is unclean I know but true ... I feel savagely crude, and almost powerfully enamoured of the child" (*Diaries* 52). This intimate link to Indigenous identity is portrayed in negative terms, in stark contrast to the romantic and sensual language she uses for her relationships to Edith K. Bendall (*Diaries* 47) and Arnold Trowell (*Diaries* 53).

In "Black/White," Rhys describes the "Riot" (directed at a neighboring newspaper editor) as "a strange noise like animals howling" and realizes "it was people" who may kill her but that "strange idea didn't frighten [her] but excited [her]..." (*Smile Please* 37). She describes how "a certain wariness did creep in when [she] thought about the black people who surrounded [her]" (*Smile Please* 38). Writing as late as the 1960s about her childhood in the 1890s–1910s, Rhys names Meta, her childhood nurse, the "Black Devil," and describes her as a malicious woman who scares her by describing how her eyes would drop out of her head because she read so much, "except the little black points," and would look at her from the page

(*Smile Please* 21). Despite this horrifying image, Rhys writes that she kept reading and lists the canonical English literature that she consumes – Irish fairy stories, *The Adventures of Ulysses*, the Encyclopedia Britannica, books by Milton, Byron, Cowper, *Robinson Crusoe*, *Treasure Island*, *Gulliver's Travels*, *Pilgrim's Progress* (*Smile Please* 20–1).

Rhys records that most of the relationships with peers are also based in racial animosity. However, the shocked distance from the animal and the explicitly hostile, based in racialized superiority, coexists with a mixture of desire and envy. At the convent, where "white girls were very much in the minority," she is fascinated by a girl who "didn't look coloured" (*Smile Please* 39). However, she sees "impersonal, implacable hatred" in the girl's face, after which she "never tried to be friendly with any of the coloured girls again … [she] was polite and that was all" (*Smile Please* 39). "We are hated" is her stunning realization. At the same time, she records hearing her mother say that "black babies were prettier than white ones" and wonders whether that was the reason for her own ardent prayers to become Black and the reason she kept running to the mirror "to see if the miracle had happened" (*Smile Please* 33). She feels envy at Black women's strength and ability to carry greater weight, their laughter, their drums and dances (of which White people had fewer); the sense that they projected of being "more alive, more a part of the place than we were" makes her envy rise "to a fever pitch at carnival time" (*Smile Please* 39–41). Envy and sublimated un-belonging mix with a tinge of moral disgust about Black women's free sexuality and fertility even as she appears to complain about the mores of marriage and virtue that bind her own life.

If Indigenous peoples are not considered other than human (animal-like or devilish), they are depicted as more than human (enigmatic, magical). In "Anna," the only chapter focusing on the Indigenous in *Beginnings*, Livesay describes the eponymous foreigner as entranced with the young man at Indian Point, who is "expressionless … so brown and silent" (47). In Mansfield's *Notebooks*, a section titled "Der Tod, das ist die kühle Nacht," contains "A True Tale," addressed to "my little Saxons" – it describes a captivating island where there are "no white people … but tall, stately, copper coloured men and women"; she tells her readers to "be glad that [they] did not live in the time that Motorua did" (1: 40, 9); Motorua is a made-up "Māori" name. Mansfield's *The Urewera Notebook*, a diary of her travels (November 23–December 17, 1907) in the area east of the volcanic plateau in the middle of the North Island – considered Māori country – includes the charming Bella, "the very dusk incarnate"; her remark trails off into an incomplete and inarticulate thought: "– The life they lead here" (*Diaries* 64). It is fittingly fleeting since Mansfield is only passing through, not burdened with any responsibility or commitment; she can thus pluck out and freeze lives into fantasized moments suspended from colonial history. In 1916, writing about Nastasya Filippovna, Mansfield admires her "almost 'technical'" knowledge of "how things are in the world ... not at all impossible. With such women it appears to be a kind of instinct. Maata was just the same – she simply knew these things from nowhere" (*Diaries* 183). This Maata is the same person for whom she describes feeling powerful and "savagely crude" feelings.[11]

Decontextualization is a frequent mode of including Indigenous references: Mansfield expresses a longing for the "authentic" English and Māori, not recognizing the hybrid as a product of the colonial history of which she herself is a part. She records meeting Prodgers on her Urewera travels, expressing that "it is splendid to see once again real English people," and being "so tired & sick of the third rate article ... [the mixed race peoples who] wear a great deal of ornament in Umuroa & strange hair fashions" (*Notebooks* 2: 141). In an earlier diary entry (1903), she describes waking up to the strains of "Swanee River," listening to it all day and hearing it as a lullaby. The fact that the song is an enslaver's nostalgia about plantation life is completely elided in her avid consumption of "American" literature. Her diaries of this period record related reading material and music – Heinrich Heine, Poe, Léon Boëllmann, and Bach; she even draws similarities between herself and John Addington Symonds. Later, her reading fully overwhelms the links to the Indigenous – de Maupassant, William Morris, Gabriel Rossetti, Arthur Symons – and her writing includes copious notes on Hawthorne, Balzac, Pater, Flaubert, and Stevenson.

If not decontextualized, Indigenous peoples are anonymous and silent and, once again, denigrated. In Bowen's review of Conrad M. Arensberg's *The Irish Countryman: An Anthropological Study* (in *The Listener*, April 28, 1937), the "countryman" of the Clare coast remains unnamed. Bowen uses the word "primitive" to mean "first" and "untouched," and romanticizes the traditions of the coastal folk, thus simulating the anthropological gaze of the author that she reviews. In *Secret Fire* (1913–14), Pauline Smith describes "[c]rowds of coloured people ... Jews and Jewesses in their Sabbath clothes," making sure to note that there was "[n]ot a face [she] knew" (8). Derogatory terms such as kaffir (the Xhosa peoples), Hottentot (the Khoikhoi peoples), and coolie (Indians and Chinese peoples) occur frequently in Smith's diary entries. Native peoples are not named unless they work in White people's homes, for example, the "quiet, staid Kaffir [Xhosa] girl, middle-aged, Judith" (Smith 4) who serves tea and cake. George and Phillida, "the Servants" (Smith 101) are given section titles, but only have first names, while the "Malay Wash-Ayahs," who are also given a short section, remain unnamed, like the anonymous "'bound girls'" (Smith 196); Smith does not comment on what is essentially conscription or enslavement. Stories about the Indigenous and other peoples are about murder, greed, ignorance, and poverty in contrast with the detailed stories of domesticity, sympathy, and affection about White South Africans who are named and given section titles; "Americans" are not racially marked and thus assumed to be White. Smith's distance from the observed is like Mansfield's in *The Urewera Notebook* and presages the ultimate disappearance of all the figures that crowd both authors' early narratives.

## White Pastoral, White Cosmopolitan

As important as Indigenous peoples in the authors' self-fashioning-in-process are the settings of their persona, especially as the backdrop to their movements between pastoral peripheries and cultural centers. Both on the page and in life, those passages constitute their "position" as they and others perceived them in their modernist milieux in the British Empire. "Pastoral" either romanticizes the reality of rural residents (often the Indigenous) or renames the rural as a romantic setting for White settlers. The authors' re-invocations recall the prevailing imperial conceptions of the pastoral, and contest but also perpetuate them: Contest them by refusing the pastoral and cosmopolitan as antitheses, and perpetuate them by parsing the pastoral as White space and the primeval as Indigenous. In their diaries, letters, and essays, the White pastoral is part of civilizational modernity, romanticized as down-to-earth and honest, while the primeval is exotic, lush but "undeveloped," untamed, and full of mystery and dread.

Livesay's paternal homestead "Woodlot," Rhys's familial home "Geneva," and Mansfield's house on Tinakori Road are sites where White pastoral and White cosmopolitan identities intersect; the Indigenous presences remain liminal in the technologies of modernist chronicles that record what is essentially settler history, but in oblique and deflected language. Livesay's father, "a young immigrant," builds Woodlot and his friends are "gentleman farmers in their colonial homestead, Benares" (*Journey* 179). She has fond memories of her own budding literary career under her mother's tutelage that extended also to "schoolchildren ... from Indian reserves and residential schools" (*Journey* 20). She extols Canada which, "for the sake of its landscape, for the sake of its youth ... is the place to live in" (*Journey* 104); however, she concludes that England is "great" because it is "small," unlike Canada which has "too many differences in each province" (*Journey* 104). Geneva, Rhys's ancestral homestead, two hours by horseback from Roseau, is the lush but declining and overgrown estate of "slave-owner the Lockharts ... [who] were never very popular ... putting it mildly" (*Smile Please* 25–6). When she returns many years later, she finds a destroyed place; "there was nothing, nothing. Nothing to look at. Nothing to say" (*Smile Please* 29). Mansfield's house in Tinakori Road is, she writes in 1915, "a big white painted square house" with a wraparound verandah that jostles with dwellings of "an endless family of halfcastes" and gardens "with empty jam tins and old saucepans and black iron kettles without lids" ("Notebook 45," *Diaries* 176–7). The Indian schoolchildren from Canada's boarding schools, the enslaved in Dominica, and the "halfcastes" on Tinakori Road fade away on the borders of narratives that move between the "old" and "new."

In their cosmopolitan life in cities such as London and New York, Rhys, Smith, and Livesay explicitly mark yet more others, Jewish and Black strangers and acquaintances, in their habitual manner of delineating similarities but accentuating differences. Rhys writes to Evelyn Scott on Sunday, February 18, 1934, about being in a Bloomsbury (London) bedsit where the owner is "a huge coloured lady" who is "[v]ery chic ... pearl earrings and everything (and I believe a compatriot)" and who comes by to demand rent (*Letters* 23). The sentence begins with exoticized difference and ends on a speculation about their possible similarity which is relegated to a parenthesis. She makes sure to note the nationality and ethnic identities of the two "German Jewish ladies (born in Wales and very sympathique)" who take over the house after the West Indian woman passes away.

In the same letter, Rhys writes: "the past exists – side by side with the present, not behind it; that what was – is" (*Letters* 23). Despite this recognition of the past, the cosmopolitan modernist diarist and letter-writer arrives more fully into their profession by utterly erasing traces of the Indigenous who were so prominent in their early years and turning to invest wholeheartedly in White Englishness, their technology of knowing themselves as literary, political, and cultural commentators. Bowen declares that she "can speak, inevitably, chiefly for England" (*Collected Impressions* 158); in "English and American Writing," she claims England as "our country" and designates America (the US) as "foreign" (*Weight* 6); she also uses the word "indigenous," by which she means (White) "home-grown" and not "Native." At the same time, an essay such as "Doubtful Subject" offers a commentary on Irish/Gaelic history and culture being neglected or denigrated by English readers (*Collected Impressions* 173ff.).[12] Smith, in her early records, takes it upon herself to analyze the cosmopolitan scene of the Dutch, the English, and the Jews – in her view, the Dutch have never forgiven the English for emancipating the slaves, and they envy but also imitate Jews who are slim, cunning, and "to be feared and hated ... somewhere vaguely between the lowest of poor Christian whites and those coloured races who ought still to be slaves" (*Secret Fire* 335). She deflects from her observations by drawing attention to the technology of writing stating that "this subject always interests [her], and it is only on paper that [she] can ever straighten out [her] thoughts about it" (*Secret Fire* 335).

Despite their proprietary tone, the cosmopolitan is cold in the colonial metropole and its pastoral realms, an expression of a deeper uneasiness and un-homeliness for some of the authors. Rhys and Smith, in particular, describe their distress frequently and in direct terms in their diaries and letters; the former, in particular, writes about her fear of the cold and the desire to get away from it, and of extended periods of illness that hamper her writing, as she becomes an itinerant across Beckenham, Croydon, Lexington, and, ultimately, a place she comes to call "Blasted Bude."[13] Both Smith and Rhys use the same phrase ("I long for warmth"), Rhys seeking to soak up the sun and Smith the comfort of both the sunshine and "the welcome of friends."[14] These experiences of the corporeal cosmopolitan who is the modernist woman author are, in their own words, crucial to their aesthetic technologies.

### Forever Foreigner, Forever but Differently White

The most immediate form of identification of these authors, in literature, has been by nationality – New Zealand, Ireland, Canada, South Africa, and the West Indies. Whiteness remains as an indelible yet unmarked race in the naming of nationality, based in settler colonialism and imperial identification. Race is subsumed into nationality for these authors, given the Dominion status for all but Rhys; when they are in their countries of origin, they already adopt the technologies of Whiteness, for instance, in their early education and in their gaze through which represent various "others." In their later diaries, when the authors are foreigners in the "Mother Country," they are keenly aware of themselves as the "other," and self-consciously practice their craft on that basis, even at the fundamental level of the response to the elements, primarily the cold. The gradual vanishing or erasure by neglect or deliberate omission of the trace of the Indigene confirms their Whiteness. Country of origin plays off against "Mother Country" in ways that Virginia Woolf described as being a "stepdaughter of England" in *Three Guineas* (1938). However, there is a difference between her claims and the status of these authors – Woolf speaks from the inside, where her citizenship and sense of cultural belonging is the very basis for her claims to create distance between her experience and dominant assumptions about her native-ness.

As a young Pākehā woman in New Zealand, Mansfield muses whether she could give a "coherent account" of the history of English literature or of English history and expresses a desire to envision and experience England in the time of Shakespeare (*Notebooks* 2: 30). This orientation toward England also marks Rhys's "Leaving Dominica" in which she, a young White Creole woman setting out from Bridgetown, Barbados, "very cheerfully," not only leaves the West Indies and her parents behind but "[forgets] them. They were the past" (*Smile Please* 76). She draws attention to her authorial inelegance ("How clumsily I'm writing") when she recalls her anxiety about her inadequate attractiveness in the eyes of the Englishman Mr. Kennaway's gaze, but also notes that now she is nearly seventeen "there is England, England, England" (*Smile Please* 137). Then, she encounters exactly the disillusion she had imagined about being in Europe – the dull streets and snobbery about "the proper pronunciation of English" (*Smile Please* 84). Similarly, in "Leaving England," Rhys reveals that she cannot actually leave England because she did not save up enough; she moves from Bloomsbury to Torrington Square and describes herself as "the only English, or pseudo-English person among Greeks, Italians, Belgian, and South Americans" (*Smile Please* 109).

Being English-identified is refracted through the author's experience of otherness; for Rhys and Mansfield, a growing sense of alienation results in a technology of dis-identification and dissociation that brings to the surface traces of that very otherness that had become submerged in their modernist praxes. Mansfield laments in 1916 that the plots of her stories leave her "perfectly cold" and that she feels "a 'sacred debt'" to make "our undiscovered country leap in to the eyes of the world" (*Diaries* 191). Writing of herself in the third person, in 1919 she calls herself "the little colonial" who is asked what she is doing in a London garden and realizes "[s]he is a stranger – an alien" (*Diaries* 277–8). Rhys writes similarly, on December 6, 1949, of being stared at in the village of "Blasted Bude," imagining that her correspondents must see her as "a raving and not too clean maniac with straws in gruesome unwashed hair" (*Letters* 64–5). In a letter to Francis Wyndham in September 14, 1959, Rhys declares that though her great-grandfather was Scot, her father was "Welsh – very," and her mother's side was "what *we* call Creole," she herself is white, as far as she knows but with "no country really now" (*Letters* 172, emphasis in original). Similarly, Smith writes to "Sarie," on October 25, 1949, that looking out over her friends' garden in Kent, she sees views that remind her of the Karoo veld and "feeling that [she] would never see S. Africa again" ("Letters" 61). She had expressed the same despair to the same correspondent, confessing that she was "*homesick* for ... that part of [her] own country," Cape Town, and for all the people she knows there (January 20, 1949, Smith, "Letters" 54, emphasis in original). Rhys uses that very word, "homesick" in a letter to Selma Vaz Dias (November 6, 1957).

For the authors in this discussion, being White (in their own cognition) is the basis for their claims to recognition and legitimacy as modernist craftswomen who use the emerging technologies of their times; yet, their Whiteness is, in the eyes of the "Mother Country," never quite English-White.

## Notes

1. See *The Shock of the New*; Donghaile; and Lewis, to name a few, about modernism's impact. In the phrase "Western European and North American modernism," I name the localities that are implied but elided in the hegemonic use of "modernism," indicate that these localities develop distinct but also related imperial histories, and signal that they are tied together in their White epistemes.
2. V-1s were the "Vergeltungswaffen" ("Vengeance weapons") that the Germans dropped on England. See Mellor for a connection between British culture, bombsites, and modernism.
3. See the writings of Walter Benjamin and Andreas Huyssen, and films such as *Metropolis* and *Modern Times* on machinic technology in the modernist period. See Armstrong; Carter and Friedman; and Maude and Nixon for some analyses of technologies in the usual sense of the term.
4. I use the capital "W" in "White" to indicate the representation and responsibility of a collective racialization.
5. Chalk; Kloepfer; and Palko address motherhood and maternity but focus primarily on gender, whereas this discussion relies on an intersection of nation, race, gender, and class.
6. The networks of correspondents and mentors in each author's career is highly impactful – Middleton Murry, Ford Madox Ford, Virginia and Leonard Woolf for Mansfield and Rhys, and Ethelreda Lewis, editor of the *Trader Horn* books, and Sarah Gertrude Millin, South African author who wrote a biography of General J. S. Smuts, for Pauline Smith, for instance.
7. Here, I interpret technology (tékhnē) as the craft of particular genres. See Aughterson; Binckes and Snyder; di Battista and Wittman; and Paquet for similar readings.
8. From Rhys (*Letters*) to Francis Wyndham (1964); Diana Athill (1966); and Selma Vaz Dias (1957). Howells (1990) comments that Rhys's stories and novels "repress her Caribbean inheritance … an irreplaceable absence," but does not include the diaries or address the racialized and Indigenous elements (373).
9. From Rhys (*Letters*) to Francis Wyndham (1958).
10. Palko analyzes "imperial maternal imperatives" that marginalize women in Bowen's and Rhys's works (89). Where Palko focuses on empire, I study Whiteness (as racialized imperial identity).
11. In the Unbound Papers (1912) and in the Newberry Notebook 2 (1913), there are stories involving Maata. She is described on August 13, 1913 as: "radiant, eager – her lovely voice like water…" (Mansfield, *Diary* 52).

12. See Moynahan for a study of Anglo-Irish as a "hyphenated culture."
13. See Smith's letters to "Sarie" (November 28, 1939) and a Mrs. Gray (December 4, 1930) about the "English Cold" not suiting her, about going to France for four months ("Letters" 18, 11), and about illness, terrible weather, and shortages of provisions – January 23, 1947 and March 13, 1947 ("Letters" 38). See Rhys's letters to her daughter Maryvonne Moerman, and to Morchard Bishop and Selma Vaz Dias, from 1949 to 1959. About Bude, see Rhys's letters to Selma Vaz Dias, November 6, 1957 (*Letters* 149) and December 15, 1959 (*Letters* 179).
14. Rhys to her daughter on April 14, 1957 (*Letters* 145). Pauline Smith, letter to Mrs. Gray, from The Moors (her mother's house) in Dorset, December 5, 1929 ("Letters" 10).

## Works Cited

Armstrong, Tim. *Modernism, Technology, and the Body*. Cambridge UP, 1998.
Aughterson, Kate. *Women Writers and Experimental Writing*. E-book, Palgrave, 2021.
Binckes, Faith, and Carey Snyder. *Women, Periodicals, and Print Culture in Britain 1890s–1920s*. Edinburgh UP, 2019.
Bowen, Elizabeth. *Collected Impressions*. Alfred A. Knopf, 1950.
   *People, Places, Things*. Edited with an introduction by Allan Hepburn. Edinburgh UP, 2008.
   *The Weight of a World of Feeling*, vol. 2. Edited with an introduction by Allan Hepburn. Northwestern Press, 2017.
Carter, Mia, and Alan Friedman. *Modernism and Literature*. Routledge, 2013.
Chalk, Bridget. *Modernism and Mobility: The Passport and Cosmopolitan Experience*. Palgrave, 2015.
di Battista, Maria, and Emily Wittman. *Modernism and Autobiography*. Cambridge UP, 2014.
Donghaile, Deaglán Ó. *Blasted Literature: Victorian Political Fiction and the Shock of Modernism*. Edinburgh UP, 2011.
Howells, Coral Ann. "Jean Rhys (1890–1979)." *The Gender of Modernism: A Critical Anthology*, edited by Bonnie Kime Scott, Indiana UP, 1990, pp. 372–7.
Kloepfer, Deborah K. *The Unspeakable Mother: Forbidden Discourse in Jean Rhys and H. D.* 1989. Cornell UP, 2018.
Lewis, Pericles, editor. *The Cambridge Introduction to Modernism*. Cambridge UP, 2007.
Livesay, Dorothy. *Beginnings*. Peguis Publishers, 1988.
   *Journey with My Selves: A Memoir 1909–1963*. Douglas & McIntyre, 1991.
Mansfield, Katherine. *The Diaries of Katherine Mansfield*, edited by Gerri Kimber and Claire Davison, Edinburgh UP, 2016.
   *Notebooks*, vol. 1, edited by Margaret Scott, Lincoln UP, 1997.
   *Notebooks*, vol. 2, edited by Margaret Scott, Lincoln UP, 1997.
Maude, Ulrike, and Mark Nixon, editors. *The Bloomsbury Companion to Modernist Literature*. Bloomsbury Academic, 2018.
Mellor, Leo. *Reading the Ruins: Modernism, Bombsites, and British Culture*. Cambridge UP, 2011.

Moynahan, Julian. *Anglo-Irish: The Literary Imagination in a Hyphenated Culture.* Princeton UP, 1995.

Palko, Abigail. "Colonial Modernism's Thwarted Maternity: Elizabeth Bowen's *The House in Paris* and Jean Rhys's *Voyage in the Dark*." *Textual Practice*, vol. 27, no. 1, 2013, pp. 89–108.

Paquet, Sandra Pouchet. *Caribbean Autobiography.* U of Wisconsin P, 2002.

Rhys, Jean. *Letters 1931–1966.* Selected and edited by Francis Wyndham and Diana Melly, Penguin, 1984.

——. *Smile Please: An Unfinished Autobiography.* Harper & Row, 1983.

Smith, Pauline. "Letters, July 1927–June 1956." *English in Africa*, vol. 23, no. 2, Oct. 1996, pp. 5–84.

——. *Secret Fire: The 1913–14 South African Journal of Pauline Smith.* Edited and introduced by Harold Scheub, U of Cape Town, 1997.

*The Shock of the New.* DVD, Ambrose Video Publishing, 2001.

## 16

JOE CLEARY

# Joyce and His Contemporaries
## Revivalism, Modernism, and Irish Anti-imperialism

### Ireland and Decolonization

The decolonization of Ireland in the late nineteenth and early twentieth-century period was accompanied by a cultural efflorescence in English unequaled in the dissolution of the British Empire. That period saw the consolidation of a modern Irish literature in English, the elaboration of a minor literature in Irish, the creation of a national theater, and the production of celebrated works in poetry, theater, the short story, and novel. Irish writers in this epoch made Dublin a notable literary city, figured among the more innovative playwrights in Anglophone drama in London and New York, and contributed to the Parisian modernist avant-garde. None of the "white" Dominions produced equivalent literary renaissances as they moved toward greater autonomy from Britain. In Africa, the Caribbean, and South Asia, decolonization's final phase came several decades after the Irish struggle and produced comparable cultural ferments, but in these situations English was often just one of the many languages and literatures involved.

In some ways, Irish decolonization set a precedent for later struggles and in other ways it was anomalous. Ireland had been part of the United Kingdom of Great Britain and Ireland since 1800, its people were white and Christian, and only a few years before the War of Independence (1918–21) campaigns for devolved Home Rule within the British Empire enjoyed popular support. Thanks to outwards migration accelerated by the Great Famine (1845–50), there were already large politicized Irish diasporic communities in Great Britain and the US, the metropoles of modern Anglophone imperialism, before Irish independence. The inwards migrations to Great Britain from Asia, Africa, and the Caribbean in contrast mostly came largely after the Second World War and the contraction of empire.

In temporal terms, Irish decolonization was out of step with wider global movements. When most North and South American colonies and Haiti gained independence from England, Spain, and France between 1776 and

1825, an Irish republican separatism was crushed and Ireland's semiautonomous Protestant Ascendancy Parliament was dissolved. Asian, African, and Caribbean decolonizations came after the Bolshevik Revolution, the dissemination of Wilsonian and Leninist doctrines of self-determination, and the global convulsions of the Second World War. Given these geopolitical and temporal divergences, it is not surprising that Irish decolonization was distinctive in several respects. Nevertheless, twentieth-century anti-imperialist movements elsewhere studied Ireland's situation with interest.

Decolonization in Ireland, as elsewhere, was a contradictory process. The Great Famine devastated the poorest peasant strata of the country and cleared the way for what historians term the "Devotional Revolution." This refers to the Catholic Church's accelerated mobilization after the Famine as it set itself to improve the moral character of the Catholic population, centralize church authority, and increase funding and personnel to administer expanding infrastructures of schools, hospitals, universities, orphanages, asylums, and missions across Ireland, the empire, and the diaspora. (Larkin; Miller) Irish tenants were organized from the 1870s onwards into national campaigns to agitate for the reform of landlord–tenant relations. Using militant and parliamentary pressure, these "Land Wars" forced major Land Acts through Westminster between 1881 and 1906. Within decades, a Protestant Ascendancy elite that had historically monopolized land ownership was replaced by a largely Catholic small farmer class (Clark).

In the same period, a well-organized Irish Parliamentary Party, under Charles Stewart Parnell, pressed Home Rule Acts through Westminster in 1886 and 1893, these narrowly defeated. Despite Parnell's downfall and the Parliamentary Party split that followed in 1890, the movement recovered sufficiently to force through a third Home Rule Bill in 1912. Militant Ulster Unionist opposition, the suspension of the Home Rule Bill after the outbreak of the First World War, and a separatist republican insurrection in Dublin in Easter 1916 inflamed a combustible situation. The Easter Insurrection was quelled but British overreaction triggered the Irish War of Independence (1918–21), the Government of Ireland Act of 1920, the Anglo-Irish Treaty of 1921, and an Irish Civil War (1921–23) when southern republicans split over the Treaty and the Free State's retention within the empire.

The Irish Revival elaborated in this wider context was never exclusively literary or narrowly cultural. After centuries of rule, British influence on Irish life was extensive; the Revival attempted to check an assimilative British culture by creating a distinctive Irish one. In 1884, the Gaelic Athletic Association was formed on the model of English amateur sporting organizations but designed to cultivate Irish sports in place of the "alien garrison games" associated with British rule. Conradh na Gaeilge, or the Gaelic League, cofounded in 1893 by Douglas Hyde and Eoin MacNeill, the one Protestant, the other Catholic, aimed to reverse the Anglicization of Ireland, to reestablish the Gaelic language declining to the verge of extinction since the Famine, and to cultivate a modern literature in Irish. In 1894, Horace Plunkett established the Irish Co-operative Organization Society to coordinate numerous farming cooperatives emerging after the Land Wars. In 1905, Arthur Griffith, a Dublin-born journalist of Catholic background, founded Sinn Féin, which joined in 1907 with the Dungannon Clubs, founded by northern nationalists Bulmer Hobson and Denis McCollough. Sinn Féin became separatist republicanism's political wing and won a landslide electoral victory over the Home Rule Party in 1918 (Mathews; Kiberd).

Five years after the establishment of the Women's Social and Political Union in Britain, the Irish Women's Franchise League was established in 1908. The League promoted "a militant suffrage society, suitable to the different political situation of Ireland, as between a subject country seeking freedom from England, and England, a free country" (James H. Cousins and Margaret E. Cousins 164, qtd. in Ward 130). The Ladies' Land League was founded in New York in 1881; Inghinidhe na hÉireann (Daughters of Erin) established in 1900; and Cumann na mBan (Irishwomen's Council) in 1914. In 1913, after an Irish Transport and General Workers' Union strike was repressed, the Irish Citizen Army, a socialist militia, was organized to defend workers from police brutality. Its leader, James Connolly, joined forces with the Irish Republican Brotherhood, a militant separatist organization, and the Irish Citizen Army took part in the 1916 insurrection.

Clearly, these movements varied significantly in methods and ambitions and all ideologically evolved in response to changing circumstances. Home Rulers, republicans, socialists, suffragists, Catholic nationalists, Irish-language campaigners, and cooperative movement activists had different conceptions of what Irish renovation might mean. Protestant unionists feared that "Home Rule means Rome Rule" and those concentrated in northeast Ulster had, with British conservative support, the means sufficient to retain the British link and to form their own secessionist Northern Irish state. The intersecting mobilizations of the Devotional Revolution, Land Wars, Revivalist, Home Rule, republican separatist and unionist movements – taking place in an era running roughly from the Scramble for Africa to the interimperial convulsions of the First World War – created a climate of extended agitation and innovation. The upshot was the emergence in the 1920s of an Ireland none had envisioned decades earlier.

## The Irish Revival

Many of the political writers, journalists, dramatists, folklorists, and intellectuals who contributed to the period's popular ferment remain notable figures in modern Irish history but are little known beyond Ireland. Today, the political writings of Michael Davitt, Patrick Pearse, Arthur Griffith, Margaret Cousins, or James Connolly are read mainly by specialists, but in the early twentieth century their writings were read across the British Empire. Griffith's "Resurrection of Hungary," for instance, was translated into several Indian languages and Gandhi acknowledged debts to Griffith when planning nonviolent resistance in India (Bourke and Gallagher; Ó Lúing 128). When Indian radical nationalists planned a more militant campaign than Gandhi's Congress, they smuggled in the writings of Dan Breen and Éamon de Valera and named themselves the Indian Republican Army (Saha).

Today, too, the literary, journalistic, or critical writings of Standish O'Grady, Augusta Gregory, George Russell (AE), Douglas Hyde, Maud Gonne, Peadar Ó Laoghaire, D. P. Moran, Daniel Corkery, Padraic and Mary Colum, Alice Milligan, Ethna Carbery, James Stephens, and others are known mainly to cultural historians. But in the early twentieth century these figures contributed to a vibrant public sphere sustained by newspapers and magazines, literary societies and theaters, language associations and political clubs, street pageants and polemics. Thanks to the Irish diaspora, the Revival was never an exclusively domestic affair. The Abbey Theatre, to take a notable example, made seven tours of the US and Canada before the Second World War: three between 1911 and 1914 and four between 1931 and 1938. The Abbey's early performances provoked controversies for Irish Americans but American and African-American theatergoers were fascinated by the company's acting styles and this contributed to new theatre movements that nurtured playwrights such as Eugene O'Neill and the Harlem Renaissance theaters (Dalsimer; Devlin).

In English literary studies, it is the Irish writers who achieved international reputation in this epoch who receive attention. For convenience, these may be divided into three generations, though their careers in practice overlapped. The first generation comprises writers already come to prominence before the First World War: here, we can count George Moore (1852–1933), Oscar Wilde (1854–1900), G. B. Shaw (1856–1950), W. B. Yeats (1865–1939), and J. M. Synge (1871–1909). The son of a Catholic landlord and Home Rule MP, Moore was educated in England, spent his early career studying painting in Paris, and then lived most of his professional life in London. His early work is associated with French naturalism, but between 1901 and 1911 he spent much of his time in Dublin involved in the Revival. Wilde, the son of Irish nationalist poet Speranza (Jane Wilde), and Shaw, the child of lower middle-class Protestants, moved as young men to England and made their theatrical careers in London. As Moore had done earlier in his Revivalist period, Shaw took considerable interest in Ireland in the turbulent period between 1912 and 1930. Yeats, whose reputation is synonymous with the Revival, spent part of his youth in London and regularly visited England throughout his long career. Synge traveled to Germany and France when he finished in Trinity College, Dublin, before returning, at Yeats's suggestion, to the remote Aran Islands, off the western Irish seacoast, to fashion his own literary vision.

Except for Moore, who converted to Protestantism, all of these writers were of Protestant descent; Protestants dominated the Irish higher professions and educated classes well into the twentieth century. That so many of this generation made their careers in England is unremarkable; London was then the uncontested capital of the English-speaking world and Irish literary expatriation to England was for centuries a well-taken route. It is more remarkable that Yeats, who might easily have assimilated into the English literary mainstream, espoused Irish cultural nationalism and contributed vigorously to Revivalist activities. Yeats's exceptional achievement was to create a body of work – poetry, drama, criticism – indisputably Irish yet equal in quality to that of any of his greatest Anglophone or European contemporaries. Moore, Wilde, and Shaw were all flamboyantly Irish in some respects, but Yeats, Synge, and Gregory made Ireland their subject matter, and their individual successes, and that of the Abbey Theatre, were formative for the generation that followed.

Sean O'Casey (1880–1964) and James Joyce (1882–1941) are the outstanding figures in the second generation of writers coming into its own after the First World War. Both were Dublin-born, belonged to downwardly mobile families, and had extended expatriate careers. O'Casey was secretary to the Irish Citizen Army and active in Gaelic League politics before taking up playwriting. Like Moore, Joyce became infamously anticlerical but his education in elite Jesuit schools and the Royal University, Dublin, was formative. Unlike Moore, Wilde, and Shaw, who had all left Ireland before the Revival gained momentum, Joyce came of age in the time of the Home Rule crises, the later land agitations, the development of the Gaelic League, the Abbey Theatre, and so on. As a cultural Catholic, he felt diffident about the mostly more upper-class Protestant figures who dominated Revivalist circles. When he left Dublin for Europe in 1904, he shunned the familiar expatriate path to London and identified with avant-garde European literary currents.

As is well known, Joyce's early career was extremely difficult. *Dubliners*, a short story collection, was completed by 1905 but rejected on numerous occasions before it was finally printed in 1914. *A Portrait of the Artist as a Young Man*, begun as *Stephen Hero* in 1904, was serialized in the English magazine *The Egoist* in 1914 and 1915, and published in book form in New York in 1916, the year of the Easter Rising. Episodes of *Ulysses* were serialized in the US in *The Little Review* from 1918 to 1920, when the publishers were prosecuted for obscenity, and the completed novel was finally published in Paris in February 1922, just weeks after the Anglo-Irish Treaty, ending the Irish War of Independence, was signed in London on December 6, 1921. *Ulysses* is steeped in Revivalist politics and faction and combines searing depictions of Dublin's Anglophile pro-imperial establishment culture and the anti-British nationalist subcultures of Joyce's youth. However, *Ulysses* made its mark not only because of its handling of its Irish subject matter but also thanks to its promotion as a classic of an emerging modernism that was in its own fashion challenging London's dominance of Anglophone literature. In *Ulysses*, Irish Revivalism and an American-dominated Anglophone modernist movement combined to complex effect (Cleary).

*Ulysses* appeared at the start of a decade when Joyce and O'Casey made their mark just as the preceding generation of Irish writers reached the height of its powers. Yeats's early "Celtic Twilight" career was distinguished from English Pre-Raphaelitism largely by its recourse to Irish mythology, history, and folk culture. However, his collections published when the Great War and the Irish crisis were most intense – "Responsibilities" (1914), "The Wild Swans at Coole" (1919), and "Michael Robartes and the Dancer" (1921) – opened an edgier late modernist style. In 1923, Yeats won the Nobel Prize for Literature; Shaw was awarded his Nobel Prize in 1925. O'Casey's *The Shadow of a Gunman* was performed in the Abbey Theatre in 1923, *Juno and the Paycock* followed in 1924, and in 1926 *The Plough and the Stars*. Two years later, in 1928, Yeats refused to take O'Casey's *The Silver Tassie*, an expressionist critique of the First World War and European imperialism, for the Abbey and O'Casey left Dublin and spent the rest of his life in England. Yeats published *A Vision*, his major aesthetic-philosophical statement, in 1925, and "The Tower," containing some of his most ambitious late poetry, in 1928. If the 1920s represented a climacteric for Anglophone high modernism, it was likewise a highpoint for Irish writing generally.

Elizabeth Bowen (1899–1973) and Samuel Beckett (1906–1989), came of age professionally in the late 1920s and early 1930s when the Free State was already established and high modernism had already made significant impact. Bowen, the child of Ascendancy gentry, made her literary career in London on the fringes of Bloomsbury. She maintained her ancestral house in Cork until the 1950s, but her family background and early English residence distanced her from the Revivalist currents that shaped Moore, AE, Synge, Yeats, Joyce, and O'Casey. Her first novel, *The Last September* (1929), is set during the War of Independence and belongs to the Big House genre cultivated in realist or gothic forms by Anglo-Irish writers from Maria Edgeworth to Edith Somerville and Martin Ross. Bowen's restrained modernism is closer to that of Henry James or Rebecca West than to the radical linguistic and stylistic experiments of Joyce, Yeats, Gertrude Stein, or William Faulkner.

Beckett was born into a middle-class Protestant family, followed Joyce's path to Paris rather than Bowen's to London, and lived permanently in France after 1928. When he graduated from Trinity College in 1927, the Revival had transitioned from an antiestablishment to establishment force and many of its earlier functions were now supported by the Irish Free State. In 1925, the Abbey Theatre had become the first state-sponsored theater in the English-speaking world and many Gaelic League ambitions had devolved to the new Free State's civil service and education systems. Beckett's "Recent Irish Poetry," published in *The Bookman* in 1934, was a broadside that identified the Revival with an ossified "antiquarian" literary current running from Samuel Ferguson and Standish O'Grady through Yeats to his 1930s successors. This blast comported well with the anti-Revivalism of Beckett's Catholic contemporaries such as Seán Ó Faoláin or Frank O'Connor working in realist forms. Aesthetically, though, Beckett's writing was already pointing toward a late modernism that was effectively departing from the more mythopoetic and maximalist dimensions of Revivalism and high modernism alike. Closer in this respect to Moore, Shaw, and Wilde than to Yeats, Joyce, or O'Casey, Bowen and Beckett were Irish writers who contributed impressively to Irish literature's international distinction but for whom the representation of Irish society was not essential to their artistic visions.

## Legacies in Ireland and Beyond

Domestically, Irish critics differ significantly as to Revival's lasting achievements. In *Inventing Ireland*, literary critic Declan Kiberd argues that:

> The enterprise achieved nothing less than a renovation of Irish consciousness and a new understanding of politics, economics, philosophy, sport, language and culture in its widest sense. It was the grand destiny of Yeats's generation to make Ireland once again interesting to the Irish, after centuries of enforced provincialism following the collapse of the Gaelic order in 1601.
> (Kiberd 3)

Taking a sterner view, Irish sociologist Joseph Ruane adjudges:

> The goal [of the Revival] was to push [British culture] back to allow a resurgent native culture to take its place. The most prominent symbols of Britishness were removed from the public domain – the national anthem, the Union flag, statues, monuments – and replaced with Irish equivalents. Irish culture in the form of Gaelic games, Irish music, dance, and theatre was supported. But there was no indigenous cultural renaissance. The attempt to revive the Irish language through the schools was a failure and the language continued to decline. British – more specifically English – influence continued much as before in business practice, public administration, scholarship, architecture, fashion and popular culture. [...] (Ruane 223)

For Kiberd, the Revival inaugurated a creative new spirit of self-reliance and a determination to reform and innovate that outweighed its limitations. For Ruane, in contrast, "Well into the 1970s, it was possible to see Ireland as still a British cultural province" and thereafter the country did not become more robustly national but was conscripted into a "global Anglo-American culture." As such, "Ireland finally emancipated itself from British colonial domination only to allow itself to be re-colonised by an even more powerful global one" (224).

Arguments like these might be extended to other postcolonial nation-states everywhere. If Kiberd downplays the Revival's failures, by Ruane's measure decolonization everywhere must be considered a "failure." Nowhere in the postcolonial world did the rollback of British or other European imperial cultures lead to the construction of robustly indigenous postindependence national cultures while the contemporary dominance of a "global Anglo-American culture" is something that by definition extends to countries almost everywhere. Ireland's axial location between the UK and the US, its large diasporic communities in other Anglophone countries, its economic dependence on both Britain and America, and the internal divisions that issued in partition ensured that the country's capacity for language revival, political independence, and cultural differentiation would be limited.

Still, even if the Revival did not achieve its maximal aims, the era's literary and political achievements were significant. However, for much of the later twentieth century, the Revival was commonly conceived by cultural historians in terms of a belated Romanticism and its more radical political, intellectual, anti-imperialist dimensions are sometimes still questioned (Howe). Irish modernism was commonly regarded as Revivalism's antithesis and valorized as a more progressive literary Europeanization or transcendent internationalism because it had supposedly elevated itself above local Irish pettiness (Nolan). In contrast, much recent scholarship stresses that modernism was less Revivalism's antithesis than its aesthetic radicalization and that the anti-imperial component in each was considerable. Domestic nineteenth-century British discourses that offered Christian, Romantic, and radical Tory-style critiques of utilitarianism, industrialism, individualism, and materialism, and socialistic critiques of capitalism and imperialist exploitation, were available to Irish writers. Revivalists and modernists drew eclectically on these critiques and often radicalized and nationalized them in the light of Ireland's subject nation situation. Thus, the negative aspects of modernity were identified with British imperialism such that the two were often conflated (Bourke and Gallagher, 233). In the more Catholic or Celticist aesthetic modes, this stimulated visions of a more spiritual anti-modern Catholic Ireland or a more heroic pagan Celtic Ireland. In its more radical socialist and republican factions, the Irish struggle supported other liberation campaigns across the empire (Deane, *Celtic Revivals*). In the pre–First World War era, Irish republicans sympathized with the Boer republics in the Boer Wars but in the later twentieth century many were supportive of African decolonization generally (O'Sullivan).

Historians of race and empire have documented the Irish struggle's significance for independence for African-American and Caribbean nationalists after the First World War and for the educated elites leading Africa's anti-imperial struggles after the Second World War. The St. Nevis-born Cyril Briggs, who emigrated to New York in 1905 and founded the African Blood Brotherhood in 1919, was an enthusiastic supporter of Irish republicanism. In 1921, he wrote in his newspaper, *The Crusader*:

> The Irish fight for liberty is the greatest Epic of Modern History. It is a struggle that should have the sympathy and active support of every lover of liberty – of every member of an oppressed group. The Negro in particular should be interested in the Irish struggle, for while it is patent that Ireland can never escape from the menace of "the overshadowing empire" so long as England is able to maintain her grip on the riches and manpower of India and Africa it is also clear that those suffering together under the heel of British imperialism must learn to CO-ORDINATE THEIR EFFORTS before they can HOPE TO BE FREE. (Bergin 52–3, emphasis in original)

Jamaican Claude McKay, another émigré and African Blood Brotherhood member, wrote in *The Liberator* in 1921:

> I react more to the emotions of the Irish than to those of any other whites, they are so passionately primitive in their loves and hates. They are quite free of the disease which is known in bourgeois phraseology as Anglo-Saxon hypocrisy. I suffer with the Irish. I think I understand the Irish. My belonging to a subject race entitles me to some understanding of them. And then I was born and reared a peasant; the peasant's passion for the soil possesses me, and it is one of the strongest passions in the Irish revolution. (Bergin 51)

## 16 Joyce and His Contemporaries

Decades later, when Kwame Nkrumah, Ghana's new Prime Minister, visited Dublin in 1960, he spoke warmly about the Irish decolonization struggle's importance for contemporary African liberation struggles. He paid tribute to "those Irish leaders of the last century who realised that the Irish struggle for independence was not the struggle of one country alone, but part of a world movement for freedom" (Nkrumah, qtd. in O'Sullivan 1). Elements of romanticism or diplomacy may heighten these comparisons, but the newly independent Irish state had played a significant role in decolonization. It did so initially by paving the way for loosening the ties of the Dominions to Great Britain as Irish society moved from the status of Free State to Republic between 1921 and 1948, and later by way of the Republic's support in the United Nations for African and Asian decolonizations (McMahon; O'Sullivan).

Literary and political discourses are constitutively different, and literary and political anti-imperialisms naturally take different forms, so it is no exaggeration to say that for much of the twentieth-century English studies largely minimized Irish literature's anti-imperial dimensions. Doctrines that stressed literature's autonomy from politics were fundamental to some modernist aesthetic ideologies and formative to the New Criticism that dominated the Anglophone humanities for decades after 1945. In the early twentieth century, Irish and American expatriate writers had sometimes shared common antipathies to literary London's domination of Anglophone letters, and American critics such as Ezra Pound, Van Wyck Brooks, or Edmund Wilson saw analogies between the Irish and American situations as their respective national literatures sought to become something more than peripheral tributaries to "English literature" (Cleary).

In the New Criticism, institutionalized in the Cold War and during the later stages of the British Empire's collapse, the matter of empire remained occluded. In this dispensation, Yeats was often conscripted to the more conservative Southern Agrarian anti-modern end of the modernist spectrum while Joyce and *Ulysses* especially were championed by a metropolitan liberal criticism that stressed Joyce's tolerant humanistic vision as opposed to Yeats's conservatism. British critics were hardly oblivious to the politics of Irish literary self-assertion, but writers such as Swift and Burke, Wilde and Shaw, Joyce and Yeats, Bowen and Beckett were nevertheless construed as essentially "British" writers, a situation that remains largely institutionally intact.

To the extent that this situation has changed, the outbreak of the Northern Irish "Troubles" after 1969 and the rise of postcolonial studies have driven that change. In this new context, Joyce and Yeats remain the talismanic figures that largely focalize debate. The Field Day Theatre Company, a collective of Northern writers and critics founded in 1980, printed a series of pamphlets that drew on then emerging postcolonial studies discourses to reassess Irish culture and society. Field Day's criticism concentrated mainly on topics such as the Irish Revival, nationalism and literature, and questions of empire. In 1986, Edward Said addressed the Yeats Summer School in Sligo in a paper later reissued in 1988 as a Field Day pamphlet, "Yeats and Decolonization," which appeared alongside Fredric Jameson's "Modernism and Imperialism" and Terry Eagleton's "Nationalism, Colonialism and Literature" (Deane, *Nationalism*). From the Marxist and postcolonial wings of English studies, these pamphlets contested an Irish revisionism for which the overlap of literature and politics represented what Conor Cruise O'Brien termed an "unhealthy intersection" and which Edna Longley contended, "like church and state[,] ought to be separated" (26).

However, in the context of a thirty-year bitter military conflict in Northern Ireland politics and literature were hard to separate. Indeed, a slew of Irish literary critical works appeared during this time attending to the ways in which Joyce and Yeats especially, but also their contemporaries, engaged with questions of nation-building and empire, race and gender, modernity and modernization. It was only in this late twentieth-century period that Irish Revivalist and modernist literature's double-edged critiques of empire and cultural nationalism first received sustained scholarly analysis. In the critical writings of Seamus Deane, Declan Kiberd, Terry Eagleton, Elizabeth Cullingford, Luke Gibbons, David Lloyd, Emer Nolan, Enda Duffy, Marjorie Howe, Maud Ellmann, P. J. Mathews, and many others, the specifically Irish and imperial dimensions of modern Irish writing were moved center stage in the academy.

The translation of Pascale Casanova's *The World Republic of Letters* (1999) in 2004 brought a new twist. In contrast to American-based conceptions of world literature attending to how great works were circulated around the globe or to paradigms that construed literary peripheries primarily as adaptive sites where metropolitan genres were repurposed to local use, Casanova posited a nationally competitive literary world system periodically renovated and extended in geo-cultural reach by means of rebellions in the literary peripheries. In Casanova's view, the European-centered modern literary world system dominated by Paris from the early modern period onwards had been expanded outwards after the French Revolution by way of a series of semi-peripheral national revolts by Britain and Germany against France. These contestations, Casanova contended, were furthered in turn by the revolts of England's, Germany's, and Spain's satellite cultures against their dominance. Thus, nineteenth-century American and Irish cultural nationalists tried to enrich their national literatures to distinguish them from British literature; Scandinavians and Russians reacted against German hegemony; and the South Americans contested Spanish dominance to enhance their own societies' literary prestige and recognition.

*The World Republic of Letters* offers the Irish case as a paradigmatic instance of a peripheral revolt in a subordinated country against a major center's historical dominance. Within the space of a few generations, Casanova argues, "the Irish literary world traversed all the stages (and all the states) of rupture with the literature of the [English] center, providing a model for the aesthetic, formal, linguistic, and political possibilities contained within outlying spaces" (304). She means by this that mid nineteenth-century Ireland had few literary resources and its literature was everywhere regarded as a minor sideshow to English literature. By turning in Herderian fashion to Irish mythology and folklore; by reviving the Gaelic language and transferring some of its riches and idioms into Hiberno-English writing; by assimilating into London's literary culture and yet satirically challenging its conventions as Wilde and Shaw, Moore and O'Casey did; by taking on London and making Dublin a national cultural capital as Yeats and the Revivalists did; and by winning recognition not just from London's but Paris's literary establishments as Joyce and Beckett did, the Irish, Casanova claims, transacted in short order a series of maneuvers that other impoverished literary peripheries would later deploy to improve their own standings in the literary world system.

Casanova's account of Irish literature is, she acknowledges, schematic and idealistic. *The World Republic of Letters* has been faulted for its eurocentrism, and while Ireland might well be exemplary for other postcolonies in some respects, the cases of South Asia, Africa, and the Caribbean, where many national cultures are comprised of multiple languages and literary traditions, present situations more complex than Ireland's. Today, a century after independence, Ireland's primary literary relations still remain largely with England and the US; despite ongoing integration into the European Union, European literary connections have arguably diminished in the aftermath of modernism. As China and India become major twenty-first-century powers, and as even small Caribbean countries reclaim heritages that are not simply Indigenous or European but also African, South Asian, and Latin American, conceptions of centers and peripheries more complex than those envisioned via the Irish case in *The World Republic of Letters* come into view.

Nevertheless, Casanova's work poses questions that remain vital. What might the literatures of a postimperial world look like? Were literatures released from the economic and cultural competitiveness of nation-states configured in a capitalist world system, what forms might they assume? These questions animated the works of Joyce and his contemporaries; they remain significant for twenty-first-century cultural studies.

## Works Cited

Bergin, Cathy. "'Unrest among the Negroes': The African Blood Brotherhood and the Politics of Resistance." *Race & Class*, vol. 57, no. 3, 2016, pp. 45–58.
Bourke, Richard, and Niamh Gallagher, editors. *The Political Thought of the Irish Revolution*. Cambridge UP, 2022.
Casanova, Pascale. *The World Republic of Letters*. Translated by M. B. DeBevoise, Harvard UP, 2004.
Clark, Samuel. *Social Origins of the Irish Land Wars*. Princeton UP, 1978.
Cleary, Joe. *Modernism, Empire, World Literature*. Cambridge UP, 2021.
Cousins, James H. and Cousins, Margaret E. *We Two Together*. Ganesh and Co., 1950.
Dalsimer, Adele. "Players in the Western World: The Abbey Theatre's American Tours." *Éire-Ireland: A Journal of Irish Studies*, vol. 16, no. 1, 1981, pp. 75–93.
Deane, Seamus. *Celtic Revivals: Essays in Modern Irish Literature, 1880–1980*. Wake Forest UP, 1985.
*Nationalism, Colonialism, and Literature*. U of Minnesota P, 1990.
Devlin, Luke. *The Trickle Down Effect: The 1911–1912 Abbey Theatre Tour and its Impact on Early African American Theatre*. 2017. University of Edinburgh, PhD dissertation, http://hdl.handle.net/1842/25684 (accessed March 6, 2025).
Howe, Stephen. *Ireland and Empire: Colonial Legacies in Irish History and Culture*. Oxford UP, 2000.
Kiberd, Declan. *Inventing Ireland: The Literature of the Modern Nation*. Harvard UP, 1995.
Larkin, Emmet. *Historical Dimensions of Irish Catholicism*. Catholic U of America P, 1984.
Longley, Edna. "Poetry and Politics in Northern Ireland." *The Crane Bag*, vol. 9, no. 1, 1985, pp. 26–40.
Mathews, P. J. *Revival: The Abbey Theatre, Sinn Féin, the Gaelic League and the Co-operative Movement*. Cork UP in association with Field Day, 2003.
McMahon, Deirdre. *Republicans and Imperialists: Anglo-Irish Relations in the 1930s*. Yale UP, 1984.
Miller, David. *Church, State, and Nation in Modern Ireland, 1898–1921*. Pittsburgh UP, 1973.
Nelson, Bruce. *Irish Nationalists and the Making of the Irish Race*. Princeton UP, 2012.
Nolan, Emer. *Joyce and Irish Nationalism*. Routledge, 1995.
O'Brien, Conor Cruise. "An Unhealthy Intersection." *New Review*, vol. 2, no. 16, 1975, pp. 3–8.
Ó Lúing, Seán. "Arthur Griffith, 1871–1922: Thoughts on a Centenary." *Studies: An Irish Quarterly Review*, vol. 60, no. 238, Summer 1971, pp. 127–38.
O'Sullivan, Kevin. *Ireland, Africa, and the End of Empire: Small State Identity in the Cold War, 1955–75*. Manchester UP, 2012.

Ruane, Joseph. "Theorising Ireland's Ambiguous Colonial Dimension: Implications for Ukraine." *Ireland and Ukraine: Studies in Comparative Imperial and National History*, edited by Stephen Velychenko, Joseph Ruane, and Liudmyla Hrynevych, Ibidem Verlag, 2022, pp. 203–36.

Saha, Poulomi. "Conspiracy Rises Again: Racial Sympathy and Radical Solidarity across Empires." *Qui Parle: Critical Humanities and Social Sciences*, vol. 28, no. 2, December 2019, pp. 307–33.

Ward, Margaret. "Conflicting Interests: The British and Irish Suffrage Movements." *The Irish Issue: The British Question*, special issue of *Feminist Review*, vol. 50, Summer 1995, pp. 127–47.

# 17

ELINOR TAYLOR

# Popular Front Aesthetics, Imperialism, and the People

## Introduction: Popular Front Politics

With the rise of fascism in Europe in the interwar years, many writers and artists began to ask how to respond to intensifying threats to freedom of speech and artistic expression. The crisis capitalism entered after the 1929 crash indeed provoked some intellectuals in Britain to ask, often with an idealized picture of the Soviet Union in mind, whether capitalism itself needed to be dismantled to secure cultural flourishing. The result was the so-called Red Decade of the 1930s, when left-wing sympathies among the intelligentsia ran high. The Third International (Comintern), a Soviet-led body that existed to promote world revolution, sponsored a range of cultural initiatives, including international literary congresses and journals that attracted many high-profile contributors (see Glaser and Lee). In Britain, the Communist Party of Great Britain, previously suspicious of intellectuals, adopted a more open approach, leading writers such as Stephen Spender, Rex Warner, Edgell Rickword, Sylvia Townsend Warner, and others to declare themselves communists (Croft). Recognizing that fascism now posed an existential threat to the still-young Soviet state, the Comintern bid communists outside the Soviet Union to focus on halting the advance of fascism in democratic states, rather than on revolution in the immediate future. While the Comintern had previously characterized fascism as a phase of the general crisis of capitalism, it was now reinterpreted as the political strategy of a particular sector of the capitalist class, what the Comintern's General Secretary Georgi Dimitrov, speaking at its Seventh Congress in 1935, called, "*the open terrorist dictatorship of the most reactionary, most chauvinistic and most imperialist elements of finance capital*" (8). This allowed for antifascist alliances between working-class groups and progressive bourgeois elements who could be persuaded that their interests were not served by fascism. This strategy was known as the Popular Front. Crucially, the Comintern proposed that the common ground of this alliance was not to

## 17 Popular Front Aesthetics, Imperialism, the People

be revolutionary aspirations, but rather a shared sense of *culture* under threat. "We want to find a *common language* with the broadest masses" (83) Dimitrov declared, "to *link up the present struggle with the people's revolutionary traditions and past*" (73) and national histories were posited as the terrain on which fascism should be combatted:

> The fascists are rummaging through the entire *history* of every nation so as to be able to pose as the heirs and continuators of all that was exalted and heroic in its past, while all that was degrading or offensive to the national sentiments of the people they make use of as weapons against the enemies of fascism (73).

Antifascism, then, implied the defense of the "national histories" of "the people." Similarly, Dimitrov instructed communists to defend existing democratic rights as bulwarks against fascism. Although Dimitrov insisted that anti-imperialist commitments remained nonnegotiable, it was apparent that for communists in Europe, their *immediate* priorities were to be directed elsewhere. World revolution receded as a goal as the Soviet Union committed to "socialism in one country," turning away from the theory of permanent revolution which held that world revolution was a single process occurring across different terrains of struggle (Morgan 6). Tom Buchanan reports that C. L. R. James and others warned that, "the logic of anti-fascism was to give priority to European over non-European interests" (664). Stuart Middleton likewise reports that George Padmore, Jomo Kenyatta, and others recognized that "the simple opposition between 'fascism' and 'democracy' within Europe [...] obfuscated the nature of colonial rule by ostensibly 'democratic' states" (202). This chapter considers these claims in relation to some of the writing produced in the Popular Front moment in Britain.

### Writing the Popular Front

Few writers in Britain were following developments in the Comintern closely, but Dimitrov's speech effectively reflected developments already taking place. From the late 1920s onwards, European intellectuals had begun exploring ways to coordinate their activities and defend intellectual freedom. The 1935 Congress of Writers for the Defence of Culture, held in Paris and attended by high-profile figures such as Henri Barbusse and Bertolt Brecht, is a notable example (Boas 1–6). A British Section of the Comintern-sponsored Writers' International was founded in 1933, launching the influential journal *Left Review* in 1934, which acted as a hub for the British literary Popular Front. Another key institution was the Left Book

Club, established by the publisher Victor Gollancz in 1936. Not everyone involved in these initiatives was a committed communist, but they were, for a time, engaged in a shared project predicated on the belief that "culture" was in profound crisis. The founding statement of the British Section, published in *Left Review*, declared that, "There is a crisis of ideas in the capitalist world to-day," a crisis amounting to "the collapse of a culture, accompanying the collapse of an economic system" (38). This crisis was characterized, so went the argument, by the disengagement of the writer from "the people" and its chief symptom was the "decadence of the past twenty years of English literature" (38). Writers were bidden to reconnect with popular life, to recover popular language and reject the formal radicalism of 1920s modernism. Not all writers on the left went along with this, but nonetheless "popularity" and an imagined audience of "the people" are woven through much leftist writing in this period. Like Dimitrov's speech, this left open the question: Which people? And on what grounds could it be assumed that "the people" was instinctively progressive and antifascist? Particularly difficult was the role of empire in shaping "the British people."

A consideration of the *Left Review* milieu brings these questions into focus. Wade Matthews argues that "contributors *to Left Review* failed to draw attention to the relationship between English culture and British imperialism; or [...] make the connection between colonialism and fascism" (46). These issues often do seem disconnected. The manifesto of the British Section proposed to include writers who would use their pens to "expose the hidden forms of war being carried on against the Indian, Irish, African and Chinese peoples" (38). But it was not clear whether these writers were assumed to be separate from the other two groups to whom the manifesto appealed – those who were antifascist and working class. *Left Review* engaged with international affairs and produced themed issues on Ireland, China, and India, bringing literature from these struggles to a British readership. But attempts to link these different struggles together were rare. An exception is Rickword's editorial for the *Left Review* issue dedicated to Indian writing, which made the connection clear. "The sincerity of our protests at fascist brutalities can only be measured by the strength of our efforts to secure the right of the colonial peoples to govern themselves," Rickword wrote, "And, as practical people, let us remember that the forces of 'law and order' kept in training on the bodies of the subject races, provide a rod in a pickle for any reactionary government to use on the backs of a militant democracy at home" ("National Liberties" 601).

A figure who was particularly insistent about the inseparability of antifascism, anticolonialism, and anti-imperialism (and, hence, resistant to nationally bounded conceptions of "the people") was Nancy Cunard. Cunard, who edited the landmark anthology *Negro* in 1934, was a regular contributor to *Left Review* and launched one of the celebrated literary initiatives of the day, the 1937 pamphlet *Authors Take Sides on the Spanish War*, which gathered responses from dozens of writers to a questionnaire. In the questionnaire, Cunard wrote that, "We have seen murder and destruction by Fascism in Italy, in Germany – the organization there of social injustice and cultural death – and how revived, imperial Rome, abetted by international treachery, has conquered her place in the Abyssinian sun. The dark millions in the colonies are unavenged" (1). Here antifascism and anti-imperialism are simultaneously articulated, with the Italian invasion of Ethiopia (Abyssinia) manifesting their interconnection. Buchanan writes that this passage "expresses a political dilemma, as the 'dark millions' were likely to remain 'unavenged' so long as authors were asked to take sides on the Spanish Civil War rather than colonial oppression" (645). But this overlooks the way that Cunard is refusing the choice between one and the other. It is furthermore noteworthy that several contributors, such as C. L. R James and George Padmore, took the opportunity to reiterate the inseparability of antifascist and anticolonial commitments.

So, in these cases at least, writers did acknowledge that antifascism could not be isolated from the global system of colonial oppression. However, what was less clear was how to give literary form to these insights, and responses ranged across forms such as historical pageants, anthologies, historical novels, and works of criticism. Consonant with Dimitrov's appeal to reclaim national histories from fascist propaganda, many writers claimed ownership of a history of resistance to capitalist social relations, domesticating left-wing positions that could otherwise be dismissed as "alien" to British tradition. These efforts were often articulated through "popular" forms, such as narrative history (most famously A. L. Morton's *A People's History of England*, 1938) and the historical pageant, such as *The March of English History*, which encouraged audiences to situate themselves in a narrative of resistance to capitalism and exploitation leading toward the achievement of communism as the realization of a centuries-old vision of a "Free and Merrie England" (Wallis 17–32). The work of the Australian-born poet, translator, critic, and novelist Jack Lindsay is especially significant for its intensive explorations of British (or more frequently, *English*) history and his questioning, through formal experiment, of how to establish new, historically informed relationships in the present between writers and audiences. Lindsay's work sought to call "the English people," as a progressive, transhistorical subject, into being, rather than presupposing its existence. His poem "not english?," published in *Left Review* in May 1936, one of several attempts to write poems for "mass declamation" by a group, called on "those who are not the english / according to the definition of the ruling class," encouraging identification between the audience and a tradition of radicals whose histories are missing from authorized narratives (353–8; see Harker for fuller discussion). It is these figures, the poem says, who have made England and will one day reclaim it as rightfully theirs. But while the poem's speaker acknowledges that they "splintered [their] bones to build an Empire" the workers of the colonized world are absent even as the poem alludes to the internationalist rhetoric of the *Communist Manifesto*. Lindsay was by no means indifferent to the role of imperialism in the history of British capitalism and the British state; indeed, his 1938 novel of the English Revolution, *1649*, identifies imperialism as an integral part of that history (Taylor 115–16). But in trying to recover the "progressive" element of this history, attention falls on the bourgeois character, the Leveller Lilburn, and his efforts to halt Cromwell's drive toward the conquest of Ireland. Like much British communist writing, the novel finds it easier to identify with individual "progressive" figures of the past than with the subjects of class and colonial violence themselves. Particular attention was paid in *Left Review* to such individuals of the past who crossed class and/or national lines; for instance, Charles Donnelly and Montagu Slater, and Ralph Fox published appreciations of Roger Casement and T. E. Lawrence respectively (Fox, "Lawrence"). *Spokesmen for Liberty*, a 1941 anthology of radical historical documents edited by Lindsay and Rickword, featured expressions of solidarity with anticolonial struggles by British writers, but (with the exception of some Irish writers), not the participants of those struggles themselves. A footnote to Rickword's editorial introduction acknowledges this limitation, but sounds a defensive note: "No single volume could adequately show the heroic resistance [...] of the many nations of Asia and Africa to that of the capitalists; but we have proved that the English people are not guilty of all the blood shed by their rulers" (xvi). There are many noteworthy innovations here – Morton pioneered the method of "history of below" that has been crucial in asserting the agency of oppressed groups and Lindsay's radical reworking of the historical novel merits further attention – yet the Popular Front turn imagined the national past as a story of struggles for the democratic liberties enjoyed in the present, a story whose terminus was an English communist utopia, but one whose connection to liberation struggles in the present was frequently obscured.

### Ralph Fox, Mulk Raj Anand, and Indian Writing in Britain

However, it is also the case that the relationship between antifascism and anticolonialism remained a central concern for writers from colonial backgrounds. The London literary scene, Priyamvada Gopal writes, "became a kind of 'junction box' for oppositional black and Asian figures from various parts of the British Empire" (212). A productive friendship that exemplifies this "junction box" of intersecting solidarities was between Ralph Fox, the journalist, translator, and literary critic, and the Indian novelist Mulk Raj Anand who had come to London as a student in 1924. For both men, Karl Marx's writings on India, which asserted the centrality of the exploitation of India to the formation of British capital, were an important influence. Fox worked as an editor on these texts during his time at the Marx–Engels–Lenin Institute in Moscow, while Anand edited a version of the text published in India, with the assistance of the British communist publishing house Martin Lawrence, in 1933 (Clark 290–2). Fox drew on the work in his 1933 book *The Colonial Policy of British Imperialism* and insisted that "in so far as they have participated in the plunder of the colonies, the English working class have strengthened their own oppressors and weakened their own chances of freedom" (108). Fox and Anand became friends in the early 1930s, and Fox influenced Anand's understanding of the intersections of class and colonial oppression (Clark 290–2). In 1934, Anand was one of a group of young Indian writers then based in London, including Sajjad Zaheer and Jyoti Ghosh, who founded the Progressive Writers' Association (PWA), established as the Indian Section of the Writers' International (Baer 582). Anand, with fellow novelist Zaheer (later to become the first General Secretary of the Communist Party of Pakistan), attended the Paris Writers' Congress in 1935 and, on their return, drafted a manifesto, published in *Left Review* in 1936, setting out their program for the creation of a modern, leftist Indian literature. In many ways, the PWA manifesto echoes the British Section's statements about the need to "reconnect" literature with "the people"; writers should aim to "bring the arts into the closest touch with the people; and to make them the vital organ which will register the actualities of life, as well as lead us to the future" (IPWA 240). Anand, however, articulated the PWA's aims in more directly anticolonial terms. Speaking in 1938, he asserted that reevaluating the Indian culture of the past was a priority, "so as to rescue it from the maligning of Imperialist archaeology on the one side and from its misuse by the reactionary element in our society" ("Progressive" 18), while in *Left Review* he traced the roots of Indian intellectuals' distance from "the people" directly to colonial policy ("Towards" 613–23). Imperialism from without and reaction from within were twin enemies. Moreover, Anand drew explicit connections between fascism and British imperialism: "[We] saw the ugly face of Fascism in our country earlier than the writers of the European countries, for it was British Imperialism which perfected the method of the

249

concentration camp, torture and bombing for police purposes which Hitler and Mussolini and the Japanese militarists have used so effectively later on" ("Progressive" 17). The connection, he wrote, was revealed to him when he witnessed the suppression of the 1926 General Strike in Britain, which "reminded me of the Seven Stripes I had got in the Martial Law days in Amritsar" (qtd. in Baer 583). It is striking that Anand's comments predate Aimé Césaire's articulation of the link in *Discourse on Colonialism* (1950) by more than a decade.

For Anand, colonial and class oppression necessarily complicated the idea of "the people" in the context of 1930s India. This placed him at a distance from more mainstream anticolonial positions invested in the claims of a national bourgeoisie to represent "the people." Anand writes that the role of the writer is to create, or call into being, such a "people," "to take an active part in preparing the people who are to read him," to engage in the "popularisation of culture" in order to "armour the people intellectually" ("Progressive" 18). There is no preexisting "people" to and for whom progressive writers may speak. For Anand, this process of popularization and intellectual armament could *only* occur through simultaneous antifascist and anticolonial action:

> The task of building up a national culture out of the debris of the past, so that it takes root in the realities of the present, is only way by which we will take our place among those writers of the world who are facing with us the bitterest struggle in history – the struggle of the peoples of the world against Imperialism, its town brother Fascism, its old aunt Feudalism, and all other aunts who refuse to let the new shoots of life from bursting into the future. ("Progressive" 20)

Here the writer has an active role in shaping "the people" and creating a new future; not simply defending existing national traditions, but struggling simultaneously against fascism and imperialism in creating an empowered and engaged public.

We may briefly consider Anand's two novels of this era, *Untouchable* (1935) and *Coolie* (1938), in light of these remarks. Ben Conisbee Baer argues that Anand's work at this time is marked by questions about which "public" it sought to address (584). Discussing *Untouchable*, Baer considers the complex negotiations Anand undertakes between "the people" and the subaltern; the novel, he argues, represents the subaltern protagonist Bakha "as potential 'people,' as becoming-people, not-quite people, public-to-come," who is distinguished from the "novel's image of the people – 'the crowd' that gathers to see Gandhi in a counter-public nationalist manifestation" (584). The novel thus registers the limitations of "the people" as it

## 17 Popular Front Aesthetics, Imperialism, the People

currently exists as a political community, but sees no solution: While the novel glimpses the hope of improved conditions through social reform, the single-day timeframe isolates Bakha from the public sphere through which such reforms might be enacted. We may read *Coolie*, by contrast, as informed by Anand's engagement with the PWA and with Fox. Indeed, Anand recalled that Fox "proposed that I write a novel about a young proletarian Indian, who managed through self-education to reach an understanding of Marxism and on his return to India he is thrown into prison, where he is literally killed by starvation" (qtd. in Clark 300). *Coolie*, tracing the life of a young boy, Munoo, does not follow the formula Fox suggested, as there is no moment of political enlightenment as such (Clark 303). But it does demonstrate a closer aesthetic alignment with the European left and – critically – emphasizes the intersection of class and imperialism: It is a more "realist" novel, examining the material conditions that might produce a sense of class consciousness in Munoo.

A kind of mirror image of Anand's work might be another novel by an Indian writer written (in Urdu, rather than, like Anand's, in English) in the atmosphere of the Popular Front: Sajjad Zaheer's *A Night in London*, published in 1938. Zaheer had contributed to the influential but controversial anthology *Angarey* (1932) and he spent time in London in the mid 1930s before returning to India in 1938 (Coppola 100–15). The novel's central characters are Indian students studying in London who gather for a party one foggy night in Bloomsbury and the novel's narrative voice and perspective move between them as they ruminate over questions of class, race, gender, caste, and religion. One character, for example, is appalled by a newspaper headline reporting the murder of Indian protesters by British troops which describes the victims as "natives," but is unable to connect his disgust at this racializing language with class oppression: "Azam's thoughts would not extend to the unfortunate poor who faced the bullets of the white man and the unemployed English workers in Hyde Park who died hungry" (Zaheer, *Night* 9). The shifting narrative style and the Bloomsbury party setting are reminiscent of modernist novels of the 1920s, but the long passages of dialogue between the characters stage the dilemmas facing the PWA, their intellectual distance from "the people," and the complicity of their class in colonial exploitation. As one character puts it, "We are no better than thieves and robbers. Who can say that we have a right to India's wealth, which we're squandering here? Of what benefit is our life to India? None!" (51). For Zaheer, these dilemmas could only be solved by returning to India ("Reminiscences" 124), but *A Night in London* also asserts the importance of solidarity between British workers and colonized peoples; early on, in a long, rather awkwardly executed scene, two characters, Azam and Rao, visit a pub and encounter two working-class British men, Tom and Jim, the former of whom surprises them with a long, Marxist lecture on the injustice and destructiveness of the British empire (Zaheer, *Night* 18–23). This episode echoes Popular Front emphases on solidarity across class and national lines; but at the same time the awkward relations between the elements of the book speak to an aesthetic challenge that mirrors (from the opposite angle) the difficulties British writers experienced. Zaheer suggests a poignant origin of this moment in his 1940 reflection on the novel. He describes writing the book onboard a ship on his way back to India. On board were several Italian workers, bound for Ethiopia, one of whom committed suicide by jumping overboard. Zaheer asks, "Why, after all, had he preferred death over going to Ethiopia and constructing a road for the Italian Empire? The question frequently arose in my mind, but who was there to answer it?" ("Reminiscences" 134). One may read the pub scene in *A Night in London* as an answer to this question. The novel's omniscience is shaped by knowledge that the characters themselves are unable to reach. It rehearses, without solving, the problems of a committed intellectual, incorporating both Popular Frontist motifs and, as its translator has it, "a modernism against modernism" in a troubled combination (Hashmi 98).

## The Novel and Which People?

These novels therefore engage with questions the PWA raised about the relationship between intellectuals and "the people," and the prospective role of the writer in calling such a people into being. But "the people" was always a vexed concept for writers in both metropolitan and colonial contexts. It is worth turning to the book that sets out to address this problem systematically, *The Novel and the People*, written by Anand and Zaheer's friend and mentor Ralph Fox, and published posthumously in 1937 after Fox's death in Spain.

Echoing the formulations Georg Lukács set out contemporaneously in such texts as "Narrate or Describe?" (1936), though in a predominantly Anglophone key, Fox's book sets out a cultural history of the European novel as epic of the bourgeois, charting the form's history in a narrative that sees it emerging in the work of Fielding, especially, as the signature form of the new commercial class, reaching its full maturity in the expansive realism of the nineteenth century, when writers, although bourgeois, were nonetheless in touch with the life of "the people," before reaching a phase of decline in literary modernism, a symptom of intellectual retreat and immobilization, to be resurrected in the Soviet Union under the sign of socialist realism, "which shall unite and re-vitalize the forces of the left in literature"

(Fox, *Novel* 26). Such a realism would express, through characters who were at once "typical" and heroic, revolutionary development toward socialism. Threaded through the argument, though, is an assertion that the novelist is connected to "the people," figured in nationally bounded terms: The "writer more than any other artist expresses his country" and the novelist, therefore, "has a special responsibility both to the present and the past of his country" and must "know his people" (23, 140). The assertiveness here contrasts with other writers' perceptions (including those of Anand and Zaheer) that "the people" was not so easily identified, particularly in contexts of colonial oppression. But Fox had conducted extensive studies of imperialism and the global development of capitalism and there is clearly a struggle going on in *The Novel and the People* to integrate the Soviet-mandated model of socialist realism with Fox's awareness of *global* development. A discussion of the French writer André Gide, for example, considers how Gide's *Travels in the Congo* (1927) records his conversion to anticolonialism through his encounter with French colonial violence, but nonetheless concludes that Gide failed to grasp the totalizing viewpoint of Marxism, so that his anticolonialism remained essentially "subjective" (Fox, *Novel* 38). Fox thus seems to recognize the centrality of anticolonial struggles to revolutionary development, but the possibility that a new "epic" might emerge from *within* those struggles themselves, rather than through the individual heroics of a bourgeois border-crosser, seems inadmissible. On this, Fox diverges from the better-known arguments of Lukács in the 1930s: Though echoing Lukács's genealogy of the novel form, Fox focuses on the heroic, world-building revolutionary, rather than the "typical" protagonist endorsed by Lukács. The book concludes with a demand for solidarity with national liberation movements, phrased in terms of the mutual interests of discrete "peoples" – "An alliance of free peoples will prove a stronger guard for the liberties of all, including our own, than the present effort to maintain Imperial tyranny" (148) – and with a quotation from Marx on India, establishing imperialism as the horizon of the argument, but the participants of anticolonial struggles themselves have an insecure place in the argument. Echoing Marx, Fox envisaged an eventual "world literature," but the possibility that the novel might be best understood as a world form, not a national-popular form, that its shifting shapes have mediated capitalism's globally uneven conditions, not merely hymned the fortunes of the bourgeoisie, is not glimpsed here.

There was, however, a strand of British writing that did envision continuities between working-class history, anticolonialism, and antifascism, mediated through narratives of "popular" heroism, in ways Fox didn't imagine. For some writers from Scotland and Wales, the Spanish Civil War spurred them to make links between their own status as members of "minor" nationalities within the British state and antifascist and anticolonial politics. As suggested earlier, much British Popular Front writing was really *English* writing, with the discrepancy between the "British people" and the "English people" largely unacknowledged. The Welsh writer Lewis Jones is one notable exception. His two novels of the life of a Welsh mining community, *Cwmardy* (1937) and *We Live* (1939), portray the village as engaged in territorial resistance to the imposed power of the British state, nowhere more clearly than in the scenes depicting a fictionalized version of the 1910 Tonypandy riots, when then-Home Secretary Winston Churchill sent troops into South Wales to quash a mining dispute. In Jones's novels, the British state functions as an occupying force, acting to violently crush "the people" of the village, who have their own laws, customs, and worldview. This anti-imperialist current leads inexorably toward Spain in the second novel, as the protagonist Len, fighting with the International Brigades, perceives that the "alien" power of the British authorities is of a piece with the Francoist forces. The Scottish novelist James Barke saw the war in similar terms in relation to the people of Scotland in his 1939 novel *The Land of the Leal*, which traces a Scottish family history of dispossession, proletarianization, and radicalization, culminating in sacrifice for the Spanish Republican cause. These novels then represent, from *within* Britain, efforts to connect anticolonial and antifascist commitments, to suggest the continuity of interests between subjects of class, colonial, and fascist violence, that in other British writing remain separate. Jones's and Barke's novels of "the people" are perhaps the most coherent realization of the Popular Front program, but both emerge from outside the normative position of middle-class Englishness.

## Conclusion

Ralph Fox died fighting in Spain in December 1936, as would hundreds of international volunteers who saw the civil war as the front of a global struggle against fascism. The outbreak of war in Spain dampened European leftist interests in struggles outside Europe and flattened complex interlocking relations into a single slogan, "For Culture against Fascism." Writers from twenty-eight nations gathered in Spain in the summer of 1937 for a congress at which they proclaimed that the "principal enemy of the culture which they have undertaken to defend is Fascism" ("Manifesto" 445). The principle of the "defense of culture" tended to elide differences in national status and bracket off questions of political autonomy. As we have seen, the Popular Front moment stimulated writers from a range of backgrounds to ask searching questions about the role of the writer in national cultural life, in social change, and in resistance to violence and exploitation; at the same time, however, it could close off analysis of the global and intersecting nature of struggles for liberation under capitalism. The outbreak of war in 1939 brought a crisis of conflicting loyalties to many communists. The questions raised in the Popular Front moment would, however, return, differently inflected, to dominate postwar debates about "commitment" in the context of a wave of anticolonial uprisings. They would be reengaged, for instance, in the Welsh Marxist thinker Raymond Williams's reflections on the dialectic between conscious commitment and the social relations in which writing occurs, given a new impetus, Williams thought, by the Chinese Revolution (203–4). The writer's relationship with "the people," whether figured in class, national, or transnational terms, would remain salient.

## Works Cited

Anand, Mulk Raj. "On the Progressive Writers' Movement." 1939. *Marxist Cultural Movement in India*, edited by Sudhi Pradhan, National Book Agency, 1960, pp. 1–22.
——. "Towards a New Indian Literature." *Left Review*, vol. 2, no. 12, Sept. 1936, pp. 613–23.
Baer, Ben Conisbee. "Shit Writing: Mulk Raj Anand's *Untouchable*, the Image of Gandhi, and the Progressive Writers' Association." *Modernism/Modernity*, vol. 16, no. 3, Sept. 2009, pp. 575–95.
Barke, James. *The Land of the Leal*. Collins, 1939.
Boas, Jacob. *Writers' Block: The Paris Antifascist Congress of 1935*. Modern Humanities Research Association, 2016.
British Section. "The Statement." *Left Review*, vol. 1, no. 1, Oct. 1934, p. 38.
Buchanan, Tom. "'The Dark Millions in the Colonies are Unavenged': Anti-Fascism and Anti-Imperialism in the 1930s." *Contemporary European History*, vol. 25, no. 4, 2016, pp. 645–65.
Clark, Katerina. *Eurasia without Borders: The Dream of a Leftist Literary Commons, 1919–1943*. Harvard UP, 2021.
Coppola, Carlo. "About the Author and His Works." *A Night in London*, by Sajjad Zaheer, Harper Perennial, 2011, pp. 100–15.
Croft, Andy. "Authors Take Sides: Writers and the Communist Party, 1920–1956." *Opening the Books: Essays on the Social and Cultural History of the British Communist Party*, edited by Geoff Andrews, Nina Fishman, and Kevin Morgan, Pluto P, 1995, pp. 83–101.
Cunard, Nancy. "The Question." *Authors Take Sides on the Spanish War*. *Left Review*, 1937, p. 1.
Dimitrov, Georgi. "The Fascist Offensive and the Tasks of the Communist International in the Struggle of the Working Class against Fascism." *Georgi Dimitrov, Selected Works*, vol. 2, 1972, pp. 7–88, https://archive.org/details/swdimitrov2/page/7/mode/2up (accessed March 7, 2025).
Donnelly, Charles, and "Ajax" [Montagu Slater]. "Connolly and Casement." *Left Review*, vol. 2, no. 7, Apr. 1936, pp. 289–95.

Fox, Ralph. *The Colonial Policy of British Imperialism*. Martin Lawrence, 1933.

"Lawrence: The 20th Century Hero." *Left Review*, vol. 1, no. 9, Jun. 1935, pp. 319–96.

*The Novel and the People*. Lawrence & Wishart, 1979.

Glaser, Amelia, and Steven S. Lee, editors. *Comintern Aesthetics*. U of Toronto P, 2020.

Gopal, Priyamvada. *Insurgent Empire: Anticolonial Resistance and British Dissent*. Verso, 2019.

Harker, Ben. "'Communism is English': Edgell Rickword, Jack Lindsay, and the Cultural Politics of the Popular Front." *Literature and History*, vol. 20, no. 2, 2011, pp. 16–34.

Hashmi, Bilal. "Translator's Afterword." *A Night in London*, by Sajjad Zaheer, Harper Perennial, 2011, pp. 97–9.

Indian Progressive Writers' Association. "Manifesto." *Left Review*, vol. 2, no. 5, Feb. 1936, p. 240.

Jones, Lewis. *Cwmardy* and *We Live*. Parthian Library of Wales, 2006.

Lindsay, Jack. "not english? A reminder for May Day." *Left Review*, vol. 2, no. 8, May 1936, pp. 353–8.

"Manifesto," *Left Review*, vol. 3, no. 8, Sept. 1937, p. 445.

Matthews, Wade. *The New Left, National Identity, and the Break-Up of Britain*. Brill, 2013.

Middleton, Stuart. "The Crisis of Democracy in Interwar Britain." *The Historical Journal*, vol. 66, no. 1, Feb. 2023, pp. 186–209.

Morgan, Kevin. *Against Fascism and War: Ruptures and Continuities in British Communist Politics, 1935–1941*. Manchester UP, 1989.

Rickword, Edgell. "Introduction: On English Freedom." *Spokesmen for Liberty: A Record of Democracy Through Twelve Centuries*, edited by Edgell Rickword and Jack Lindsay, Lawrence & Wishart, 1941, pp. vii–xxii.

"National Liberties." *Left Review*, vol. 2, no. 12, Sept. 1936, pp. 601–3.

Taylor, Elinor. *The Popular Front Novel in Britain, 1934–1940*. Brill, 2018.

Wallis, Mick. "The Popular Front Pageant: Its Emergence and Decline." *New Theatre Quarterly*, vol. 11, no. 41. 1995, pp. 17–32.

Williams, Raymond. *Marxism and Literature*. Oxford UP, 1977.

Zaheer, Sajjad. *A Night in London*. Translated by Bilal Hashmi, Harper Perennial, 2011.

"Reminiscences." 1940. *Marxist Cultural Movement in India*, edited by Sudhi Pradhan, National Book Agency, 1960, pp. 33–47.

PART IV

# Pathways and Legacies: 1945–2020

# 18

ANDREW HAMMOND

# British Fiction, Decolonization, and the Cold War

## The Cold War and British Fiction

The independence movements that spread across the Global South after 1945 had a profound effect on the course and conduct of the Cold War. Significantly, the retreat of Western European imperialism began at the same time that conflict was emerging between the US, the Soviet Union, and the People's Republic of China, with each viewing the vacated territories as key sites in the struggle for supremacy.[1] Over the following decades, it was the postcolonial nations of Asia, Africa, Oceania, and Latin America where the so-called proxy wars were conducted, where propaganda agencies intensified their campaigns of disinformation, and where the most aggressive policies of diplomatic and economic coercion were pursued. As Roger Kanet writes, the "free world" and the communist bloc understood the processes of decolonization as "a zero-sum game [...] in which even the slightest gain in presence or influence for one side was seen as transforming immediately into a comparable loss of presence or influence for the other" (334). While containment was largely focused on superpower adversaries, it also worked to disempower other players in the global struggle, a fact that was as relevant to the former European empires as it was to members of the nonaligned movement. For Washington, support for independence was necessary both for retaining the sympathy of the new postcolonial elites and for destroying colonial monopolies, evidenced in the opening up of "Third World" markets and resources by the Bretton Woods institutions. In George Orwell's *Nineteen Eighty-Four* (1949), crucially, the three-way fight for global control impacts most heavily on the nominally decolonized countries but also devastates the nations of Western Europe, now reduced to impoverished outposts of either the US or the Soviet bloc.

This is not to say that the former empires had any intention of relinquishing power. For the UK, there was certainly no wish to surrender a 400-year history of political and material gain that had not only consolidated the nation's standing in the world but had also become a fundamental factor in the nation's sense of self (White 100). Imperial power had involved both the direct administration of some 400 million subjects spread over 60 colonies and dependencies and the indirect practices of "informal empire," a vast network of trading companies, financial services, and communications systems that had accrued much of the nation's wealth. The ruthless acquisition and expropriation of resources was achieved through theft, oppression, massacre, impoverishment, forced displacement, and environmental destruction, not to mention the policies of "divide and rule" which continued to create social discord after national liberation had been gained. Indeed, the condition of the colonies at the moment of independence offers some of the clearest evidence of the failures of the imperial mission. In the final decade of British rule in India, for example, the average life expectancy was under twenty-seven years, 88 percent of people were illiterate, 55 percent lived below the poverty line, and only 13 percent had the right to vote (Penier 20; Washbrook 48–9). Naturally, "the obscenities of colonialism," in Abdulrazak Gurnah's phrase, were obscured by a self-aggrandizing mythology that literary culture did much to circulate (*By the Sea* 135). As Edward Said points out, British writing of the sixteenth century onwards "fixes socially desirable space in metropolitan England or Europe and connects it by design, motive, and development to distant or peripheral worlds [...] conceived of as desirable but subordinate" (61). In popular culture, similarly, the tales of adventure published by Rudyard Kipling, H. Rider Haggard, G. A. Henty, A. E. W. Mason, and others formed "the energizing myths of English imperialism," presenting a glorified model of athletic masculinity set off by depraved and backward subjects (Green 3). Over the centuries, writers had established such a deep connection between the British Empire and British identity, with their overlapping notions of democracy, liberalism, rationality, orderliness, and decency, that imperial ideologies were never likely to vanish after 1945.

During the postwar Labour government, the Colonial Development and Welfare Act (1945) and Colonial Development Corporation (1948) indicated the revival of imperial ambition, one that found particular scope in the extraction of agricultural produce and raw materials from the African possessions. For Ernest Bevin, there was even a sense that, "if we only pushed on and developed Africa, we could have the US dependent on us, and eating out of our hands in four or five years" (qtd. in Hopkins 474). That the Conservative opposition concurred was seen in Churchill's notion of the "three great circles" of the Western world – the British Empire, the English-speaking countries, and the emergent federation of Western Europe – and of the huge prestige that Britain gained from being "the only country which

## 18 British Fiction, Decolonization, and the Cold War

has a great part in every one of them" (qtd. in May 9). Even the initial withdrawals from Jordan, India, Ceylon, Burma, and Palestine in the latter half of the 1940s were understood to be a rationalization, rather than a termination, of the imperial project, a strategic retreat that would allow a more practical allocation of resources. Yet the lack of funding for investment, combined with ongoing pressure from Washington, soon took a toll. The ten years from 1948 to 1958 also saw a series of nationalist upheavals in Egypt, Kenya, Malaya, Cyprus, British Guiana, and the Central African Republic of Rhodesia and Nyasaland, as well as violent counterinsurgencies on the part of the British military that help to explain Nadeem Aslam's withering comment that "'[t]he Cold War was cold only for the rich and privileged places of the planet'" (37). Over the next two decades, the imperial retreat was confirmed by the loss of nearly fifty territories across Africa, Asia, the Caribbean, and the Pacific, with Hong Kong being the only remaining colony of economic import. Acknowledgment of the new realities came in a speech delivered by Harold Macmillan to the South African Parliament in 1960: "The wind of change is blowing through this continent," he intoned, and in the light of Soviet expansionism the only hope is that "the balance will come down in favor of freedom and order and justice" (qtd. in White 125–6). In part, the nation's contribution to US-led containment was the entirely self-serving British Commonwealth, the last gasp of its age-old belief in the right to guide and manage the Global South.[2] As ineffectual as the Commonwealth was, the institution helped to retain the population's sense of imperial nationhood for the length of the Cold War. The fact that the British Empire remained a motif of board games and food packages, a subject of films, documentaries, and radio broadcasts, and a predominant theme in national events from the Victory Parade of 1946 to the Falklands/Malvinas conflict of 1982 showed how successfully imperial identity outlasted imperial actuality.

For all the political and economic impact of decolonization, its influence on British literature remains an under-researched topic.[3] Mirroring the complex transformations taking place in wider society, the forty-five years of the Cold War marks a literary period caught between the confident imperialism of Victorian writing and the anti-imperialism of so much twenty-first-century writing. In part, the complexity of the period results from a rift that existed between the retrograde views of "the Caucasian fictional world," as Dominic Head terms the literary mainstream, and the progressive ideologies of diasporic authors from the Global South (18). The latter participated in a history of oppositional writing that stretched back to such nonfiction authors as Ignatius Sancho, Olaudah Equiano, and Mary Prince in the eighteenth and nineteenth centuries and that helped to produce the "internationalization" of British literary culture after 1945, a shift that Bruce King considers to be as significant as those of Romanticism and modernism (1). For the "Caucasian" mainstream, conversely, there was a profound ambivalence about the advent of postimperial nationhood. Despite the enduring influence of interwar modernism, which had included a current of anti-imperial sentiment, the majority of Cold War writers struggled to accept the realities and implications of decolonization, particularly those who had lived and worked in the Global South. If most diasporic writing of the period exists within the general category of postcolonial literature, the mainstream is an early stage in what could be called postimperial fiction, a stage taking place in the final stages of empire that is starting to realize the redundancy of imperial ideologies without managing to take a position beyond them. The current is particularly important to examine as its approach to the imperial theme has received far less attention than that of diasporic authors. Elleke Boehmer captures this critical oversight when noting the "occlusion of empire from discussion of the ethnically defined 'Anglo-British' novel, as against the overriding preoccupation with empire and its cognate issues in postcolonial [...] writing" (240). The aim of the following essay is to sketch out some of the general patterns in both literary categories, bearing in mind Graham MacPhee's argument "that all British literature needs to be read with a consciousness of the continuing relevance of the imperial legacy" (3). It is also a contention of the essay that diasporic authors, despite offering the most cogent and insightful commentaries on Britain and the wider world, were almost entirely unheeded by nondiasporic contemporaries.

## The 1940s and 1950s

In the late 1940s and 1950s, literary engagement with empire was dominated by novels that repeated the key tropes of Victorian adventure fiction. Rather than acknowledge the decolonization taking place in South Asia and the Middle East, Gerald Hanley's *Monsoon Victory* (1946), Paul Scott's *Johnnie Sahib* (1952), and John Masters's *The Lotus and the Wind* (1953) returned to earlier periods of history, concealing the real-world loss of imperial agency behind the imagined agency of imperial characters. At the same time, a crude dichotomy was maintained between the courage and decency of imperial overlords and the barbarism of colonized populations, commonly dismissed as "strangers from another planet," "useless, corruptible masses," and "[s]tupid cow-like crowds" (Unwin 16; Bates, *Purple* 49; Bates, *Scarlet* 16). Such discourse was repeated in novels with contemporary colonial settings, particularly those where British rule was weakening. The sense of vulnerability caused by Japan's military successes in the Far

East during the Second World War did not lessen after 1945 but resurfaced in the Palestine of Olivia Manning's *School for Love* (1951), the East Africa of Simon Raven's *The Feathers of Death* (1959), and the Malaya of Mary McMinnies's *The Flying Fox* (1956) and Anthony Burgess's *The Malayan Trilogy* (1956–59). Typically, the literary response to Indigenous dissent was vehement: Cypriots are "the scum of the earth," East Africa is marked by "savagery and violence," and Kenyans are "the laziest bunch in the whole of Africa" (Raven, *Judas* 19; Kaye 31; Mackenzie 76). The fact that support for empire continued into the 1960s and 1970s is evidenced in the work of Paul Scott, whose *The Raj Quartet* (1966–75) treated British India with nostalgia and later contributed – in a fourteen-part television adaptation – to the "Raj revival" that Salman Rushdie located in screen culture of the 1980s.[4] An imperialist to the last, Scott's valedictory *Staying On* (1977) even had Indians themselves "regrett[ing] the passing of the days of the *raj*" (30).

One of the major reasons for the persistence of imperial nostalgia was the Suez Crisis of 1956. Here, the nationalization of the Suez Canal Company by the Egyptian president, Gamal Abdul Nasser, threatened British interests in the Middle East and led to a full-scale invasion by Britain, France, and Israel. The US, fearful that events would aggravate nationalist tendencies elsewhere in the region, sought a United Nations (UN) resolution for a ceasefire and forced a withdrawal of the invading armies by the threat of sanctions. There were few commentators who didn't take the humiliation of Suez to be "Britain's imperial endgame" (Rylance 137). The wave of anti-Egyptian sentiment that appeared in British political life, typified by Anthony Eden's view "that Colonel Nasser was another Hitler," was mirrored in British fiction, which obsessed about Egypt from Evelyn Waugh's *The Ordeal of Gilbert Pinfold* (1957) to John Fowles's *Daniel Martin* (1977), and Olivia Manning's *The Battle Lost and Won* (1978) (Marwick 101). Literary novels and thrillers alike were flooded with Orientalist clichés about "criminal misgovernment," "authoritarian gangsters," and "Muslim gun-lovers," as well as about "tottering backward-looking feudalisms" that apparently made Egypt "'the Communist's dream'" (Durrell, *Constance* 10; Thomas 237; Newby, *Picnic* 229; Durrell, *Mountolive* 94; Enright 21). The scale of resentment was best illustrated by P. H. Newby's award-winning *Something to Answer For* (1968). Set shortly after Nasser's nationalization of the Canal Zone, the novel follows the misadventures of James Townrow, a financial advisor and former soldier, who travels to Port Said to sort out the affairs of an English widow and is immediately endangered by the new regime. Not only is he mysteriously attacked upon arrival but the widow suspects that the government has murdered her husband in an attempt to sequester his capital, a symbol of corrupt authorities that want "'everything that's British, French or Jewish in their pockets'" (68). The economic opportunism of the new elite is only one facet of this "stinking country" and its "'crazy, treacherous people'" (130, 132). Equally significant is the nationalist fervor displayed in aggressive political rallies and heightened antagonism toward British and Jewish communities, culminating in Townrow being detained under suspicion of espionage. While the Anglo-French invasion offers hope of a return to imperial control, Britain's capitulation to the UN ceasefire is confirmation of Nasser's victory: "'I'm ashamed of being British,'" the widow exclaims: "'Why start an invasion if you don't mean to go through with it?'" (260). The novel's receipt of the inaugural Booker Prize in 1969 was an indication of both the popularity of Newby's views and the continued imperialism of British literary institutions.

As continual as imperial sentiment was in the period, it was rarely expressed with the confidence of a Haggard, Henty, or Kipling. By the 1950s, the sheer scale of anti-British feeling charted in Gerald Hanley's *The Consul at Sunset* (1951), John Masters's *Bhowani Junction* (1954), and David Unwin's *The Governor's Wife* (1954) seemed a tacit acceptance that the empire had entered its terminal years. More significantly, novels were emerging that characterized late imperial elites less by the self-sacrificing heroism of Victorian protagonists than by vice, pettiness, and enervation. Amongst the attributes of the imperial psyche explored in Hanley's *The Consul at Sunset* are even doubts about the value of British rule: "The sun was never allowed to set on the Union Jack," one of the characters thinks, "[b]ut it had begun to set in the hearts of those who saluted it" (254). Nonetheless, such novels failed to allow for any genuine alternative. The literary treatment of imperial identity in an age of decolonization may have raised questions about British notions of superiority but repeated the age-old tendency to reduce a colonized population to a backdrop, denied narrative relevance. An example is the fictional territory described in Muriel Spark's *Robinson* (1958). Here, a plane carrying a group of European travelers in the mid 1950s crashes on a small, remote island which, while located somewhere in the North Atlantic, conjures up the exotic landscapes of Defoe's *Robinson Crusoe* (1719) and Ballantyne's *The Coral Island* (1857), associating the characters' experiences with those of early explorers. While the steady decline in their moral character inverts the standard imperial narrative, the absence of an Indigenous population precludes discussion of the complex transformation of imperial–colonial relations taking place in the period (which included the independence of Sudan, Ghana, and Malaysia in the years before the book's publication and of large swathes of Africa, East Asia, and the Caribbean in the following decade). The same obfuscation appeared in Graham Greene's *The Heart of the Matter* (1949), Angus Wilson's "Union Reunion" (1949), and William Golding's *Lord of the Flies* (1954), with the first concealing its West African setting to such an extent that George Orwell was led to complain that "the whole thing might as well be happening in a London suburb" ("Review" 498). As such, the texts perfectly illustrate what Paul Gilroy terms "postimperial melancholia": That is, the "inability even to face, never mind actually mourn, the profound change in circumstances and moods that followed the end of the Empire and consequent loss of imperial prestige" (98).

## Mainstream Fiction

A similar inability was evident in mainstream literature set in the metropolis, a strand of writing that is as essential for understanding early postimperial fiction as the colonial tales of Spark and Newby. However distanced it seemed from colonial locations, such writing insisted on the continuing relevance of the empire through accounts of its all-pervasive influence on the culture and society of the homeland and through the unbridled enthusiasm with which that influence is described. Examples extend from the minutiae of dress codes, interior furnishings, reading materials, and advertisements to aspects of public space, such as hospital wards named "Clive of India," streets named "Kabul Avenue," and houses named "Mefeking, Ladysmith, Pretoria, Omdurman" (Berger, *Foot* 9; McEwan 26; Hartley 266). In terms of narrative event, the steady loss of colonies around the world does not stop characters attending political meetings about Nyasaland, giving broadcasts on the BBC's West African service, teaching schoolchildren the history of the empire, and recalling military service in Kenya or India (Amis 177; Frayn, *Towards* 9; Storey 154; Waugh, *Men at Arms* 128–9; Mitford 277). Nor does it prevent glowing allusions to the "benevolent paternalism" and "unflinching devotion to duty" that make up "[t]he spirit of the empire-builders" (Lively, *Oleander* 13; Durrell, *Constance* 16; Taylor 96). Such features not only typified the literary culture of the early Cold War but continued into the 1970s and 1980s, when characters were still recalling imperial service and still traveling to (former) colonies in search of adventure or opportunity. In Margaret Drabble's *The Middle Ground* (1980), for example, an account of an anthropologist who is taken prisoner by Kurdish separatists while conducting research in Iraq shows the kind of narrative interest that former British territories had to offer (173). Crucially, the foregrounding of British activity in the "Third World" ran alongside a refusal to acknowledge the increasingly multicultural nature of British society. Between 1948 and 1958, the reconstruction drive that followed the Second World War was assisted by labor from (post)colonial countries, including some 125,000 people from the Caribbean and 55,000 from India and Pakistan, many of whom worked in transport, industry, hospitality, and the health service. Nonetheless, apart from occasional, fleeting references to a "black street-sweeper" or "West Indian conductor," the migrant presence was largely denied in mainstream writing, as were the later waves of refugees from Cold War crisis in Uganda, Kenya, Vietnam, Chile, and Iran, which, by the late 1980s, had increased the number of postcolonial migrants to some 4.5 percent of the UK population (Frayn, *Sweet* 14; Lively, *According* 58).[5]

On occasion, the resistance to demographic change led to overtly racist portrayals of migrant communities, typically evoking a metropolitan center in territorial competition with the peripheries. As Wendy Webster has argued, the anxieties about ownership recreated labor migration as "a Colonial problem with a difference," one evidenced by a "convergence of the language of white settler communities [...] and white opponents of immigration in the metropolis, as both identified themselves as beleaguered, vulnerable and embattled" (160, 152). Accordingly, one finds complaints about how migrants in a West Riding town are making it impossible "for a professional man to live in the district," about a neighborhood in Birmingham turning into "a twilight area with a severe problem of immigrant overcrowding," and about "those ethnically indefinable races which colonise Soho and interbreed there" (Braine 117; Bradbury 39–40; Powell 33). The imagined battle for territory was even more explicit in science fiction, a genre long associated with imperial ideologies. For John Rieder, the proliferation of tales of intergalactic conquest in the late nineteenth century was linked to the completion of European global conquest: "Having no place on Earth left for the radical exoticism of unexplored territory," Rieder states, authors needed to "invent places elsewhere" (4). Although novels of space exploration continued during the Cold War, the retreat of empire also produced more pessimistic strands of science fiction, as seen in the numerous accounts of alien incursion. Even more pertinently, John Christopher's *The World in Winter* (1962), J. G. Ballard's *The Drowned World* (1962), Christopher Priest's *Fugue for a Darkening Island* (1972), and Anthony Burgess's *1985* (1978) represented a new form of invasion fiction in which Britain is taken over by formerly subjugated populations, a sort of narrative of "reverse colonization" (Luckhurst 131). Margot Bennett's *The Long Way Back* (1954) expands on the theme by envisaging the loss of the entire system of global capitalism. After a nuclear calamity wipes out much of the northern hemisphere, the center of the "'civilised world'" shifts to Africa and gradually develops into a Huxleyan anti-utopia of mechanical labor and state-organized leisure

(27). After some centuries have passed, a group of Kenyan scientists is sent to Britain to seek new sources of wealth, aiming to "'fire the heart of the nation'" with news of great discoveries, particularly a golden city that is reputed to exist in the interior (26). What they find, however, is an entirely forested land plagued by packs of mutated animals and inhabited by tribes of "'savage Britons'" engaging in barbarous rites (73). As the Kenyans discover, the mythical golden city is little more than a scattering of broken stones, the only sign of a people that had once "'conquered the world'" but now has "no civilisation to destroy" (172). For Bennett, a supporter of the Campaign for Nuclear Disarmament, there is no greater illustration of the idiocy of ultimate weapons than the possibility of African supremacy.[6]

## Oppositional Writing

The racist imaginings of mainstream fiction were in stark contrast to the work that emerged from the Windrush generation, a collective term for the hundreds of thousands of people who arrived in Britain from the (former) colonies between the late 1940s and early 1970s. As part of the postwar recruitment drive, the Labour government passed the Nationality Act in 1948, which aimed to offset labor shortages by giving full right of entry and citizenship to all subjects of the British Empire and which helps to explain why so many migrants "felt themselves to be British and had high expectations of their reception, treatment and future in the 'mother country'" (Layton-Henry 9). The new arrivals included future writers who took up permanent or short-term residency, amongst them Wilson Harris (British Guiana), George Lamming (Barbados), V. S. Naipaul (Trinidad), Buchi Emecheta (Nigeria), Tayeb Salih (Sudan), Lauretta Ngcobo (South Africa), Roy Heath (British Guiana), Wole Soyinka (Nigeria), Ngũgĩ wa Thiong'o (Kenya), Kamala Markandaya (India), and Zulfikar Ghose (Pakistan). The creative output of those who arrived between 1952 and 1967 – which included the publication of 137 novels, as well as poems, plays, and short stories – was assisted by the creation of various support networks (James 35). Alongside journals such as the *West Indian Gazette* and publishing houses such as Bogle-L'Ouverture, New Beacon Press, and Allison and Busby were the Caribbean Artists Movement, set up by Kamau Brathwaite, Jonathan La Rose, and Andrew Salkey, and the BBC's *Caribbean Voices*, which received contributions by V. S. Naipaul, Edgar Mittelholzer, Una Marson, Sam Selvon, and John Figueroa. Crucially, the Windrush writers introduced into national culture alternative viewpoints onto a range of global events, from the struggles of anti-imperial nationalism to the ravages of superpower expansionism and European imperialism. For Beryl

Gilroy, who arrived from British Guiana in 1951, the opposition to empire was a key feature of diasporic intellectual life: "The world of the young Commonwealth immigrant of the early fifties was full of political talk," she later wrote: "The federation of the Rhodesias, the independence of the Gold Coast, and British exploitation of the Colonies were burned into our throats. We were all going to put this world to rights in five or six moves" (*Black Teacher* 103).[7]

In the 1950s and 1960s, much of the oppositionalism was directed at the discriminatory attitudes of the majority population. Despite the liberal terms of the Nationality Act, migrants were experiencing verbal and physical abuse in cities across the country, including full-scale "race riots" in Nottingham and Notting Hill and a "color bar" in pubs, lodging houses, and workplaces. Blaming the violence on migrants themselves, right-wing newspapers and politicians pushed for restrictions on new arrivals, even recommending a system of racial segregation similar to that of South Africa (Panayi 229). While the campaign achieved a measure of success in the work permit system introduced by the Commonwealth Immigrants Act (1962), the right wing continued to press for an end to immigration and for wide-scale repatriation, most notoriously in the vision of "unparalleled invasion" and the "transformation of whole areas into alien territory" contained in Enoch Powell's "Rivers of Blood" speech (qtd. in Layton-Henry 139). The outcome was the second Commonwealth Immigrants Act of 1968 and the Immigration Act of 1971, which, by limiting the right of residency to migrants who had had a grandparent born in the UK, effectively ended the automatic right of citizenship that defined the Windrush generation. Inevitably, the antagonism expressed in political discourse worked to exacerbate public prejudice, as charted in Lamming's *The Emigrants* (1954), Selvon's *The Lonely Londoners* (1956), Naipaul's *The Mimic Men* (1967), and Emecheta's *Second-Class Citizen* (1974). In Selvon's work, the discriminatory tenor of official rhetoric was addressed directly through scathing references to "'that fellar Enok Power'" and to the way "he make things rough for black people" (Selvon, *Plains* 14; Selvon, *Moses* 145). Similarly, Salkey's *Escape to an Autumn Pavement* (1960) condemns the circulation of racist pamphlets which assert that the nation's "'greatest treasure has been its native stock, its Anglo-Saxon blood,'" and that the result of "'the Coloured invasion is miscegenation and the debasement of our race'" (110, 121). As the novel's protagonist points out, the prejudice is not limited to racist organizations but extends to "'textbooks in schools, advertisements, saying things like "worked like a nigger," documentary films improperly slanted, B.B.C. features and plays, West End plays, novels, the bloody lot!'" (62). Given the extent of these exclusionary practices, it is unsurprising that many writers' careers would be damaged. As Sandra Courtman relates, almost no Black Caribbean women had works published in the UK before the late 1970s, with even Beryl Gilroy, a hugely significant figure in British culture, education and community work, having a novel and memoir turned down by publishers (52–3).

An author who managed to evade much of the period's intolerance was the Indian-born Attia Hosain. After moving to Britain during the Partition of 1947, Hosain combined work as a broadcaster on the BBC Eastern Service with the publication of *Phoenix Fled* (1953) and *Sunlight on a Broken Column* (1961), the latter addressing the national and personal traumas caused by the violent breakup of British India. The issue is further explored in "No New Lands, No New Seas," a fragment of an unfinished novel written in the 1960s and published posthumously in 2013. This deals with the exile of two British-Indian friends – Murad and Isa – who were displaced in 1947 and have struggled to achieve a sense of belonging during their ten years in London. While content to leave behind them "the constraint of custom," their lingering attachment to Indian culture and society, combined with distaste for the individualism of British life, still suggests that home lies elsewhere (Hosain, "No Land" 33). For Murad, the feeling is aggravated after Isa is killed in a racist attack at a London nightspot. Not only does he lose his primary companion in London but he also assumes that Isa's widow Aziza – a Muslim woman who gained little fulfillment in her arranged marriage – will return to her family in India or Pakistan: "He could see her as a real person only if he placed her in her own setting," we are told, "and not, as now, incongruous […] among the uncaring Molls and Megs and Harrys and Smiths and Jones" (39, 40). Yet Aziza has an entirely different future in mind. Rejecting Murad's traditionalist attitudes, she considers Britain to be the most suitable place to bring up her children and has already organized child allowance and secured a steady source of income from renting out rooms. The fact that "she was planning her life in this environment from which he was fleeing" leads Murad to question further whether his yearning for India is merely "the blurred vision of nostalgia," a false attachment that stems from "an exaggerated assumption of personal and national identity" (45, 32, 32). In dramatizing the liminality of its central character, the text shows the suffering that public prejudice was causing (post)colonial migrants while simultaneously asserting their right of residency. As C. L. Innes relates, Hosain and her contemporaries forged a significant change in diasporic literature: Whereas previous work had "primarily addressed a white British audience," the work of the 1950s and 1960s not only "spoke of and to a black and south Asia community" but also aimed "to *create* [that] community here and now in Britain" (234).

## The 1970s and 1980s

Such themes remained central to the writing in the 1970s and 1980s, when established authors were continuing to publish and a new generation was coming of age. Among the latter were Amon Saba Saakana (Trinidad), Ben Okri (Nigeria), Farrukh Dhondy (India), Dambudzo Marechera (Rhodesia), Barbara Burford (Jamaica), and Salman Rushdie (India), as well as Grace Nichols, David Dabydeen, Pauline Melville, and Mike Phillips from British Guiana. As with the earlier generation, their success was often due to the development of local or nationwide support networks. These included the publishing company Karnak House, the magazines *Wasafiri*, *Echo*, and *Artrage*, and organizations such as the Black Writers' Workshop and the Asian Women Writers' Collective, the latter involving Ravinder Randhawa, Rukhsana Ahmad, and Leena Dhingra. While authors occasionally returned to the experiences of the Windrush generation, as seen in Joan Riley's *Waiting in the Twilight* (1987) and Caryl Phillips's *The Final Passage* (1985), they tended to focus on more contemporary issues, particularly the latest manifestations of racist and ethnic prejudice. During the economic recession of the 1970s, a new wave of violence was not only being incited by right-wing parties like the National Front and the British Movement but also appearing in the low-tolerance policing directed at ethnic minorities in many of the larger cities. Again, the prejudices of the public were partly encouraged by those of politicians, typified by Margaret Thatcher's claim, in the lead-up to the 1979 election, that Britain was "swamped by people with a different culture" (qtd. in Goodfellow 87). In response, Wilson Katiyo's *Going to Heaven* (1979), David Simon's *Railton Blues* (1983), Ravinder Randhawa's "Sunni" (1987), Amon Saba Saakana's *Blues Dance* (1985), and Abdulrazak Gurnah's *Pilgrim's Way* (1988) detailed the afflictions caused by institutional and interpersonal racism. At the same time, authors were insisting on the social and cultural hybridity that increasingly defined the nation. The point is illustrated by the work of Hanif Kureishi, one of a number of British-born writers with family ties to the Global South, who captured his own mixed heritage in the first-person narrator's famous statement in *The Buddha of Suburbia* (1990): "I am an Englishman born and bred, almost. I am often considered to be a funny kind of Englishman, a new breed as it were, having emerged from two old histories" (3).[8] The transnational flow of cultures, languages, histories, and identities was also dramatized stylistically. This appeared in the textual inclusion of mixed locations, such as the British and Indian settings of Rushdie's *The Satanic Verses* (1988), and in the usage of mixed cultural forms, previously seen in the Caribbean calypso of Selvon's "Calypso in London" (1957) and the

Arabic *mu'aradah* of Salih's *Mawsim al-Hijrah ilâ al-Shimâl* (*Season of Migration to the North*, 1966). As John McLeod asserts, this was a strand of literature determined to "re-conceptualiz[e] the creation of British culture, if not British nationhood, in transnational terms" (103).

Alongside its more inclusivist understanding of Britishness, diasporic writing continued to challenge dominant assumptions about the benefits of British involvement in the Global South. Examples are the depictions of neocolonialism in Emecheta's *The Rape of Shavi* (1983), in which British characters retain the power to exploit resources in Africa, and the accounts of poverty in Gilroy's *Frangipani House* (1986), in which the hardships of life in South America show how little has been gained from the empire and Commonwealth. Amongst the novels dealing with historic violence and subjugation were Lamming's *Natives of My Person* (1972), Nichols's *Whole of a Morning Sky* (1986), and Phillips's *Higher Ground* (1989), each condemning "the years of slavery and gruesome tortures" and "[t]he bloody excesses of colonialism" (Selvon, *Moses*, 91; Phillips, *European*, 54). In *Whole of a Morning Sky*, Nichols returns to the British Guiana of the early 1960s and charts the ongoing effects of a 150-year-old plantation economy, one initially based on slave labor and latterly dominated by the exploitative practices of Booker Brothers & Co. (a trading company that would go on to establish the Booker Prize for Fiction).[9] The lives of common people, who struggle to make a living from small-scale farming or trade, are in clear contrast to those of "'expatriates [who] have built their empires on sugar and tea'" and who frequent "'exclusive clubs [and] swimming pools'" (79). For the schoolteacher Archie Walcott, employment in the British education system has brought a measure of personal security but also an awareness of the hardships of others, as displayed by the "tumbledown buildings and [...] teeming humanity" of the Georgetown slums (41). The country's move toward independence, however, fails to bring any optimism. On the one hand, Guyanese politics are dominated by the National Labour Party, a lightly fictionalized version of Cheddi Jagan's People's Progressive Party, whose Marxist leanings threaten a Soviet takeover: For the country "[t]o cut itself off from the apron strings of the British," Archie supposes, "was to leave the way open for the Russians to walk in" (35). On the other hand, the colonial authorities are attempting to manage decolonization in a way that secures British Guiana for the "free world." This is seen most clearly when British troops are brought into the capital to retain order during a general strike, although also seen in the way that local government is starved of funds by the Colonial Office and placed under CIA surveillance. Despite the diminished power of British officials in the 1960s, one character is adamant that "'the American government, in its anti-Soviet campaign and anti-Cuba propaganda, will stop at nothing to help them'" (73). Yet *Whole of a Morning Sky* is not entirely without hope. Illustrating the significance of stylistic choices in diasporic writing, the way that the cadence, grammar, and diction of Guyanese Creole is drawn into the text, particularly such native words and phrases as "jumbies," "proud-proud," "shave-ice," and "logie-shacks," evokes the nation as an enduring entity that is influenced by, but also autonomous of, outside forces (6, 10, 53, 79).

Given the power of diasporic writing during the latter half of the twentieth century, its failure to impact on the styles and attitudes of mainstream fiction is one of the most notable features of the period. A strand of anti-imperialism certainly appeared in the latter, running through the work of George Orwell, Colin MacInnes, Barry Unsworth, and Jonathan Coe and achieving particular intensity in the writings of Doris Lessing and Jean Rhys, whose status both as canonized British writers and as disruptive voices from the colonial peripheries shows how the mainstream is never a fully stable category. Yet the vast majority of authors were still failing to question dominant attitudes at the end of the 1980s.[10] In a piece of autobiographical writing from the 1990s, Penelope Lively wonders whether her childhood fondness for H. E. Marshall's *Our Island Story* (1905), with its "glossy romantic pictures of national heroes," has deposited within her "some unreconstructed layer which believes pink is best and that it has been uphill all the way from brave Boadicea to good Lord Kitchener" (Lively, *Oleander* 18–19, 19). It is a remarkable admission when considering the empire's involvement in exploitation and genocide. Elsewhere, Lively's uncertainty was exchanged for a forthright denigration of the Global South, a feature seen in popular thrillers such as Frederick Forsyth's *The Dogs of War* (1974), Denis Pitts's *The Predator* (1977), and Denis Cleary and Frank J. Maher's *Sahara Strike* (1980), and in literary works such as Bruce Chatwin's *The Viceroy of Ouidah* (1980), William Boyd's *A Good Man in Africa* (1981), J. G. Ballard's *The Day of Creation* (1987), and Julian Barnes's "The Visitors" (1989). There also remained a disregard for diasporic communities and their transformative influence on British culture. Indeed, the claim made by one of John Wain's characters – that "'the thing to be nowadays, if you want fat grants and subsidized publication, is a playwright from Marrakesh or a novelist from Barbados or a poet from the Seychelles'" – only acknowledges diasporic communities in order to condemn their search for cultural equality (208). Such patterns of representation have had a predictable effect on contemporary attitudes. Priya Satia, speaking of a 2016 survey that found that 43 percent of British people still retained a belief in empire, is convinced of how "redemptive myths about colonial upliftment persistently mask the empire's abysmal history of looting and pillage, policy-driven famines, brutal crushing of rebellion, torture, concentration camps, aerial policing, and everyday racism and humiliation" (4). There is no doubt that mainstream fiction, in conjunction with British educational institutions and publishing houses, helped to conceal the iniquities of empire for the length of the Cold War.[11]

## Notes

1. As John Lewis Gaddis points out, the fact that "colonialism was ending as the Cold War was intensifying" was understood by the superpowers, who knew that "the choices newly independent states made could yet tip the balance of power" (123).
2. In the 1950s, Leopold Amery, a former Secretary of State for the Colonies, repeated the optimism of Bevin and Churchill when suggesting that the Commonwealth "may yet become the nucleus around which a future world order will crystallize" (qtd. in Porter 344).
3. As Stuart Ward points out, "[t]here remains a firmly entrenched assumption that the broad cultural impact of decolonisation was confined to the colonial periphery, with little relevance to post-war British culture" (1).
4. The revival mainly appeared in film and television and, as Rushdie details, involved a "refurbishment of the Empire's tarnished image" and a "recrudescence of imperialist ideology" ("Outside," 91, 92).
5. As A. Robert Lee comments, the literary mainstream "rarely [...] tackled multicultural Britain with any degree of appetite," preferring instead to restrict the fictional landscape to "white middle-England" (74).
6. The novel offers support for critics such as David Pringle and W. Warren Wagar, who associate the mass catastrophes depicted in dystopian fiction with "Britain's decline as a world power throughout the twentieth century" and with "British feelings of impotence over the loss of Empire" (in Ruddick 99–100).
7. Such political radicalism was not new to the 1950s but had been present for decades. The temporary British resident Roger Mais, for example, was jailed in Jamaica in 1944 for his fulmination against Britain's imperial motives during the Second World War: "what we are fighting for," he proclaimed, "is that England [sic] might retain her exclusive prerogative to the conquest and enslavement of other nations" and that "the sun may never set upon aggression and inequality and human degradation" (2).
8. Amongst the writers who began publishing fiction, drama and poetry in the 1980s were the British-Jamaican Norman Samuda Smith, the British-Indian Meera Syal, the British-Sudanese Jamal Mahjoub, and the British-Guyanese Fred d'Aguiar.
9. John Berger, after winning the Booker Prize for the novel G. (1972), donated half of his prize money to the British Black Panthers in protest at Booker's involvement in the Caribbean (Sperling 139–41).
10. For example, see Orwell's *Nineteen Eighty-Four* (1949), MacInnes's *Absolute Beginners* (1959), Unsworth's *Sugar and Rum* (1988), Coe's *A Touch of Love* (1989), Lessing's *The Grass Is Singing* (1950), and Rhys's *Wide Sargasso Sea* (1966).

11. The big publishing houses were still failing to support diasporic writing at the turn of the twenty-first century. Writing in 2000, James Procter noted that of the wave of fiction that appeared in the twenty years after the docking of the SS *Empire Windrush*, only Selvon's *The London Londoners* was still in print (9).

## Works Cited

Amis, Kingsley. *Take a Girl Like You*. Victor Gollancz, 1960.
Aslam, Nadeem. *The Wasted Vigil*. 2008. New ed., Faber and Faber, 2009.
Ballantyne, R. M. *The Coral Island: A Tale of the Pacific Ocean*. 1857. New ed., T. Nelson and Sons, 1901.
Ballard, J. G. *The Day of Creation*. 1987. New ed., Grafton Books, 1988.
—. *The Drowned World*. 1962. New ed., Penguin, 1965.
Barnes, Julian. "The Visitors." *A History of the World in 10½ Chapters*. 1989. New ed., Picador, 1990, pp. 31–58.
Bates, H. E. *The Purple Plain*. 1947. New ed., Penguin, 1956.
—. *The Scarlet Sword*. 1950. New ed., Penguin, 1958.
Bennett, Margot. *The Long Way Back*. The Bodley Head, 1954.
Berger, John. *The Foot of Clive*. 1962. New ed., Penguin, 1970.
—. *G*. 1972. New ed., Penguin, 1973.
Boehmer, Elleke. "Afterword: The English Novel and the World." *End of Empire and the English Novel since 1945*, edited by Rachael Gilmour and Bill Schwarz, Manchester UP, 2011, pp. 238–43.
Boyd, William. *A Good Man in Africa*. 1981. New ed., Penguin, 1982.
Bradbury, Malcolm. "Who Do You Think You Are?" *Who Do You Think You Are? Stories and Parodies*. 1976. New ed., Arrow Books, 1979, pp. 37–53.
Braine, John. *The Jealous God*. Eyre & Spottiswoode, 1964.
Burgess, Anthony. *1985*. 1978. New ed., Arrow Books, 1980.
—. *The Malayan Trilogy: Time for a Tiger; The Enemy in the Blanket; Beds in the East*. 1956, 1958, 1959. New ed., Penguin, 1972.
Chatwin, Bruce. *The Viceroy of Ouidah*. 1980. New ed., Picador, 1982.
Christopher, John. *The World in Winter*. 1962. New ed., Penguin, 2016.
Cleary, Denis, and Frank J. Maher. *Sahara Strike*. 1980. New ed., Severn House, 1981.
Coe, Jonathan. *A Touch of Love*. 1989. New ed., Sceptre, 1990.
Courtman, Sandra. "Not Good Enough or Not Man Enough? Beryl Gilroy as the Anomaly in the Evolving 'Black British Canon.'" *A Black British Canon?* edited by Gail Low and Marion Wynne-Davies, Palgrave Macmillan, 2006, pp. 50–73.
Defoe, Daniel. *The Life and Adventures of Robinson Crusoe*. 1719. New ed., Penguin, 1985.
Drabble, Margaret. *The Middle Ground*. 1980. New ed., Penguin, 1981.
Durrell, Lawrence. *Constance: Or Solitary Practices*. 1982. New ed., Faber and Faber, 1983.
—. *Mountolive*. 1958. New ed., Faber and Faber, 1963.
Emecheta, Buchi. *The Rape of Shavi*. Ogwugwu Afor, 1983.
—. *Second-Class Citizen*. 1974. New ed., Heinemann, 2004.
Enright, D. J. *Academic Year*. 1955. New ed., Oxford UP, 1985.

Forsyth, Frederick. *The Dogs of War*. 1974. New ed., New American Library, 2012.
Fowles, John. *Daniel Martin*. 1977. New ed., Triad/Panther, 1978.
Frayn, Michael. *Sweet Dreams*. 1973. New ed., Penguin, 1976.
   *Towards the End of the Morning*. 1967. New ed., Flamingo, 1985.
Gaddis, John Lewis. *The Cold War*. 2005. New ed., Penguin, 2007.
Gilroy, Beryl. *Black Teacher*. Cassell, 1976.
   *Frangipani House*. Heinemann International, 1986.
Gilroy, Paul. *After Empire: Melancholia or Convivial Culture?* Routledge, 2004.
Golding, William. *Lord of the Flies*. 1954. New ed., Faber and Faber, 1958.
Goodfellow, Maya. *Hostile Environment: How Immigrants became Scapegoats*. 2019. New ed., Verso, 2020.
Green, Martin. *Dreams of Adventure, Deeds of Empire*. Basic Books, 1979.
Greene, Graham. *The Heart of the Matter*. 1949. New ed., The Reprint Society, 1950.
Gurnah, Abdulrazak. *By the Sea*. 2001. New ed., Bloomsbury, 2002.
   *Pilgrim's Way*. Jonathan Cape, 1988.
Hanley, Gerald. *The Consul at Sunset*. 1951. New ed., The Reprint Society, 1952.
   *Monsoon Victory*. Collins, 1946.
Hartley, L. P. *Eustace and Hilda*. 1952. New ed., Faber and Faber, 1965.
Head, Dominic. *The Cambridge Introduction to Modern British Fiction, 1950–2000*. Cambridge UP, 2002.
Hopkins, A. G. *American Empire: A Global History*. 2018. New ed., Princeton UP, 2019.
Hosain, Attia. "No New Lands, No New Seas." *Distant Traveller: New and Selected Fiction*, edited by Aamer Hussein and Shama Habibullah, Women Unlimited, 2013, pp. 28–71.
   *Phoenix Fled and Other Stories*. 1953. New ed., Virago, 1988.
   *Sunlight on a Broken Column*. Chatto & Windus, 1961.
Innes, C. L. *A History of Black and Asian Writing in Britain*. 2002. New ed., Cambridge UP, 2008.
James, Louis. "The Disturbing Vision of George Lamming." *Other Britain, Other British: Contemporary Multicultural Fiction*, edited by A. Robert Lee, Pluto P, 1995, pp. 35–47.
Kanet, Roger E. "The Superpower Quest for Empire: The Cold War and Soviet Support for 'Wars of National Liberation.'" *Cold War History*, vol. 6, no. 3, 2006, pp. 331–52.
Katiyo, Wilson. *Going to Heaven*. 1979. New ed., Harlow, 1982.
Kaye, M. M. *Death in Kenya*. 1958. New ed., Penguin, 1984.
King, Bruce. *The Oxford English Literary History. Vol. 13: 1948–2000: The Internationalization of English Literature*. Oxford UP, 2004.
Kureishi, Hanif. *The Buddha of Suburbia*. Faber and Faber, 1990.
Lamming, George. *The Emigrants*. 1954. New ed., Allison & Busby, 1980.
   *Natives of My Person*. 1972. New ed., Allison & Busby, 1986.
Layton-Henry, Zig. *The Politics of Immigration: Immigration, "Race" and "Race" Relations in Post-War Britain*. Blackwell, 1992.
Lee, A. Robert. "Changing the Script: Sex, Lies and Videotapes in Hanif Kureishi, David Dabydeen and Mike Phillips." *Other Britain, Other British: Contemporary Multicultural Fiction*, edited by A. Robert Lee, Pluto P, 1995, pp. 69–89.
Lessing, Doris. *The Grass Is Singing*. 1950. New ed., Penguin, 1961.

Lively, Penelope. *According to Mark.* 1984. New ed., Penguin, 1985.
  *Oleander, Jacaranda: A Childhood Perceived.* 1994. New ed., Penguin, 1995.
Luckhurst, Roger. *Science Fiction.* Polity P, 2005.
MacInnes, Colin. *Absolute Beginners.* 1959. New ed., Penguin, 1964.
Mackenzie, Compton. *Thin Ice.* 1956. New ed., Penguin, 1959.
MacPhee, Graham. *Postwar British Literature and Postcolonial Studies.* Edinburgh UP, 2011.
Mais, Roger. "Now We Know." *Public Opinion,* July 11, 1944, p. 2.
Manning, Olivia. *The Levant Trilogy: Volume One: The Danger Tree; Volume Two: The Battle Lost and Won; Volume Three: The Sum of Things.* 1977, 1978, 1980. New ed., Penguin, 1982.
  *School for Love.* 1951. New ed., Penguin, 1982.
Marshall, H. E. *Our Island Story: A History of England for Boys and Girls.* 1905. New ed., Frederick A. Stokes Company, 1920.
Marwick, Arthur. *British Society since 1945.* 1982. New ed., Penguin, 1996.
Masters, John. *Bhowani Junction.* 1954. New ed., Sphere Books, 1983.
  *The Lotus and the Wind.* 1953. New ed., Penguin, 1956.
May, Alex. *Britain and Europe since 1945.* Longman, 1999.
McEwan, Ian. "Jack Flea's Birthday Celebration." *The Imitation Game: Three Plays for Television.* 1981. New ed., Picador, 1982, pp. 19–42.
McLeod, John. "Fantasy Relationships: Black British Canons in a Transnational World." *A Black British Canon?* edited by Gail Low and Marion Wynne-Davies, Palgrave Macmillan, 2006, pp. 93–104.
McMinnies, Mary. *The Flying Fox.* Collins, 1956.
Mitford, Nancy. *Love in a Cold Climate and Other Novels.* 1945, 1949, 1951. New ed., Penguin, 2000.
Naipaul, V. S. *The Mimic Men.* 1967. New ed., Picador, 2002.
Newby, P. H. *The Picnic at Sakkara.* Jonathan Cape, 1955.
  *Something to Answer For.* Faber and Faber, 1968.
Nichols, Grace. *Whole of a Morning Sky.* Virago, 1986.
Orwell, George. *Nineteen Eighty-Four.* 1949. New ed., Penguin, 1983.
  "Review: The Heart of the Matter by Graham Greene." *The Collected Essays, Journalism and Letters of George Orwell. Vol. 4: In Front of Your Nose 1945–1950,* edited by Sonia Orwell and Ian Angus. 1968. New ed., Penguin, 1970, pp. 497–501.
Panayi, Panikos. *An Immigration History of Britain: Multicultural Racism since 1800.* Longman, 2010.
Penier, Izabella. "*Anglobalisation* and the Making of the Third World: The British Empire in India." *Romanian Journal of English Studies,* vol. 12, no. 1, 2015, pp. 10–21.
Phillips, Caryl. *The European Tribe.* 1987. New ed., Faber and Faber, 1988.
  *The Final Passage.* Faber and Faber, 1985.
  *Higher Ground.* 1989. New ed., Penguin, 1990.
Pitts, Denis. *The Predator.* Robert Hale, 1977.
Porter, Bernard. *The Lion's Share: A Short History of British Imperialism 1850–1995.* 1975. New ed., Longman, 1996.
Powell, Anthony. *Casanova's Chinese Restaurant.* 1960. New ed., Fontana Books, 1970.

Priest, Christopher. *Fugue for a Darkening Island*. 1972. New ed., New English Library, 1973.
Procter, James. "General Introduction: '1948'/'1998': Periodising Postwar Black Britain." *Writing Black Britain 1948–1998: An Interdisciplinary Anthology*, edited by James Procter, Manchester UP, 2000, pp. 1–12.
Randhawa, Ravinder. "Sunni." *Dynamite*. CreateSpace, 2014, pp. 41–54.
Raven, Simon. *The Feathers of Death*. 1959. New ed., Panther Books, 1964.
  *The Judas Boy*. 1968. New ed., Panther Books, 1969.
Rhys, Jean. *Wide Sargasso Sea*. 1966. New ed., Penguin, 1997.
Rieder, John. *Colonialism and the Emergence of Science Fiction*. Wesleyan UP, 2008.
Riley, Joan. *Waiting in the Twilight*. Women's P, 1987.
Ruddick, Nicholas. *Ultimate Island: On the Nature of British Science Fiction*. Greenwood P, 1993.
Rushdie, Salman. "Outside the Whale." *Imaginary Homelands: Essays and Criticism 1981–1991*. 1991. New ed., Granta Books, 1992, pp. 87–101.
  *The Satanic Verses*. 1988. New ed., Vintage Books, 2006.
Rylance, Rick. "1956, Suez and Sloane Square: Empire's Ebb and Flow." *The Edinburgh Companion to Twentieth-Century Literatures in English*, edited by Brian McHale and Randall Stevenson, Edinburgh UP, 2006, pp. 137–49.
Saakana, Amon Saba. *Blues Dance*. Karnak House, 1985.
Said, Edward W. *Culture and Imperialism*. Chatto & Windus, 1993.
Salih, Tayeb. *Season of Migration to the North*. 1966. Translated by Denys Johnson-Davies, Penguin, 2003.
Salkey, Andrew. *Escape to an Autumn Pavement*. Four Square Books, 1960.
Satia, Priya. *Time's Monster: How History Makes History*. Cambridge UP, 2020.
Scott, Paul. *The Day of the Scorpion*. 1968. New ed., Panther Books, 1973.
  *A Division of the Spoils*. 1975. New ed., Panther Books, 1977.
  *The Jewel in the Crown*. 1966. New ed., Panther Books, 1973.
  *Johnnie Sahib*. 1952. New ed., Panther Books, 1979.
  *Staying On*. 1977. New ed., Panther Books, 1978.
  *The Towers of Silence*. 1971. New ed., Panther Books, 1973.
Selvon, Sam. "Calypso in London." *Ways of Sunlight*. 1957. New ed., Longman, 1987, pp. 113–19.
  *The Lonely Londoners*. 1956. New ed., Hodder Education, 1979.
  *Moses Migrating*. Longman, 1983.
  *The Plains of Caroni*. MacGibbon & Kee, 1970.
Simon, David. *Railton Blues*. Bogle-L'Ouverture, 1983.
Spark, Muriel. *Robinson*. 1958. New ed., Penguin, 1964.
Sperling, Joshua. *A Writer of Our Time: The Life and Work of John Berger*. Verso, 2018.
Storey, David. *Flight into Camden*. 1960. New ed., Penguin, 1964.
Taylor, Elizabeth. *Mrs Palfrey at the Claremont*. 1971. New ed., Virago, 1982.
Thomas, Hugh. *The World's Game*. Eyre & Spottiswoode, 1957.
Unwin, David. *The Governor's Wife*. Michael Joseph, 1954.
Unsworth, Barry. *Sugar and Rum*. 1988. New ed., Penguin, 1990.
Wain, John. *A Winter in the Hills*. 1970. New ed., Penguin, 1974.
Ward, Stuart. "Introduction." *British Culture and the End of Empire*, edited by Stuart Ward, Manchester UP, 2001, pp. 1–20.

Washbrook, David. "The Indian Economy and the British Empire." *India and the British Empire*, edited by Douglas M. Peers and Nandini Gooptu, Oxford UP, 2012, pp. 44–74.

Waugh, Evelyn. *Men at Arms*. 1952. New ed., Penguin, 1964.

*The Ordeal of Gilbert Pinfold: A Conversation Piece*. Chapman & Hall, 1957.

Webster, Wendy. *Englishness and Empire 1939–1965*. 2005. New ed., Oxford UP, 2007.

White, Nicholas J. *Decolonisation: The British Experience since 1945*. Longman, 1999.

Wilson, Angus. "Union Reunion." *The Wrong Set and Other Stories*. 1949. New ed., Penguin, 1959, pp. 25–46.

# 19

LISA TOMLINSON

# Beyond the Empire
## Black Caribbean British Writing

### Introduction

Although many Black Caribbean writers continued to work within the empire's literary tradition, they incorporated an African Caribbean writing style and a Black diaspora sensibility to advance their literary activism further. Later generations of Black Caribbean Britons who sought to make their presence felt in British society inherited a unique and diverse literary style. Their themes were no longer concerned with the struggle of belonging or the task of recreating a new Caribbean space in a foreign land. Anticolonial poems, such as those by Linton Kwesi Johnson (LKJ), reflected the narratives of their resistance against British cultural imperialism and institutionalized racism. While the questions of identity and self-determination remained a haunting factor in the literature, the newer generation of writers also departed from the biographical narratives found in the works of postwar Caribbean writers like George Laming and Samuel Selvon, whose writing spoke to a direct experience with the home country (Weedon 46). The new generation tackled different political and social issues and used various genres of fiction and poetry to capture new complexities of the Black experience in Britain.

The first section of this chapter focuses on the legacies and continuities of African Caribbean writing. I discuss the dub poetry of LKJ and consider Black diaspora sensibility, showing how Black writers of Caribbean descent critically analyze the complex nuances of race, gender issues, and sexuality and their use of new literary styles and forms. This chapter also focuses on Jean "Binta" Breeze, Joan Riley, and Andrea Levy, with minor references to other Caribbean British writers.

### The Legacies and Continuities of African Caribbean Writing

"Postcolonial fiction dealing with the experience of migration often focuses on both the place left behind and the new home. In the case of British fiction, both spaces can be islands not only emblematizing centre–periphery relations but also unsettling colonial history" (Vlasta 233). This quotation speaks to how Black Caribbean writers vacillate between two histories, migration and the legacy of colonial identity. The Black British writer's presence in England was met with opposition. Coming to the mother country, many Caribbean immigrants felt a sense of pride and security in the metropolitan center, believing they shared similarities with their British counterparts. Common Christian religious values, speaking a similar language, and a shared indoctrination in British education might have accounted for these expectations. The two cultures shared these commonalities due to the assimilation of colonization. However, there were some noticeable differences that the Caribbean population found challenging to get used to, namely the climate and the high degree of industrialization and urbanization (Heide 80–83). However, these cultural differences were easier to overcome than the discrimination and racism from the white British population. The awakening to the racial rift and the tension within "de homeland" is heard in Una Marson's poem "Nigger." Like her earlier Caribbean countrymen and women, it is only when Marson travels to England for the first time that she experiences a shattered illusion of Britishness and is forced to question her British identity, as revealed in the persona's rage:

> The called me "Nigger,"
> Those little white urchins,
> They laughed and shouted
> As I passed along the street,
> They flung it at me:
> "Nigger! Nigger! Nigger!"
> What made me keep my fingers
> From choking the words in their throats? (Marson 8–9)

The poem captures the culture shock that many Caribbeans experienced in their "mother country" that excluded them from a culture they, in many ways, perceived as their own. Fortunately, many immigrants could attain some level of success as artists and entertainers. Their creative works could provide a buffer and express the pains of integrating into their new home. They created a Black British culture that drew from the migrants' backgrounds and the distinct realities of life in Britain, shaped by their interactions with the country's multicultural environment. This outlet also made them more visible in the British cultural landscape and became one of the primary voices of Black British people who sought to carve out a home in the new host country. Black Caribbean literature, for instance, made its way into the British mainstream through the BBC radio show, *Caribbean Voices*,

## 19 Beyond the Empire

created by Una Marson. The weekly BBC program featured upcoming and established writers and intellectuals from the Caribbean.

Undoubtedly, literature became one of the surest ways to vocalize Black British immigrants' plight and gave the Caribbean community some visibility in the British metropolis. In addition to the personal narratives, it was through the Caribbean writers' literary work that more was learnt about the maladjustment and alienation of many Caribbean people. It did not matter the period in which these writers wrote. Their stories captured the complexities of the Black British experience and the goal to one day call Britain their home while maintaining their African Caribbean roots and identity. Dub poets became one of the main sources to speak against social injustices toward Black British people. They drew on the Indigenous forms of Caribbean aesthetics (i.e., oral tradition, spirituality, and nation language[1]) and adapted them to their new British environment. Dub poets used their diverse art forms to resist racist oppression and give their community visibility.

The most popular of the early dub poets was LKJ, a Jamaican-born activist who migrated to England in his early teens. The racism Black people faced in the Windrush period persisted decades later when Johnson came of age. His poems politicize issues impacting the Black Caribbean population in England. For instance, some of his poems engaged the antagonistic and violent relationship between Black people and the police. "Sonny's Lettah (Anti-sus Poem)" shows continuity with the Jamaican language and remains a critical piece as it protests police brutality in London. The poem best exemplifies the state's violence in the imposition of the "sus" laws and conveys the damage this had on the Black community.[2]

LKJ uses the diasporic literary trope of letter writing to retell the Black immigrant's experience in Britain. However, unlike Una Marson's speaker in "Quashie to London," who comically recounts his journey throughout the metropolitan center (using the literary device of the foodway), Johnson gives an account of the bitter reality of racial violence by the police. The speaker, a young Black man, is writing a letter to his mother from behind bars. He relates a gruesome reenactment of being arrested in a confrontation resulting from his brother's unwarranted arrest:

> Mama,
> I really doan know how fi tell y'u dis,
> cause I did mek a salim pramis [solemn promise]
> fi tek care a lickle Jim
> an' try mi bes' fi look out fi him (Johnson 25)

Sonny, the persona, turns to a narrative about the events that led to the accidental murder of one of the police officers who assaulted his brother.

The rhythmic Jamaican sound alliteration and end rhyme further stress the violent impact of the police's attack on Jim and Sonny's response to the police.

"Inglan is a Bitch," another poem by LKJ, speaks to the feelings of the empire's betrayal and the frustration the Black British population experienced. LKJ's persona embodies the dissatisfied first-generation immigrant who struggles to make a living doing odd jobs. Speaking in the nation language, "the sort of English spoken by the Jamaican-born Black British immigrant" (Volkmann 247), the worker complains about labor exploitation and grumbles about the low pay that does not allow him to make ends meet:

> dem
> have a
> lickle factri up inna Brackly
> inna disya factri all dem ahu is pack crackery
> fi dis laas fifteen years get mi laybah (Johnson 38)

Unlike the characters of the Windrush generation, there is a gradual sense of assimilation into British society wherein the speaker reluctantly realizes that England has become his permanent home. The persona concedes to this thought as he admits: "dere's no escaping it / Inglan is a Bitch / dere's no runnin' whey fram it" (39).

Johnson's poems illustrate the expression of Black British identity through two strands. First, he uses the nation language that distinctly shapes Black British linguistic identity by deviating "from standard or generally accepted forms of English" (Volkmann 247). LKJ, like many of the writers, consciously rejects Standard English to include the functional use of Caribbean Creole to express cultural identity and subvert the power of Standard English (Brathwaite 42–8). In doing so, he reluctantly declares his final resignation to become a part of British society, assuming British "citizenship" in his nativized accent.

The speaker's hesitancy to integrate into the host country echoes similar sentiments in the poem "Wherever I Hang" by British-Guyanese poet Grace Nichols. In Nichols's poem, an expatriate speaker assertively confirms England as "home" despite her occasional homesickness for her "home" country. She confesses in her cadenced Guyanese nation language:

> I get accustomed to de English life
> But I still miss back-home side
> To tell you de truth I don't know really where I belaang
> Yes, divided to de ocean
> Divided to de bone ... (Nichols 169–70)

Johnson's poems also embody the sounds of Jamaican reggae music and dub performance, like the way in which Nichols blends the Guyanese nation language with the pulsating Caribbean Calypso.

Like the postwar writers, LKJ's poems reflect Stuart Hall's notion of "collective identity." Hall defines collective identity as a construct against racism that aims to create a unified identity (146, 200–202). Therefore, the writer's use of the nation language and Caribbean music to shape the poetic structure invokes a strong group identity informed by the persona's shared history of migration and racism. The persona speaks on behalf of the community and helps to create a distinct Black British identity.

## Gendering Dub

In contrast to male-dominated dub poetry, Jean "Binta" Breeze uses the art to intersect race and gender. She addresses the concerns affecting immigrant women who were also experiencing alienation and discrimination albeit less in the form of police brutality. Breeze combines Black diasporic sensibility in her poems, such as jazz, Caribbean cultural traditions, the Jamaican vernacular, and proverbs. In her poem "Atlantic Drift," Breeze highlights the theme of transnational motherhood. The speaker in the poem is miles away from her children, whom she was forced to leave in the Caribbean. She expresses her longing to see and hear them. She laments:

> When I hear
> children's voices
> thrilling through
> my window
> they are not
> water voices
> carried by the trade
> they are here now
> just outside my skin. (37)

The "ice queen" character that Breeze introduces can further be read as London's unbearable cold weather and "the chill of separation and loneliness" (Tomlinson 120) faced by Caribbean immigrant mothers separated from their children.

In "Testament," Jean "Binta" Breeze also engages with the first-generation Caribbean immigrant who still has an attachment to their native country and wishes to return "home." The poem tells the story of a Black Caribbean woman who has labored her entire life under poor working conditions in England while still caring for her children and husband. Breeze also underscores the difficulty faced by second-generation British children who have little to no attachment to their parents' homeland. As the daughter gets older, she is embarrassed by her Caribbean parents – her father, who smells like train oil, and her mother, who keeps her local Jamaican language. The mother, who cannot fully adjust to the cold that "does bad tings to [her] knee," finds comfort in the Caribbean "memories of back home" with "her [we] regular Sunday church/in de back a de local hall" (Breeze, "Testament" 7–11). Like the disgruntled laborer we meet in LKJ's poem, "Inglan is a Bitch," the mother-speaker has no choice but to make England her new home. This outcome is contrary to the mother-speaker's daughter, who is already assimilated into British culture because of her education and socialization. Novelist Caryl Phillips points out that although this generation struggled with racism and discrimination like their parents, they were not allowed to dream of returning home. This generation, Phillips states, "was home in England" (224). He observes that their major challenge was negotiating the question of identity (275). Unlike the earlier speakers who hesitated to embrace England as their home, the second generation asserted their British identity and rejected a marginalized status (275).

## Centering Women and Children Narratives in Black Caribbean British Novels

In the post-dub poet period, Black British writers continued to shed light on the discrimination and marginalization in Britain. By this period, Black British citizens had a better sense of belonging and began to see Britain as their home. Therefore, the work of Black British novelists also took a similar trajectory. However, many of the stories were child-focused and dealt with the challenges of early adulthood. These narratives contrasted with the adult experiences generally depicted in the earlier dub poems of LKJ and Jean "Binta" Breeze. In Joan Riley's novel, *The Unbelonging*, the central character arrives in England from Jamaica at an early age with little memory of Jamaica. The readers, therefore, get a fictional account of young people's challenges adjusting to the hostile British society. The theme centered on a generation of British youths who neither felt at home in England nor in the Caribbean. This is a stark contrast to characters who still have some contact back home, highlighted through the letter-writing technique used to express ties to the place of origin. *The Unbelonging* was also a groundbreaking novel, the first to be published since Jean Rhys's *Voyage in the Dark* highlighting the Caribbean migration from a woman's perspective (Riley 13). Although both stories are about coming of age in a foreign place, the protagonists are separated by time, race, and experience.

## 19 Beyond the Empire

Other women writers from earlier generations also engaged in different subject matters related to Caribbean migration. Beryl Gilroy's work, for example, centered on the "fate of family and friends the emigrants leave behind" (Weiss 305).

Additionally, novelists from this generation began to interrogate the complexity of how young Black British Caribbeans took "from a literary perspective, the Bildungsroman or coming-of-age narrative," which essentially provided "fruitful ground for the analysis of citizenship, belonging, and the relation between the individual and state/community/society" (Beushausen 60). Therefore, since the mid-1980s, the coming-of-age novel, narrated typically from a first-person point of view, became a salient motif in Caribbean women's fiction in the Caribbean and its diaspora (61). This motif served as a coping mechanism "to come to terms with the self, to negotiate identity between at least two cultures perceived as different, the Caribbean countries of origin and new diaspora homes" (61).

Hyacinth, the protagonist in *The Unbelonging*, migrates to England as a young girl. Because of the racism she faced, Hyacinth had difficulties settling into her new "home." The character's failure to adapt to her new environment is compounded by living with an abusive father who sexually abuses her. Therefore, racism is not the only challenge the character must overcome. These challenges further exacerbate Hyacinth's longing to return to Jamaica, where she feels the most "belonging." As such, Hyacinth convinces herself that her blackness has no bearing in Jamaica and she romanticizes that everyone is treated equally on the island. Jamaica becomes an idealized nostalgic "home" for Hyacinth. Olive Senior notes, "If you are invisible and silenced in the country to which you have journeyed, then home, the place you left behind, functions at least in your mind as the place … where you are both seen and heard" (19). Hyacinth, therefore, finds consolation in her childhood memories, reminiscing on the times spent playing with her friends in the community and the images of the close relationship she shared with her aunt Joyce. Memories of her idyllic Jamaican reality allow her to recreate a temporary feeling of belonging away from her abusive environment. It also gives her an imagined visibility that she cannot achieve in England. Sadly, when she returns to Jamaica as a teenager, Hyacinth is confronted with the ugly reality that Jamaica no longer represents the paradise she imagined. Even more disappointing, Jamaica is no longer the place she envisioned as "home." Hyacinth cannot relate to contemporary Jamaica. She suddenly loses her only visibility and is excluded because of her language and how she dresses. Being told to return to England, she realizes that she is perceived as a "farigner [foreigner] … and rejected even among her own kind" (Riley 142).

## Post-90s Black British Writing: Reconstructing Identities in Andrea Levy

The post-90s writers continue to highlight their negotiation with Caribbean identities, but they take a different approach to articulating this "Caribbeanness." Their challenge in negotiating identities widens to include the racism Black British youths continue to face, coupled with the tension between their parents' cultural tradition, hinted in Breeze's poem "Testament." Hence, the conflict between the first and second generation becomes evident in their attitudes toward identity and Britishness. Andrea Levy's novel *Fruit of the Lemon* fits appropriately within this discourse in Black British post-90s literature.

Faith Jackson, the protagonist, is a second-generation immigrant born and raised in England. Unlike the speakers in the previous work discussed, she considers England her home and considers herself British. The feeling of belonging to the empire contrasts with Caribbean-born immigrants who share a different relationship with England. Faith's parents, Wade and Mildred, leave Jamaica for opportunities but are met with poor social and economic conditions as they struggle to achieve a better life for their children. In addition, her parents worked for long hours and were subjected to racial insults, "Everyone called them 'Wog' and 'Darkie.' Everyone told them they were from the jungle" (Levy 390). Therefore, the experience of migrating to England and the cultural uprootedness they face cause immigrant parents to have the burning desire to assimilate their children into British culture, usually at the expense of detaching them from their Caribbean background:

> My mum and dad never talked about their lives before my brother Carl, and I were born. They didn't sit us in front of the fire and tell long tales of life in Jamaica of palms trees and yams and playing by the rivers. There was no "oral tradition" in our family. Most of our childhood questions to them were unanswered with "that was a long time ago" or "What you want to know about that?" (4)

According to Ole Laursen, Caribbean immigrants were prepared to forget the "histories of slavery and colonial subordination" to reestablish a new life in their new country (57–8). Further, he argues that "[they] have repressed their history in Jamaica because it is too traumatic to be told" (59). So, for Caribbean parents, burying the painful realities of back home and assimilating into the host country act as coping mechanisms to shield their children from the marginalization they experience. Faith's parents had good intentions when they attempted to assimilate their children; they were hopeful "that their children will adjust as 'true' British to their motherland"

(Toplu 3). Sadly, this is not the case because Faith is left to find her identity alone. This search proves crucial for Faith as she "suffers from her unknown personal history, and she cannot define her cultural self" (Ozun and Kuzgun 306–7). Paradoxically, her parents firmly cling to their Caribbean culture. However, "they expect their children to settle down in England" (Toplu 2). Boxes upon boxes are stacked up all over the family home. Faith tells the readers: "My parents' hobby was collecting empty boxes…. Brown cardboard boxes mostly" (Levy 13). Toplu points out that these boxes are an "explicit metaphor of the parents' immigrant selves" (2). In other words, the parents are still tied to their birthplace and consider England their short-term residence. In addition, Faith is horrified by the idea that her parents want to relocate to Jamaica and she innocently shuns their dream by telling the reader: "I'd stopped listening. Because what I meant by why, the question I wanted answering was, why Jamaica? Why is Jamaica home?" (Levy 49). Faith's attitude toward Jamaica is telling in that it reveals her disconnection from her parents' birthplace. She also naively sees England as the "home" of her parents despite the many symbolic attachments to Jamaica apparent throughout the house. Faith's obliviousness to her parents' wish to return home is due to the absence of stories they shared of Jamaica with their children. Faith does not know about her parents' birthplace and why Caribbean people like her parents migrated to England. This situation is entirely different from Hyacinth, who, although young, still has fond memories of Jamaica and desires to return.

In addition, Wade and Mildred do not share experiences of racial discrimination with Faith and they talk very little about their birthplace. Weihsin Gui reminds us that at the start of the novel, Faith is uninformed of "any racial discrimination because her … parents … raised her to assimilate into mainstream British society" (82). As Faith struggles to find herself in British society, she lacks a cultural anchor. Even as a second-generation immigrant born and raised British, she is not spared from the racism her parents experienced. She is bullied by the schoolchildren, who remind her of her Caribbean history: "[y]our mum and dad came on a banana boat" (Levy 1). Faith is also called "darkie" (390).

To make matters worse, Mildred verifies that they traveled to England by boat. Bewildered, Faith concludes that "the little white boys were right" (Levy 3), which further emphasizes her detachment from her parents' past or knowledge of Caribbean immigrant history to the UK. However, even before Mildred corrects the stereotyped stories of Caribbean people arriving in England on a "banana boat," Faith believes otherwise. Mildred questions Faith: "What, you think we sit among the bananas?" Faith admits that "[she] didn't tell her but, yes, that was exactly what [she] thought" (2).

Therefore, the banana boat is "resignified as a derogatory insult, one that highlights Faith's racial difference and otherness – she is essentially told that she does not belong" (Machado Sáez 1).

Similarly, Laursen suggests "that the generation of West Indians who grew up in societies shaped by the historical experiences of slavery and colonialism did not pass on those histories to their children" (58). Consequently, these children, like Faith, lack an understanding of how modern-day racism underpins the painful history of colonialism and slavery (58). Furthermore, Levy includes other instances of racism that Faith encounters despite being second-generation British.

Faith finally gets to visit her parents' country, allowing her to redefine a sense of cultural self. This redefinition of self via an ancestral journey is a thread in later Black diasporic literature. However, this sojourn to the home country is not without its challenges. As Levy retraces Faith's origins, Faith encounters difficulties in learning about a culture she barely knows. When she arrives in Jamaica, she experiences a cultural shock. She has trouble understanding the local Jamaican language and, more significantly, she is surprised to find herself surrounded in an environment where nearly everyone around her is Black. In this way, Faith's lack of knowledge of her Caribbean roots excludes her from Jamaica in the same way she is excluded from her British society. Faith experiences double diaspora consciousness in this instance, two kinds of dispossession or unbelonging.

In his essay "Double Consciousness of the Diaspora," Samir Dayal argues that multiculturalism and transnationalism create "the state-centric model of allegiance to the host vs. the home country" (46). Therefore, the diasporic subject expresses a sense of not belonging while at the same time longs for a place they can call "home." As a result, the protagonist further represents the double consciousness of the diaspora, where both nationalist and anti-nationalist feelings converge with the ideas of belonging.

In the end, Faith understands her Jamaican heritage and family. She gets a sense of her identity and gains knowledge of her Caribbean roots through the oral histories supplied by her Jamaican relatives. She learns about her family background, plantation slavery, and colonialism. Faith confidently asserts:

> Let those bully boys walk behind me in the playground. Let them tell me, "You're a darkie. Faith's a darkie." I am the granddaughter of Grace and William Campbell. I am the great-grandchild of Cecelia Hilton. I am descended from Katherine whose mother was a slave. I am the cousin of Africa. I am the niece of Coral Thompson and the daughter of Wade and Mildred Jackson. Let them say what they like. Because I am the bastard child of Empire and I will have my day. (Levy 326–7)

Ironically, Hyacinth, who was born and spent her formative years in Jamaica, cannot recover "home" the same way as Faith. For Hyacinth, "The complexities of return are particularly pronounced" (Tomlinson 159). After returning to Jamaica, instead of a warm welcome, Hyacinth is chased away from the family home by angry relatives.

## Conclusion

As depicted in the literature of Black Caribbean British writers, each generation moved closer to integrating and claiming a sense of belongingness in mainstream British society. The postwar generation put to pen their cultural shock of unlearning their presumed "Britishness," attacks of racial discrimination, and nostalgic memories of their home country. As such, they used their Caribbean artistic expressions to mark a distinct cultural presence in the empire. In addition to exposing these harsh economic conditions of immigrant lives, this Windrush generation also used their literary work to "educate a largely ignorant English public, who could not readily distinguish, for example, Africa and the Caribbean" (Ellis 69). The next generation of writers would forcefully take up the mantle of resisting systemic racism by confronting the institutions and calling them out on racist practices, as highlighted in LKJ's poems. Johnson holds the police accountable for the assault against his poetic persona and implicates the workplace for their exploitation of immigrant labor. Likewise, Breeze thoughtfully critiques the immigration policy that forces Caribbean mothers to leave their children behind. Conversely, the post-90s writers represent a complete sense of belonging by illustrating the identity issues or crisis that the second-generation Black British endured.

Regardless of the period in which they wrote, Black British writers all shared the desire to use Black Caribbean aesthetics to tell their own stories. The Caribbean Creole remained a signifier of identity. Black Caribbean creative writers saw the need to make the Creole language visible in their new space as a cultural expression tied to their linguistic or cultural identity and community. This desire is because, according to Tzu-Yu Lin, "Oral features in the Caribbean Creole language are important; thus, Caribbean community could not easily be constructed if there are no 'sound' and rhythm in the language" (165). Lin further acknowledges the power of Caribbean nation languages in literature and the use of music as a metaphor in defining a linguistic identity in the diaspora. He claims that in addition to Caribbean Creoles, "There is also an appreciation for a spatial creation in constructing an imaginative diasporic space of immigrant community in London" (165). While Lin directs his comment to the Windrush generation, these aesthetic features can be found across the creative works of different generations of Black Caribbean British writers.

Significantly, the post-90s writers also shared a similar approach with women writers of the mid-80s to the early-90s in centralizing the narratives of Black Caribbean British immigrants or their female offspring. These writers often touched on taboo subjects such as sexual abuse and Caribbean patriarchy witnessed in *The Unbelonging*. This approach is where the generation of writers faintly depart in style. Ellis observes that Caribbean writers like Joan Riley do not use social realism established by C. L. R. James "as the dominant mode of expression of the West Indian novel in the 1930s" (69). Instead, Riley diverges from realism and commits to social reality. Ellis comments that Riley's stylistic approach evokes discomfort in white readers because she dealt with material that was too painful for readers despite their positioning (71). For Riley, realism does not challenge her readers because she insists it "provides a sense of closure" (71), allowing them to retreat to their comfortable world with no solutions. As such, Riley's plot has no redemptive potential, as Hyacinth is as "dispossessed at the end of the narrative as she was at the start" (71). Likewise, post-90s writers were committed to social reality rather than realism because their works bluntly exposed Black British life – such as the unprovoked killing of LKJ's persona by racist police. Consequently, Riley's commitment to social reality instead of realism has been described as "washing dirty laundry in public" (Bishop 27).

The post-90s writers have presented commonalities with the generation before them – thematically and aesthetically. However, they have critically shifted the conversation from the questions of identity and belonging, offering new thematic perspectives on a multicultural England. Andrea Levy mirrors this diversity by pairing her character, Faith, with a white best friend, entirely removing her from the Black community. It is worth mentioning that other well-known post-90s writers, such as Zadie Smith, similarly engage the Caribbean and their second-generation children. However, Smith's themes also reflect multiculturalism in Britain. Smith's novel, *White Teeth*, tells the stories of three ethnically diverse families. Similarly, Caryl Phillips's works uniquely fall within two generations of Black Caribbean British writers. So, while Phillips writes about postwar immigration and settlement, some of his work engages multicultural themes. His novel, A *Distance Shore*, features two main characters, Solomon, an African political refugee, and Dorothy, a white Englishwoman, who become friends. The different literary responses by each generation reveal that Black British Caribbean writing cannot be restricted to a singular voice or literary style. This traversing of the various generations can only result in a deeper understanding of the complex nature of the Black British experience.

## Notes

1. Historian and playwright Edward Brathwaite introduces the term "nation language" and describes it as "the language which is influenced very strongly by the African model, the African aspect of our new World/Caribbean heritage ..." (Brathwaite 13).
2. The sus ("suspected person") was a stop and search law that allowed police officers to stop, search, and potentially arrest persons suspected of loitering.

## Works Cited

Beushausen, Wiebke. "Sexual Citizenship and Vulnerable Bodies in Makeda Silvera's *The Heart Does Not Bend* and Joan Riley's *The Unbelonging*." *Meridians*, vol. 13, no. 2, 2016, pp. 56–78.
Bishop, Maria. "Interview with Joan Riley." *Spare Rib*, Jul. 1989, p. 27.
Brathwaite, Edward. *History of the Voice: The Development of Nation Language in Anglophone Caribbean Poetry*. New Beacon Books, 1984.
Breeze, Jean "Binta." "Atlantic Drift." *Spring Cleaning*, Virago P, 1992, p. 37.
"Testament." *Spring Cleaning*, Virago P, 1992, pp. 7–11.
Dayal, Samir. "Diaspora and Double-Consciousness." *Journal of the Midwest Modern Language Association*, vol. 29, no. 1, 1996, pp. 46–62.
Ellis, David. "'Wives and Workers': The Novels of Joan Riley." *Contemporary British Women Writers*, edited by Emma Parker, D. S. Brewer, 2004, pp. 68–84.
Gui, Weihsin. "Post-Heritage Narratives: Migrancy and Travelling Theory in V. S. Naipaul's *The Enigma of Arrival* and Andrea Levy's *Fruit of the Lemon*." *Journal of Commonwealth Literature*, vol. 47, no. 1, 2012, pp. 73–89.
Hall, Stuart. "Old and New Identities, Old and New Ethnicities." *Theories of Race and Racism: A Reader*, edited by Les Back and John Solomon, Routledge, 2020, pp. 199–208.
Heide, H. Ter. "West Indian Migration to Great Britain." *Nieuwe West-Indische Gids / New West Indian Guide*, vol. 43, 1963, pp. 75–88.
Johnson, Linton Kwesi. *Mi Revalueshanary Fren*. Ausable P, 2006.
Laursen, Ole Birk. "'Telling Her a Story': Remembering Trauma in Andrea Levy's Writing." *EnterText*, special issue on Andrea Levy, vol. 9, 2012, pp. 53–68.
Levy, Andrea. *Fruit of the Lemon*. 1999. Tinder P, 2017.
Lin, Tzu-Yu. "Sam Selvon's *Lonely London* and Diasporic Caribbean Identity." *Diasporic Identities and Empire: Cultural Contentions and Literary Landscapes*, edited by Anastasia Nicéphore and David Brooks, Cambridge Scholars Publishing, 2013, pp. 157–76.
Machado Sáez, Elena. "Bittersweet (Be)Longing: Filling the Void of History in Andrea Levy's *Fruit of the Lemon*." *Anthurium: A Caribbean Studies Journal*, vol. 4, no. 1, 2006, pp. 1–14.
Marson, Una M. "Nigger." *The Keys*, Jul. 1933, pp. 8–9.
"Quashie to London." *The Moth and the Star*, 1937, pp. 17–21.
Nichols, Grace. "Wherever I Hang." *The Heinemann Book of Caribbean Poetry*, edited by Stewart Brown and Ian McDonald, Heineman, 1992, pp. 169–70.
Ozun, Sule, and Canan Kuzgun. "Diasporic Subjectivity and Homing Desire in *Fruit of the Lemon*." *Neophilologus*, vol. 102, 2018, pp. 301–15.

Phillips, Caryl. *A New World Order*. Secker & Warburg, 2001.
Riley, Joan. *The Unbelonging*. The Women's P, 1985.
Senior, Olive. "Crossing Borders and Negotiating Boundaries." *Jamaica in the Canadian Experience: A Multiculturalizing Presence*, edited by Carl E. James and Andrea Davis, Fernwood Publishing, 2012, pp. 14–22.
Tomlinson, Lisa. *The African-Jamaican Aesthetic: Cultural Retention and Transformation across Borders*. Brill, 2017.
Toplu, Şebnem. "Home(land) or 'Motherland': Transnational Identities in Andrea Levy's *Fruit of the Lemon*." *Anthurium: A Caribbean Studies Journal*, vol. 3, no. 1, 2005, article 7.
Vlasta, Sandra. "Islands to Get Away From: Postcolonial Islands and Emancipation in Novels by Monica Ali, Andrea Levy and Caryl Phillips." *Shipwreck and Island Motifs in Literature and the Arts*, edited by Brigitte Le Juez, Brill, 2015, pp. 233–46.
Volkmann, Laurenz. "The Quest for Identity in Benjamin Zephaniah's Poetry." *Embracing the Other: Addressing Xenophobia in the New Literatures in English*, edited by Dunja M. Mohr, Brill, 2008, pp. 245–63.
Weedon, Chris. "British Black and Asian Writing since 1980." *The Cambridge Companion to British Black and Asian Literature (1945–2010)*, edited by Deirdre Osborne, Cambridge UP, 2016, pp. 40–56.
Weiss, Timothy. "Postcolonial Fiction of the West Indian/Caribbean Diaspora." *The Encyclopedia of Twentieth-Century Fiction Volume 1*, edited by Brian Shaffer, Wiley-Blackwell, 2011, pp. 303–308.

## 20

NADIA ATIA

# Reimagining the First World War in Contemporary British-Arab Writing

Five empires fought the First World War; none would emerge unscathed. While scholars have made significant progress in reconceptualizing the war as a global conflict, in Britain the First World War's literary legacies remain rooted in a much older tradition (see, e.g., Anderson; Barrett; Das). Perhaps the best known and most prominent of these are the white, British, and largely middle-class poets whose voices still conjure the First World War as a pointless war of attrition that destroyed a generation. There is no denying the continued dominance of the poetry of Rupert Brooke, Robert Graves, Wilfred Owen, Siegfried Sassoon, and their contemporaries. They sit alongside Virginia Woolf's Septimus Smith and Vera Brittain's wartime memoirs in educational curricula (Walter; Woolf; Brittain). More recently, Pat Barker's *Regeneration* trilogy (1991, 1993, 1995) offered a reimagination of the experiences of some of these war poets and of the psychologist W. H. R. Rivers's intervention in the treatment of traumatized soldiers. Award-winning, best-selling, and now also part of the canon, the reception of Barker's trilogy reaffirms the poets' continued significance in the popular imagination.

In recent years, however, the literary landscape of the war has also begun to shift. Increasing attention is being paid to the war beyond the Western Front, perhaps in a reflection of slowly shifting popular conceptions of the war's global and imperial scope.[1] Men from around the world fought the First World War and they fought it around the globe. The war also hastened the end of centuries of Ottoman rule and its outcomes would, quite literally, shape the map of the modern Middle East. In this chapter I examine the literary representation of the war in two twenty-first-century texts by British-Arab authors: Ruqaya Izzidien's *The Watermelon Boys* (2018) and, more briefly, Isabella Hammad's *The Parisian* (2019). Published at the centenary of the war's end, not only do these texts reframe our understanding of past events but, in their insistence on the vulnerability and fragility of Arab lives, they should also be read as counternarratives to the islamophobia and dehumanization of the present moment.

Perhaps the best-known representation of the war in the Middle East remains T. E. Lawrence's problematic and self-aggrandizing *Seven Pillars of Wisdom* (1926), popularized in David Lean's epic, multi-award-winning film, *Lawrence of Arabia* (1962). As James Canton outlines, *Seven Pillars* only became widely available after Lawrence's death in 1935, but it was an "instant best seller" (69). Less well known is the Mesopotamian campaign, which Izzidien's text reimagines. It was fought in the region that would become modern-day Iraq and has largely been remembered as the site of one of the British army's most humiliating defeats, as I discuss in more detail later in this chapter. Hammad's *The Parisian* explores the legacies of Britain's war in Palestine. Though little remembered today, contemporary representations of the Sinai and Palestine campaign drew inevitable comparisons with the medieval wars of the Crusades. When General Edmund Allenby's troops marched into Jerusalem in 1917, the capture of the city was hailed by Prime Minister David Lloyd George as a Christmas present for the British people and evoked as the final, victorious crusade. As *The Times* put it in December 1917, "SALADIN entered [Jerusalem] in triumph as GENERAL ALLENBY enters it to-day." Hammad and Izzidien reconceptualize the geography of the First World War. Their novels focus our attention to these often-neglected fronts of the war, resisting the dehumanizing discourses of erasure by turning our reluctant gaze to the suffering of Arab civilians, activists, and soldiers.

Like other Anglophone Arab texts, both novels are written in English, but contain significant words and phrases of transliterated, but not translated, Arabic. Conforming to Yasir Suleiman's description of a literature that is Arab, but not necessarily Arabic, the authors' use of English and opaque, untranslated Arabic reflects the "evolving betweenness" that he attributes to authors who straddle more than one language, identity, and literary heritage (Suleiman 24). Critics have argued that we should understand diasporic writing as always hybrid, forming part of a "new Arabic literature" (Salhi 3). Such texts exploit the advantages of their liminality to offer new perspectives, often highlighting underrepresented or forgotten stories, "constructing hybridity and deterritorialising their English writing" (Nash 34). I would situate Hammad and Izzidien's novels in this critical context and argue that the authors use their "betweenness" to redefine what aspects of the historical record are worthy of our attention. They insist on the longue durée of the war; in neither text does the action begin in 1914 and simply end at the armistice in 1918. Rather, by insisting that the events that should most demand our attention begin before 1914 and end in the years after 1918, they illuminate the prolonged contestations between the British, French, and Ottoman empires, as well as linkages between European and Zionist colonialisms.

## The Watermelon Boys

Izzidien explains that, for her, "historical accuracy is fundamental to the integrity of this story" (ArabLit). The fifteen years or so that the novel encompasses take us from the Tonypandy pit strikes in South Wales and their brutal suppression in 1910–11, to the Arab Revolt in Mesopotamia in 1920 and the introduction of aerial "policing" and communal punishment by air bombardment in the years that followed the uprising. *The Watermelon Boys* tells the story of the war in Mesopotamia from the perspective of Ahmad, Dabriya, and their children, Emad, Yusuf, and Luma. A significant subplot centers on Carwyn, a proud Welshman from a mining community. The novel twins Carwyn's Welsh nationalism with the Mesopotamian family's own fight for self-determination. We might read *The Watermelon Boys* as two parallel stories: Ahmad's repeated, but ultimately futile, attempts to fight for Arab independence, and Carwyn's personal journey from Welsh nationalist dissent to his conflicted position as part of the British Army's imperialism cloaked as liberation in Mesopotamia.

Literary representations of the Mesopotamian campaign, most of which were written during or just after the war, were almost exclusively about the siege of Kut, and, later, General Sir Stanley Maude's capture of Baghdad in 1917. A combination of romances and boys' own-type children's literature told the story from the perspective of British central protagonists and echoed the racial prejudices and accepted politics of their day (Brereton, *Scouts*; Brereton, *With Allenby*; Stonehouse). These novels represented Mesopotamia as a place filled with untrustworthy, filthy Arabs, often described as "budoos," and the occasional noble Arab, usually a sheikh, who was naturally an ally of the righteous British forces who had come to liberate the land between rivers from its Ottoman overlords. When they appeared, Indian servicemen formed part of the exotic background of the campaign like the bazaars, souks, and vestiges of long-long Abbasid grandeur. I have written elsewhere on these popular representations of Mesopotamia and its people during the First World War (Atia, *World War*).

Ruqaya Izzidien describes herself as an "Iraqi writing about my own history, and reclaiming the dominant English narrative about Iraq" in order "to reframe British chronicles of the war in Mesopotamia" (ArabLit). She contrasts the flat and homogenizing gaze of early twentieth-century fictional representations with a multifaceted and diverse population. The Mesopotamia she brings to life is an idealized one where Armenians, wealthy Baghdadi Jews, and humble Arab watermelon sellers live in relative harmony until the war intrudes into their lives and disrupts their equilibrium. Nevertheless, her text offers an important revision to extant literary representations. *The Watermelon Boys* replaces predictable racial stereotypes with three-dimensional, flawed human beings in whom the reader becomes emotionally invested

The novel begins with a traumatized Ahmad who has fled the Ottoman ranks and returned to his family on the outskirts of Baghdad in 1916. We meet him suffering from amnesia and overwhelmed in a Baghdad market. He rocks back and forth and hums "his favorite Sherif Muhiddin melody," reassuring himself that he will "remember and it will be all right" until he realizes that the woman he thinks is calling him mad is actually his wife calling his name: Ahmad (Izzidien 349). In the weeks to come, Ahmad begins to settle back into life with his family. Though delighted to be back with them, he is plagued by nightmares and flashbacks – classic symptoms of what we might now understand as post-traumatic stress.

Ahmad is haunted by his belief that he abandoned Karim, a fellow Ottoman soldier with whom he'd become close. Karim is wounded in battle and begs Ahmad to put him out of his misery by killing him, but Ahmad refuses and carries Karim until he is knocked unconscious. When he wakes, Karim has been left behind in the retreat, presumed dead. Ahmad flees the army and returns to Baghdad where his wife Dabriya finds him. While many First World War literary studies have focused on the psychological toll of warfare, rarely has this been extended to nonwhite combatants. It is undoubtedly the case that men of many ethnicities suffered the effects of wartime trauma, but because colonial combatants were so often dehumanized the psychological impact of the violence of warfare is rarely seen in representations of them. A comparison to recent scholarship on slavery is salutary here; in his recent study of depression, Jonathan Sadowsky argues that slavers denied the possibility that enslaved Africans could feel depressed. He links such arguments to imperial discourses and argues that "the image of Africans as immune to depression ... served a purpose. It allowed a denial of the inhumanity of slavery by diminishing the full humanity of the enslaved" (12). A similar argument can be made in relation to the colonial soldiers, carriers and laborers of the First World War who no doubt suffered the trauma of war, but whose trauma is mostly hidden from our understanding. In foregrounding the psychological cost of battle, Izzidien offers a rare literary example of the psychological effects of warfare on all those who saw service during the First World War.

Reparative attention to the hitherto overlooked is mirrored in relative neglect of the hitherto celebrated in Izzidien's writing. While early twentieth-century accounts of the war in Mesopotamia were dominated by the battle and subsequent siege at Kut al Amara, we learn very little about it in *The Watermelon Boys*. The failure of relief efforts and the surrender of the long-suffering garrison in April 1916 came to define the campaign in Britain and to dominate its literary representation. In contrast, in *The Watermelon Boys* we learn only that "Ahmad could recall only snapshots from the battle of Ctesiphon," the defining battle that led to the siege of Kut. Although Ahmad too describes it as "a graveyard to his Ottoman comrades and English enemies," the novel's focus is on Karim's injury and Ahmad's ongoing guilt, not the battle itself (Izzidien 14).

Initially, Izzidien uses Carwyn's narrative to voice a more traditional British perspective on the siege. As he and his colleagues reach Kut on their way to conquer the city of Baghdad in 1917, the narrator tells us that the year before "thirty thousand besieged British and Indian forces had perished" (Izzidien 169). But in a marked shift from traditional narratives, as Carwyn reaches Kut he is struck for the first time by the fact that the inhabitants of the town would also have suffered. As he stares at the "unreadable gaunt faces, beneath ghutras and fezzes," Carwyn guiltily reflects that he too had been "so absorbed in the siege of Kut […] that he had not thought about the residents who were caught up in it too" (169). These brief reflections offer an important revision to the extant dominant British narrative, which barely acknowledged the people of the town. Izzidien is careful to underline suffering beyond the loss of British and Indian lives. She insists on the civilian cost of the war, the suffering caused by the war effort, and asserts that Arab lives were also lost and should also be acknowledged.

Ahmad's traumatized state, his inability to shake the guilt of what he believes he has done, is part of what fuels him to join the rebellion that would later be called the Arab Revolt (1916–18). As Eugene Rogan outlines, British authorities used "the budding Arab nationalist movement against the Ottomans" (199). Ahmad reluctantly decides to fight again, to aid the British forces in defeating the Ottomans in the belief that after the war the Arabs would gain their own independent homeland. The promises made between Henry McMahon and the Sharif of Mecca, or what came to be known as the Hussein–McMahon correspondence, are some of the most reviled in the Arab World and came to shape the fate of all the former Ottoman territories, not least Mesopotamia and Palestine. The correspondence is described by Victor Kattan as a "secret treaty" (98) wherein "His Majesty's Government conveyed its intention to recognise and support the independence of the Arabs on condition that they assisted in fighting the Turks" (99). Instead, after the war, the spheres of influence agreed by Sir Mark Sykes and Georges Picot during the conflict would largely be formalized into mandates. Colonies by another name, mandated territories were to be overseen by European powers until they were deemed ready for independence.

As Ustad Saad explains to Ahmad's son, Yusuf, "the Sykes–Picot Agreement directly contradicted guarantees made to the Arab people in the Hussein–McMahon Correspondence" (Izzidien 230). Historians have argued over exactly what was promised to whom for over a century, but Arab popular conceptions are well summarized in Yusuf's explanation that "while the English were trying to rally us to fight with them, to liberate Arab lands from the Turks, they had made an agreement with the French to divide the region between them, leaving them in colonial control" (229). This widely shared perception of Allied betrayal resonates throughout the narrative as we follow Ahmad to the ranks of the Arab Revolt. Ahmad goes to fight to create a free Baghdad, ruled by its own people. But Emad, Ahmad and Dabriya's eldest child, is always suspicious: "'I don't like him fighting for the English,'" he tells his mother, "'Baba is fighting for our freedom, but we'll walk away with nothing when the English win'" (58).

In the final third of the novel, Izzidien follows resistance movements as they grow in Baghdad and beyond. Illicit petitions circulate, men gather in mosques to hear leaders preach rebellion even as presses are shut down, mosques raided, and those who resist British rule peacefully are "beaten, detained, or [forced to make] unlikely escapes during a British raid" (253). These voices of dissent offer Ahmad a "glimmer of hope in a world that had betrayed him" (227). But when he meets with Civil Commissioner Sir Arnold Wilson as part of a Baghdadi delegation, Wilson merely reads them the published Anglo-French declaration, issued in November 1918 after the Armistice of Mudros, which formally concluded the war against the Ottoman Empire. Frustrated and ignored by the British authorities, nationalist dissent soon turns to violent rebellion.

In the wake of the formal award of the mandates for Mesopotamia, Palestine, and Transjordan to Britain (and of the mandate for Greater Syria to France) in April 1920, violent raids spread across Mesopotamia. Railroad and telegraph lines were vandalized, compromising British communications and supply lines (Omissi 1994). When increasing numbers of ground troops failed to suppress the rebels, the Royal Air Force was used to bring an end to the rising. Rogan writes that "the British were relentless in pursuing the insurgents and refused all negotiations" (226). As Jafna Cox and others have shown, this set a controversial precedent in the methods used to police Mesopotamia. Well into the 1920s, aerial bombardment was being used to enforce British taxation policy, often indiscriminately killing civilian women and children in their wake (Cox; Dodge; Satia). Charles Tripp estimates that "the revolt cost the lives of an estimated 6,000 Iraqis and roughly 500 British and Indian troops" (44).

In Baghdad, Izzidien highlights British racism and the bullying and humiliation of Mesopotamia's civilian population. A beating from Lieutenant Morgan leaves Yusuf in a terrible state. When Ahmad finds him "[c]artilage pierced the bridge of Yusuf's nose and his skinny torso was twisted at an odd angle" (246). Morgan seeks Yusuf out because the boy made fun of him and lied about the content of a leaflet inciting Baghdadis to revolt against British occupation. He leaves Yusuf with severe bruising and what seem to be broken ribs, and urinates on him. Morgan cuts Yusuf's dishdasha (a long gown worn by Arab men) in half, creating "trousers," and declares, echoing the language of earlier British representations of Mesopotamia: "'Typical budoo, scared of a fight,' [...] 'Maybe it's those dresses. It's hard to fight like a man when you're dressed like a woman.'" When his subordinate tries to restrain him, he shuts him down: "'Quiet, Williams. I'm teaching them gratitude'" (244). Incidents such as these enable Izzidien to show the disdain with which the Arab population was treated. Yusuf's child's-eye view further underlines the racism and brutality with which the civilian population, including women and children, were treated.

Carwyn's war service enables Izzidien to highlight two strands of British imperial violence, which might otherwise appear disparate. Carwyn's personal experiences of repression, his memories of the violence of the British state, whether in the form of soldiers mobilized against their own civilian population after the riots that killed his father, or in an educational system designed to replace Welsh with English, mean that he cannot help but see the "liberation" of Mesopotamia as a conquest. Carwyn's attempts to learn the Arabic language, to protect or stand up for Iraqi civilians, especially the children whom he befriends, are nothing compared to his role in burning villages as part of the invading force. In one incident, Carwyn is confronted by an old man who pleads with him. "'I have no choice,'" Carwyn tells him, but the man refuses this explanation: "'You have a choice, and you chose to ruin me,'" he tells Carwyn (Izzidien 284). Carwyn is mortified that he is now "killing on behalf of [his] father's murderers" (284). Later he tells Yusuf that "'This is the worst thing I've ever done in my life,' [...] 'I've stopped sleeping.'" But Yusuf is also unsympathetic and retorts only: "'Must be really hard for you,' [...] 'All that killing and burning'" (288).

Through Carwyn, Izzidien underscores the indiscriminate burning of civilian villages and crops, but it is the use of aerial bombardment against the civilian population that is most shockingly and movingly portrayed in *The Watermelon Boys*. These brutal and inhumane practices, used to suppress the rebels and to punish those who failed to pay newly introduced British taxes, form the culmination of Izzidien's narrative. Dabriya rides furiously to warn her son, Emad, that British forces intend to bomb the rebels into submission during the Arab rebellion of 1920 and although he accompanies her home, he is not safe. Dabriya and the family hide in terror as their home and neighborhood are bombed by RAF planes and mustard gas is deployed against the civilian population (Izzidien 333).

Again, Izzidien uses the terror of uncomprehending children to underline the brutality and amorality of British policy in Mesopotamia. We see a traumatized young Luma escape the mustard gas and the bombs only to watch her brother die. Despite his mother's efforts, Emad is killed when their home is raided. Emad is shot with no warning and his family prevented from trying to save him or bury his body. As the Lieutenant explains to Carwyn when he attempts to intervene, "'Do you think that family will dare to defy us now that they've seen the cost of rebellion?'" (Izzidien 339). Carwyn finally breaks, deciding that it is better to be shot as a traitor than to continue to be part of an army that behaves this way. But even his rebellion fails, and we leave him powerless to resist or leave the army. Emad, however, is allowed two small acts of resistance. He dies telling his family not to stop fighting and his final act is to raise "two defiant fingers at [his] thieving, spineless murderers" (343).

## The Parisian

Isabella Hammad's *The Parisian* begins on a ship from Alexandria to Marseille in October 1914. Midhat, an Ottoman-educated son of a Nabulsi merchant, heads to France to pursue a degree in medicine. His trip helps his father "put him out of war's way" by avoiding conscription into the Ottoman army (24). The Ottoman Empire would enter the war less than two weeks after Midhat's arrival in France, but the war rarely intrudes upon the story Hammad tells. We become aware of it as deaths are reported and in the increasing privations in food and supplies, but the First World War remains largely in the background of Hammad's text. The only time the war significantly impacts Midhat's life in France is when his friend Laurent enlists as a doctor in the French army (61) and is later killed (118). Although the war is interlaced through the narrative, rendering Midhat "a citizen of the enemy," our focus is on Midhat's love for and desire to marry Jeannette, the daughter of his French host, Frederic Molineu, not on the ongoing war either in Europe or in the Middle East (70).

Laurent's death and Midhat's own reservations about his position as a foreigner in French society, his conflicted relationship to the study of medicine, and – most importantly – Midhat's discovery that his host, the anthropologist Docteur Molineu, has been secretly studying him, lead him to leave Montpellier for Paris (Hammad 129). Molineu wishes to show that an Arab can be taught to be more civilized, to appreciate concepts such as liberty, thereby bucking the accepted limitations of his race. When Midhat drunkenly demands if Molineu believes him to be "*uncivilised*," Molineu insists that he was "'attempting, on the contrary, to humanise you!'" (134), but this is no consolation to Midhat. On arrival, Midhat seeks out the only Arab he knows in Paris, a Syrian called Faruq al-Azmeh whom he met on the ship to France. Through Faruq, he meets and becomes friends with a group of Arab intellectuals.

The men meet as penniless students who share what food and resources they have and come together to discuss Arab politics, to argue about Arab nationalism and the clash of empires that the war presents. Some of them go on to be agitators for Arab independence; advisers and interlocutors of Prince Faisal, son of the Sharif Hussein, one of the leaders of the Arab Revolt and would-be leader of an independent Arab homeland. In Hammad's novel, the outcome of the First World War is only relevant in relation to questions of Arab independence. The men are drawn from what would then have been known as Bilaad al-Shaam or Greater Syria – the countries that would become modern-day Syria, Lebanon, Palestine, and Jordan, but which might equally have been imagined as an independent Arab province united under shared leadership and collective identity. Every debate, including the pressing questions around growing Jewish migration to Palestine and of a future independent Arab state or states, is analyzed through the lens of imperial power – whether Ottoman or European. As Raja Abd al-Rahman says one evening, "Yahud, Musulmeen, we're all the same to them, they don't trust us. Just put us over there. So it's not a matter of colonialism. It's more a matter of disposal" (Hammad 164). Midhat and his friends are preoccupied with the key issues of their time: "Has Faisal made a deal with the French or not? Will Syria be independent?" (204).

In Paris, Midhat studies philosophy and literature at the Sorbonne. He learns to move between Arab intellectual life and Parisian society, and to woo French women, though his heart belongs to Jeannette. But the most significant thing that happens in Paris is the Peace Conference of 1919. Midhat's friend Hani is unceremoniously corralled to help Prince Faisal's delegation at the last minute because, as his friends explain, "'ya 'ni, we're at a disadvantage.' […] 'They only told us last week that Faisal was welcome at the Conference. So it was last minute, ya 'ni'" (Hammad 168). Hammad paints a picture of a peace conference where Faisal is placated by polite reassurances, but not taken seriously despite the promises implied in the Hussein–McMahon correspondence and the prince's own personal role in the Arab revolt. The delegation attends meetings that offer "not a word of politics, all smiles and politesse and sitting down and standing up and holding hands and admiring his robe" (171). Eventually Hani must take Faisal to a tailor to fit him for a suit. As the narrator describes, "since the emir removed his abaya and donned a trouser suit things had begun to improve" (172). Here, as in Izzidien's emphasis on Yusuf's dishdasha in the bullying tactics of Lieutenant Morgan, the markers of Arab identity are objects of fascination, ridicule, and disdain. One cannot be taken seriously wearing the clothing of an Arab prince.

Midhat returns to Nablus after the war. The impact of Balfour's 1917 declaration promising a Jewish homeland in the Palestinian territories has already begun to change the city of his birth, accelerating the rate of Jewish migration from Europe and giving ever greater concessions to the Jewish population. While, in *The Watermelon Boys*, the narrative is poised between Ottoman and British imperial power, in *The Parisian* it is Zionism, under the protection of British imperialism, that poses the greatest threat. Once again, the impact of imperial power plays out on a personal, intimate stage in Hammad's text. We see the effort of Palestinian resistance fighters through the story of Midhat's cousin Jamil, escalating surveillance through the subplot of Father Antoine, and clashes between Jews and Muslims at the Nebi Musa festival in Jerusalem in 1920 form part of Midhat and his future wife, Fatima's, love story (Hammad 292).

Britain's inability or unwillingness to make good Balfour's contradictory promises of a Jewish homeland, which would not compromise the rights of existing non-Jewish communities, shapes much of Hammad's plot. Pan-Arab voices and the cause of Arab self-determination, which we first see in Paris, continue to form an important backdrop to the Palestinian narrative. Local committees organise to send "Palestinians to fight in Faisal's army, against the French" (Hammad 251). But even these matters of state are filtered through Midhat's ongoing friendship with Hani, which means that he receives regular updates on the prince's failed rebellion in Syria and ongoing nationalist struggles in the region. I want now to focus on just one example to instantiate the many ways in which we see colonial power intertwined with the ordinary lives of the central protagonists of Hammad's novel.

When Midhat's father receives a letter in French addressed to his son he turns to Colonel John Hubbard, the British military governor of Nablus. It is the Colonel who translates Jeannette's love letter to Midhat for Haj Taher (Hammad 185–8). Haj Taher decides to hide the letter from his son and marry him to a suitable Palestinian girl. After many years, Midhat discovers Jeannette's letter hidden in his father's old house. This chance discovery shocks Midhat into a breakdown. As Midhat reads the letter and realizes that Jeannette had been in love with him, had asked him to return to her in Montpellier, and that his father had kept all this from him, he collapses. The

French language, which only moments earlier had felt like "dry objects in his mouth" (424), becomes his primary mode of communication. He suffers a complete psychological breakdown and is cared for first by the French nuns at the hospital in Nablus and later at an institution from which his family must rescue him.

As Fatima hears of her husband's collapse, a British RAF plane patrols the skies in search of wanted Palestinian rebels. The airplane seems to foreshadow disaster as Fatima walks to her parents' home where she finds Father Antoine, chronicler of Nablus and spy, discussing the political situation in Palestine and the Palestinian resistance with her unsuspecting father and uncle (Hammad 432). Like a harbinger of doom, the airplane still circles the skies as Fatima finds her husband resting after his collapse (440). In each instance, imperial power and surveillance are not the foci of our attention. Like the escalating violence and political unrest, these form the backdrop to the real narrative of the novel, which predominantly focuses on the human relationships it evokes, rather than the historical context in which these are rooted. Hammad's subtle intertwining of the operation of imperial power with the minutiae of the everyday emphasizes the inseparability of these seemingly disparate strands of her story.

## Conclusions

In the last thirty years, the two Gulf wars and the invasion of Iraq (1990–91 and 2003) have highlighted the long history of Western nation-building in the Middle East and its largely disastrous consequences.[2] In an interview, Hammad has been clear that she sees the ongoing violence in Palestine/Israel today as "a continuation of the issues covered by the novel" (Dwyer). She explains that "good literature" can also be "a powerful domain of truth-telling, and of examining the world from a different vantage – via the imagination, and affect" (Dwyer). Like Izzidien's *Watermelon Boys*, Hammad's text creates real people where once numbers and two-dimensional caricatures dominated. Her narrative stands as a corrective to the imperial gaze that has its roots in the racist discourses that Frederic Molineu personifies early in the novel.

In *The Question of Palestine* Edward Said asserts that "Palestine does not exist, except as a memory or, more importantly, as an idea, a political and human experience, and an act of sustained popular will" (5). Reflecting on her writing process, Hammad emphasizes the importance of writing a novel that imagines Palestinian life in the years before the now defining and catastrophic *nakba* during which the Palestinian people were disenfranchised and dispossessed. Hammad stresses the importance of oral history and especially of stories to make lost traces of a now largely forgotten people and way of life "live again" (Dwyer). To return to Said once more, we might remind ourselves of his insistence that stories are one of the ways that people "assert their own identity and the existence of their own history" in the face of colonial erasure (9). Hammad's text should be read as a form of resistance, an example of a mode of cultural production that, as Said explained in a 2003 interview, can be "a way of fighting against extinction and obliteration. Culture is a form of memory against effacement" (qtd. in Barsamian 159).

Izzidien also draws a line from the events of the First World War, and the creation of the Iraqi state under British auspices in its aftermath, to the geopolitical reality of the contemporary Middle East. She tells one interviewer that "The crimes of that era, even if they have been forgotten by Britain, haven't been forgotten by Iraqis [....] We need to address the fact that, whether we like it or not, British actions in Iraq during the First World War were used as an instrumental tool for ISIS recruitment" (Hawksley). In her emphasis on the human cost of the war in Mesopotamia, and on Iraqi lives, we can place Izzidien alongside other Iraqi authors and artists whose writing resists the dehumanizing logic that writes the lives of Black and Brown civilians off as merely "collateral damage," not worthy of mourning or regret and therefore not human (Atia, "Death"; Butler).

The logic of colonial discourse homogenizes and erases difference. In place of individuals, it sees only colonial types whose behavior can be predicted and controlled. These texts intervene to replace such hackneyed types with human beings. They assert the suffering of the people of Iraq and of Palestine, but they see beyond this too. While these texts are necessarily suffused with the violence of war and resistance, and the inevitable pain that they leave behind, they are also filled with other human emotions. The people they bring to life for us are feeling, caring, sentient beings. They are not always likeable or laudable. They laugh and they cry, they fall in and out of love, sometimes inappropriately. They are filled with longing and desire. They can become traumatized and suffer the injustices and violence of colonial rule. It is by evoking this full and varied spectrum of human experience that they assert the humanity of the people whose stories they tell.

## Acknowledgments

I am enormously grateful to Ed Charlton for alerting me to Jonathan Sadowski's work, and to Sam Halliday, Tiffany Page, and kitt price whose generous feedback on this chapter was invaluable.

## Notes

1. For instance, David Diop's *At Night All Blood is Black*. A brutal evocation of the psychological impact of the violence and trauma of war combined with the equally traumatizing imperial discourses of race and civilization on African men fighting alongside the allies during the First World War. Diop's visceral reimagining of the war in Africa from the perspective of a traumatized Senegalese soldier fighting alongside French troops won the *Prix Goncourt* in 2018 and the English translation won International Booker Prize in 2021.
2. This chapter was written in May 2023, long before the genocidal war in Gaza. It is impossible at these late stages of production to adequately reflect on how the ongoing humanitarian crisis in Gaza must shape our understanding of the ideas briefly outlined in this chapter.

## Works Cited

Anderson, Ross. *The Forgotten Front: The East African Campaign 1914–18*. History P, 2014.
ArabLit. "'Watermelon Boys' Author Ruqaya Izzidien on Writing Iraqis into Iraqi Historical Fiction." *ArabLit Quarterly*, Apr. 24, 2017, https://arablit.org/2017/04/24/watermelon-boys-author-ruqayya-izzidien/. Accessed Mar. 18, 2025.
Atia, Nadia. "Death and Mourning in Contemporary Iraqi Texts." *Interventions*, vol. 21, no. 8, 2019, pp. 1068–86.
*World War One in the Middle East: The British and the Ottomans in Iraq*. I. B. Tauris, 2016.
Barrett, Michèle. "Subalterns at War: First World War Colonial Forces and the Politics of the Imperial War Graves Commission." *Interventions*, vol. 9, no. 3, 2007, pp. 451–74.
Barsamian, David and Edward W. Said. *Culture and Resistance: Conversations with Edward W. Said*. Pluto P, 2003.
Brereton, Frederick Sadleir. *Scouts of the Baghdad Patrol*. Blackie and Son, 1921.
*With Allenby in Palestine*. Blackie and Son, 1919.
Brittain, Vera. *Testament of Youth*. 1933. Virago, 1992.
Butler, Judith. *Precarious Life: The Powers of Mourning and Violence*. Verso, 2004.
Canton, James. *From Cairo to Baghdad: British Travellers to Arabia*. I. B. Tauris, 2014.
Cox, Jafna L. "A Splendid Training Ground: The Importance to the Royal Air Force of Its Role in Iraq, 1919–32." *Journal of Imperial and Commonwealth History*, vol. 13, 1985, pp. 157–84.
Das, Santanu. *India, Empire, and First World War Culture: Writings, Images, and Songs*. Cambridge UP, 2018.
Diop, David. *At Night All Blood is Black*. Translated by Anna Moschovakis, Pushkin, 2020.
Dodge, Toby. *Inventing Iraq: The Failure of Nation Building and a History Denied*. Hurst, 2003.

Dwyer, Mary. "The Parisian: An Interview with Isabella Hammad," January 15, 2021. The quote appears here too; https://litofexile.nd.edu/news/the-parisian-br-an-interview-with-isabella-hammad/ (accessed April 23, 2025).

Hammad, Isabella. *The Parisian*. Penguin, 2019.

Hawksley, Rupert. "Ruqaya Izzidien on Challenging the 'Rose-Tinted View of Empire' in Her Debut Novel," *The National*, Sept. 3, 2018, www.thenationalnews.com/arts-culture/books/ruqaya-izzidien-on-challenging-the-rose-tinted-view-of-empire-in-her-debut-novel-1.766113. Accessed Mar. 18, 2025.

Izzidien, Ruqaya. *The Watermelon Boys*. Hoopoe, 2018.

Kattan, Victor. *From Co-existence to Conquest: International Law and the Origins of the Arab–Israeli Conflict 1891–1949*. Pluto, 2009.

*Lawrence of Arabia*. Directed by David Lean, Horizon Pictures, 1962.

Nash, Geoffrey. *The Anglo-Arab Encounter: Fiction and Autobiography by Arab Writers in English*. Peter Lang, 2007.

Omissi, David. *The Sepoy and the Raj: The Indian Army, 1860–1940*. Macmillan, 1994.

Rogan, Eugene. *The Arabs: A History*. Penguin, 2009.

Sadowsky, Jonathan. *The Empire of Depression: A New History*. Polity, 2021.

Said, Edward W. *Culture and Imperialism*. Alfred. A Knopf, 1993.

―. *The Question of Palestine*. Routledge, 1992.

Salhi, Zahia Smail. "Introduction: Defining the Arab Diaspora." *The Arab Diaspora: Voices from an Anguished Scream*, edited by Zahia Smail Salhi and Ian Richard Netton, Routledge, 2006, pp. 1–10.

Satia, Priya. "The Defense of Inhumanity: Air Control and the British Idea of Arabia." *American Historical Review*, vol. 111, no. 1, 2006, pp. 16–51.

Stonehouse, Patricia Ethel. *The Gates of Kut: A Novel*. Cassell & Co. 1917.

Suleiman, Yassir. "The Betweenness of Identity." *The Arab Diaspora: Voices from an Anguished Scream*, edited by Zahia Smail Salhi and Ian Richard Netton, Routledge, 2006, pp. 11–25.

Tripp, Charles, *A History of Iraq*. Cambridge UP, 2007.

Walter, George, editor. *The Penguin Book of First World War Poetry*. Penguin, 2006.

Woolf, Virginia. *Mrs Dalloway*. 1925. Oxford World Classics, 2000.

# 21

AMINA YAQIN

# Multiculturalism and Muslim Writing after Brexit

The impact of Brexit on the UK has been challenging, and a rapidly changing environment in the arts and culture sector has led to new adaptabilities and responses (Faucher). The publishing industry is a major player in this sector and literary fiction, in particular, has been a part of critical and cultural responses to Brexit. When it comes to culture, the questions of Britishness and Englishness have been central to how fiction, and particularly the novel, narrates identity. This is tied to notions of time and space in the narration of the nation in an increasingly globalized world as well as the "invention of tradition" (Hobsbawm). In this chapter, I will look at the novel's exploration of identity, and in particular, Muslim identities in relation to Englishness in the aftermath of Brexit and how Muslim characters navigate multicultural city spaces and the countryside as transnational actors. I refer to the multicultural city through the lens of globalization. As Saskia Sassen has noted, the processes of immigration and technological innovation are integral to the global system, and cities are transformed through transnational actors making new claims in a changing political economy ("The Global City"). Reflecting on the tensions of globalization and the transformation of cities through digitization, I explore how imagined transnational Muslim identities in Britain form digital interconnections and face disruptions in an increasingly securitized global architecture where the digital serves as a site of contestation and surveillance in urban and rural topographies (Sassen, "Reading the City"). What I wish to emphasize is how Muslim writers translate the limits of a national English identity for migrant groups after Brexit through new representations of enclosed spaces such as gardens and parks.

One way of understanding the perceived tension between Englishness and Islam is offered by Jo Carruthers, who identifies an anti-ritualistic Protestantism at the heart of the mythologized English sense of self. For Carruthers, Englishness can be read through the novel form and its representation of ideas of simplicity tied to Protestantism and "located in the

English landscape" (2). She views the garden trope in English mythography as representative of two features, the "appealing simple life of spiritual sustenance" and "an island state that's safe and secure, manicured and controlled" (2). Carruthers notes how "The garden's boundaries enclose and protect those inside, strengthening the group's identity" against supposed undesirables. Quoting Zygmunt Bauman, she observes that gardening is:

> a practice "in the service of the construction of an artificial social order through cutting out the elements of the present that neither fit the visualized perfect reality, nor can be changed so that they do." The alien threatens, he claims, "by blurring the boundary of the familiar (right) and the alien (wrong) way of life." The garden is, then, a space that specifically keeps out those identities that threaten those inside. (Qtd. in Carruthers 2)

Referring to this particularity of Englishness when it comes to borders, I highlight how post-Brexit Muslim writing responds to as well as complicates a patriotic pastoral and genteel English national identity that defines itself in opposition to the labor of migrants. In the novels I analyze, bounded green spaces – gardens, parks, and container gardens enclosed by hedges, bushes, or perched on balconies in suburban apartment blocks – provide spaces of safety and belonging for Muslim characters who otherwise experience marginalization. Yet these spaces are always sites of conflict precisely to the extent that they enact a sealing off from the surrounding community and those nativist forces that lay claim to England's "green and pleasant land." By exploring such tropes, I hope to demonstrate how writers such as Zaffar Kunial, Mohsin Hamid, Kamila Shamsie, and Ayisha Malik are contesting the essentialization of Englishness, tied to a growing culture of anti-Muslim prejudice fed by what Nathan Lean has referred to as the Islamophobia industry.

Muslim writing that came out in the immediate aftermath of Brexit included Mohsin Hamid's *Exit West* (2017), winner of the Aspen Words Literary Prize and the LA Times Book Prize, Kamila Shamsie's *Home Fire* (2017), recipient of the Women's Prize for Fiction, and Ayisha Malik's *This Green and Pleasant Land* (2019), awarded the Diverse Book Awards Prize.[1] These writers of South Asian origin were among those who gained global recognition after 9/11, responding to a need in the literary marketplace for an authentic insight into the world of Islam. Shamsie is a well-known and established British-Pakistani author who has been publishing award-winning fiction since 1998. Hamid, based in Pakistan after long periods of residence in the US and the UK, rose to fame with the publication of *The Reluctant Fundamentalist* in 2007 and subsequent novels thereafter. Malik began her career in the publishing industry in the UK and has earned a reputation for

## 21 Multiculturalism and Muslim Writing after Brexit

writing witty and humorous genre novels, making her mark as a national writer of diverse fiction.²

Malik's romantic comedy is set in the English countryside and narrates the story of how a married Muslim couple from the West Midlands cope with the pressures of bereavement, family life, and feeling at home. Endorsements of the novel mention its relevance for Brexit. It is a highly self-conscious parody of the English countryside novel, imagining what happens when a Muslim family moves from the city to a rural village. In contrast, Mohsin Hamid's *Exit West*, is a magical realist novel about borders that captures the refugee crisis in the backdrop of Calais in 2015 and Brexit in 2016. The novelist offers a humanist response to Brexit built on the idea that "we are all migrants through time" (209). Migrant journeys are represented through magical doorways and the novel focuses on the human stories of refugees as survivors. In her rewriting of the Greek tragedy *Antigone*, Kamila Shamsie's *Home Fire* encapsulates ideological post-truth narratives about Muslims through the representation of two Muslim families, the Pashas and the Lones, and how Islamophobia becomes legitimized by the British state as a response to Islamism. In these novels there are multiple movements across time and space and characterizations define transnational interconnections; meanwhile, digital technologies are used to convey nonphysical networks across the country and the city while also allowing for the exploration of the structural imbalances of life in Britain for Muslim immigrants. All three novels address the question of borders as part of spatial negotiations within and outside the nation (Diener and Hagen 121; Jay 33). In doing so, these novelists query the border-fixated politics of Brexit and a cultural nationalism imbued with imperial nostalgia. Borders in the novels take form through hedges, bushes, arterial roads, and airports. Bounded space in these texts signifies order, but also the threat of infiltration. I contrast this physical topography with digital connections and disruptions.

Historically, the English novel has been a form in which cultural and national values have been debated and read globally. The dialogic form of the novel allows for a multiplicity of voices and readerships opening it up to new expressions. When it comes to nationalism, works such as Benedict Anderson's *Imagined Communities* (1983) and Homi Bhabha's edited collection, *Nation and Narration* (1990), have studied how the novel form, in tandem with the English language, helped build the idea of a homogenous cultural identity leading to national cohesion. Anderson identifies the English novel and its spatiotemporal plotlines as successfully representing an imagined community over the seventeenth, eighteenth, and nineteenth centuries, while Bhabha explores the contradictions of an ambivalent English consciousness – haunted by acts of migration – that subverts the myth of nationalism. In these works, the form of the novel remains tied to the idea of Englishness. On the other hand, Raymond Williams has argued that the novel, like poetry, reproduces a structure of feeling between the country and city that has been a defining feature of English national identity linked by capitalism. His selected critical readings of poetry and prose across the centuries reiterate the pastoral as an intrinsic quality of Englishness under threat from urbanization and globalization. More recently, these threats include changes to British society in the twentieth century following its earlier imperial encounters, and especially post–Second World War immigration to metropolitan centers, including large numbers of people coming to England from South Asia, Africa, and the Caribbean. Historical tensions over race and nation have bubbled up over time and resurfaced again since the Brexit vote in the forms of increased racism and a "hostile environment."[3]

Brexit was a return to ideological "British values" which included suspicion of immigrants and multiculturalism. Connected to this was a rise in anti-Muslim prejudice fueled by the far right.[4] According to a YouGov poll conducted by Hope Not Hate Reports in July 2018, 49 percent Conservative voters in the 2017 election believed Islam was incompatible with British values (BBC News).[5] In an article for *The Telegraph* in August 2018, Boris Johnson – then a backbench MP and yet to mount his successful campaign for the Conservative leadership, employing the mantra "Get Brexit Done" – referred to Muslim women wearing burkas as "bank robbers" and described them as looking like "letter boxes." The community charity, Tell MAMA, in their 2018 Annual Report, noted a spike in anti-Muslim hate crimes of 375 percent in the week after Johnson's intervention, exacerbating and further normalizing Islamophobia. In 2018, Sajid Javid took helm at the Home Office. Despite being the first Muslim to hold one of the highest offices of state, Javid rejected demands made by the Muslim Council of Britain among others for an inquiry into allegations of Islamophobia within the Conservative Party.[6] Javid was the earliest of a series of minority ethnic politicians to double down on narrow definitions of Britishness wherein the loyalties of some, most notably Muslim, minorities were to be always held in question.

In literary studies, Brexit has informed critical debates on national identity and the English language (Eaglestone). Kristian Shaw reiterates that the issues that led to Brexit were problems that were already being explored by writers before 2016, including Euroskepticism, immigration, devolution, and post-truth narratives. These different perspectives have in common a return to a conservative Englishness that retreats to the pastoral as an authentic space symbolizing cultural nationalism.[7] In her exploration of the invention of the idea of countryside and how it became attached to

## 21 Multiculturalism and Muslim Writing after Brexit

the nation, Donna Landry argues that this can be found in late seventeenth and eighteenth-century perceptions of the English landscape, as "the very term countryside became a symbolic repository of all that was and is most cherished about being English" (1). The country became synonymous with gentility and "politeness" (2). Further, "the great estate, the landscaped park and the country house may have depended on the toil of many, but these places were designed to minimize the visibility of labour" (10). In post-Brexit writing, the critique of "little England" prevails as bounded spaces such as parks and fences become exaggerated symbols of securitized borders.[8] Additionally, hedges have been used as markers of boundaries in rural and urban Britain.

An alternative to the canonized English pastoral can be seen in the Birmingham-born poet Zaffar Kunial's latest collection *England's Green*. Kunial visualizes a landscape dominated by hedges in Britain marking the frontier between public and private, the urban and the rural. At the start of the poem "The Hedge" he references England and Britain and at the end "England and beyond," suggestive of a shift from a national to a global perspective inclusive of others within it. The poet narrator's voice personalizes the experience of the hedge from the perspective of someone who has been inside it and can understand the nuances of "a disappeared wicket," "a book with cursive black swords," "a bricked up church door," "a truant morning," and "Birmingham" (5). While these city hedges are not the same as hedgerows of the English countryside, what they seem to indicate is a contradictory mix of borders and biodiversity (Ross):

> This place is full of them. England. Britain.
> Its green envelope. Hedges.
> ...
> I know the scratches that come from seeking
> the lost in a hedge.
> ...
> England and beyond (Kunial 5)

Kunial's narrative poem is structured around images and shades of dark and light, and his poetic voice has a brooding quality that is subtle and disquieting. Although the urban is central to his ideas, referencing Ted Hughes, T. S. Eliot, William Shakespeare, and Emily Brontë in epigraphs to poems, he emphasizes a comparative link to the pastoral in his descriptions of place and nature. The urban hedges in Kunial's poetry mark property and territorial borders and are symbolic of unseen changing realities through which he envisions the misty midlands. There is an England behind and beyond these hedges which is not orderly and is unknown. He also deliberately juxtaposes the figure of his father, the immigrant Pakistani Muslim, throughout the collection from which this poem comes from. Kunial's poetic voice disturbs the idealism of the simple English pastoral through the complexities of difference.

This connection and rearticulation of the English countryside can be seen in Ayisha Malik's *This Green and Pleasant Land*, which features a Muslim family who relocate to a coastal village in the countryside away from the spatial confusion of the city of Birmingham. By placing a Muslim family in the heart of rural Britain, Malik creates a pastiche pastoral novel set in Babbel's End, an imaginary village not far from Birmingham, where Bilal Hasham has chosen to settle with his journalist wife, Maryam, and their teenage son. Bilal's mother, who dies in her city home in Birmingham at the start of the novel, bequeaths her son a last wish to build a mosque in his village to "[s]how these people our Islam" (Malik 6). Her sister Rukhsana, who lived with her, moves in with Bilal and his family. Bilal decides to go ahead with the mosque-building project in the village, which creates suspicion and unrest in the local community and brings him into direct conflict with the village busybody and leader of the parish council, Shelley Hawking. The novel revolves around exaggerated misrecognitions and misunderstandings in the countryside. One of these incidents centers on trimming an overgrown bush belonging to English villager Tom Lark's property, which obstructs traffic on Coowood Lane. Shelley ruthlessly cuts down the bush with a hedge cutter when she discovers that Tom is the secret donor for Bilal's mosque project. She is caught on camera and the video posted on YouTube. The news goes viral and, subsequently, Babbel's End is caught up in a media storm. Through such technological interventions, Bilal's local project turns into a national story and Muslim activists and city dwellers march into the village to protest. Malik captures the outrage, racial prejudice, and discord that centers around the hedge-cutting incident through social media responses. Digital technologies are shown to be a means of protest and solidarity but also instruments contributing to trolling and hate speech couched in the form of an exaggerated patriotism.

Rural England is portrayed through an "everyday Englishness" that is encapsulated in the power of linguistic coding that favors an in-group over the out-group. Shelley's character symbolizes a particular idea of rural England that considers itself authoritative. As chair of the parish council, she feels at home writing letters and petitions serving the local community. She embodies privilege, but also a certain polite, middle-class decorum. When Bilal first puts forward his idea of building a mosque in a parish meeting, her response is: "We're civil people and we'll take the civilized

## 21 Multiculturalism and Muslim Writing after Brexit

approach. We'll let the Hashams know, via petition, that we're against *anything* new that threatens to spoil our land" (Malik 115, emphasis in original). However, uncivil things do happen, such as painted graffiti at Bilal's place of work saying, "*FUCKING MUSLIMS, GO HOME*" (148). This is closer to his childhood experiences of growing up in Birmingham, where his mother tried to fit in the culture of English schools but never could because she didn't get the nuances of language. An avid gardener, toward the end of her life she dug a six-foot hole in the ground resembling a grave, where she would retreat in order to be closer to her Muslim self. She is literally the kind of Muslim outsider that Shelley is worried will "bring foreign ideas into their green spaces" (113). Emulating his mother, Bilal digs a grave in his garden in Babbel's End and it is here that he has his epiphany to build the mosque. The grave symbolizes death and a material connection with Islam and nature. This enclosed space, within the space of the landscaped garden, comes to epitomize the experience of immigration and Bilal's ideas about home and belonging.

In contrast to the rural setting of *This Green and Pleasant Land*, Kamila Shamsie's *Home Fire* is set primarily in cities such as London, New York, Karachi, and Istanbul, with plane journeys over and across the Indian and Atlantic Oceans. An adaptation of Sophocles' play *Antigone*, it tells the story of Aneeka Pasha's efforts to bury her twin brother Parvaiz's body in his British homeland after he has been stripped of his citizenship by the Home Secretary, Karamat Lone, following his recruitment by ISIS. To gain access to the Home Secretary, Aneeka builds a relationship with his son Eammon Lone and, in the process, the two fall in love. Parvaiz's coffin is transported to a park in Karachi and Aneeka goes there to demand his burial in England. The park becomes a liminal space representing the distance between their Pakistani Muslim heritage and their British citizenship rights. Eammon joins Aneeka and, as they reunite, they are both killed in a suicide bombing. London provides a key setting for physical character interactions and is home to both the Pasha and Lone families, who live in different parts of the city. Isma, Parvaiz, and Aneeka live in the working-class area of Alperton near Wembley, while the British-Pakistani/Irish-American Eammon has grown up in the upper-middle-class comforts of Kensington.

Geographically, the novel traces affluence through Karamat Lone's residence in Holland Park while precarity defines the Pashas' residence in Preston Road. There are barriers to entering the Holland Park residence, which requires security approval, whereas the Pasha house is in an area hospitable to migrants from different communities. The Pasha siblings eke out a living by renting a portion of their house while they are studying, while Eammon lives off the generosity of his parents and has an independent flat in Notting Hill. Aneeka and Eammon's first meeting occurs when he visits her home in Preston Road on the pretext of delivering a parcel from Isma, whom he met in New York. Intrigued and curious to meet Aneeka, Eammon travels from his flat to the Pasha residence by foot. This walk is significant as it reflects the centrality of transnational identities to the city landscape. Beginning from Little Venice, his walk incorporates the geography of canals, the North Circular road and bridges, including a reference to an IRA bomb in 1939 to convey the circularity and unpredictability of the city that has "other Londons" in London (Shamsie 57). His stroll reflects the topography of the country in the city as he walks along "curved side streets" built over "country roads" (60). As he ambles toward Preston Road, he is reminded of his father's ambitions that transported him from his upbringing in Bradford to emulate the extended affluent family in Wembley. In a multicultural environment of Hindu temples, Halal meat shops, a Jewish bakery, a Romanian butcher's, and an Islamic bookshop, Eammon has little consciousness of his class and race privilege. This comes through in his conversation with Aneeka at the house. In a bid to sound interesting, he mentions the history of the canal and recommends looking up "North Circular canal bomb" to which she responds, "because that's a good idea if you're GWM, isn't it?" (65). Aneeka has to spell out the acronym, "Googling While Muslim" as Eammon is nonplussed by it. Through their dialogue, the novel interconnects a digital spatial consciousness for immigrant Muslim characters on the borders of citizenship despite being British citizens.

Eammon is attracted to Aneeka's beauty and her rebelliousness. His relationship with her is, on the one hand, stereotypical as their sexual encounters seem to satisfy his fantasies about veiled women, and on the other hand, she brings him closer to a part of his identity that he has ignored. Their union is based on impromptu secretive meetings, without phone calls and messaging, cocooned from the prying eyes of family and friends in Eammon's flat. At Aneeka's instigation, they transform the flat roof next to the bedroom window into a small private garden retreat. The privacy is managed by placing tall plants on the border, shielding them from the view of the communal garden below. Aneeka adds colorful cushions to sit on, making it a place where she feels at home. This outside space, claimed by Aneeka as their safe space for intimate moments, is where she tells him that her brother, Parvaiz, is in Raqqa, Syria, with ISIS and needs her help. Eammon, realizing the premise of their relationship in her confession, reacts violently by kicking out and dismantling the order of the carefully constructed roof garden:

## 21 Multiculturalism and Muslim Writing after Brexit

The kumquat fell straight, flowerpot shattering as it hit the ground; for an instant the root-entangled soil held its shape, and then the plant leant forward and collapsed, orange fruit rolling around the garden patio. The cactus, by contrast, wheeled in the air, upturning itself as it fell, never before so anthropomorphised as with arms outstretched in a headfirst plummet, its necks snapping in two on impact. (Shamsie 95)

The harmony of the makeshift rooftop garden is unable to sustain the weight of Aneeka's confession: The cactus takes on the shape of a human figure crashing to the ground, showing its fragility, as does the kumquat tree detached from its roots. This in turn disturbs the peace of the communal garden, attracting the neighbors' attention. The garden as a microcosm of England's carefully cultivated green is once again under threat as things take a turn for the worse. The roof garden, a place of safety and sustenance, is disrupted by Aneeka's confession, and her carefully calculated plan to rescue her brother falls apart in the face of Eammon's reaction; he feels he can no longer trust her. By the time Eammon comes around to her plan to rescue Parvaiz, it is too late, as his transgression with Aneeka has been "discovered" by the security services and reported to his father. Aneeka's communications often take the form of WhatsApp messages connecting her to her siblings, extended family, and Eammon. It is through a text that she informs Parvaiz that she is on her way to meet him in Istanbul. But surveillance technology betrays her as Parvaiz is killed, Eammon is locked in by his father, and her passport is taken away.

The novel is focalized by the various main characters. Aneeka's section is composed of a fragmentary, formally innovative mix of tabloid news reports, trending twitter hashtags, and tweets (Ahmed). We are told that she is not compliant like her sister Isma and is unafraid to call out racial prejudice. To demand justice, she digs out her expired National Card for Overseas Pakistanis to get a Pakistani passport to recover Parvaiz's body from Karachi and take his remains back to London, registering her protest against the Home Secretary's actions. Her characterization is formed through movements across digital and built spaces and crisscrossing networks of local and transnational interconnections across city spaces through which families are isolated and communities divided. Phones, laptops, and SIM cards play a vital function in how relationships are navigated but these are all subject to a power dynamic in which surveillance and communications serve the interests of the British state and resistance is punished. In the end, the Karachi park near the securitized British Deputy High Commission compound becomes a site of localized transnational resistance enacted by Aneeka as she makes her televised appeal for justice to the Home Secretary standing next to Parvaiz's coffin (Yaqin). The scene ends explosively as she is reunited with Eammon and they are simultaneously killed in a suicide bombing.

The theme of borders is also at the heart of Mohsin Hamid's *Exit West*, in which he narrates the story of two protagonists, Saeed and Nadia, in an unnamed city on the brink of civil war (Yadav). As life becomes unbearably violent, they decide to relinquish family ties and become refugees as they travel through magical doorways to a succession of locations: Mykonos in Greece; London; and Marin, San Francisco. As readers, we are given insights through the refugees' eyes of how they encounter city spaces and navigate their social and economic relationships to it. From the novel's start, cell phones and social media help the two protagonists to inhabit two parallel worlds, the digital and the physical (Naydan). We are told in the first part of the novel that the two were "always in possession of their phones" (Hamid 31).

The novel's representation of the refugee experience in London is articulated through inequalities. London is visualized through an organized landscape of parks, houses and disused lots. "It seemed the more empty a space in the city the more it attracted squatters, with unoccupied mansions in the borough of Kensington and Chelsea particularly hard-hit" (Hamid 126). This extends to the parklands of London including "Hyde Park and Kensington Gardens ... between Westminster and Hammersmith" (126). These places are referred to as "black holes in the fabric of the nation" (126). They are representative of a national border protected by "soldiers," "armoured vehicles," "drones" and "helicopters" (135). The people who inhabit this world are said to belong to a "dark London" – a term with racial connotations as well as a reference to their lack of amenities such as electricity. They are also forcibly reminded of majority power: "Every day a flight of fighter aircraft would streak through the sky, screaming a reminder to the people of dark London of the technological superiority of their opponents, of the government and nativist forces" (150). Nadia and Saeed survive this precarious zone, thriftily using data bundles on their phones as a lifeline, networking them into other spaces.

However, Nadia has for some time felt that her actions and behavior are inauthentic in the virtual sphere; for instance, when reading the news on her phone in dark London, she has the "bizarre feeling of time bending all around her" (Hamid 154) as she sees herself projected in the news report despite being outside. In contrast, Saeed moves away from the digital sphere and becomes more religiously drawn to his own community. The community house in Vicarage Gate has a back garden where they pray together, and in this space Saeed feels most comfortable speaking his own language and eating homemade food. This garden space, like the one in *This Green and Pleasant Land*, is a safe space where transnational communities

## 21 Multiculturalism and Muslim Writing after Brexit

are not looked at from the outside and come together on "religious principles" (152). But as the narrator points out in a general commentary on world affairs and Brexit, "Without borders nations appeared to be becoming somewhat illusory …. Even Britain was not immune from this phenomenon, in fact some said Britain had already split … Britain was an island, and islands endure, even if the people who come to them change …" (155). Hamid's Britain is not a pastoral paradise, and migrants and squatters punctuate his description of nature and England's green.

Things change when a nativist mob attacks the street Palace Gardens Terrace near where Nadia and Saeed are occupying a house with other migrants. Chaos sets in the city and communities are fractured as the army is deployed to deal with the nativists and the migrants. This setting is a signifier of how Brexit has torn through the fabric of the country even in a multicultural city like London. In contrast to the violence of the nativist mob, Palace Gardens Terrace, a microcosm of the English garden, offers blossoming hope through its natural environment of cherry trees "bursting into white blossoms, the closest thing many of the street's new residents had ever seen to snow" (Hamid 136). Nadia and Saeed occasionally come together at night to watch a fox in the garden of the house in which they are staying. The actions of the fox seem to symbolize the predatory atmosphere of fox hunting, an elite sport amplifying class differences and the elite-dominated countryside (Landry 12–15). As the fox chases a nappy in the garden, dragging it around, "fouling the grass, changing course again and again, like a pet dog with a toy, or a bear with an unfortunate hunter in its maw, in any case moving with both design and unpredictable wildness, and when it was done the nappy lay in shreds" (Hamid 139) its movements mimic the fox hunt in which the chase is paramount. It symbolizes the nonhuman treatment of the refugee. Eventually Nadia and Saeed find themselves in a dystopian "worker camp" on the peripheries of London, a development called the "London Halo." Here the garden is replaced by "a perimeter fence" (168) and they labor under constant surveillance so they can have shelter. Nadia and Saeed work on laying pipes that "would run the lifeblood and thoughts of the new city" (181) in which there are no trees, gardens, or birds, and migrants are promised a home on "forty square metres of land" (167) with a connecting pipe. Any disruptions by the migrants are dealt with through "an invisible network of surveillance that radiated out from their phones, recording and capturing and logging everything" (188–9), with drones dotting the skyline. It is a place that dehumanizes them.

In conclusion, the texts I have discussed offer different insights into Brexit through representations of gardens, hedges, and other liminal spaces acting as borders within and at the edges of the nation. These borders are defined around a renewed idea of "Britishness" that is insular and weighed down by imperial nostalgia. Britishness gets integrated with an older cultural construct of Englishness tied to rural nostalgia, which is shown to be complacent with racial prejudice and makes easy associations with Islamophobia. Across the texts, pastoral spaces are reimagined in the country and the city showing how globalization and modern technologies pave the way for ecological disaster and an inhuman world where information is weaponized to spread false news. On the other hand, social media and the digital realm allow for interconnections and hyperrealities across local and global cultural communities. Shamsie's *Home Fire* narrates a sociocultural landscape of exclusion, patriotism, and surveillance for Muslims in Britain. News headlines, digital media, securitization, and internet trolling in the novel contribute to a conservative nationalism tightening its borders to protect so-called British values. Hamid's *Exit West* references a motif of windows and fences closing in on migrants and doors that act as liberatory portals in a desperate globalized world. Malik's *This Green and Pleasant Land* ends on a more hopeful note with a coming together of the local community, but here there are no class differences to contend with as such. At the heart of the novel is the question "*What exactly does it mean to be English?*" (Malik 296, emphasis in original). Overall, post-Brexit Muslim writing offers a new aesthetic of the pastoral across different genres, reiterating the closing borders of the new nation alongside ecological wastelands. It shows us that technological interconnections create innovations and cause spatial disruptions and inequalities for transnational migrants.

## Notes

1. I'm using Muslim writing as defined in the introduction to *Culture, Diaspora and Modernity in Muslim Writing* by Ahmed, Morey and Yaqin. We define it as writing produced both by writers of Muslim background and non-Muslims writing about Muslims.
2. Malik worked in the publishing industry prior to becoming a published author. She has built her literary reputation around romantic comedy with her novels, *Sofia Khan is Not Obliged* (2015), *The Other Half of Happiness* (2017), and most recently, *Sofia Khan and the Baby Blues* (2022). She is a ghost writer for *The Amir Sisters* trilogy by The Great British Bake Off winner Nadiya Hussain.
3. On race in Britain, see Gilroy, *There Ain't No Black* and *Postcolonial*. On May 25, 2012, Theresa May, then Home Secretary, announced in an interview to the *Daily Telegraph* that Britain would create a hostile environment for illegal immigrants, which led to a number of policies targeting migrants (see Gentleman).
4. According to the 2021 Census, the areas with the largest Muslim populations are Birmingham, Bradford, London, and Manchester. In an analysis by the Muslim Council of Britain, 40 percent Muslims live in the most deprived areas (Muslim Council of Britain).

5. While it has been noted that there are many factors that contribute to the statistics, including new ways of reporting and gathering information, it confirms the outsider status of Muslim communities within Britain, showing they are vulnerable to acts of hostility in the name of patriotism.
6. In June 2019, a Hope Not Hate poll tracking Islamophobia in the Conservative Party confirmed 47 percent thought that "Islam was a threat to the British way of life" (see Hope Not Hate Reports).
7. The notion of an authentic pastoral is referred to by Raymond Williams in relation to "structures of feeling" in different literary forms (12).
8. The novelist Zadie Smith gives the example of how fence building proliferates in city spaces, amplifying capital investment in projects that are built on the principle of preserving middle-class detachment from laboring classes who service them at home and work. This hostile environment is reflected in a number of novels that came out after Brexit, a prominent example is Ali Smith's *Autumn*. Here the securitized fence is symbolized as a marker of national borders in the countryside.

## Works Cited

Ahmed, Rehana. "Towards an Ethics of Reading Muslims: Encountering Difference in Kamila Shamsie's *Home Fire*." *Textual Practice*, vol. 35, no. 7, 2021, pp. 1145–61.

Ahmed, Rehana, Peter Morey, and Amina Yaqin. "Introduction." *Culture, Diaspora and Modernity in Muslim Writing*, edited by Rehana Ahmed, Peter Morey, and Amina Yaqin, Routledge, 2012, pp. 1–17.

Anderson, Benedict. *Imagined Communities: Reflections on the Origins and Spread of Nationalism*. Verso, 1983.

BBC News. "Islamophobia behind Far-Right Rise in UK, Report Says," Feb. 18, 2019, www.bbc.co.uk/news/uk-47280082. Accessed Aug. 15, 2023.

Bhabha, Homi K., editor. *Nation and Narration*. Routledge, 1990.

Carruthers, Jo. *England's Secular Scripture: Islamophobia and the Protestant Aesthetic*. Continuum, 2011.

Diener, Alexander C., and Joshua Hagen. *Borders: A Very Short Introduction*. Oxford UP, 2012.

Eaglestone, Robert, editor. *Brexit and Literature: Critical and Cultural Responses*. Routledge, 2018.

Faucher, Charlotte. "Resilience and Adaptation of the UK's Arts Sector during the Process of the UK's Withdrawal from the EU." *International Journal of Cultural Policy*, vol. 29, no. 2, 2023, pp. 231–46.

Gentleman, Amelia. "UK's Hostile Environment Policies 'Disproportionately Impact' People of Colour." *The Guardian*, Feb. 9, 2023, www.theguardian.com/uk-news/2023/feb/09/uks-hostile-environment-policies-disproportionately-impact-people-of-colour. Accessed Aug. 15, 2023.

Gilroy, Paul. *Postcolonial Melancholia*. Columbia UP, 2006.

———. *There Ain't No Black in the Union Jack: The Cultural Politics of Race and Nation*. Hutchinson, 1987.

Hamid, Mohsin. *Exit West*. Penguin Random House, 2018.

Hobsbawm, Eric. "Introduction." *The Invention of Tradition*, edited by T. Ranger and E. Hobsbawm, Cambridge UP, 1983, pp. 1–14.
Hope Not Hate Reports. "The Deep Roots of Islamophobia in the Conservative Party," Sept. 30, 2020, hopenothate.org.uk/2020/09/30/the-deep-roots-of-islamophobia-in-the-conservative-party/. Accessed Mar. 18, 2023.
Jay, Paul L. *Transnational Literature: The Basics*. Routledge, 2021.
Johnson, Boris. "Denmark Has Got It Wrong. Yes, the Burka Is Oppressive and Ridiculous – But That's Still No Reason to Ban It." *The Telegraph*, Aug. 5, 2018, www.telegraph.co.uk/news/2018/08/05/denmark-has-got-wrong-yes-burka-oppressive-ridiculous-still/. Accessed May 12, 2023.
Kunial, Zaffar. *England's Green*. Faber and Faber, 2022.
Landry, Donna. *The Invention of the Countryside*. Palgrave Macmillan, 2001.
Lean, Nathan. *The Islamophobia Industry: How the Right Manufactures Fear of Muslims*. Pluto P, 2012.
Malik, Ayisha. *This Green and Pleasant Land*. Zaffre, 2019.
Muslim Council of Britain. "Census 2021: First Look," Nov. 29, 2022, https://mcb.org.uk/wp-content/uploads/2022/12/MCB-Census-2021-%E2%80%93-First-Look.pdf. Accessed May 12, 2023.
Naydan, Liliana M. "Digital Screens and National Divides in Mohsin Hamid's *Exit West*." *Studies in the Novel*, vol. 51, no. 3, 2019, pp. 433–51.
Ross, Peter. "How Hedges Became the Unofficial Emblem of Great Britain." *Smithsonian Magazine*, Nov. 2020, www.smithsonianmag.com/arts-culture/history-hedges-scotland-england-180976023/. Accessed Aug. 15, 2023.
Sassen, Saskia. "The Global City: Introducing a Concept." *Brown Journal of World Affairs*, vol. 11, no. 2, 2005, pp. 27–44.
   "Reading the City in a Global Digital Age: The Limits of Topographic Representation," Selected Papers of Beijing Forum 2006, *Procedia Social and Behavioural Sciences*, vol. 2, 2010, pp. 7030–41.
Shamsie, Kamila. *Home Fire*. Bloomsbury, 2017.
Shaw, Kristian. *Brexlit: British Literature and the European Project*. Bloomsbury, 2021.
Smith, Ali. *Autumn*. Hamish Hamilton, 2016.
Smith, Zadie. "Fences: A Brexit Diary." *New York Review*, Aug. 18, 2016.
Tell MAMA. "Tell MAMA Annual Report 2018: Normalising Hatred," Sept. 2, 2019, tellmamauk.org/tell-mama-annual-report-2018-_-normalising-hate/. Accessed May 12, 2023.
Williams, Raymond. *The Country and the City*. The Hogarth P, 1993.
Yadav, Kanak. "The Poetics of the (Un)named City in Mohsin Hamid's *Exit West*." *Journal of Postcolonial Writing*, vol. 59, no. 1, 2023, pp. 100–12.
Yaqin, Amina. "Necropolitical Trauma in Kamila Shamsie's Fiction." *The Muslim World*, vol. 111, no. 2, 2021, pp. 234–49.

# FURTHER READING

Ahmed, Rehana. *Writing British Muslims: Religion, Class and Multiculturalism.* Manchester UP, 2015.
Aljoe, Nicole N. *Creole Testimonies: Slave Narratives from the British West Indies, 1709–1838.* Palgrave Macmillan, 2011.
Aravamudan, Srinivas. *Enlightenment Orientalism: Resisting the Rise of the Novel.* U of Chicago P, 2014.
Armitage, David. *Ideological Origins of the British Empire.* Cambridge UP, 2000.
Atia, Nadia. *World War One in the Middle East: The British and the Ottomans in Iraq.* I.B. Tauris, 2016.
Banerjee, Sukanya. *Becoming Imperial Citizens: Indians in the Late-Victorian Empire.* Duke UP, 2010.
Barker, Samuel. *Written on the Water: British Romanticism and the Maritime Empire of Culture.* U of Virginia P, 2010.
Belich, James. *Replenishing the Earth: The Settler Revolution and the Rise of the Anglo-World, 1783–1939.* Oxford UP, 2009.
Bell, Duncan. *The Idea of Greater Britain: Empire and the Future of World Order, 1860–1900.* Princeton U P, 2007.
Boehmer, Elleke. *Indian Arrivals, 1870–1915: Networks of British Empire.* Oxford UP, 2015.
Bohls, Elizabeth A. *Slavery and the Politics of Place: Representing the Colonial Caribbean, 1770–1833.* Cambridge UP, 2015.
Brannigan, John. *Race in Modern Irish Literature and Culture.* Edinburgh UP, 2009.
Brantlinger, Patrick. *Taming Cannibals: Race and the Victorians.* Cornell UP, 2011.
Carruthers, Jo. *England's Secular Scripture: Islamophobia and the Protestant Aesthetic.* Continuum, 2011.
Chakravarty, Gautam. *The Indian Mutiny and the British Imagination.* Cambridge UP, 2005.
Chambers, Claire. *Britain through Muslim Eyes: Literary Representations, 1780–1988.* Palgrave Macmillan, 2015.
Chander, Manu S. *Brown Romantics: Poetry and Nationalism in the Global Nineteenth Century.* Bucknell UP, 2017.
Chatterjee, Ronjaunee. *Feminine Singularity: The Politics of Subjectivity in Nineteenth-Century Literature.* Stanford UP, 2022.
Childs, Peter. *Modernism and the Post-colonial: Literature and Empire, 1885–1930.* Continuum, 2007.

Christoff, Alicia M. *Novel Relations: Victorian Fiction and British Psychoanalysis*. Princeton UP, 2020.

Clark, Katerina. *Eurasia without Borders: The Dream of a Leftist Literary Commons, 1919–1943*. Harvard UP, 2021.

Cleary, Joe. *Modernism, Empire, World Literature*. Cambridge UP, 2021.

Cohen, Ashley. *The Global Indies: British Imperial Culture and the Reshaping of the World, 1756–1815*. Yale UP, 2021.

Colley, Linda. *Captives: Britain, Empire, and the World, 1600–1850*. Random House, 2002.

Dadabhoy, Ambereen. *Shakespeare through Islamic Worlds*. Routledge, 2024.

Daly, Suzanne. *The Empire Inside: Indian Commodities in Victorian Domestic Novels*. U of Michigan P, 2011.

Das, Santanu. *India, Empire, and First World War Culture: Writings, Images and Songs*. Cambridge UP, 2018.

Daut, Marlene. *Tropics of Haiti: Race and Literary History of the Haitian Revolution in the Atlantic World, 1789–1865*. Liverpool UP, 2015.

Davies, Dominic. *Imperial Infrastructure and Spatial Resistance in Colonial Literature, 1880–1930*. Peter Lang, 2017.

Dentith, Simon. *Epic and Empire in Nineteenth-Century Britain*. Cambridge UP, 2006.

DeWispelare, Daniel. *Multilingual Subjects: On Standard English, Its Speakers, and Others in the Long Eighteenth-Century*. U of Pennsylvania P, 2017.

Donnell, Alison. *Twentieth-Century Caribbean Literature: Critical Moments in Anglophone Literary History*. Routledge, 2006.

Doyle, Laura. *Freedom's Empire: Race and the Rise of the Novel in Atlantic Modernity, 1640–1940*. Duke UP, 2008.

Eltis, David, and David Richardson. *Atlas of the Transatlantic Slave Trade*. Yale UP, 2010.

Esty, Jed. *Unseasonable Youth: Modernism, Colonialism, and the Fiction of Development*. Oxford UP, 2011.

Evans, Elizabeth F. *Threshold Modernism: New Public Women and the Literary Spaces of Imperial London*. Cambridge UP, 2019.

Ferris, Ina. *The Romantic National Tale and the Question of Ireland*. Cambridge UP, 2002.

Freedgood, Elaine. *The Ideas in Things: Fugitive Meaning in the Victorian Novel*. U of Chicago P, 2006.

Fuchs, Barbara. *Mimesis and Empire: The New World, Islam, and European Identities*. Cambridge UP, 2001.

Garrity, Jane. *Step-daughters of England: British Women Modernists and the National Imaginary*. Manchester UP, 2003.

Gibbons, Luke. *Gaelic Gothic: Race, Colonization, and Irish Culture*. Arlen House, 2004.

Gibson, Corey. *The Voice of the People: Hamish Henderson and Scottish Cultural Politics*. Edinburgh UP, 2015.

Gibson, Mary Ellis. *Indian Angles: English Verse in Colonial India from Jones to Tagore*. Ohio UP, 2011.

Gikandi, Simon. *Slavery and the Culture of Taste*. Princeton UP, 2011.

Gilroy, Paul. *After Empire: Melancholia or Convivial Culture?* Routledge, 2005.

Goodfellow, Maya. *Hostile Environment: How Immigrants Became Scapegoats.* Verso, 2020.
Gopal, Priyamvada. *Insurgent Empire: Anticolonial Resistance and British Dissent.* Verso, 2019.
Hames, Scott. *The Literary Politics of Scottish Devolution: Voice, Class, Nation.* Edinburgh UP, 2019.
Hanley, Ryan. *Beyond Slavery and Abolition: Black British Writing c.1770–1830.* Cambridge UP, 2019.
Hensley, Nathan K. *Forms of Empire: The Poetics of Victorian Sovereignty.* Oxford UP, 2016.
Hogan, Sarah. *Other Englands: Utopia, Capital and Empire in an Age of Transition.* Stanford UP, 2018.
Hoock, Holger. *Empires of the Imagination: Politics, War, and the Arts in the British World, 1750–1850.* Profile Books, 2010.
Innes, Lynn. *A History of Black and Asian Writing in Britain, 1700–2000.* Cambridge UP, 2002.
Jackson, Joseph H. *Writing Black Scotland: Race, Nation and the Devolution of Black Britain.* Edinburgh UP, 2020.
Joshi, Priya. *In Another Country: Colonialism, Culture, and the English Novel in India.* Columbia UP, 2002.
Kaisary, Philip. *The Haitian Revolution in the Literary Imagination: Radical Horizons, Conservative Constraints.* U of Virginia P, 2014.
Kalliney, Peter J. *Commonwealth of Letters: British Literary Culture and the Emergence of Postcolonial Aesthetics.* Oxford UP, 2013.
Kapila, Shuchi. *Educating Seeta: The Anglo-Indian Family Romance and the Poetics of Indirect Rule.* Ohio State UP, 2010.
Kaufman, Miranda. *Black Tudors: The Untold Story.* Oneworld Publications, 2017.
Kaul, Suvir. *Poems of Nation, Anthems of Empire: English Verse in the Long Eighteenth Century.* University of Virginia P, 2000.
King, Bruce. *The Internationalization of English Literature. The Oxford English Literary History Volume 13. 1948–2000.* Oxford UP, 2004.
Koditschek, Theodore. *Liberalism, Imperialism, and the Historical Imagination: Nineteenth-Century Visions of a Greater Britain.* Cambridge UP, 2011.
Kohlmann, Benjamin. *Committed Styles: Modernism, Politics, and Left Wing Literature in the 1930s.* Oxford UP, 2014.
Leask, Nigel. *Curiosity and the Aesthetics of Travel Writing, 1770–1840: From an Antique Land.* Oxford UP, 2002.
Lee, Julia Sun-Joo. *The American Slave Narrative and the Victorian Novel.* Oxford UP, 2010.
Lehner, Stephanie. *Subaltern Ethics in Contemporary Scottish and Irish Literature: Tracing Counter-Histories.* Palgrave Macmillan, 2011.
Lennon, Joseph. *Irish Orientalism: A Literary and Intellectual History.* Syracuse UP, 2004.
Lesjak, Carolyn. *The Afterlife of Enclosure: British Realism, Character, and the Commons.* Stanford UP, 2021.
Loomba, Ania. *Shakespeare, Race, and Colonialism.* Oxford UP, 2002.
MacPhee, Graham. *Postwar British Literature and Postcolonial Studies.* Edinburgh UP, 2011.

Magennis, Caroline. *Northern Irish Writing after the Troubles: Intimacies, Affects, Pleasures.* Bloomsbury, 2021.
Makdisi, Saree. *Making England Western: Occidentalism, Race, and Imperial Culture.* U of Chicago P, 2014.
Mallipedi, Ramesh. *Spectacular Suffering: Witnessing Slavery in the Eighteenth-Century British Atlantic.* U of Virginia P, 2016.
Markley, Robert. *The Far East and the English Imagination, 1600–1730.* Cambridge UP, 2006.
Matthews, Wade. *The New Left, National Identity, and the Break-Up of Britain.* Brill, 2013.
Mellor, Leo. *Reading the Ruins: Modernism, Bombsites and British Culture.* Cambridge UP, 2011.
Moreton-Robinson, Aileen. *The White Possessive: Property, Power, and Indigenous Sovereignty.* U of Minnesota P, 2015.
Morey, Peter. *Islamophobia and the Novel.* Columbia UP, 2018.
Mufti, Nasser. *Civilizing War: Imperial Politics and the Poetics of National Rupture.* Northwestern UP, 2017.
Mukherjee, Upamanyu P. *Natural Disasters and Victorian Empire: Famines, Fevers and the Literary Cultures of South Asia.* Palgrave Macmillan, 2013.
Mulholland, James. *Before the Raj: Writing Early Anglophone India.* Johns Hopkins UP, 2021.
Mullen, Mary L. *Novel Institutions: Anachronism, Irish Novels and Nineteenth-Century Realism.* Edinburgh UP, 2019.
Nash, Geoffrey. *The Anglo-Arab Encounter: Fiction and Autobiography by Arab Writers in English.* Peter Lang 2007.
Nasta, Susheila. *Home Truths: Fictions of the South Asian Diaspora in Britain.* Palgrave, 2002.
Ng, Su Fang. *Alexander the Great from Britain to Southeast Asia: Peripheral Empires in the Global Renaissance.* Oxford UP, 2019.
Nocentelli, Carmen. *Empires of Love: Europe, Asia, and the Making Early Modern Identity.* U of Pennsylvania P, 2013.
Olusoga, David. *Black and British: A Forgotten History.* Picador, 2016.
Parsons, Cóilín. *The Ordnance Survey and Modern Irish Literature.* Oxford UP, 2016.
Pearl, Jason. *Utopian Geographies and the Early English Novel.* U of Virginia P, 2014.
Plasa, Carl. *Slaves to Sweetness: British and Caribbean Literatures of Sugar.* Liverpool UP, 2009.
Ranasinha, Ruvani. *South Asian Writers in Twentieth-Century Britain: Culture in Translation.* Oxford UP, 2007.
Rawson, Claude. *God, Gulliver, and Genocide: Barbarism and the European Imagination, 1492–1945.* Oxford UP, 2001.
Rieder, John. *Colonialism and the Emergence of Science Fiction.* Wesleyan UP, 2008.
Salton-Cox, Glyn. *Queer Communism and the Ministry of Love: Sexual Revolution in British Writing of the 1930s.* Edinburgh UP, 2018.
Sandler, Matt. *The Black Romantic Revolution: Abolitionist Poets at the End of Slavery.* Verso, 2020.

Sanghera, Sathnam. *Empireland: How Imperialism Has Shaped Modern Britain.* Viking, 2021.
Sarker, Sonita. *Women Writing Race, Nation, and History: N/native.* Oxford UP, 2022.
Satia, Priya. *Empire of Guns: The Violent Making of the Industrial Revolution.* Stanford UP, 2018.
Schiebinger, Londa. *Plants and Empire: Colonial Bioprospecting in the Atlantic World.* Harvard UP, 2004.
Smith, Ian. *Black Shakespeare: Reading and Misreading Race.* Cambridge UP, 2022.
Snaith, Anna. *Modernist Voyages: Colonial Women Writers in London, 1890–1945.* Cambridge UP, 2014.
Snyder, Carey J. *British Fiction and Cross-Cultural Encounters: Ethnographic Modernism from Wells to Woolf.* Palgrave Macmillan, 2008.
Stasi, Paul. *Modernism, Imperialism and the Historical Sense.* Cambridge UP, 2012.
Steer, Philip. *Settler Colonialism in Victorian Literature: Economics and Political Identity in the Networks of Empire.* Cambridge UP, 2020.
Stein, Mark U. *Black British Literature: Novels of Transformation.* Ohio UP, 2004.
Taylor, Elinor. *The Popular Front Novel in Britain, 1934–1940.* Brill, 2018.
Thomas, Helen. *Romanticism and Slave Narratives: Transatlantic Testimonies.* Cambridge UP, 2000.
Tickell, Alex. *Terrorism, Insurgency and Indian-English Literature, 1830–1947.* Routledge, 2012.
Turhan, Filiz. *The Other Empire: British Romantic Writings about the Ottoman Empire.* Routledge, 2003.
Veličković, Vedrana. *Eastern Europeans in Contemporary Literature and Culture: Imagining New Europe.* Palgrave Macmillan, 2019.
Ward, Candace. *Crossing the Line: Early Creole Novels and Anglophone Caribbean Culture in the Age of Emancipation.* U of Virginia P, 2017.
Warren, Andrew. *The Orient and the Young Romantics.* Cambridge UP, 2014.
Webster, Wendy. *Englishness and Empire 1939–1965.* Oxford UP, 2005.
Wester, Maisha L. *African American Gothic: Screams from Shadowed Places.* Palgrave Macmillan, 2012.
Whitaker, Cord J. *Black Metaphors: How Modern Racism Emerged from Medieval Race-Thinking.* U of Pennsylvania P, 2019.
Wong, Amy R. *Refiguring Speech: Late Victorian Fictions of Empire and the Poetics of Talk.* Stanford UP, 2023.

# INDEX

abolition, 93, 95, 96, 100–1, 142, 152
Adorno, Theodor, 24
  and Max Horkheimer, 27–8
adventure fiction, 10, 122, 175–6, 189–99, 262
Agard, John, 12
agriculture, 162, 165. *See also* countryside
Alexander, Ziggi, 94
alhambraism, 114
America, Latin, 3, 241, 259
America, United States of, 6, 7, 9–12, 22, 37, 93, 126, 151, 208–9, 219, 233, 237, 241, 259, 263
  Revolutionary War, the American, 140
Anand, Mulk Raj, 10, 248–53
Anglophone, 5, 9, 77, 78, 89, 230, 235, 239, 252, 294
Anim-Addo, Joan, 94
anti-fascism, 245–7, 253
anti-imperialism, 239, 246, 261, 272
Apartheid, 12, 37, 192
Arab. *See also* Middle East
  Arab independence, 295, 301
  Arab Revolt, 295, 297–8, 301
  Arabic language, 80, 294, 299
Aryan, 11
Asian Women Writers Collective, 270
Aslam, Nadeem, 261
Atlantic, 5, 7, 9, 37, 68, 110, 128, 264, 313
  Black Atlantic, 93–5, 103
  transatlantic, 102, 110, 150–1, 154
Australia, 67, 126, 161–71
avant-garde, 10, 230, 234

Baartman, Saartjie, 142
Bacon, Francis, 27–8, 66
Balfour Declaration, the, 302
Ballard, James Graham, 266, 272
Barbados, 64, 202, 226, 267, 272

Barke, James, 254
Barnes, Julian, 272
Baynton, Barbara, 163, 170–1
Beckett, Samuel, 235–6, 239, 241
Beckford, William, 138
Behn, Aphra, 65, 68, 93, 96–7, 99
Bengal, 6, 79, 82, 130–4, 143, 179, 195, 197, 205
Bennett, Louise, 212–13
Bennett, Margot, 266
Bermuda, 26–7
Bevin, Ernest, 260
Bible, the, 102
Bildungsroman, 124, 285
Birmingham, 266, 311–13
Black Writers' Workshop, 270
Blackburn, Robin, 37
blackness, 3, 7, 38, 54, 136, 153, 285
Blauner, Robert, 37
Bloomsbury Group, 10
Boehmer, Elleke, 189, 205, 262
Boer War, 190, 193, 238
Bogle-L'Ouverture Publications, 267
Boldrewood, Rolf (Browne, Thomas Alexander), 163, 168
Bon Saàm, Moses, 98–9
Bonaparte, Napolean I, 109
Booker Brothers & Co., 271
  Booker Prize, 264, 271
Bowen, Elizabeth, 216–19, 222, 224, 235–6, 239
Boyd, William, 272
Braddon, Elizabeth, 156
Braithwaite, Kamau, 267
Breeze, Jean Binta, 279, 283–6, 289
Brexit, 13, 307–11, 317–18
Britain
  British Commonwealth, 261
  British Isles, 2, 4, 51, 123

326

British Movement, 270
Greater Britain, 7, 126, 128, 163
British Broadcasting Corporation (BBC), 265, 269
Caribbean Voices, 267, 281
British Guiana, 261, 267–8, 270–1
Brontë, Charlotte, 155–6, 219
Brooke, Rupert, 293
Brooke, Sir James, 125
Buchan, John, 176, 190–6
Burford, Barbara, 270
Burgess, Anthony, 263, 266
Burma (Myanmar), 261
Burton, Robert, 21
Byron, George Gordon, 109, 116, 118, 221

Calcutta, 79, 81, 179
Campaign for Nuclear Disarmament, the, 267
Campbell, Roy, 10
Campo-Bell, John Talbot, 93, 97–9
Canada, 3, 7, 9, 10, 123, 128–9, 161, 191, 223, 225, 233
capitalism
  early, 3
  racial, 4, 37, 38, 44, 151
Caribbean Artists Movement, 267
Casanova, Pascale, 240–1
Central African Republic of Rhodesia and Nyasaland, 261
Césaire, Aimé, 3, 250
Ceylon (Sri Lanka), 261
Chatterjee, Bankim Chandra, 130–4
Chatwin, Bruce, 272
Cheddi, Jagan, 271
China, 69, 82, 84, 116, 155, 241, 246, 259
cholera, 155
Christianity, 55, 58, 67, 101
Christopher, John, 266
Churchill, Winston, 128, 254, 260
Clarke, Marcus, 163, 166
Coe, Jonathan, 272
Cold War, 6, 12, 25, 239, 259–73
Coleridge, Samuel Taylor, 64, 114
Colonial Development Corporation, 260
colonial discourse, 6, 10, 196, 205, 304
colonialism
  dominions, 2, 79, 122, 191, 217, 225, 239
  internal, 7, 123
  penal, 164, 167
  protectorates, 2
  settler, 3, 14, 67, 163, 169, 225
Comintern, 244–5

communism, 24–6, 30, 247
Conrad, Joseph, 185, 190
Cook, James, 65–7
counter-hegemonic, 114–15, 119
countryside, 39, 307, 309–12, 317
criminality, 13, 163, 166–8, 171
critical race theory, 6
Cuba, 3, 272
Cugoano, Ottobah, 93, 101
Cunard, Nancy, 12, 246
Cuthbertson, Catherine, 136–8, 140
Cyprus, 46, 261

Da Gama, Vasco, 55, 80
Daborne, Robert, 45
Dabydeen, David, 270
Dacre, Charlotte, 142
Dampier, William, 65–7, 69
Day, John, 54
Deane, Seamus, 238, 240
decolonization, 12, 31, 237–8, 259–65
  Africa, Caribbean, and South Asia, 230
  Ireland, 230–1
  Irish, African, and Asian, 239
Defoe, Daniel, 45, 65, 69, 71, 264
Dekker, Thomas, 41
Derrida, Jacques, 184
Dhondy, Farrukh, 270
diaspora, 95, 128, 231, 233, 279, 285, 288–9
Dickens, Charles, 149, 152, 154, 157, 162, 184
Diggers, the, 28–30, 32
digital space, 309–18
Dilke, Charles Wentworth, 7, 126
Dimitrov, Georgi, 244–7
Diodorus Siculus, 4
Disraeli, Benjamin, 149
domesticity, 100, 155–6, 216, 223
Douglass, Frederick, 93, 95, 99
Doyle, Arthur Conan, 127, 181
Drabble, Margaret, 265
Drake, Francis, 50
Drennan, William, 138
Dryden, John, 50, 52, 58–60, 220
dub poetry, 13, 279, 281, 283
Dutch. *See* Netherlands, the

early modern, 19, 28, 36–8, 46, 51–2, 57, 84, 240
East India Company (British), 5, 51, 58, 77–8, 110, 131–2
ecology, 25, 29–30, 32, 88, 110, 150, 318

economics, 6, 38, 236
Eden, Anthony, 263
Edgeworth, Maria, 138, 142–4, 236
education, 1, 12, 46, 65, 84, 122, 133, 175, 217, 225, 234, 236, 251, 269, 271, 273, 280, 284, 293, 299
Egypt, 4, 83, 111, 261, 263
Eliot, George, 122, 149
Eliot, Thomas Stearns, 10, 203–4, 206–8, 212, 311
Elizabeth I, Queen, 45, 50, 56–7
Emecheta, Buchi, 267–8, 271
Emmet, Robert, 137, 140
enclosures, 20, 36, 43, 193
Engels, Friedrich, 151, 153, 249
Englishness, 54, 81, 224, 254, 307–8, 310, 312, 318
enslaved. *See* slavery
Eora (Indigenous Australian), 165–6
epic, 5, 77–81, 88–90, 124–5, 132, 210, 238, 252–3
Equiano, Olaudah, 101, 261

factory, 58, 149–52, 154, 157. *See also* industry
Faisal I, King, 301–3
Falklands, the, 261
Fanon, Frantz, 177
feminism, 6, 11, 210
Figueroa, John, 267
First World War/World War I, 293, 296, 300
First, Ruth, 12
Form, Literary, 28, 50, 77–8, 124, 174–5, 189, 204, 247
Forster, Edward Morgan, 190, 195–9
Forsyth, Frederick, 272
Fowles, John, 263
Fox, Ralph, 248–55
France, 19, 36, 42, 110, 209, 217, 230, 234, 240, 263, 300
Franklin, Miles, 10
Freedgood, Elaine, 125, 155
Frobisher, Martin, 50
Frye, Northrop, 174–7
Fryer, Peter, 94

gardens, 78, 84, 87–8, 113, 226, 307–8, 312–17
Gaskell, Elizabeth, 149–50, 153, 157
Gaspé, Philippe Aubert de, 128–130
Gates, Henry Louis, Jr., 96
genocide, 7, 125, 219, 272

genre, literary, 2, 5, 8, 13, 60, 65, 71, 95, 99–100, 123, 128, 149, 164, 174, 181, 191, 194, 236, 279
Gerzina, Gretchen, 94
Ghana, 68, 239, 264
Ghose, Zulfikar, 267
Gibbon, Edward, 111, 113
Gilroy, Beryl, 268–9, 271, 285
Gilroy, Paul, 103, 265
Global South, 30, 110–11, 259, 261, 270–2
Goethe, Johann Wolfgang von, 9
Gold Coast, 268
Golding, William, 265
Gopal, Priyamvada, 119, 189, 203, 249
gothic, the, 7, 81, 136–45, 236
Grattan, Henry, 138
Great Britain. *See* Britain
Greece, 83, 114–15, 184, 316
  and Rome, 79, 81, 87
Greenblatt, Stephen, 24, 52
Greene, Graham, 265
Gresham, Thomas, 50
Gronniosaw, James Albert Ukawasaw, 96, 101
Gurnah, Abdulrazak, 260, 270

Haiti, 230
  Haitian Revolution, the, 12, 25, 31, 110, 142
Hakluyt, Richard, 50–2
Hall, Joseph, 26
Hall, Stuart, 12, 94, 283
Hamid, Mohsin, 308–9, 317
Hammad, Isabella, 293–4, 304
Hanley, Gerald, 262, 264
Harrington, James, 19, 28
Harris, Wilson, 267
Heath, Roy, 267
hegemony, 7, 12, 114, 118, 192–3, 197, 241. *See also* counter-hegemonic
Hemans, Felicia, 109, 114, 118
Henty, George Alfred, 125, 260, 264
Heywood, Thomas, 42–7, 50, 52, 56
Highlands. *See* Scotland
Hinduism, 5, 78, 80–9, 112–13, 131–2, 180, 210
Hobsbawm, Eric, 12
Home Rule, 230–4
Hong Kong, 261
Hosain, Atia, 269
Hudson, William Henry, 127
humanism, 1, 5, 14, 205, 217, 239, 309
Hume, Fergus, 163, 167

# INDEX

ideology, 25, 28, 40, 99, 174, 192, 198
imperialism. *See also* colonialism
  new imperialism, 122, 189
  post-imperial, 241, 262, 265
India
  Indian independence, 196
  Indian Uprising of 1857, 178, 196
  Indian writers, 249
Indians (Native Americans). *See* indigenous
indigenous. *See also* Eora, Māori
  population, 8, 130, 161–2, 171, 264
Industrial Revolution, 149–51
industry, 130, 266, 307–8
  coal mining, 152
  cotton, 150–6
  textiles, 40, 150, 152, 155
Iran, 266. *See also* Persia
Iraq, 265, 294–5, 298–9, 303–4
Ireland
  Irish republican, 231, 232, 238
  Irish Revival, 11, 231, 235, 240
irony, 25, 83, 166
Irwin, Eyles, 78–9
Islam. *See also* Muslim
  Islamic, 5, 50, 53–4, 60, 111–14, 179, 314
  islamophobia, 293, 308–10, 318
Israel, 263, 303
Izzidien, Ruqaya, 293–300, 303–4

Jacobite Risings, 123, 128–9
Jacobs, Harriet, 93, 95, 99
Jamaica, 3, 68, 98, 208, 211–12, 238, 270, 281–9
James, Cyril Lionel Robert, 12, 202, 204, 207, 245, 247
Jameson, Fredric, 24, 175, 189, 240
Jamestown Colony, Virginia, 51
Japan, 58, 250, 262
Johnson, Linton Kwesi, 279, 281–2
Jones, Claudia, 12
Jones, Lewis, 254
Jones, William, 78, 80, 84
Jordan, 261, 298, 301
journals, 11, 66, 244, 267
Joyce, James, 10, 11, 65, 189, 208, 234–5

Karnak House, 270
Katiyo, Wilson, 270
Kaufman, Miranda, 94
Kenya, 261, 263, 265–7
Kiberd, Declan, 236, 237, 240
Kiernan, Victor, 12

King, Bruce, 262
Kingsley, Charles, 125–7, 149, 162
Kipling, Rudyard, 2, 7, 125, 176, 181, 190, 207, 209–11, 260, 264
Kopf, David, 6
Kunial, Zaffar, 308, 311
Kureishi, Hanif, 270

La Rose, Jonathan, 267
labor, 9, 11, 45, 47, 71, 123, 149, 152–3, 155, 169, 171, 266, 271, 308. *See also* working class
Lamming, George, 267–8, 271
Lancaster, G.B. (Lyttleton, Edith), 163, 169
Landor, Walter Savage, 114
Las Casas, Bartolomé de, 45
Lawrence, Thomas Edward, 248, 294
Le Fanu, Sheridan, 138
*Left Review*, 245–9
Legassick, Martin, 37
Lessing, Doris, 272
liberalism, 8, 30, 162–4, 171, 260
Lindsay, Jack, 247–8
Lively, Penelope, 266, 272
Livesay, Dorothy, 10, 216–24
Locke, John, 162, 170
London, 4, 10, 39–45, 50–2, 163, 166, 192, 202–3, 208, 212, 216, 233–6, 239, 241, 249, 269, 283, 313–17
Lukács, Georg, 122, 124, 252–3

MacInnes, Colin, 272
Macmillan, Harold, 261
Macmillan's Colonial Library, 168
Madura (Madurai), 78–88
magazines, 233, 270
Malaya, 261, 263
Malik, Ayisha, 13, 308–9, 312, 318
Malynes, Gerard, 21, 29
Manchester, 153, 156
Manning, Olivia, 263
Mansfield, Katherine, 10, 216–27
Māori, 125, 161, 166
Marechera, Dambudzo, 270
Markandaya, Kamala, 267
Marlowe, Christopher, 52–4
Marshall, Henrietta Elizabeth, 272
Marson, Una, 10, 203, 210–12, 267, 280–1
Marx, Karl. *See* Marxism
Marxism, 6, 32, 37, 251, 253
  class conflict, 38
  Marx, Karl, 36, 203, 249
masculinity, 54, 169–70, 211, 260

329

Mason, Alfred Edward Woodley, 260
Massinger, Philip, 45, 47
Masters, John, 262, 264
Mather, Cotton, 21–2
Maturin, Charles, 138, 140, 144
McKay, Claude, 207–10, 238
McMinnies, Mary, 263
Melbourne, 166–8
Melville, Pauline, 270
Mesopotamia. *See* Iraq
metropole, 7–8, 177, 190, 203, 216–17, 220, 225, 230
Middle East, the, 6, 13, 113, 117–19, 262–63, 293, 300, 303–4. *See* Arab
migration, 5, 24–25, 29, 32, 57, 145, 207–8, 230, 266, 279, 283–5, 301–2, 307, 309–10, 313
miscegenation, 8, 136, 174, 177, 180, 268
Mittelholzer, Edgar, 267
modernism, 10, 188–227, 230
More, Thomas, 13, 19, 22, 69, 109, 116
Moreton-Robinson, Aileen, 29, 162
Morocco, 44, 57
Moryson, Fynes, 141
Mosley, Oswald, 128
Mosse, Henrietta Rouvière, 138, 143
Mughal Empire, 45, 51, 79–84, 131
Muslim, 53, 54, 57, 83–4, 112–13, 131–2, 269, 302, 307–18
Mutiny. *See* Indian Uprising

Naidu, Sarojini, 203–14
Naipaul, Vidiadhar Surajprasad, 267–8
*nakba,* the, 303
Nasser, Gamal Abdul, 263
National Front, 270
nationalism, 10, 13, 38, 40–1, 47, 59, 137, 207, 234, 240, 267, 295, 301, 309–10, 318
Needham, Joseph, 12
Netherlands, the, 4, 19, 41, 51, 58–9, 224
New Beacon Press, 267
new historicism, 6
New Left, 6
New Spain, 125
New Zealand, 8, 10, 125–6, 161–72
Newby, Percy Howard, 263–5
newspapers, 7, 154, 233, 268
Ngcobo, Lauretta, 267
Nichols, Grace, 270–1, 282
Nigeria, 267, 270
Nkencho, George, 139

novel
  historical, 7, 13, 122–23, 127–8, 132, 139, 247–8
  industrial, 8, 149–57
  mutiny, 178
  regional, 139
  and travel narratives, 64–8

Oastler, Richard, 151
Oceania, 259
Ohajuru, Michael, 94
Okri, Ben, 270
Olusoga, David, 94
orientalism, 6, 89, 113, 137, 176, 205
Orwell, George, 259, 265, 272
Ottoman Empire, 45, 48, 51, 53–5, 81, 83, 111–18, 293–302
Owenson, Sydney, 123, 138, 142

Pacific, 6–7, 66, 126, 261
A Pakeha Maori (Maning, Frederick Edward), 161, 163, 165–6, 171
Pakistan, 249, 266–7, 269, 308, 313, 315
Palestine, 12, 13, 261, 263, 294, 297–8, 301, 303–4
Pankhurst, Sylvia, 12
Parry, Benita, 6, 196–7, 199
pastoral, 13, 84, 88, 162, 223, 225, 310, 312, 318
periphery, 8, 52–3, 164, 208, 217, 280
Persia, 44, 53–5, 79, 87, 116
Phillips, Caryl, 270, 290
Phillips, Mike, 270
Pitts, Denis, 272
Popper, Karl, 24
post-colonial, 6, 12, 78, 89, 203, 237, 239, 259, 262, 266
Pound, Ezra, 10, 203–4, 206–8, 239
Powell, Enoch, 268
Priest, Christopher, 266
Prince, Mary, 101, 261
private property, 3, 19–32, 162
  abolition of, 20
Progressive Writers Association, 249–52
Protestants, 26, 125, 234, 307

race. *See also* critical race
  racism, 37–8, 122, 137, 279, 288–9
Radcliffe, Ann, 142, 144
Raleigh, Walter, 57, 126
Randhawa, Ravinder, 270
Raven, Simon, 263

Reeve, Clara, 142
Reeves, William Pember, 164
renaissance. *See* early modern
Retamar, Roberto Fernández, 3
Rhys, Jean, 216–18, 220, 223–7, 272, 284
Rickword, Edgell, 244, 246, 248
Rider Haggard, Henry, 126–7, 174, 176–7, 180–4, 189, 260
Rieder, John, 266
Riley, Joan, 270, 279, 284, 290
ritual, 67, 132, 174, 177, 180, 184
Robinson, Cedric, 37–8
Roche, Regina Maria, 142, 145
Rodó, José Enrique, 3
romanticism, 10, 110–11, 137, 139, 237
Rowley, William, 54
Ruane, Joseph, 237
Rushdie, Salman, 263, 270

Saakana, Amon Saba, 270
Safavid Empire. *See* Persia
Said, Edward, 6, 150, 176, 204–5, 240, 260, 303
Salih, Tayeb, 267, 271
Salkey, Andrew, 267–8
Sancho, Ignatius, 261
Schreiner, Olive, 190, 196
science fiction, 266
Scotland, 4, 7, 19, 41, 51, 67, 122–5, 128, 193, 253–4
Scott, Francis Reginald, 10
Scott, Paul, 262
Scott, Walter, 118, 122–4, 128, 132
Scottish. *See* Scotland
Scythian, 52–4
Second World War/World War II, 216, 230, 238, 263, 266
Seeley, John Robert, 127, 130, 161, 171
Selvon, Sam, 212–13, 267–8, 270, 279
Selwyn, George Augustus, 125
Shakespeare, William, 3, 5, 27, 47, 209, 220, 226, 311
Shamsie, Kamila, 308–9, 313, 318
Shelley, Percy Bysshe, 4, 109, 114, 117–18
Shyllon, Folarin, 94
Simon, David, 270
Sinn Féin, 232
Sivanandan, Ambalavaner, 12
slavery, 36–7, 93, 137, 150–1, 212, 286, 296. *See also* abolition
  slave narratives, 103
Smedley, Agnes, 12

Smith, Arthur James Marshall, 10
Smith, Pauline, 216, 219, 222
Smith, Thomas, 22
Solomon, Job Ben, 96
South Africa, 10, 37, 190, 192, 219, 225, 267–8
South Asia. *See* India, Pakistan
Southey, Robert, 109, 112, 114, 118, 138
Soviet Union, 6, 12, 244–5, 252, 259
Soyinka, Wole, 267
Spain, 11, 19, 36, 41, 45, 69, 113, 125, 154, 230, 254
  Hapsburg, 51
  Spanish Armada, 50, 57, 125
  Spanish Civil War, 247, 253
Spanish. *See* Spain
Spark, Muriel, 264
Spivak, Gayatri Chakravorty, 150, 176
stadialism, 122–3, 162, 166, 171
Starling, Marion, 96
Stead, Christina, 10
Steele, Richard, 64
Stevenson, Robert Louis, 128, 181
Stoker, Bram, 138
Sudan, 264, 267
Suez Crisis, 263
Swift, Jonathan, 65–6, 69–70, 239

Tagore, Rabindranath, 190, 195–6, 203, 205–7, 209
Taylor, Philip Meadows, 174, 178
technology, 156, 217–18, 224, 226
television, 7, 263
Thackeray, William Makepeace, 127, 204
Thatcher, Margaret, 12, 270
Thiong'o, Ngũgĩ wa, 267
Third World, 6, 12, 259, 265
Thompson, Edward John, 190, 194–9
Timur (Tamerlane), 53
Tirumala Nayaka, 78, 85
trade
  commodities, 157
  opium, 156
Travers, William Thomas Locke, 161
Trinidad, 203–4, 267, 270
Trollope, Anthony, 171
Trollope, Frances Milton, 149, 151–2
Tyndal, John, 128

Uganda, 266
United Kingdom. *See* Britain
United Nations, 239

Unsworth, Barry, 272
Unwin, David, 264
utopia, 19–31, 65, 71, 175, 181, 248, 266.
    *See also* More, Thomas

vagabondage, 44
Vietnam, 266
Vijayanagara Empire, 84–5
Virgil, 50, 89, 220
Volney, Comte de, 111, 113

Wafer, John, 66–7
Wain, John, 272
Wales, 4, 11, 218, 253–5, 295
Warrane/Sydney Cove, 164
Warren, George, 68
*Wasafiri*, 270
Waugh, Evelyn, 263
Webster, Wendy, 266
Welsh. *See* Wales
*West Indian Gazette*, 267
whiteness, 10, 54, 219, 225, 227

Whittington, Richard, 4, 39–48
Wilkins, George, 54
Williams, Eric, 12, 94
Williams, Raymond, 12, 24, 157, 176, 204, 213, 255, 310
Wilson, Angus, 265
Windrush generation, 12, 267–8, 270, 282, 289
Wordsworth, William, 114
working class, 5, 8, 11, 43, 56, 149–57, 191, 244, 246, 249, 252–3, 313
world literature, 205, 240, 253
    *Weltliteratur*, 9
world-systems theory, 6, 189, 240–2. *See also* capitalism
Wynter, Sylvia, 3, 20

Yeats, William Butler, 10, 204–5, 207, 209, 233–6, 239–41

Zaheer, Sajjad, 249, 251–3
Zionism, 12–13, 294, 302

# Cambridge Companions to ...

## AUTHORS

Edward Albee edited by Stephen J. Bottoms
Margaret Atwood edited by Coral Ann Howells (second edition)
W. H. Auden edited by Stan Smith
Jane Austen edited by Edward Copeland and Juliet McMaster (second edition)
James Baldwin edited by Michele Elam
Balzac edited by Owen Heathcote and Andrew Watts
Beckett edited by John Pilling
Bede edited by Scott DeGregorio
Aphra Behn edited by Derek Hughes and Janet Todd
Saul Bellow edited by Victoria Aarons
Walter Benjamin edited by David S. Ferris
William Blake edited by Morris Eaves
Boccaccio edited by Guyda Armstrong, Rhiannon Daniels, and Stephen J. Milner
Jorge Luis Borges edited by Edwin Williamson
Brecht edited by Peter Thomson and Glendyr Sacks (second edition)
The Brontës edited by Heather Glen
Bunyan edited by Anne Dunan-Page
Frances Burney edited by Peter Sabor
Byron edited by Drummond Bone (second edition)
Albert Camus edited by Edward J. Hughes
Willa Cather edited by Marilee Lindemann
Catullus edited by Ian Du Quesnay and Tony Woodman
Cervantes edited by Anthony J. Cascardi
Chaucer edited by Piero Boitani and Jill Mann (second edition)
Chekhov edited by Vera Gottlieb and Paul Allain
Kate Chopin edited by Janet Beer
Caryl Churchill edited by Elaine Aston and Elin Diamond
Cicero edited by Catherine Steel
John Clare edited by Sarah Houghton-Walker
J. M. Coetzee edited by Jarad Zimbler
Coleridge edited by Lucy Newlyn
Coleridge edited by Tim Fulford (new edition)
Wilkie Collins edited by Jenny Bourne Taylor
Joseph Conrad edited by J. H. Stape

H. D. edited by Nephie J. Christodoulides and Polina Mackay
Dante edited by Rachel Jacoff (second edition)
Daniel Defoe edited by John Richetti
Don DeLillo edited by John N. Duvall
Charles Dickens edited by John O. Jordan
Emily Dickinson edited by Wendy Martin
John Donne edited by Achsah Guibbory
Dostoevskii edited by W. J. Leatherbarrow
Theodore Dreiser edited by Leonard Cassuto and Claire Virginia Eby
John Dryden edited by Steven N. Zwicker
W. E. B. Du Bois edited by Shamoon Zamir
George Eliot edited by George Levine and Nancy Henry (second edition)
T. S. Eliot edited by A. David Moody
Ralph Ellison edited by Ross Posnock
Ralph Waldo Emerson edited by Joel Porte and Saundra Morris
William Faulkner edited by Philip M. Weinstein
Henry Fielding edited by Claude Rawson
F. Scott Fitzgerald edited by Ruth Prigozy
F. Scott Fitzgerald edited by Michael Nowlin (second edition)
Flaubert edited by Timothy Unwin
E. M. Forster edited by David Bradshaw
Benjamin Franklin edited by Carla Mulford
Brian Friel edited by Anthony Roche
Robert Frost edited by Robert Faggen
Gabriel García Márquez edited by Philip Swanson
Elizabeth Gaskell edited by Jill L. Matus
Edward Gibbon edited by Karen O'Brien and Brian Young
Goethe edited by Lesley Sharpe
Günter Grass edited by Stuart Taberner
Thomas Hardy edited by Dale Kramer
David Hare edited by Richard Boon
Nathaniel Hawthorne edited by Richard Millington
Seamus Heaney edited by Bernard O'Donoghue
Ernest Hemingway edited by Scott Donaldson
Hildegard of Bingen edited by Jennifer Bain
Homer edited by Robert Fowler

*Horace* edited by Stephen Harrison
*Ted Hughes* edited by Terry Gifford
*Ibsen* edited by James McFarlane
*Kazuo Ishiguro* edited by Andrew Bennett
*Henry James* edited by Jonathan Freedman
*Samuel Johnson* edited by Greg Clingham
*Ben Jonson* edited by Richard Harp and Stanley Stewart
*James Joyce* edited by John Nash (third edition)
*Kafka* edited by Julian Preece
*Keats* edited by Susan J. Wolfson
*Rudyard Kipling* edited by Howard J. Booth
*Lacan* edited by Jean-Michel Rabaté
*D. H. Lawrence* edited by Anne Fernihough
*Primo Levi* edited by Robert Gordon
*Lucian* edited by Simon Goldhill
*Lucretius* edited by Stuart Gillespie and Philip Hardie
*Machiavelli* edited by John M. Najemy
*David Mamet* edited by Christopher Bigsby
*Thomas Mann* edited by Ritchie Robertson
*Christopher Marlowe* edited by Patrick Cheney
*Andrew Marvell* edited by Derek Hirst and Steven N. Zwicker
*Ian McEwan* edited by Dominic Head
*Herman Melville* edited by Robert S. Levine
*Arthur Miller* edited by Christopher Bigsby (second edition)
*Milton* edited by Dennis Danielson (second edition)
*Molière* edited by David Bradby and Andrew Calder
*William Morris* edited by Marcus Waithe
*Toni Morrison* edited by Justine Tally
*Alice Munro* edited by David Staines
*Nabokov* edited by Julian W. Connolly
*Eugene O'Neill* edited by Michael Manheim
*George Orwell* edited by John Rodden
*Ovid* edited by Philip Hardie
*Petrarch* edited by Albert Russell Ascoli and Unn Falkeid
*Harold Pinter* edited by Peter Raby (second edition)
*Sylvia Plath* edited by Jo Gill
*Plutarch* edited by Frances B. Titchener and Alexei Zadorojnyi
*Edgar Allan Poe* edited by Kevin J. Hayes
*Alexander Pope* edited by Pat Rogers
*Ezra Pound* edited by Ira B. Nadel

*Mary Prince* edited by Nicole N. Aljoe
*Proust* edited by Richard Bales
*Pushkin* edited by Andrew Kahn
*Thomas Pynchon* edited by Inger H. Dalsgaard, Luc Herman and Brian McHale
*Rabelais* edited by John O'Brien
*Rilke* edited by Karen Leeder and Robert Vilain
*Philip Roth* edited by Timothy Parrish
*Salman Rushdie* edited by Abdulrazak Gurnah
*John Ruskin* edited by Francis O'Gorman
*Sappho* edited by P. J. Finglass and Adrian Kelly
*Seneca* edited by Shadi Bartsch and Alessandro Schiesaro
*Shakespeare* edited by Margareta de Grazia and Stanley Wells (second edition)
*George Bernard Shaw* edited by Christopher Innes
*Shelley* edited by Timothy Morton
*Mary Shelley* edited by Esther Schor
*Sam Shepard* edited by Matthew C. Roudané
*Spenser* edited by Andrew Hadfield
*Laurence Sterne* edited by Thomas Keymer
*Wallace Stevens* edited by John N. Serio
*Tom Stoppard* edited by Katherine E. Kelly
*Harriet Beecher Stowe* edited by Cindy Weinstein
*August Strindberg* edited by Michael Robinson
*Jonathan Swift* edited by Christopher Fox
*J. M. Synge* edited by P. J. Mathews
*Tacitus* edited by A. J. Woodman
*Henry David Thoreau* edited by Joel Myerson
*Thucydides* edited by Polly Low
*Tolstoy* edited by Donna Tussing Orwin
*Anthony Trollope* edited by Carolyn Dever and Lisa Niles
*Mark Twain* edited by Forrest G. Robinson
*John Updike* edited by Stacey Olster
*Mario Vargas Llosa* edited by Efrain Kristal and John King
*Virgil* edited by Fiachra Mac Góráin and Charles Martindale (second edition)
*Voltaire* edited by Nicholas Cronk
*David Foster Wallace* edited by Ralph Clare
*Edith Wharton* edited by Millicent Bell
*Walt Whitman* edited by Ezra Greenspan
*Oscar Wilde* edited by Peter Raby
*Tennessee Williams* edited by Matthew C. Roudané

*William Carlos Williams* edited by Christopher MacGowan
*August Wilson* edited by Christopher Bigsby
*Mary Wollstonecraft* edited by Claudia L. Johnson
*Virginia Woolf* edited by Susan Sellers (second edition)
*Wordsworth* edited by Stephen Gill
*Richard Wright* edited by Glenda R. Carpio
*W. B. Yeats* edited by Marjorie Howes and John Kelly
*Xenophon* edited by Michael A. Flower
*Zola* edited by Brian Nelson

## TOPICS

*The Actress* edited by Maggie B. Gale and John Stokes
*The African American Novel* edited by Maryemma Graham
*The African American Slave Narrative* edited by Audrey A. Fisch
*African American Theatre* edited by Harvey Young
*Allegory* edited by Rita Copeland and Peter Struck
*American Crime Fiction* edited by Catherine Ross Nickerson
*American Gothic* edited by Jeffrey Andrew Weinstock
*The American Graphic Novel* edited by Jan Baetens, Hugo Frey and Fabrice Leroy
*American Horror* edited by Stephen Shapiro and Mark Storey
*American Literature and the Body* edited by Travis M. Foster
*American Literature and the Environment* edited by Sarah Ensor and Susan Scott Parrish
*American Literature of the 1930s* edited by William Solomon
*American Modernism* edited by Walter Kalaidjian
*American Poetry since 1945* edited by Jennifer Ashton
*American Realism and Naturalism* edited by Donald Pizer
*American Short Story* edited by Michael J. Collins and Gavin Jones
*American Travel Writing* edited by Alfred Bendixen and Judith Hamera
*American Utopian Literature and Culture since 1945* edited by Sherryl Vint
*American Women Playwrights* edited by Brenda Murphy
*Ancient Rhetoric* edited by Erik Gunderson
*Arthurian Legend* edited by Elizabeth Archibald and Ad Putter
*Australian Literature* edited by Elizabeth Webby
*The Australian Novel* edited by Nicholas Birns and Louis Klee
*The Beats* edited by Steven Belletto
*The Black Body in American Literature* edited by Cherene Sherrard-Johnson
*Boxing* edited by Gerald Early
*British Black and Asian Literature (1945–2010)* edited by Deirdre Osborne
*British Fiction: 1980–2018* edited by Peter Boxall
*British Fiction since 1945* edited by David James
*British Literature of the 1930s* edited by James Smith
*British Literature of the French Revolution* edited by Pamela Clemit
*British Romantic Poetry* edited by James Chandler and Maureen N. McLane
*British Romanticism* edited by Stuart Curran (second edition)
*British Romanticism and Religion* edited by Jeffrey Barbeau
*British Theatre, 1730–1830* edited by Jane Moody and Daniel O'Quinn
*Canadian Literature* edited by Eva-Marie Kröller (second edition)
*The Canterbury Tales* edited by Frank Grady
*Children's Literature* edited by M. O. Grenby and Andrea Immel
*The City in World Literature* edited by Ato Quayson and Jini Kim Watson
*The Classic Russian Novel* edited by Malcolm V. Jones and Robin Feuer Miller
*Comics* edited by Maaheen Ahmed
*Contemporary African American Literature* edited by Yogita Goyal
*Contemporary Irish Poetry* edited by Matthew Campbell
*Creative Writing* edited by David Morley and Philip Neilsen
*Crime Fiction* edited by Martin Priestman
*Dante's 'Commedia'* edited by Zygmunt G. Barański and Simon Gilson
*Dracula* edited by Roger Luckhurst

*Early American Literature* edited by Bryce Traister

*Early Modern Women's Writing* edited by Laura Lunger Knoppers

*The Eighteenth-Century Novel* edited by John Richetti

*Eighteenth-Century Poetry* edited by John Sitter

*Eighteenth-Century Thought* edited by Frans De Bruyn

*Emma* edited by Peter Sabor

*English Dictionaries* edited by Sarah Ogilvie

*English Literature, 1500–1600* edited by Arthur F. Kinney

*English Literature, 1650–1740* edited by Steven N. Zwicker

*English Literature, 1740–1830* edited by Thomas Keymer and Jon Mee

*English Literature, 1830–1914* edited by Joanne Shattock

*English Melodrama* edited by Carolyn Williams

*English Novelists* edited by Adrian Poole

*English Poetry, Donne to Marvell* edited by Thomas N. Corns

*English Poets* edited by Claude Rawson

*English Renaissance Drama* edited by A. R. Braunmuller and Michael Hattaway (second edition)

*English Renaissance Tragedy* edited by Emma Smith and Garrett A. Sullivan Jr.

*English Restoration Theatre* edited by Deborah C. Payne Fisk

*Environmental Humanities* edited by Jeffrey Cohen and Stephanie Foote

*The Epic* edited by Catherine Bates

*Erotic Literature* edited by Bradford Mudge

*The Essay* edited by Kara Wittman and Evan Kindley

*European Modernism* edited by Pericles Lewis

*European Novelists* edited by Michael Bell

*Fairy Tales* edited by Maria Tatar

*Fantasy Literature* edited by Edward James and Farah Mendlesohn

*Feminist Literary Theory* edited by Ellen Rooney

*Fiction in the Romantic Period* edited by Richard Maxwell and Katie Trumpener

*The Fin de Siècle* edited by Gail Marshall

*Frankenstein* edited by Andrew Smith

*The French Enlightenment* edited by Daniel Brewer

*French Literature* edited by John D. Lyons

*The French Novel: From 1800 to the Present* edited by Timothy Unwin

*Gay and Lesbian Writing* edited by Hugh Stevens

*German Romanticism* edited by Nicholas Saul

*Global Literature and Slavery* edited by Laura T. Murphy

*Gothic Fiction* edited by Jerrold E. Hogle

*The Graphic Novel* edited by Stephen E. Tabachnick

*The Greek and Roman Novel* edited by Tim Whitmarsh

*Greek and Roman Theatre* edited by Marianne McDonald and J. Michael Walton

*Greek Comedy* edited by Martin Revermann

*Greek Lyric* edited by Felix Budelmann

*Greek Mythology* edited by Roger D. Woodard

*Greek Tragedy* edited by P. E. Easterling

*The Harlem Renaissance* edited by George Hutchinson

*The History of the Book* edited by Leslie Howsam

*Human Rights and Literature* edited by Crystal Parikh

*The Irish Novel* edited by John Wilson Foster

*Irish Poets* edited by Gerald Dawe

*The Italian Novel* edited by Peter Bondanella and Andrea Ciccarelli

*The Italian Renaissance* edited by Michael Wyatt

*Jewish American Literature* edited by Hana Wirth-Nesher and Michael P. Kramer

*The Latin American Novel* edited by Efraín Kristal

*Latin American Poetry* edited by Stephen Hart

*Latina/o American Literature* edited by John Morán González

*Latin Love Elegy* edited by Thea S. Thorsen

*Literature and Animals* edited by Derek Ryan

*Literature and the Anthropocene* edited by John Parham

*Literature and Climate* edited by Adeline Johns-Putra and Kelly Sultzbach

*Literature and Disability* edited by Clare Barker and Stuart Murray

*Literature and Food* edited by J. Michelle Coghlan

*Literature and the Posthuman* edited by Bruce Clarke and Manuela Rossini

*Literature and Religion* edited by Susan M. Felch

*Literature and Science* edited by Steven Meyer

*The Literature of the American Civil War and Reconstruction* edited by Kathleen Diffley and Coleman Hutchison

*The Literature of the American Renaissance* edited by Christopher N. Phillips

*The Literature of Berlin* edited by Andrew J. Webber

*The Literature of the Crusades* edited by Anthony Bale

*The Literature of the First World War* edited by Vincent Sherry

*The Literature of London* edited by Lawrence Manley

*The Literature of Los Angeles* edited by Kevin R. McNamara

*The Literature of New York* edited by Cyrus R. K. Patell and Bryan Waterman

*The Literature of Paris* edited by Anna-Louise Milne

*The Literature of World War II* edited by Marina MacKay

*Literature on Screen* edited by Deborah Cartmell and Imelda Whelehan

*Lyrical Ballads* edited by Sally Bushell

*Manga and Anime* edited by Jaqueline Berndt

*Medieval British Manuscripts* edited by Orietta Da Rold and Elaine Treharne

*Medieval English Culture* edited by Andrew Galloway

*Medieval English Law and Literature* edited by Candace Barrington and Sebastian Sobecki

*Medieval English Literature* edited by Larry Scanlon

*Medieval English Mysticism* edited by Samuel Fanous and Vincent Gillespie

*Medieval English Theatre* edited by Richard Beadle and Alan J. Fletcher (second edition)

*Medieval French Literature* edited by Simon Gaunt and Sarah Kay

*Medieval Romance* edited by Roberta L. Krueger

*Medieval Romance* edited by Roberta L. Krueger (new edition)

*Medieval Women's Writing* edited by Carolyn Dinshaw and David Wallace

*Modern American Culture* edited by Christopher Bigsby

*Modern British Women Playwrights* edited by Elaine Aston and Janelle Reinelt

*Modern French Culture* edited by Nicholas Hewitt

*Modern German Culture* edited by Eva Kolinsky and Wilfried van der Will

*The Modern German Novel* edited by Graham Bartram

*The Modern Gothic* edited by Jerrold E. Hogle

*Modern Irish Culture* edited by Joe Cleary and Claire Connolly

*Modern Italian Culture* edited by Zygmunt G. Baranski and Rebecca J. West

*Modern Latin American Culture* edited by John King

*Modern Russian Culture* edited by Nicholas Rzhevsky

*Modern Spanish Culture* edited by David T. Gies

*Modernism* edited by Michael Levenson (second edition)

*The Modernist Novel* edited by Morag Shiach

*Modernist Poetry* edited by Alex Davis and Lee M. Jenkins

*Modernist Women Writers* edited by Maren Tova Linett

*Narrative* edited by David Herman

*Narrative Theory* edited by Matthew Garrett

*Native American Literature* edited by Joy Porter and Kenneth M. Roemer

*Nineteen Eighty-Four* edited by Nathan Waddell

*Nineteenth-Century American Literature and Politics* edited by John Kerkering

*Nineteenth-Century American Poetry* edited by Kerry Larson

*Nineteenth-Century American Women's Writing* edited by Dale M. Bauer and Philip Gould

*Nineteenth-Century Thought* edited by Gregory Claeys

*The Novel* edited by Eric Bulson

*Old English Literature* edited by Malcolm Godden and Michael Lapidge (second edition)

*Performance Studies* edited by Tracy C. Davis

*Piers Plowman* edited by Andrew Cole and Andrew Galloway

*The Poetry of the First World War* edited by Santanu Das

*Popular Fiction* edited by David Glover and Scott McCracken

*Postcolonial Literary Studies* edited by Neil Lazarus

*Postcolonial Poetry* edited by Jahan Ramazani

*Postcolonial Travel Writing* edited by Robert Clarke

*Postmodern American Fiction* edited by Paula Geyh

*Postmodernism* edited by Steven Connor

*The Pre-Raphaelites* edited by Elizabeth Prettejohn

*Pride and Prejudice* edited by Janet Todd

*Prose* edited by Daniel Tyler

*Queer Studies* edited by Siobhan B. Somerville

*Renaissance Humanism* edited by Jill Kraye

*Robinson Crusoe* edited by John Richetti

*Roman Comedy* edited by Martin T. Dinter

*The Roman Historians* edited by Andrew Feldherr

*Roman Satire* edited by Kirk Freudenburg

*The Romantic Sublime* edited by Cian Duffy

*Romanticism and Race* edited by Manu Samriti Chander

*Science Fiction* edited by Edward James and Farah Mendlesohn

*Scottish Literature* edited by Gerald Carruthers and Liam McIlvanney

*Sensation Fiction* edited by Andrew Mangham

*Shakespeare and Contemporary Dramatists* edited by Ton Hoenselaars

*Shakespeare and Popular Culture* edited by Robert Shaughnessy

*Shakespeare and Race* edited by Ayanna Thompson

*Shakespeare and Religion* edited by Hannibal Hamlin

*Shakespeare and War* edited by David Loewenstein and Paul Stevens

*Shakespeare on Film* edited by Russell Jackson (second edition)

*Shakespeare on Screen* edited by Russell Jackson

*Shakespeare on Stage* edited by Stanley Wells and Sarah Stanton

*Shakespearean Comedy* edited by Alexander Leggatt

*Shakespearean Tragedy* edited by Claire McEachern (second edition)

*Shakespeare's First Folio* edited by Emma Smith

*Shakespeare's History Plays* edited by Michael Hattaway

*Shakespeare's Language* edited by Lynne Magnusson with David Schalkwyk

*Shakespeare's Last Plays* edited by Catherine M. S. Alexander

*Shakespeare's Poetry* edited by Patrick Cheney

*Sherlock Holmes* edited by Janice M. Allan and Christopher Pittard

*The Sonnet* edited by A. D. Cousins and Peter Howarth

*The Spanish Novel: From 1600 to the Present* edited by Harriet Turner and Adelaida López de Martínez

*Textual Scholarship* edited by Neil Fraistat and Julia Flanders

*Theatre and Science* edited by Kristen E. Shepherd-Barr

*Theatre History* edited by David Wiles and Christine Dymkowski

*Transnational American Literature* edited by Yogita Goyal

*Travel Writing* edited by Peter Hulme and Tim Youngs

*The Twentieth-Century American Novel and Politics* edited by Bryan M. Santin

*Twentieth-Century American Poetry and Politics* edited by Daniel Morris

*Twentieth-Century British and Irish Women's Poetry* edited by Jane Dowson

*The Twentieth-Century English Novel* edited by Robert L. Caserio

*Twentieth-Century English Poetry* edited by Neil Corcoran

*Twentieth-Century Irish Drama* edited by Shaun Richards

*Twentieth-Century Literature and Politics* edited by Christos Hadjiyiannis and Rachel Potter

*Twentieth-Century Russian Literature* edited by Evgeny Dobrenko and Marina Balina

*Utopian Literature* edited by Gregory Claeys

*Victorian and Edwardian* Theatre edited by Kerry Powell

*The Victorian Novel* edited by Deirdre David (second edition)

*Victorian Poetry* edited by Joseph Bristow

*Victorian Women's Poetry* edited by Linda K. Hughes

*Victorian Women's Writing* edited by Linda H. Peterson

*War Writing* edited by Kate McLoughlin

*Women's Writing in Britain, 1660–1789* edited by Catherine Ingrassia

*Women's Writing in the Romantic Period* edited by Devoney Looser

*World Crime Fiction* edited by Jesper Gulddal, Stewart King and Alistair Rolls

*World Literature* edited by Ben Etherington and Jarad Zimbler

*Writing of the English Revolution* edited by N. H. Keeble

*The Writings of Julius Caesar* edited by Christopher Krebs and Luca Grillo

For EU product safety concerns, contact us at Calle de José Abascal, 56–1°, 28003 Madrid, Spain or eugpsr@cambridge.org.

www.ingramcontent.com/pod-product-compliance
Ingram Content Group UK Ltd.
Pitfield, Milton Keynes, MK11 3LW, UK
UKHW020050301125
465360UK00039B/806